Coppola

virgin film

COPPOLA

James Clarke

First published in Great Britain in 2003
by Virgin Books Ltd
Thames Wharf Studios
Rainville Road
London
W6 9HA

A catalogue record for this book is available from the British Library.

ISBN 0 7535 0866 4

Typeset by TW Typesetting, Plymouth, Devon
Printed and bound in Great Britain by Mackays of Chatham PLC

For my brother, Andrew. Stay gold.

Contents

Acknowledgements

First I would like to thank Kirstie Addis, my editor at Virgin Books, for her patient and thorough guidance and enthusiasm but most importantly for making a dream come true in giving me the chance to write this book.

A great big thank-you to hero of the hour Elaine Lenton at the film department of The University of Warwick. Thumbs up as ever to the fine folks at Movie Mail, the finest video and DVD outlet in the galaxy.

A smile goes out to Julie Harries.

Introduction: Zoetrope Soul

'Most of my life has been influenced by romantic preconceptions.'

Francis Ford Coppola

The world needs stories. Stories that remind us of ourselves and that reinvigorate our thoughts and senses about the world. Stories that put our own emotional lives up on the screen with that bit more intensity and grace than we might actually experience. In those films that work their charms and connect with audiences we see the world as it is and as we wish it could be and maybe even hope it never will be. We want to see life reflected, but also improved, on the movie screen. We want to feel the emotions common to all of us underscoring the essential strain of fantasy and dream on the screen. The indelible films are the ones that capture these things: moments of family and togetherness, moments of victory and moments of loss, times of honour and times of confusion; moments of great joy and moments of great fear and loneliness. Behaviour, choices, colours, places and far-off spaces all tend towards a richness and vivid quality just that bit out of reach here in the world outside the sacred darkness and light of the movie theatre. In essence, the best movies succeed in compressing all the highs and lows that define our lives.

Francis Ford Coppola's cinema charts all of these emotional valleys and mountain peaks and has done so for thirty years. Coppola is a film director's film director, his work orchestrating all the tools and techniques within the film maker's reach and sometimes just beyond it. He is a favourite of Gillian Armstrong, Andrew Bergman, Yiwen Chen, Roger Corman, John Dahl, Milos Forman, Jonathan Glazer, Sidney Lumet, Michael Mann and Sam Mendes. On the set of his film *Hook* (1991), director Steven Spielberg praised Coppola for the breadth and depth of his film-making know-how, ranking him alongside Stanley Kubrick in the extent of his knowledge.

As with so many directors whose work endures, Coppola's storytelling extends in many directions, and he has had a particular influence on films about crime and war that have followed in the mesmerising wake of Coppola's *The Godfather* trilogy and *Apocalypse Now*. Just consider *Once Upon A Time in America* (Sergio Leone, 1984), *The Road to Perdition* (Sam Mendes, 2002) and the TV series *The Sopranos* to see the spirit of *The Godfather* at work. *Apocalypse Now* has become part of pop culture and Coppola's name has become synonymous with a certain level of creative ambition. While it may not always have been completely successful, it is to be valued greatly when set in the context of so much cautious mediocrity.

1

The films of Francis Ford Coppola have always found some affecting way to fuse the personal with the spectacular. Intense, sprawling, resonant, thoughtful, playful, charming: these are the kinds of words that can be used to describe Coppola's cinema.

Several of Coppola's films have defined an era (the 1970s) and continue to thrive as touchstones of the artful and expressive possibilities of popular movie-making. Coppola, at least based on the voluminous accounts of his work and life, emerges as bullish, committed, humble, aware of his creative failings, idealistic and generous. The expansive quality of so many of his films seems to embody his essential personality. If film, art and creativity generally are an expression of temperament – even more so than of imagination – then Coppola's work surely clues audiences in to the kind of person he is. Intriguingly, Coppola still feels he has yet to truly satisfy his own creative spirit and make his best film.

Creative challenges and struggles are part of the legend of Coppola's career. There is a very appealing let's-put-on-a-show quality to Coppola, a sense that, even as an older man, he remains a plucky, young film maker rather than someone who, in the 1970s, once bestrode Hollywood like a Colossus. Coppola has achieved all that could be dreamed of in a film-making career, yet his quest is to make at least one more truly personal film in an age of spectacle. In a 1993 interview, Coppola said, 'I'm more like a kid trying to be enthusiastic, and enthusiasm is often mistaken for megolamania ... I have less self-confidence now ... because I've been hit a few times.'

Compellingly, there is a sadness to Coppola's career after thirty years of sincere, brave and refreshingly bold endeavour. His sense of self suggests he feels he has failed in some way, that he has not truly capitalised on his original ambition for personal cinema and that he has not matched the achievements of his own film-making heroes, Akira Kurosawa, Francesco Rosi, Sergei Eisenstein and Bernardo Bertolucci. Of his varied and extensive output, Coppola's personal favourites are perhaps unexpected though certainly justified: *The Conversation* and *Rumble Fish*. For Coppola these films more closely conformed to his notion of personal cinema than either *The Godfather* or *Apocalypse Now*. Big on ideas and cinematic fervour, *The Conversation* and *Rumble Fish* suggest the kind of film maker Coppola really is. Coppola has rightly prided himself on his screenwriting skills but the reality is that many of his movies have been adaptations of source novels. In *Sight and Sound*'s 2002 poll of the greatest films ever made, *The Godfather Part II* was on the list, and Coppola was the only living American director to be included in its ten best directors list. Time, it seems, will be kinder to Coppola than the commercial imperative. This book hopes to redress the balance between the louder and the quieter films and also to highlight several other lesser known pieces of Coppola movie magic. Whether taking audiences into the shadows of the Corleone compound or the Vietnam jungle, the backstreets of sunbaked Tulsa or the energetic fizz of a car designer's factory, Coppola's body of work has the quality of a dream, moving with delight across the possibilities found in enriching genres and creating fascinating generic fusions. For example *The Godfather* puts gangsters and loving family life alongside one another; in *Apocalypse Now* war and psychedelia form a combustible vision; and in *One From the Heart* a relationship meltdown is carefully detailed and set against the backdrop of a modern movie musical. Coppola's closest contemporary in creative terms is Steven Spielberg, both of them sharing a playfulness and joy in telling their stories. While their commercial success and the overall span of their careers is quite different, they share a fascination with spectacle, and frequently and overtly infuse fairy-tale forms into their work.

Spielberg and Coppola have a mutual friend and collaborator in George Lucas, also known for the fairy-tale strain in some of his films, notably the *Star Wars* series, and Lucas has often said that all he learned about film making he learned from Coppola. Lucas and Coppola have, all through their careers, waved the flag for independent film making and have committed themselves to the integration of video and digital technology into film. Coppola's belief in his own work has led him to fund several movies from his own pocket, just as George Lucas uses his own funds to finance his projects. As directors synonymous with making big pictures, they have made astute observations about where cinema is heading. In the early 1980s they both spoke enthusiastically of films needing to become ever more operatic in order to combat the influence and variety of home entertainment forms that were burgeoning at that time. In one sense Coppola has become a victim of his own success rather like George Lucas with the success of the *Star Wars* films. Could it be that *The Godfather* movies created an audience perception of Coppola that caused them to neglect his more personal work?

For Coppola, his proposed *Megalopolis* project (see **Works Still to Come**) is something of a tease. Coppola seems compelled to bring it to the screen and remind audiences and himself of his capacity for intelligent spectacle. Yet, the more whimsical, screenwriter side of him seems content for the project to exist in its perfect-world form as a screenplay.

At the age of sixty-four, after a lifetime improving the art of film making, Coppola still has to wrestle with the movie studios and prove himself, a situation that vexes his more recent regular producer, Fred Fuchs, who worked on *Tucker: The Man and His Dream*, a film that major studios were reluctant to finance. (Ultimately George Lucas financed it through LucasFilm and Paramount agreed to distribute it.)

3

Coppola feels that he dented the movie-making system, but did not revolutionise it (with American Zoetrope) as he had always dreamed. One senses that that young movie maker's desire remains very much intact even now. When *The Rainmaker* was released, Coppola talked wistfully about the time remaining in which to make films; it is an all too painful awareness of opportunity passing by that infuses several of his finest films with their great and very real sadness.

In 1990, during the filming of *The Godfather Part III*, Coppola commented on his own failure saying, 'You know, I have been a "promising" film maker for years. I'm still promising. Zoetrope is still promising. That's what keeps us young.' Around the time of the release of *Jack*, Coppola commented that he still felt he owed himself one epic-scaled, original piece of writing that he would then go on to direct.

There is an appropriate and enlightening parallel to be repeated here which is that Coppola's career has a particular analogue to that of Orson Welles' experience. Both directors impacted hugely on the Hollywood industry at the start of their careers (in their twenties) and then seem to have spent the rest of their careers fighting battles to maintain and recover the glory of their early days. Of course, this belies the integrity and artistic success of their later work and also testifies to creative courage on their part. In an article for *Salon* online magazine, writer Michael Sragow talks of Coppola's 'ravaged Hollywood genius' and draws a parallel between Coppola and Orson Welles. Both experienced great film-making success as young men but subsequently, and ironically, spent much of their career battling the studio system that had initially embraced them. More specifically Welles had attempted to adapt Joseph Conrad's *Heart of Darkness*, which, of course, Coppola did in the shape of *Apocalypse Now*.

Coppola has often talked of cinema rather than film, alluding to his interest in the experience of watching a film, communally, rather than simply making films. In some way the use of the term cinema also suggests a more European sensibility and adds to the mounting evidence of Coppola's brave quest to combine the sensibility of the American cinema with that of the European. Consider the Hollywood splash of *One From the Heart* which makes huge efforts to detail a contemporary relationship (somewhat in the manner of a European realist film), as it crumbles in the kitchen and the bedroom, before taking the relationship apart and setting it against the format of an updated take on the Hollywood musical.

It is tragic that Coppola seems only to be remembered for *The Godfather*, *The Godfather Part II* and *Apocalypse Now*. Perhaps Coppola's films do not move fast enough for the twenty-first century audience. Perhaps they do not dramatise the easier emotions. Coppola's glory days of the 1970s must seem long gone to the contemporary audience. His efforts to make accessible films with their fair share of thought and complexity and his often deliberate storytelling pace may now seem tedious in an age of relentless spectacle where more is considered better. Yet, more than once in his career, he has been the trailblazer. Coppola's battle to negotiate and survive in cinema is mirrored by his contemporary, Martin Scorsese. Where Scorsese is seen as having resurrected himself, however, for some, Coppola has yet to do so. Perhaps everyone is rooting for *Megalopolis* to happen and to happen with verve, energy, rich emotion and universal resonance. That's how Coppola began.

Since the early 1980s Steven Spielberg has been dubbed the Peter Pan of popular cinema. This claim can equally be made for Francis Ford Coppola, who has frequently brought a sense of the playful and inventive to film making, often telling intimate stories on large palettes. In many ways, Coppola makes some of the most human films, and he certainly has the most European sensibility of his equally legendary contemporaries. Many photos of Coppola, taken in the 1970s, also confirm his very welcome sense of the bohemian. In a cluster of them Coppola looks very much like the Beat poet, Alan Ginsberg – and that sense of a creative movement, rooted in San Francisco, makes the connection plain.

During the late 1960s Coppola headed for San Francisco where he wished to base his company. Like the Beats, Coppola has maintained a genuine commitment to the notion of youth, and several of his films carry a very real sense of someone, with a focus on youth, experimenting with the possibilities of popular film. Now, in 2003, the word is that Coppola will finally produce a movie version of Jack Kerouac's landmark novel *On The Road*. Coppola's Beat sensibility shines through in his films *The Outsiders* and *Rumble Fish* and, in *Peggy Sue Got Married*, one character – an aspiring writer – is clearly indebted to the spirit of Jack Kerouac. Coppola has also committed himself to supporting film makers like Hans Jurgen Syberberg, Jean-Luc Godard, Akira Kurosawa and Kidlat Tahimik. When interviewed at the turn of the new millennium, Coppola made links between the power of cinema to express issues of global concern but expressed frustration that nobody really seemed to be taking up this challenge, at least within the American movie-making matrix.

For all Coppola's epic movie-making struggles there is a very appealing warmth to his film director persona. In the winter of 1982 at a preview screening of *One From the Heart*, he ensured that all the people queuing around the block to see his long-awaited new movie were served with hot soup. At a 1979 preview screening of *Apocalypse Now*,

Coppola handed out a photocopied letter he penned for the audience to explain the nature of his project and that it was still a work-in-progress. These gestures are not just grandiose but quite humble. Coppola wants the viewer to enjoy spending time with his work, to feel welcome. In the countless interviews Coppola has given since the late 1960s, there is an appealing honesty to his expressions of self-doubt and creative insecurity. He has avoided becoming some kind of iron-clad super-king of creativity for whom there is never a wavering moment or cloud of fallibility over his choices.

When Coppola steps up to direct a new movie, people want him to hit a home run, an appropriate American pop-culture term for an American pop-culture hero. They want to see Coppola remind them of why they were so taken by his work early in his career. For many, Coppola's winning streak burned brightly but briefly in the 1970s, and ever since he has only allowed us glimpses of this rather than any sustained involvement and human drama. As such he has been regarded as an inconsistent director. *Apocalypse Now* is seen as a creative watershed for Coppola, capping a ten-year period of energy, focus and brilliance. Perhaps his most ambitious and acute cinematic vision was expended with that film, but though his subsequent films may lack the overwhelming virtuosity of his 1970s output they still register as inventive and fresh attempts at familiar genres, in several cases with outstanding results. A film does not have to be big, brash and socially significant to be marvellous. The achievement of such Coppola films as *Rumble Fish* and *Gardens of Stone* is equivalent to the differently scaled craft of *The Godfather Part II* and *Apocalypse Now*. In each case there is an ambition to explore human frailty and to imbue familiar forms with something fresh. Often, Coppola's characters fail rather than achieve, and in mainstream American cinema this is an anomaly. For Coppola's characters, perhaps their admission of failure is their victory. Incredibly, when Michael Corleone repents in *The Godfather Part III*, the audience want to see it work, despite the atrocities he has committed. In *Gardens of Stone*, when Clell Hazard makes his decision to overturn his perceived failure, the audience feel for him and know that he hasn't failed.

Coppola's work thrives on sincere feeling and certainly an affecting strain of melancholy offset by gentle playfulness. For all the laughs and chuckles of *Jack*, an ultimately minor entry in his work, Coppola still invests the film with a sense of time passing and opportunities fading that brings some sense of genuine sadness to a film that, on the surface, is light-hearted.

The concept of cool has always been a way for movie marketeers to promote their product. In 2003, sadly, it seems to be the only way. How many movie magazines can there be with top 100 lists of cool guns, cool action scenes, cool war movies? But beyond the adolescent infatuation of film fans and their association of cool with violence there are Coppola's other, quieter films. As a media personality (and Coppola has had his frustrations with the media, particularly in the 1970s and early 1980s), Coppola remains a figure of great interest. He has become legendary, his name conjuring very specific images of his kind of cinema, a point equally true, of course, for many other film makers.

His life generally has been the source of much coverage. Even as recently as the summer of 2002 Coppola took a railroad vacation with fellow film maker George Lucas across Canada. The Canadian media covered the event with great excitement – this just for a holiday. Just imagine if the two were planning a new collaboration. Audiences can maybe live in hope.

Of all the dazzling new film maker stars that came to light in American cinema in the early 1970s none shone brighter than Francis Ford Coppola. Arguably, the warmest and most human of the brilliant gang of wonder boys, Coppola led the way for his compadres: Scorsese, Spielberg, Lucas, Milius and Murch, to pursue their movie-making dreams.

The early 1970s saw Coppola achieve and secure a major place in American mainstream cinema, incorporating a Hollywood scale and technical razzle-dazzle with a European sensibility towards character and emotional resonance within his stories. With *The Godfather*, *The Conversation*, *The Godfather Part II* and *Apocalypse Now*, Coppola charted American dreams as American nightmares of paranoia, anger and violence. He has also charted a contrasting course through a series of projects which owe much to fairy tales and youth: *The Outsiders*, *Rumble Fish*, *Peggy Sue Got Married*, *Jack*, *Faeirie Tale Theatre*, *Rip van Winkle*, and the abandoned *Pinocchio* plan. Some of Coppola's movies thrillingly engage with more mythological notions, as evidenced by *Apocalypse Now* and *Rumble Fish* (with its associations to the Fisher King), and the proposed *Megalopolis* movie. In a very hi-tech, looking-to-the-future age, Coppola retains an awareness of, and ability to, integrate classical and folk elements into his work, proving ultimately that the fundamental concerns, and maybe even the rules of drama, do not change that much.

As a producer, Coppola has been a defender of the movie-making faith, most famously at a test-screening of *American Graffiti* (George Lucas, 1973). When Universal Pictures baulked at the film and suggested they would put it on TV rather than in movie theatres, Coppola berated the executives, reminded them how hard George Lucas had worked on the film to bring it in on time and budget, and then offered to buy the film from Universal there and then.

Coppola is perhaps the most literary of film makers and maybe one of the few contemporary film makers openly expressive of a wish to be thoughtful in his work. As a whole, Coppola's cinema is not focused on stunning kinetic activity and visceral thrills, though parts of his most famous films undeniably play to these features. His films are highly visual, but Coppola's beginnings as a writer has led to finely structured stories with nimble handling of multiple storylines and richly drawn characters. It is a very novelistic sensibility and there is something old-fashioned about Coppola's faith in a well-crafted tale.

But Coppola's love of technology and its potential as a storytelling device cannot be overlooked. There are special effects in Coppola's films, though not so much in terms of creating the never-before-seen or impossible, but rather in terms of the spectacle of editing and lighting. Coppola's films tend towards the carnivalesque and, in the austere and solemn *The Godfather* trilogy, Coppola finds opportunities to reference the older storytelling traditions and devices that mirror the drama of the characters in the film. In *One From the Heart, Tucker: The Man and His Dream* and *Jack* there is a playful quality built around images of parades and play as important communal activities that strengthen groups. Inevitably, Coppola (like all of us) has a creative vibe informed by childhood and then a wider cultural sense. His Italian heritage tends towards melodrama and this makes a nice contrast to the New World narrative dynamics of popular cinema.

In the 1970s, Coppola was seemingly able to do no wrong, and by the early 1980s his brave attempts at reinvigorating the Hollywood form with *One From the Heart, The Outsiders* and *Rumble Fish* were, for many, his last gasp of excellence. These three films are fascinating and are real highlights of his career. They are quixotic movies that feel like the work of a new director excited by the possibilities of technology and technique to vividly express aspects of human experience. The films that followed were almost always work-for-hire rather than personally developed projects and for many observers the work did not shine as brightly any more. *Peggy Sue Got Married* had plenty of charm and nostalgia but audiences must have asked how this could be from the same director who had made *Apocalypse Now*. And then, some years later, gasps of derision were to be heard when Coppola directed the heartfelt and very small movie *Jack*, starring Robin Williams. For all the film's immersion in childish humour *Jack* has its welcome moments of warmth and honesty and an appealing melancholy. Coppola's most recent feature was *The Rainmaker*, his most anonymous film since *The Cotton Club*. Without a strong screenplay, Coppola's visual know-how is not enough to invest weak material with sufficient interest and energy. In both *The Cotton Club* and *The Rainmaker* it feels as though only pieces, but not all, of the respective stories engaged and excited Coppola.

By the mid-1970s Coppola, adopting a healthy and understandably positive attitude in the warm glow of his early successes, began to energetically back and support film makers in his capacity as producer. It was in this role that he had worked with George Lucas on his first two movies, *THX-1138* (1971) and *American Graffiti* (1973). By the early 1980s, Coppola was not only a director but also a presenter and sponsor – a cinematic Master of Ceremonies – through the offices of his American Zoetrope studio.

At the time of writing, anyone with an interest in film, and especially American film, must ask the question, O Coppola Where Art Thou? He has certainly not been idle and there is a real sense of anticipation about his magnum opus, *Megalopolis*. The title alone immediately suggests Fritz Lang's landmark science-fiction film *Metropolis* (1921), albeit on an even vaster scale, combining the personal statement and the social comment. Coppola has been building the *Megalopolis* movie project since 1983 and it certainly sounds like the personal project he has always wanted to realise. Without wishing to sound downbeat, is he perhaps considering it his cinematic ride into the sunset as a director?

At the Morocco Film Festival in the autumn of 2002, Coppola talked about how best to figure out who is running the world; it is, he said, to discover who is employing the artists. Thirty years on, Coppola continues to kick against the notion of the establishment and he knows that the corporate-financed movie studios probably will not want to back his personal, most authentic movies or indeed the personal and challenging visions of many directors currently working or yet to emerge.

Coppola the Trailblazer

The American writer and thinker Ralph Waldo Emerson wrote, in 1841, 'Nothing great was ever achieved without enthusiasm.' He must have known that one day there would be films and that Francis Ford Coppola would come along to make some of them.

As far back as the early 1980s, Coppola was experimenting with integrating video and digital technology into the film-making process to maximise its efficiency and malleability. It was George Lucas who accelerated the push for digital production, in part riding it in on the commercial success of his *Star Wars* serial, and, in the age of digital visual effects, who can imagine the vistas that Coppola might present with his new project. Coppola is at a point where he is secure enough to pursue once more his own vision and not kowtow to studio opinion. Because the commercial track record of Coppola's movies has been mixed, he has had to struggle; his early 1980s experiment of American Zoetrope showed that it is financial independence and not the ownership of the means of production that counts most. Coppola's battles, some won, some lost, endear him to film fans, and in the process he assumes the identity of the struggling artist. However, his non-film ventures have come together to allow him creative independence. He may have lost battles, but now it seems that the war is won.

Coppola is one of the great makers of personal, mainstream cinema – intelligent, resonant and memorable. Failure is an often underrated achievement, and Coppola's so-called movie failures make very engaging viewing. In almost every case they prove far more of a treat than those films that achieved more popularity at the time. It is these smaller, often quieter films that make a welcome relief to the cult that has built up around *The Godfather* and *Apocalypse Now*. Every director has their greatest hits, but that is no reason to ignore the less high-profile films, some of which deserve resurrection, re-evaluation and a little bit of banner waving on the part of film fans everywhere. The release of *Apocalypse Now Redux* in 2001 reminded people just how quixotic and inventive a film maker he is and in 2002 *Film Comment* magazine honoured him with a cover story as part of its tribute issue.

While Coppola's friends and contemporaries have frequently built repeatedly on their commercial and artistic success, Coppola seems to have lurched from heroic victory to heroic failure. Yet, it is precisely this roller-coaster aspect that makes his work so intriguing, compelling and exciting. In many ways, there is a warmth to his movie-making persona that only adds to his appeal.

Themes of family, history, loyalty and betrayal fuel his movies, all of them brimming with a thrilling combination of cinematic flair and theatrical know-how. He truly is a major figure on the pop-culture landscape.

Coppola, the most fragile and human of the Movie Brats in his apparent willingness to acknowledge failings and insecurities, even now regards himself foremost as a writer. His love of the word and of theatre are the tributaries that feed the river of his cinema work, they are the source of his style. Whereas his contemporaries are all children of the TV set and the movie theatre, Coppola is distinct. He may yet remain the showman of the group, in both the conduct of his career and the aesthetic of his work.

Coppola is a vibrant American film maker and entrepreneur. His Zoetrope studio made a brave effort to utilise digital video technology, twenty years ahead of the game, with his film *One From the Heart*, and he has also been committed to advances in camera and sound applications. He has a massively successful winery (Niebaum Coppola), runs a short story magazine (*Zoetrope: All Story*), once owned a theatre and, most significantly, continues with American Zoetrope, based in San Francisco just as it always was, producing feature films and television projects.

Just as Coppola was nurtured by B movie maestro Roger Corman, so too has he nurtured the careers of young talent, notably that of George Lucas. In the 1970s and 1980s Coppola went on to support and sponsor film makers such as Wim Wenders, Werner Herzog and, one of Coppola's great heroes, Akira Kurosawa. Coppola has also showcased many of mainstream cinema's acting greats.

Coppola's impact is vast but people's memories are short and unforgiving. Yes, *The Godfather* triptych and *Apocalypse Now* are greats of modern cinema, but let's not forget *The Conversation*, *Rumble Fish*, *Gardens of Stone* and *Tucker: The Man and His Dream*. Throughout his career, Coppola has pushed new acting talent into the foreground and espoused digital technology.

Film history has allowed Coppola's so-called failures to obscure his great contributions. Though some may say he has never recovered as an industry figure since the collapse of Zoetrope with the release of *One From the Heart* in 1982, Coppola has frequently *not* played it safe in his choice of material. For that he should be applauded. Perhaps *One From the Heart* was one movie that was years ahead of its time, rather like *Blade Runner* (Ridley Scott, 1982) released in the same year. Adventure and sunny moods were the prevailing tone of American movies back then.

Just because Coppola's films did not hit the big time *every* time does not necessarily mean he lost his way. If anything, perhaps he found his way, constantly shifting the kinds of projects he made. To borrow from a phrase used by David Lean at Coppola's American Film Institute Lifetime Achievement Award ceremony, Coppola has not come out of the same rabbit hole every time.

Whereas technology has frequently triumphed over technique in the last twenty years, Coppola's flair for writing and directing performances has an appeal to enduring notions of classical narrative in an age where spectacle, sound and fury often reign supreme. Coppola's films are occasionally whimsical, frequently melodramatic and intense, and always visually inventive and memorable. From the iconic image of Don Corleone sitting in the shadows of his office in *The Godfather* to shots of jungles exploding into flame in *Apocalypse Now*, and on to the smoke and mirror effects of *Dracula*, and the clouds as they race across the sky in *Jack*, Coppola can capture the intimate and the epic with great verve.

Growing Up

Born on 7 April 1939 in Detroit, Michigan, Francis Ford Coppola had asthma and found solace in reading and theatre as a counter to not being an outdoorsy, sporty child. Coppola's contemporaries, Scorsese, Spielberg and Lucas also had similar developments.

Unlike his other film-making contemporaries, however, Coppola's interest in theatre has an important influence on his movie work, yielding nuanced and affecting performances and also, more tritely, contributing to that sense of putting on a show, of producing something memorable. Coppola attended Hofstra University and then went to the University of California, Los Angeles (UCLA). Coppola was the first of his young film maker confrères to make the break into Hollywood, which he would soon help to reinvent itself, by accident or design. The great battle, mission and vocation of Coppola's career has been to work himself free of studio financing, thereby allowing him to make the personal cinema he longs for. It has not been easy.

Coppola's father Carmine was a flautist with Arturo Toscanini's NBC Symphony Orchestra and for many years longed for acknowledgement in his own right as a musician and composer. In one of the most poetic turns of Coppola's movie-making career, he was able to give his father the chance to realise his dreams, inviting him to compose music for *Apocalypse Now* and some of his other films. Francis Coppola's mother, Italia, was the daughter of Neopolitan musician Francesco Pennino, and she went on to act in some of the films of Italian director Vittorio de Sica.

Home for Francis Ford Coppola was in Bayside, Queens, before a move to Great Neck. In the near-classic creative-type manner, Coppola's childhood had some fragility to it. An introspective and inquisitive child, Coppola's interior life was compounded by the onset of polio that kept him in bed for around a year. During this time he became enamoured of puppetry. Many years later a long-held ambition to adapt *Pinocchio* to the live action format fell through. Ironically, Spielberg *was* able to fold the *Pinocchio* motif into his astonishing film *AI:Artificial Intelligence* (2001). From every tragedy comes its strain of joy and it was during his childhood bout of polio that Coppola immersed himself in an imaginative life, getting to grips with the family's 8mm projector and tape recorder. He would synchronise new music for the home movies to run against. Coppola also recalled how he enjoyed screening these revised home movies – a telling point given his affinity for showmanship. In his movie *Jack*, true to his efforts to always keep a film personal in some way, the title character spends part of the movie in his bedroom unable to be visited by his friends. In *The Conversation*, the main character Harry Caul had polio. The other key element in young Francis's life was his elder brother August who Coppola always regarded as brilliant, if not near-perfect, being both handsome *and* smart. Coppola began to develop an interest in writing partly in order to emulate his brother. August went on to be a university professor at Berkeley.

After recovering from polio, the young Coppola was sent to military school, and it was here, in an event that could easily be from a story, that Coppola flexed his storytelling wings. Charging a dollar a page, Coppola would write love letters on behalf of his more creatively challenged fellow students.

At school, Coppola became president of the school radio club. In 1956, he was admitted to Hofstra College (now University) where he studied theatre and stagecraft, reasoning that this would be a strong grounding prior to pursuing film. It was partly this decision which, Coppola attests, led to the emphasis of consistently strong acting and a confident theatricality in his films. His film interests developed at Hofstra where, initially, he became a more willing student of content than technique. Science and technology and stories were Coppola's favourite things and these are, of course, the fundamental elements of cinema. At Hofstra, Coppola became president of the drama society and his imagination and ambition became apparent to all-comers. He staged HG Wells's play *The Man Who Could Work Miracles*, and it was at Hofstra that Coppola met long-standing colleague James Caan, and also Robert Spiotta, who would become the head of American Zoetrope in later years.

In 1960, Coppola headed west and enrolled at UCLA as a student on their graduate film programme. It was the start of something big – the film school student revolution, or at least evolution. Coppola blazed the way for his friends and associates (George Lucas, Martin Scorsese, Steven Spielberg, Brian De Palma et al) to follow. Walter Murch has called Coppola the 'ice breaker'. Unlike Lucas, for example, Coppola did not find film school the nurturing place he had hoped it would be. Interestingly, in England at roughly the same time, director-to-be Ridley Scott was immersing himself in some film making at the Royal College of Art, while in Europe the tendency towards independent, realist cinema had made its impact, a wave that was about to hit Hollywood. And, like so many stories of great achievers, it is their early years, prior to that moment of hitting the big time, that are the most interesting.

The Dream Begins

Coppola's slight unease at the film school experience was remedied by a small twist of fate that may yet be the key moment in his career trajectory; the classic, at the time low-key, collision of careers that history would record as momentous. There on the noticeboard was an advertisement placed by the low-budget Hollywood producer Roger Corman (himself a movie-making legend deserving of his Hollywood Walk of Fame star). Corman was looking for someone to write English dialogue for a Russian science-fiction film, entitled *Battle Beyond the Sun*. Many years later Corman would produce *Battle Beyond the Stars* (Jimmy T Murikami, 1980), featuring a screenplay by indie king John Sayles, production design by James Cameron and a score by James Horner. Coppola took the job and soon after found himself working in an assistant capacity to Corman. Another side to the story goes like this: Dorothy Arzner (a Hollywood director) had been tutoring at UCLA; Coppola had been a student of hers and had impressed. When Corman contacted her, looking for new editors, she recommended Coppola. At Zoetrope today, Coppola has a screening theatre called *The Dorothy Arzner Theatre*, named in her honour.

Whatever route Coppola took to get to Corman, the aspiring director soon found his assistant duties extending to being dialogue director on *The Tower of London* (1962) and working as sound recordist on *The Young Racers* (1963). Regardless of scale, budget or prestige, Coppola was working in the industry. If the Corman noticeboard ad had been a break, then the big break came when Corman gave Coppola the chance to realise his dream and direct a feature. As with later film makers, Joe Dante, Ron Howard and Martin Scorsese, Corman became the paterfamilias. The feature was B movie material, in this case a horror movie called *Dementia 13*. Corman gave Coppola twenty thousand dollars and, in an early display of will, courage and a facility for getting people to back him, Coppola raised another twenty thousand from an English producer called Raymond Strose. Coppola sold the English rights to the film to Strose before the movie had even been shot. The script for *Dementia 13* was written by Coppola in three nights and, even in such an early piece, the emphasis on family is central to the story. Coppola enjoyed making the film, which was shot on location in Ireland and, for a few days, at Aardmore Studios in Dublin. *Dementia 13* told the story of the Haloran family, a highly dysfunctional bunch, headed by a mad mother haunted by the death of one of her children. Coppola's affinity for staging 'rituals' shines through, in this case a memorial service. It was during the *Dementia 13* shoot that Coppola met his wife-to-be Eleanor Neil. On 2 February 1963 they married.

Mr Young Movie Director

Soon after, Coppola won the Samuel Goldwyn writing award, while still at UCLA, and he was hired as a staff writer for Seven Arts. The award alerted the studios to new talent in town. Coppola worked on three feature screenplays in a year, including *Is Paris Burning?* (René Clément, 1966) and *Patton* (Franklin J Schaffner, 1970). (See also **Coppola the Writer**.) The third was his own original project: he had been working on a screenplay about a young man's adventures in the world when he read a novel by David Benedictus called *You're a Big Boy Now*. When Coppola saw that the novel and his own work were on similar lines he bought the rights to the novel and fused the material together.

Canadian actor Peter Kastner starred in *You're A Big Boy Now* alongside Karen Black and Rip Torn, an actor who has achieved late career success in *Men In Black* (Barry Sonnenfeld, 1997). Coppola had fourteen days to shoot the film, for Warner Seven Arts, on a budget of $800,000. The plot of the film follows nineteen-year-old Bernard Chanticleer who wants to live free of his suffocating mother and authoritarian father. At the library Bernard meets a librarian called Amy. The film follows Bernard's misadventures, which include him being jailed and a chase down Fifth Avenue. The film is essentially about a young man growing up. It was premiered on 21 March 1967 and was the only American entry at Cannes that year.

When he was denied access to film in New York public library, because of their previous bad experiences with other film shoots, Coppola, in a display of confidence and bravura, called New York Mayor John Harding who granted permission. Amazingly, during the three-week rehearsal period Coppola used an early videotape to record the rehearsals for reference. It is a technique he continues to use and which would become a very important production tool in the early 1980s for his work and the development of what is now known as digital cinema. *You're A Big Boy Now* received some warm reviews and showed that Coppola could direct with energy and wit, though some felt the film was a little too close to Richard Lester's work. Coppola had emerged as a director to watch, and his commitment to the notion of artistry has extended throughout his career. Referring to his work on *The Conversation*, Coppola has said that, 'I was very anxious to try to be a writer, to try to be an artist.' For Coppola, the resulting film, *You're A Big Boy Now*, was perhaps less important to his own development than the experience of dealing with Hollywood's commercial processes. Deal-making was as important as shot-making. The film's other significance was that it marked the first, and certainly not the last, time that Coppola had adapted novel source material. Some of his most celebrated movies would find their wellsprings in novels and novellas. The process of making the film was intimidating for Coppola as it was the first time he had worked with union crews. This too, marked the first of several run-ins with the unions throughout his career. Coppola's maverick status was already developing and when better than as a young film maker whose pluck and vision remains an inspiration to so many.

Following an encouraging reception for *You're A Big Boy Now* (available on VHS in America), with its theme song courtesy of The Lovin' Spoonful, Coppola headed into the movie major leagues when he agreed to direct *Finian's Rainbow* for Warner Brothers.

Coppola's Cinema

What makes a Coppola film? What is it about his movies that make them endure and translate so powerfully worldwide? His thematic concerns centre on time passing, mortality, youth, family (blood and adopted), history and faith. His motifs zero in on ritual, violence, whimsy and loneliness. 'Characters are always nesting in Coppola, getting comfy . . . they're looking for shelter,' wrote Kent Jones.

Grand images, intimate small shots and tableaux are Coppola mainstays in his visual language. Coppola's movies also cover an astonishing range of terrain, from seeing Harry Caul in his mundane San Francisco apartment in *The Conversation*, to the snaking river of Vietnam, to the mountains of Transylvania in *Bram Stoker's Dracula*, and the sanctuary of a man-boy's bedroom in *Jack*. Coppola's films are romantic, theatrical, and sometimes chime with the times. The classical and literary are vital to his sense of film as is his theatre background, emphasising strong performances. Coppola's images are often beautifully simple, and the offbeat sensibility present in most of his work is worth noting. Dazzling sequence construction, compositional elegance and a tone of regret bind his output together.

Many of Coppola's male protagonists experience great loneliness, sometimes imposed on them, other times their own doing and punishment. Over the years, noting the references to Catholicism in Martin Scorsese's films has become a pastime for some people. Coppola's films also possess a similarly thematic line that riffs on Catholic imagery and dogma as *The Conversation* and *The Godfather* trilogy demonstrate. Broader than the references to Catholicism is an interest in the spiritual and the philosophical. *Apocalypse Now* clearly gives credence to this and it is a vital part of Coppola's sense of personal cinema. In that film, Coppola integrated the ancient and modern fury of war and showed how the clash of civilisation with the wilderness is both within the soul of man and in the world around us. It is a clash that reverberates in *The Outsiders* and *Rumble Fish*, too, and which is disguised by the smart suits and intricate business deals of the world shown in *The Godfather* films. Why should it not be emotionally true and indicative of the dilemmas that confront us all? Coppola's movies are very much about men, and women tend to feature as idealised mother figures, literally or figuratively.

Coppola's long-time collaborator, and one of the great practitioners and teachers of film, Walter Murch, recently commented that his sense of a Coppola film was of an individual's face set against an expansive backdrop, something epic. For Murch, Coppola's great strength is to fuse the experiences and concerns of his personal life with the film material he is working with at a given time. Murch considers Coppola's lesser films to be those where that fusion and conjunction of interests, passions, insecurities and aspirations has not occurred so vividly. Murch has called it Coppola's 'personal battleground'.

And what of Coppola's detractors? What is the kernel of their reservation about his work? First they see an inconsistency in his output, symptomatic of his being pulled between the big, and the small, budget. His storytelling, they feel, is actually fairly superficial, dressed up on great visual style. They tend to recognise the great creative magic of *The Conversation* and *The Godfather Part II* but *Apocalypse Now* is thought to take Coppola back to neat image-making and fairly trite philosophising. By the mid-1980s, Coppola's output is seen as derivative and lacking real emotional subtlety and range. He is seen less as an intellectual film maker and more as the builder of believable realities on film.

Often Coppola wraps up these predispositions in very slickly produced enterainments, but like other Hollywood directors he finds a way to plug his personal sense into the circuitry of the film. He is a director and writer who loves ideas and certainly *Apocalypse Now* is perhaps strongest in its closing act as a compendium of ideas than a film with its own philosophical aspect. Coppola is a classicist, and certainly a humanist, who is at home with stories about the powerless as readily as he is with stories of the powerful. They endure; they remind us of our sensitivities and failings and potential for both love and hate. Coppola's movies for the most part emphasise what is inside. A hug can give you life or take it from you. A kiss can be the kiss of life or the kiss of death. A sunset can be an end and a glorious beginning and, thankfully, in Coppola's movie world, there is always the possibility of redemption.

In an interview in May 2003 about his career, John Milius, co-writer of *Apocalypse Now*, said of Coppola, 'I think Francis was far and away the best of the lot. He was the real thing.'

In keeping with the other titles in the Virgin Film series, each chapter focuses on one film, arranged in chronological order. Any significant re-edits or Special Editions of Coppola films will be noted accordingly in the relevant film chapter.

CAST AND CREW LIST: A listing of all key crew and cast (characters).

TAGLINE: The words that sold the movie on posters and in print.

SUMMARY: A detailed summary of the film's story.

COPPOLA'S CONCEPT: This section details the genesis of the film and its development.

INFLUENCES: A consideration of those materials that helped to shape the thinking behind the film. Source material, other films, art and music all play their part in informing a vision.

COSTUME: A brief look at particular points of interest and practical challenges in costuming a given film.

TEAM COPPOLA: This section notes any special information regarding the crew, such as when they worked with Coppola or other notable films.

CASTING: Coppola's theatrical background means that casting is a typically vigorous process. This section details the casting process and decisions, and subsequent cast members.

I KNOW THAT FACE: A look at the key actors in each film and where they have been seen elsewhere.

THE FILMING: An overview of the production history of each film including information on location and design.

PROMOTION: A section detailing the marketing of each film, its poster campaign and any other 'stunts' used to promote the movie.

THE OPENING: A detailed look at the opening moments or sequence of a film, including stylistic and narrative points.

HEROES AND VILLAINS: A breakdown of the main characters and how their behaviour and motivation develops through the drama. This section also cross-references characters and their types between films, emphasising the unity across the director's body of work.

COPPOLA STYLE: How the director and his collaborators use images and sounds to create atmosphere, character and meaning. Coppola's fusion of the theatrical and the cinematic means that his body of work is rich with storytelling style and magic.

IMAGE: An appreciation of the visual elements of each film: camera placement, movement and lighting.

SOUND: An appreciation of the sound element of each film.

COPPOLA TUNES: The music for the film under discussion, including a list of source music where applicable.

HUMOUR: An acknowledgement of humorous moments and scenes.

AWARDS: A list of awards a given film was nominated for and won.

COPPOLA MAGIC: This section concerns any technical or technological innovations/applications.

MOVIE SPEAK: Memorable or especially poignant dialogue is acknowledged in this section.

HOME VIEWING: A section detailing the availability of each Coppola film and also noting their DVD status and any supplementary material.

DELETED SCENES: Where appropriate, those scenes that were filmed but excised and listed and described.

TRIVIA: Information about quirks of production and/or of the finished film.

COPPOLA'S VIEW: The themes of the films: honour, family, tradition, the mythological, the political, the military, the maverick and youth.

CRITICAL COPPOLA: A selection of review excerpts from newspapers and magazines. This section also includes other appropriate comment drawn from reviews and other material.

VERDICT: An assessment of the film's strengths and weaknesses and how it fits into the larger body of the director's work.

COPPOLA NOW: A quote from Coppola about the film under discussion.

Appendices:

SHORT FILM PROJECTS: A look at three Coppola shorts of the 1980s.

WORKS STILL TO COME: A look at three long-in-the-works projects including *Megolopolis*.

COPPOLA THE PRODUCER AND SHOWMAN: Coppola has also produced a lot of films – this chapter lists and summarises the story of each film, making any special note about Coppola's contribution. In the early 1980s he was particularly engaged in this way through Zoetrope. Coppola has also held interests in publishing and the presentation and sponsoring of film makers long gone or maybe neglected, such as Akira Kurosawa with *Kagemusha* (1980) and Coppola's presentation of Abel Gance's *Napoleon* (1927).

COPPOLA THE WRITER: Details of films for which Coppola wrote the screenplay, such as *Patton* (Franklin J Schaffner, 1970) and *The Great Gatsby* (Jack Clayton, 1974).

Making His Mark: Two Minor Majors

Prior to hitting career-making, legendary success with *The Godfather*, Francis Ford Coppola directed two feature films of very different kinds. One was a musical for Warner Brothers, entitled *Finian's Rainbow* and the other project was based on an original screenplay by Coppola called *The Rain People*.

The spectacle of the musical and the personal inflection of the road-movie drama clearly point the way to key artistic approaches in his later, more well-known and celebrated films. *Finian's Rainbow* and *The Rain People* mark the beginning of Coppola's professional work, transforming him from the enthused newcomer, working on obscure low-budget horror such as *Dementia 13* and quirky low-key comedy like *You're A Big Boy Now*, to the much more crafted and artistic work that followed.

Finian's Rainbow (1968)

(Colour – 144 minutes)

Warner Brothers – Seven Arts
Producer: Joseph Landon
Associate Producer: Joel Freeman
Screenplay: EY Harburg and Fred Saidy, based on the
Broadway play (book by EY Harburg and Fred Saidy, lyrics
by EY Harburg, music by Burton Lane)
Cinematographer: Philip Lathrop
Editor: Melvin Shapiro
Music Direction: Ray Heindorf
Production Designer: Hilyard M Brown
Choreography: Hermes Pan
Costume Design: Dorothy Jeakins
Sound: MA Merrick and Dan Wallin

CAST: Fred Astaire (*Finian McLonergan*), Petula Clark (*Sharon McLonergan*), Tommy Steele (*Og*), Don Francks (*Woody*), Barbara Hancock (*Susan the Silent*), Keenan Wynn (*Senator Billboard Rawkins*), Al Freeman Jr (*Howard*), Ronald Colby (*Buzz Collins*), Dolph Sweet (*Sheriff*), Wright King (*District Attorney*), Louil Silas (*Henry*), Brenda Arnau (*Sharecropper*), Avon Long, Roy Glen, Jerster Hairston (*Passion Pilgrim Gospellers*)

BUDGET: $3.5 million

THE BOX OFFICE: $11,600,000

RELEASE DATE: 9 October 1968

MPAA: G

BBFC: U

TAGLINE: If all you want out of a movie is a great, big, wonderful time just follow the rainbow, whistle the songs and join in the fun.

SUMMARY: Old Irishman Finian McLonergan believes he can yield riches by burying a pot of gold near Fort Knox. He steals a leprechaun's pot of gold and moves with his daughter Sharon to Missitucky where all people live peacefully. Missitucky, though, is ruled by Senator 'Billboard' Rawkins, a racist who is trying to shut down Woody Mahoney's tobacco farm. Finian offers to help Woody by paying off his debts. Sure enough, Woody falls in love with Sharon. The pot of gold has magical powers that keep its guardian Og alive. However, without the pot, Og will be cursed and become mortal, so Og pursues Finian in order to retrieve the pot. It becomes a race against time when geologists discover gold in the area. The gold, it is said, can grant three wishes. Og falls in love with Woody's mute sister and gives up his immortality to live with her. She regains speech. Woody and Sharon marry and Woody becomes very wealthy.

COPPOLA'S CONCEPT: Coppola headed into the movie major leagues when he agreed to direct *Finian's Rainbow* for Warner Brothers. It was his biggest-budgeted movie to date. It was based on the 1947 Broadway musical and Coppola wrote the screenplay, albeit uncredited. All his life Coppola had been a fan of musicals and was keen to direct one when the opportunity came up. Warner Brothers wanted the film to be made relatively inexpensively but Coppola pushed for location filming to expand the scope and interest.

INFLUENCES: The major influence on *Finian's Rainbow* was Coppola's memory and familiarity with the movie musical format that had been such a part of his growing up.

COSTUME: The costumes befit the fanciful tone of the film.

TEAM COPPOLA: The most important collaborative opportunity on Finian's Rainbow occurred in the margins of its production when Coppola met a young film school graduate named George Lucas, who was observing the production: it was to be one of Coppola's most important friendships and collaborations; it has also become one of the most legendary. George Lucas was a graduate of the University of Southern California film department and an aspiring film maker. He was on a scholarship to Warner Brothers at the time *Finian's Rainbow* was being filmed. Coppola spotted Lucas quietly surveying the shoot. From all accounts, he saw in Lucas a young man with whom he could collaborate; everybody else on the set was over 40.

CASTING: Fred Astaire was 68 and Coppola just 28. Significantly, in the original Broadway production the character of Finian was a non-singing role. Of course, casting Fred Astaire imbued the film with a vital energy and charm.

Petula Clark had developed a very big European following by the mid-1960s. Clark was a big hit on the Warner Brothers record label and this must certainly have partially informed their choice of her as the female lead. Tommy Steele's casting was based on his star turn in the movie musical *Half a Sixpence* (George Sidney, 1967). Whereas Coppola wanted the character of leprechaun Og to be introverted, Tommy Steele played him as an extrovert. The role of Buzz Collins was played by Coppola's friend and future production associate Ron Colby. As has now become famous with Coppola, there was a thorough rehearsal period before filming; it lasted three weeks during which Coppola's flautist father played alongside a pianist and a drummer.

I KNOW THAT FACE: Fred Astaire is a Hollywood legend, famous for his dancing partnership with Ginger Rogers. Astaire's film credits include *Top Hat* (Mark Sandrich, 1935), *Broadway Melody of 1940* (Norman Taurog, 1940), *Holiday Inn* (Mark Sandrich, 1942), *Yolanda and the Thief* (Vincente Minnelli, 1945), *Easter Parade* (Charles Walters, 1948), *Funny Face* (Stanley Donen, 1957) and *Silk Stockings* (Rouben Mamoulian, 1958). Petula Clark has also appeared in *Goodbye, Mr Chips* (Herbert Ross, 1969).

THE FILMING: The film began shooting on 26 June 1967 and production continued for twelve weeks. Coppola was able to secure more location-based shooting which meant eight days shooting in San Francisco, Modesto (George Lucas's hometown), Carmel and Monterey. His ambition had been to shoot on location in the South but the studio insisted on filming on the Warner Brothers lot. Coppola was given three weeks to rehearse the film and three months to shoot it. He was dissatisfied with the work of choreographer Hermes Pan, whom Fred Astaire had insisted work on the film, so Coppola staged most of the dance numbers himself. Warner Brothers loved the finished film and in their enthusiasm decided to blow the print up to 70mm. This resulted in a movie that literally cut off Astaire's feet so they could not be seen during his dance numbers. While working on the movie, Coppola had plans to move on to a far more personal piece of work entitled *The Rain People*, based on a short story he had written called *Echoes*. With production on *Finian's Rainbow* finished, Coppola was happy for the studio to complete it while he began work on *The Rain People*.

Finian's Rainbow was released in October 1968 and, despite its Broadway popularity as a stage musical, it failed to engage the movie audience. For Coppola, though, the biggest lesson of the project was partly self-inflicted. Tired of the studio process he left the project as soon as possible after shooting but, in hindsight, believed that the studio put the film together in a bad way. From that he learned the importance of overseeing his own post-production to ensure the tone of a film is consistent and correctly gauged.

HEROES AND VILLAINS: The forces of good and bad in *Finian's Rainbow* are broadly drawn. Finian is an idealistic character who is confronted by the corruption of the world: it is old man Finian who steps in with his wealth to save the property of Woody Mahoney. This is a Coppola line of thought that was replayed more fully in the *Godfather* films, *Apocalypse Now*, *Tucker: The Man and His Dream* and *The Rainmaker*. The strain of social commentary that the film has the space to hold is contained in the character of Sharon, who is more aware than her father of the challenge of poverty in the promised land of America.

Senator Rawkins and Buzz Collins are the villains, greedy and racist by turn. Rawkins is a traditional old South figure and he has no interest in change or equality. (See also **HUMOUR.**)

COPPOLA STYLE: Coppola adheres to an established movie musical style but manages to inject it with his trademark crosscutting technique at certain points. His belief in the value of shooting some of the film on location enhances its charm and vitality. Coppola's signature device, the intercutting of action, is evident in the song 'Woody's Here!', which intercuts between the song being performed and shots of a fast-moving train.

IMAGE: The film alternates between stage-bound sets (trees, groves and streams) and location exteriors of plantations and fields (see **THE FILMING**).

COPPOLA TUNES: The musical score for the film, in its buoyancy, energy and whimsy, adheres strongly to the material laid down in the Broadway stage version. EY (Yip) Harburg wrote the lyrics for *The Wizard of Oz* (Victor Fleming, 1939).

The soundtrack for the film is as follows: 'Look to the Rainbow'/'How Are Things in Glocca Morra?', 'This Time of the Year', 'How Are Things in Glocca Morra?', 'Look to the Rainbow', 'Old Devil Moon', 'Something Sort of Grandish', 'If This Isn't Love', 'That Great Come and Get It Day', 'When the Idle Poor Become the Idle Rich', 'Old Devil Moon', 'Rain Dance Ballet', 'The Begat', 'Look to the Rainbow', 'When I'm Not Near the Girl I Love', 'Look to the Rainbow', 'How Are Things in Glocca Morra?'

COPPOLA Finian's Rainbow

HUMOUR: As Og, Tommy Steele provides much of the film's comedy. More interestingly the film also finds a space for humour to make a clear and simple point about the injustice of racial inequality.

AWARDS: The film was nominated for a Writers Guild of America Award in the category of Best Written Musical. At the 1969 Golden Globes the film was nominated for Best Motion Picture Musical/Comedy, Best Motion Picture Actor (Fred Astaire), Best Motion Picture Actress (Petula Clark) and Best Supporting Actress (Barbara Hancock). Ray Heindorf was nominated for an Oscar at the 1970 awards ceremony in the category of Best Music and Score (Original or Adaptation) and was also nominated for Best Sound. In 1970, Petula Clark was nominated for a Golden Laurel award in the Female New Face category.

COPPOLA MAGIC: Within his limited technical resources, Coppola's invention and flair shines through, notably in the location-set material. The strength of these sequences contrasts with the obviously stage-bound scenes.

Coppola's magic with this film is in investing it with sincere emotion: Petula Clark singing the famous 'How are Things in Glocca Morra' is a good example of this.

MOVIE SPEAK:

Og: 'Fairy land was never like this!'

Finian: 'Now that you're half mortal, you're indecent!'

HOME VIEWING: *Finian's Rainbow* is available on VHS in both North America and the UK.

TRIVIA: The title sequence for the film was shot by long-time Coppola colleague, Carroll Ballard, who would go on to direct *The Black Stallion* (1979) which Coppola produced.

COPPOLA'S VIEW: *Finian's Rainbow* marks certain preoccupations that continued to develop through Coppola's career, notably the meaning of family and community. Tonally, the film hints at Coppola's storytelling playfulness and engagement with a fairy-tale sensibility that is present in much of his work, notably in *Peggy Sue Got Married*, *Captain Eo*, *Bram Stoker's Dracula*, and *Jack*. The power of song and dance to bring people together is a staple of the musical form and Coppola would rework this idea most famously in *One From the Heart*.

CRITICAL COPPOLA: In *Sight and Sound* Tom Milne described the film as 'a demonstration of the naturalness of the musical as a means of expression . . . with singers actually experiencing the emotions they celebrate.'

VERDICT: Although it received a run of positive reviews which emphasised the film's charm and Warner Brothers backed the film with enthusiasm, ultimately the film suffers from technical weaknesses in its choreography, sound recording and editing.

When produced for the stage in the 1940s *Finian's Rainbow* was considered ahead of its time. By the time of the late 1960s its style and tone may have seemed a little outdated. Nonetheless it remains an energetic and consistently entertaining musical, made at a time when the musical tradition was virtually in its sunset. Coppola's affinity for the musical shines through and his efforts to give the film the texture of the American South work well.

COPPOLA NOW: 'I was like a fish out of water among all these old studio guys . . .'

The Rain People (1969)

(Colour – 101 minutes)

Warner Brothers – Seven Arts
Producer: Bart Patton and Ronald Colby
Screenplay: Francis Ford Coppola
Cinematographer: Wilmer Butler
Editor: Barry Malkin
Music: Ronald Stein
Production Designer: Leon Ericksen
Art Direction: Leon Ericksen
Sound: Nathan Boxer
Sound Montage: Walter Murch
Production Associates: Mona Skager, George Lucas

CAST: James Caan (*Jimmie Kilgannon*), Shirley Knight (*Natalie*), Robert Duvall (*Gordon*), Marya Zimmet (*Rosalie*), Tom Aldredge (*Mr Alfred*), Laurie Crews (*Ellen*), Andrew Duncan (*Artie*), Margaret Fairchild (*Marion*), Sally Gracie (*Beth*), Alan Manson (*Lou*), Robert Modica (*Vinny*)

BUDGET: $750,000.00

RELEASE DATE: 27 August 1969

MPAA: R

BBFC: 15

TAGLINE: 'Rain people are very fragile . . . one mistake in love and they dissolve.'

SUMMARY: It is the late 1960s. A young woman, Natalie, leaves her husband when she discovers she is pregnant. He does not know where she is going or whether she will return. En route she picks up Jimmie, a brain-damaged former college football star, who is hitchhiking to West Virginia looking for work and who becomes dependent on her. She is intrigued by his childlike manner and they strike up a rapport.

On their arrival in West Virginia, Jimmie's girlfriend wants nothing to do with him now that he has a mental condition. Jimmie travels on with Natalie to Nebraska where she finds work for him at an animal farm. She leaves him there.

Natalie meets a cop named Gordon who fines her for speeding and is taken into town where she sees that Jimmie has liberated all the animals. Jimmie's attachment to Natalie remains strong though she goes on a date with Gordon. He has a young daughter, Rosalie. Gordon tries to force himself on Natalie; Jimmie intervenes and beats Gordon. Rosalie comes to her father's defence and shoots Jimmie dead.

COPPOLA'S CONCEPT: *The Rain People* represented Coppola's dream of independent film making and it furnished the developing director with the genesis of his ambition for his own studio. Just as digital video is marking a movie-making evolution in the early twenty-first century, so too in the mid- and late 1960s were film cameras and sound recording equipment becoming more portable – the very reason the European cinema had pushed for realism over artifice, shooting on real streets.

The Rain People was a road movie genuinely made on the road, with some of the improvisation that any road trip is a celebration of. Coppola's source material was his own short story *Echoes*, which tells the tale of three housewives who all take off in a station wagon to escape the monotony of their domestic lives. Other films that have followed along similar lines are *Stand Up and Be Counted* (Jackie Cooper, 1972), *An Unmarried Woman* (Paul Mazursky, 1978), *Alice Doesn't Live Here Anymore* (Martin Scorsese, 1974) and *Thelma and Louise* (Ridley Scott,

1991). There is an air of melancholy in the film as with most of
Coppola's films. Even the title comes from a poetically downbeat line of
dialogue spoken by Jimmie: 'The rain people are made of rain, and when
they cry they disappear altogether.' The film also established Coppola's
preoccupation with family that has marked so many of his films.

In broader thematic terms (that certainly receive expression in his later
movies), *The Rain People* came at a time when Coppola was reading a
lot of existentialist literature and the idea of being responsible for one
another really took shape in his creative mind. For Coppola, a film has
the potential to follow a novelistic form in that it can contain a wealth of
ideas. One of the principal ideas at work in *The Rain People* is that of
responsibility, a preoccupation that reverberates most powerfully
through *The Godfather* trilogy, *The Conversation* and *Gardens of Stone*.

For Coppola *The Rain People* stands as a genuine little art film and is
even more poignant for him as, alongside *The Conversation*, it is directed
from his own screenplay. All Coppola's other movies have been either
literary adaptations of novels or films based on other writers' screenplays.

INFLUENCES: Coppola's long-standing affinity for the quietness and
deliberate pacing of much European cinema, as opposed to the
muscularity and fast energy of so much American film making, clearly
impacts on the design of *The Rain People*. It is an approach so vital to
The Godfather films and to *The Conversation* as well. One could cite
Ingmar Bergman's film *Persona* (1966) as a key influence.

COSTUME: The film's contemporary setting demands a naturalistic
costume design for all the characters.

TEAM COPPOLA (and the Birth of a Studio): *The Rain People* allowed
Coppola to sow the seed for his dream of independent film making: with
George Lucas, Mona Skager, Bill Butler and Walter Murch on the crew,
Coppola had a core team of people who were to become long-standing
collaborators. Coppola has said that with the success of the *Star Wars*
saga American film making lost one of its smartest directors.

As with *You're A Big Boy Now*, *The Rain People* also served as
another rung on Coppola's industry ladder. It was during the shoot of
The Rain People that George Lucas proposed San Francisco as a base for
the company Coppola wanted to build. Lucas suggested a name for the
company: Transamerican Sprocket Works. Coppola eventually went for
the more grandiose and less cute sounding American Zoetrope. Coppola
wanted to be somewhere beautiful, with poetry and a bohemian
sensibility. Lucas describes the group at the heart of American Zoetrope
as 'a loose confederation of radicals and hippies'.

Once *The Rain People* was completed Coppola and his movie-making gang looked to establish a rural film-making base in northern California. They looked around Sonoma county and found a country house that was then bought while Coppola was still raising funds to secure it. Eventually, it was decided to put the rural retreat idea on hold and set up shop in San Francisco. Three floors of a building on Folsom Street served the purpose. On 14 November 1969, American Zoetrope officially went into business. A faux art nouveau brochure was produced to promote the company, playing up its combination of European and American cinematic sensibilities. Every Thursday night, as part of the bohemian ambition, a film was screened at the premises. Coppola was president of Zoetrope with Lucas as vice president. Before establishing things in San Francisco, Coppola took a trip to Denmark and visited Lanterna Film in Copenhagen where he saw that the operation was an old mansion that now housed a film company. It appeared bucolic, and inspired American Zoetrope and, beyond that, George Lucas's Skywalker Ranch base in rustic northern California. In his foreword to Charles Champlin's book about George Lucas, *The Creative Impulse*, Coppola writes that Lucasfilm 'remains American Zoetrope's younger and dazzling brother'.

Coppola ordered film kit and returned to San Francisco. John Korty, a local film maker, only fuelled Coppola and Lucas's dreams when he showed them where he worked: a barn-studio at Stinson Beach.

As a comparison, Coppola, Lucas and their cohorts were the equivalent of today's directors Wes Anderson (*Rushmore*, 1998, *The Royal Tenenbaums*, 2001), PT Anderson (*Boogie Nights*, 1997, *Magnolia*, 1999) and David Fincher (*Se7en*, 1995, *Fight Club*, 1999). Coppola had begun to encourage and nurture new film makers, rather like a doting father. At the Sorrento film festival in 1970, in attendance with Martin Scorsese, Coppola's theatrically phrased comment 'Have I become an old man of film already?' unwittingly alluded to his status by the early 1980s. Indeed, it was at that Sorrento festival that Coppola scoured the town for hole reinforcers for his notepad as he was about to start work on a screenplay for a new project – *The Godfather* – that was to make him that old man of film. At Sorrento, Coppola recommended Scorsese as the potential director of *Alice Doesn't Live Here Anymore* (1974) when its star Ellen Burstyn quizzed Coppola about new talent. Scorsese did go on to direct the feature.

Filled with optimism for the future, Zoetrope struck a multi-picture development deal with Warner Brothers for seven features. During this time Orson Welles contacted Coppola about making a film on 16mm. The films that were pitched to Warners included *THX-1138*, *Vesuvio* (about life in northern California, to have been directed by Carroll Ballard), *The Conversation* and a film called *Apocalypse Now*. Warners lent Zoetrope $300,000 and a further $300,000 in development money. This was a loan to be repaid by Zoetrope if they backed out. On 2 September 1969, *THX-1138* went into production with a ten-week shoot on a budget of $800,000. New writer-director George Lucas was at the helm.

On Thursday 19 November 1970, Warners rejected all Zoetrope's screenplays on a day that became known as Black Thursday at Zoetrope. Film makers left the company and the rent went up. For the moment, Coppola's dreams had fallen, but all this was just a prelude to what would unfold over the next few years, when Francis Ford Coppola would emerge as one of the finest American directors of all time.

In the early 1980s, Coppola reinvented the Zoetrope concept with a studio base in Hollywood. His concept was to re-create the studio world of the 30s, 40s and 50s using the studio as a safe haven for more maverick directors. Even the great Michael Powell had an office there.

The Rain People was shot by Bill Butler, who went on to *Jaws* (Steven Spielberg, 1975), *Rocky* (John Avilsden, 1976) and *One Flew Over The Cuckoo's Nest* (Milos Forman, 1976). Butler recently received the ACE award.

CASTING: Coppola had long admired the acting of Shirley Knight and, though it may be apocryphal, the story of how he offered her the lead in his proposed film is funny, bold and whimsical. Coppola saw Knight crying at a film festival after someone had upset her. To immediately cheer her, Coppola went up to the actress and claimed that he would write a film for her to star in. Knight was on board. During the filming, Knight was pregnant, matching the screen reality of her character Natalie.

Joining Coppola on his road-movie adventure were James Caan, Robert Duvall (as a motorcycle cop) and behind the camera the ground-floor guys of what would become American Zoetrope.

The most significant hurdle for Coppola, contrary to his initial hopes, was that working with Shirley Knight became difficult, as she was uneasy with Coppola's emphasis on improvisation. (Later in his career, this emphasis on improvisation would be at the heart of the opening scene of *Apocalypse Now* with Willard (Martin Sheen) going into a soul-meltdown in a Saigon hotel room.) Subsequently, reworking the screenplay on location, Coppola skewed the story towards James Caan's character. Coppola later expressed dissatisfaction at the way he resolved the story, which gave the character of Natalie (Shirley Knight) nowhere to go.

I KNOW THAT FACE: Shirley Knight went on to a major American TV career. Her most recent appearance in a feature film was *Divine Secrets of the Ya-Ya Sisterhood* (Callie Khouri, 2002).

James Caan went on to star in *The Godfather* and *Gardens of Stone* and also appeared in *Red Line 7000* (Howard Hawks, 1965), *El Dorado* (Howard Hawks, 1967), *Cinderella Liberty* (Mark Rydell, 1973), *Freebie and the Bean* (Richard Rush, 1974), *Rollerball* (Norman Jewison, 1975), *Comes A Horseman* (Alan J Pakula, 1978), *Thief* (Michael Mann, 1981), *Alien Nation* (Graham Baker, 1988), *Honeymoon in Vegas* (Andrew Bergman, 1992), *Flesh and Bone* (Steve Kloves, 1993) and *Dogville* (Lars von Trier, 2003).

Robert Duvall appeared as Boo Radley in *To Kill A Mockingbird* (Robert Mulligan, 1962). He has become a Coppola regular, appearing in *The Godfather*, *The Godfather Part II*, *The Conversation* and *Apocalypse Now*. He has also appeared in *Countdown* (Robert Altman, 1968), *Bullitt* (Peter Yates, 1968), *True Grit* (Henry Hathaway, 1969), *The Great Northfield Minnesota Raid* (Philip Kaufman, 1972), *Network* (Sidney Lumet, 1976), *Colors* (Dennis Hopper, 1989), *Tender Mercies* (Bruce Beresford, 1983), *Lonesome Dove* (Simon Wincer, 1989), *Days of Thunder* (Tony Scott, 1990), *Gods and Generals* (Ronald F Maxwell, 2003) and *Open Range* (Kevin Costner, 2003). He is now also a film director having directed *The Apostle* (1998), and *Assassination Tango* (2003), on which Coppola was executive producer.

THE FILMING: Coppola had been paid $80,000 for directing *Finian's Rainbow* and with that money he invested in sound and film equipment and convinced Warner Brothers to finance *The Rain People* – they agreed to $275,000.

George Lucas worked on the project as camera assistant, sound assistant and, from all accounts, assistant to everybody. Alongside this production role he also shot a documentary about the making of the movie, called *filmmaker*. A clip from it, showing Coppola arguing on the telephone, was included in BBC1's 1987 documentary series *Talking Pictures*, written and presented by Barry Norman.

The Rain People began shooting in early April 1968 at Long Island, NY. Lucas, Caan and a small crew filmed some football footage at Hofstra University prior to the larger film unit heading into the Midwest. Filming ran for eighteen weeks, ranging across eighteen states, over 105 shooting days.

A much-published photo of the film makers on location shows Coppola up on a ladder with George Lucas on the roof of the station wagon in the background, tellingly already standing out from the crowd.

Coppola delighted in the concept of a movie made away from Hollywood, confirming his commitment to a group of film makers separate from the 'frenzy business' of a mass media community. Grasping the spirit of the adventure, Coppola included real-life events in the movie such as a parade marching by. It was the first of several long-running film shoots of Coppola's career whereby real life folded into the movie world being created, leaving the resulting film all the better for this conjunction.

Easy Rider (Dennis Hopper, 1969) became a big hit at around the same time and, unfortunately, despite its critical recognition, *The Rain People* slipped away almost unnoticed soon after its release on 27 August 1969. However, with *The Rain People*, Coppola established himself as 'godfather' to a generation of film makers. Over thirty years later, Coppola's affinity for nurturing and supporting creative people continues.

HEROES AND VILLAINS: Natalie is the focus of the story. Rarely have Coppola's films centred on women; the next time a woman would be central to the drama of a Coppola film was in *Peggy Sue Got Married*. In both stories the dilemma for the woman is to find some kind of freedom and happiness from the pall of domesticity.

Like so many of Coppola's characters, the protagonists of *The Rain People* remain lonely.

COPPOLA STYLE: As with *Finian's Rainbow*, Coppola was really beginning to appreciate the emotive power of a close-up. In narrative terms, the film's style is that of a road movie; Coppola would arrange his themes and interests around the journey motif again in *Apocalypse Now*.

Complementing Coppola's unfussy visual style, the dialogue of the film is low-key and lacking in any kind of pretension. The meaning comes in the choices and actions of the characters, rather than in what they say. There is not much space for humour within the film.

IMAGE: There is an austere and muted quality to the visuals.

AWARDS: The one recognition the film received was a win (the Golden Seashell) for Coppola at the 1969 San Sebastian International Film Festival.

MOVIE SPEAK:
Natalie: 'I just want to be free even for five minutes.'

HOME VIEWING: *The Rain People* is available on VHS in America.

TRIVIA: Amusingly, to give an air of respectability to the crew, those men with beards (Coppola and Lucas's movie-making trademark in later years) shaved. However, without his beard, Coppola's air of authority was compromised.

COPPOLA'S VIEW: The film demonstrates Coppola's long-standing interest in dramatising the ties and complications of family commitment.

CRITICAL COPPOLA: *Time Out*'s Tom Milne described *The Rain People* as 'a fascinating early road movie . . . Symbolism rumbles beneath the characterisation but is never facile.'

VERDICT: *The Rain People* is a very strong early Coppola film that proves his facility for eliciting subtle performances and also maintaining a controlled tone throughout.

COPPOLA NOW: 'I wanted the film to be understanding of those issues in a woman that would cause her to want her own freedom, and yet at the same time trying to collide them with a sense of family.'

The Godfather (1972)

(Colour – 175 minutes)

Paramount Pictures
Producer: Albert S Ruddy
Associate Producer: Gray Frederickson
Screenplay: Mario Puzo, Francis Ford Coppola, based on the novel *The Godfather* by Mario Puzo
Cinematographer: Gordon Willis
Editor: William Reynolds, Peter Zinner
Music: Nino Rota (additional music by Carmine Coppola)
Production Design: Dean Tavoularis
Art Direction: Warren Clymer
Costume Design: Anna Hill Johnstone
Sound: Christopher Newman
Make-up: Dick Smith
Visual Effects: AD Flowers

CAST: Marlon Brando (*Don Vito Corleone*), Al Pacino (*Michael Corleone*), James Caan (*Sonny Corleone*), Richard Castellano (*Clemenza*), Robert Duvall (*Tom Hagen*), Sterling Hayden (*McCluskey*), John Marley (*Jack Woltz*), Richard Conte (*Barzini*), Al Lettieri

(*Sollozzo*), Diane Keaton (*Kay Adams*), Abe Vigoda (*Tessio*), Talia Shire (*Connie*), Gianni Russo (*Carlo Rizzi*), John Cazale (*Fredo Corleone*), Rudy Bond (*Cuneo*), Al Martino (*Johnny Fontane*), Morgana King (*Mama Corleone*), Lenny Montanna (*Luca Brasi*), John Martino (*Paulie Gatto*), Salvatore Corsitto (*Bonasera*), Richard Bright (*Neri*), Alex Rocco (*Moe Greene*), Tony Giorgio (*Bruno Tattaglia*), Vitto Scotti (*Nazorine*), Tere Livrano (*Theresa Hagen*), Victor Rendina (*Philip Tattaglia*), Jeannie Linero (*Lucy Mancini*), Julie Gregg (*Sandra Corleone*), Ardell Sheidan (*Mrs Clemenza*), Simonetta Stefanelli (*Apollonia*), Angelo Infanti (*Fabrizio*), Corrado Gaipa (*Don Tommasino*), Franco Citti (*Calo*), Saro Urzi (*Vitelli*)

BUDGET: $6 million

THE BOX OFFICE: $101.5 million (the 1997 reissue earned a further $53 million)

RELEASE DATE: 14 March 1972

MPAA: R

BBFC: X

TAGLINE: The film's poster simply carried the title *Mario Puzo's The Godfather*, indicative of how embedded the source novel was in the imagination of the audience by the time of the film's release. The film poster's image was of the Don's face, and the logo incorporated a marionette, emphasising the drama of people being controlled like puppets.

The film was immensely popular around the world, proving the rightness of Coppola in emphasising the story's family dynamic.

SUMMARY: New York, 1946. A local businessman, Bonasera, has come to speak to the aging Don Vito Corleone, the Godfather, about an attempted rape of his daughter. Don Bonasera hopes that Don Vito will be able to deal with the attackers appropriately as they have only received a suspended sentence for their crime. Sitting in Corleone's den are his son, Sonny (Santino) and Vito's consigliere (lawyer), Tom Hagen. Outside the den, the wedding party of the Don's daughter Connie is in full swing. Vito's youngest son, Michael, and his fiancée Kay, sit and watch the celebrations. Fredo, Vito's eldest son, is drunk. At their table, Kay asks Michael about his family. Michael explains that Tom Hagen is his 'brother' in so far as Michael's father adopted Tom as a baby and

raised him as family. Another of Don Vito's associates, Luca Brasi, goes
for counsel with him, nervously reciting what he will say before going in.
Johnny Fontane, a singer, then arrives at the wedding and asks the Don
for his help. Fontane's career is failing and Fontane needs to reassert his
popularity in films. Vito helped Fontane in the past. He says he will deal
with Hollywood for Fontane.

In Hollywood Tom Hagen visits Woltz Studios, the company where
Johnny Fontane has been having problems. Hagen issues a veiled threat
in an effort to force studio head Woltz to hire Fontane. Woltz baulks at
the notion. The next morning, Woltz wakes up to find the severed head
of his prized racehorse lying at his feet.

Back at the Corleone home and base, Hagen goes through a file with
Vito on the subject of a family enemy, Sollozzo. Vito arranges to meet
Sollozzo. After the meeting and wanting to know more about Sollozzo,
Vito instructs Luca Brasi to investigate. An attempt is then made on Don
Vito's life and Fredo fails to protect his father.

It is Christmas and Michael and Kay shop for gifts. Hagen goes to see
Sollozzo and is held by him for a number of hours before being released.
Sollozzo tells Hagen that Vito is dead; Hagen says that Sonny will swiftly
seek revenge. Michael arrives at the house having seen in a newspaper
that his father is in hospital after an attempt on his life. Hagen explains
that if Vito dics then much of the Corleone family power and influence
dies too; Michael should not get involved in family business at this level.
But Michael feels differently, the loyalty he feels to his father is
uppermost in his mind regardless of the implications. He has come out of
the army with military honours but wants nothing to do with his family's
criminal business operation. Luca goes to meet with Sollozzo but is
killed. A fish is sent to the Corleone home as a Sicilian symbol of Brasi's
death: he 'sleeps with the fishes'. Sonny is eager for revenge. Michael
does not want Kay to get involved in the life of the family in this way. He
visits Vito in hospital and has him moved to another room for safety. As
Michael stands at the entrance to the hospital he is beaten by a corrupt
police captain called McCluskey, who is being paid by Sollozzo.

Back home, Michael decides that, for his own safety, he, McCluskey
and Sollozzo should meet in a public place. At the meeting, Michael will
kill both men. Rocco, a family associate, teaches Michael how to handle
a gun and later Michael has the meeting and kills both McCluskey and
Sollozzo at close range. Vito is brought home from hospital to continue
recovering in a safer environment. Fredo is put up to go and learn the
casino business and run the operation in Las Vegas.

Michael is now the prime suspect in the murder of Sollozzo and
McCluskey and goes to Sicily for about a year, hiding out until the
conflict between the Mafia families dies down. In New York, his sister

Connie endures a painful marriage of violence and abuse and Sonny takes matters into his own hands, beating up her husband, Carlo. When Carlo continues to abuse Connie, Sonny makes another journey to see him. This time Sonny is gunned down by family rivals in a revenge attack on the Corleone family for the killing of Sollozzo.

In Sicily, Michael falls in love with a young woman called Apollonia and marries her. She is then killed in retaliation for Michael's killing of Sollozzo. Michael returns to New York and goes back to Kay, who has no idea of where he has been for the past year. To Kay, the outsider, this secrecy amplifies the strangeness of the Corleone life.

Vito, recovered but weak, organises a meeting of the five Mafia families and insists the vengeance must end. Kay tells Michael how much she objects to the violence in the family and he says that it will take five years to divest the family of its illegitimate business interests. Vito makes Michael the head of the family and Tom Hagen is sent out to Vegas to work as consigliere there. Vito becomes Michael's consigliere.

In Las Vegas Fredo deals with kingpin Moe Green who wants Johnny Fontane under contract as a singer at his casino. Michael then arrives in Vegas and informs Moe that the Corleone family want to buy him out. Moe is furious and says that will never happen.

Back in New York, Connie and Carlo's child is soon to be baptised and Michael is to be godfather to the child. Vito then dies in his garden. Following the funeral, Connie and Carlo's daughter is baptised while simultaneously, as Michael has ordered, the Corleone's key rivals are all executed.

Michael is now in full control. The house is sold and the family are to move to Lake Tahoe in Nevada. Kay confronts Michael about the business and Michael refuses to tell her anything. He is the new Godfather.

COPPOLA'S CONCEPT: Coppola won his first Oscar for screenwriting for *Patton* (Franklin J Shaffner) in 1970, but Robert Evans, the Production head at Paramount Pictures, had chosen him as director for *The Godfather* mainly because of his Italian background. Evans felt sure this would make the re-creation of the Italian/Sicilian homelife as authentic as possible. He could not have been more right. Alongside the guns and gangsters, Coppola enriches the world of *The Godfather* with domestic, historical and linguistic details that lend the fiction an element of truth. For Coppola the overriding theme that he wanted to extract from the material was that of America seen as a metaphor of the Mafia's modus operandi. After all, they were an immigrant culture that had been marginalised by the establishment and yet, in certain cases, were still able to maximise the opportunities offered by America's capitalist mindset.

Beyond the narrative appeal of *The Godfather*, Coppola considered that the opportunity to be paid for working on a major Hollywood film would allow him to secure enough capital to go on and make his own, more personal, material. He had taken *The Godfather* project in part to pay off debts incurred by Warners' rejection of American Zoetrope's plans for seven feature films. It was George Lucas and Coppola's father Carmine who encouraged the hesitant Coppola to sign up to direct the film. Concern about his personal kind of movie making was all that worried Coppola.

Coppola, on *The Godfather* trilogy DVD, declares that 'Kurosawa is the father of all violence' in the movies and then goes on to link that tradition back to Shakespeare. Given Coppola's enthusiasm for the theatre and an awareness of classical narratives, he sought to emphasise the sense of Greek tragedy that the source material suggested. In *The Godfather Part II* and *The Godfather Part III* these qualities are developed further still. Just as his feature *The Rain People* had dramatised the pressure of domesticity and the responsibility of family, so *The Godfather* relished in the notion of a family as a protective network of trust and dependability. Alongside the personal narratives of the film, Coppola and co-screenwriter and author of the novel, Mario Puzo, aimed to explore the privatisation of justice in America as expressed in the film through the relationship between McCluskey and Sollozzo.

One of the most famous artefacts of *The Godfather* is Coppola's bible for the project. This document is a vast biblically scaled annotated version of the novel. On *The Godfather* DVD set, there is a fascinating chapter in which Coppola talks through his creation of this document – the left page contains each page from the novel and the right page a corresponding series of notes and comments. Coppola's biographer and chronicler of *The Godfather* trilogy and *Apocalypse Now*, Peter Cowie, remarks, 'If ever proof were needed that auteurist theory – and practice – was alive and well in North America in 1971, this hefty volume proved it.' The notebook was broken into five elements for each chapter that Coppola was working on: there was a synopsis of each part of the story; a note about the times (the social context); imagery and tone; the core (the dramatic heart of each scene); and finally a segment called pitfalls, which was a series of notes to guide Coppola away from cliché and so forth. Coppola has said that this notebook, created prior to the screenplay, rendered the screenplay unnecessary. Coppola's notebook testifies to just how carefully designed a great film is, how much thought is put into it to draw out the resonance of the film.

The film has been criticised for romanticising the Mafia in that it never depicts harm and negative influence on innocent people beyond the enclaves of the families. Coppola did concede that the film was a 'romantic conception of the Mafia'.

Coppola's emphasis on the biblical issues of atonement and guilt are present. Interestingly, one shot was not included at the end of *The Godfather*. It was a moment that appeared in the original novel in which Kay lights a candle for Michael at the close of the story. The scene is included in the TV edition of *The Godfather* and *The Godfather Part II*.

INFLUENCES: *The Godfather*'s expansive, multi-character narrative recalls a theatrical tradition, and its period setting and criminal milieu suggest the Warner Brothers movies of the 1930s, such as *Angels with Dirty Faces* (Michael Curtiz, 1938) and *Scarface* (Howard Hawks/Richard Rosson, 1932), infused with a more European sensibility towards depth of characterisation. With its patriarchal centre in the form of Don Vito, one cannot help but think of a king or an emperor. Kurosawa's samurai films, such as *The Seven Samurai* (1954), *Throne of Blood* (1957), *The Hidden Fortress* (1958) and *Yojimbo* (1961), all feed into *The Godfather*. Kurosawa is one of Coppola's film director gurus. The samurai code and disciplined image-making of Kurosawa's movies is ever present in *The Godfather*, albeit within a very different setting and culture.

Coppola's other influences include Sergei Eisenstein's innovative early cinema and experiments with intercutting various stories so that they propel the narrative at a furious pace. American early cinema director DW Griffith also experimented with this now all too familiar way of structuring a story. In films such as *Birth of A Nation* (1915), *Intolerance* (1916) and *Way Down East* (1920), Griffith was also a genius with spectacle and historical settings, features that play their part in the evocation of the world of *The Godfather*.

COSTUME: The costumes for *The Godfather* are historically accurate and speak powerfully about the characters. Kay's bright orange dress at the start of the film is conspicuous, suggesting her outsider status.

Marlon Brando's rough, brown jacket and shirt have a humility to them that belie his power and recall his Sicilian roots.

Michael is first seen in his military uniform. As the film progresses he assumes a darker dress code that suggests the overwhelming shadow cast by Don Vito. Michael's clothes are more traditional, suggesting his connection to the older values that the family abides by and which the film suggests have been corrupted by modern business interests and practice.

Sonny is the most flamboyant character of the three brothers. His machismo is made evident by his tendency towards strutting around in his vest; even his shirts are monogrammed in a display of his confidence and flair. By contrast, Fredo, the eldest brother, possesses none of the bullishness of Sonny; he is a weak character, pathetically so at times. In his scenes in Las Vegas, the kind of low-key dress code that marks out both Vito and Michael is ignored by Fredo, who wears an almost comically gauche jacket, suggesting a serious absence of good taste.

Consistent with his powerfully ultra-low-key presence in the story, Tom Hagen wears sombre suits at all times, only adding to his calm and shadowy place in the action.

Michael is first seen, as a perfectly groomed war veteran, at the wedding of his sister Connie. Later in the film, for the sequence where he hides out in Sicily, he adopts the waistcoat and flat cap of the rural people. When he returns from Sicily, his life ravaged by tragedy, Michael looks funereal in his long coat and hat.

TEAM COPPOLA: With the genesis of American Zoetrope, Coppola had assembled a close network of colleagues and friends around him, but had to leave them behind for work on *The Godfather* before returning to his San Francisco base after the project's completion. Coppola's interest in the place of family on screen is mirrored in his working life by a repeated collaboration with trusted associates. It was George Lucas who shot the newspaper footage for the film. Coppola's most significant collaborators were Mario Puzo and cinematographer Gordon Willis. As a writer Coppola relished working on the screenplay with the author of the source novel.

Teaming with Coppola in the day-to-day battle of making the film was a young Canadian producer, Albert S Ruddy, who had produced two films of note: *Little Fauss and Big Halsey* (1970) and *Making It* (1971). Gordon Willis, who has been nicknamed The Prince of Darkness because of the emphasis on shadow and silhouette in his work, also shot *Klute* (Alan J Pakula, 1971), *Bad Company* (Robert Benton, 1972), and *All the President's Men* (Alan J Pakula, 1976), and had collaborated with Woody Allen on *Annie Hall* (1977), *Interiors* (1978), *Manhattan* (1979), *Stardust Memories* (1980), *A Midsummer Night's Sex Comedy* (1982), *Broadway Danny Rose* (1984) and *The Purple Rose of Cairo* (1985). With Coppola, he produced some of his finest and most memorable work, which has, arguably, transcended the movies themselves.

Coppola's other key collaborators were Gray Frederickson who would go on to work with Coppola on *Apocalypse Now* and Dean Tavoularis, who came on board as the production designer and has remained a vital Coppola comrade ever since. He has worked on *The Conversation, The Godfather Part II, The Godfather Part III, Apocalypse Now, The Outsiders, Rumble Fish, One From the Heart* and *Tucker: The Man and*

His Dream. Tavoularis is also collaborating with Coppola on the developing project *Megalopolis*. Tavoularis has also worked on *Zabriskie Point* (Michelangelo Antonioni, 1970), *Little Big Man* (Arthur Penn, 1970), *Rising Sun* (Philip Kaufman, 1993), *I Love Trouble* (Charles and Nancy Shyer, 1994), *CQ* (Roman Coppola, 2001) and *Angel Eyes* (Luis Mandoki, 2001).

Finally, there was Fred Roos, who has also remained close to Coppola since *The Godfather*, starting as a casting agent and then moving into a role as producer on later films. Fred Roos went on to collaborate almost exclusively with Coppola, working on *The Godfather Part II, The Conversation, Apocalypse Now, The Outsiders, Rumble Fish, Gardens of Stone, Tucker: The Man and His Dream, The Godfather Part III* and *Jack*.

CASTING: In casting *The Godfather* the effort was exhaustive but resulted in providing pop culture with a range of iconic actors and characters. As with most films, many actors were considered in an 'unofficial' way prior to work commencing on the movie. Anthony Quinn and Ernest Borgnine (both Oscar winners for *Zorba the Greek* (Michael Cacoyannis, 1964) and *Marty* (Delbert Mann, 1955), respectively) were possibles for the role of Don Vito Corleone. That these actors were considered for the role seems an aberration given the way in which Brando is now so readily associated with the character. Indeed, *The Godfather* is so embedded in the popular imagination that it is important to remember there was a time when it did not exist. The same thing occurs with pop songs that lodge themselves in the mass consciousness. Like the moon and the stars, these works have just always been there and are taken for granted. At one point Burt Lancaster had wanted to buy the rights to the novel and portray the Don. Despite the iconic status of his eventual performance in the role of Don Vito, Marlon Brando was not considered the obvious choice. At the time of the film's pre-production his commercial popularity was in bad shape. Paramount had hopes for Anthony Quinn playing the role. It was Coppola who suggested Brando. Studio head, Robert Evans, felt that Brando was too young for it as he was only 47. Soon an effort was being made to dissuade Coppola from his Brando ambition. Tellingly, and unsurprisingly, Coppola persisted in his belief that Brando was the ideal candidate. Paramount came to a compromise – Coppola would have to screen-test Brando. The studio hoped that the idea of a screen test for such a big star might dilute Brando's enthusiasm for the film. Coppola went to Brando's house on Mulholland Drive. Improvising, Brando slicked his hair back with boot polish and stuffed tissue paper in his mouth and even wrinkled the tips of his shirt collar. He then pencilled in a moustache after Coppola had mentioned his own uncle's moustache. The effort and detail of this screen test convinced Paramount to back Coppola's conviction.

In the period since the mid-1970s when he worked with Coppola again on *Apocalypse Now*, Brando was, sadly, more famous for the size of his pay cheques than the integrity of his performances. He signed up for *The Godfather* for $50,000, plus $10,000 per week in expenses. He was due to work six weeks on the film and take 1 per cent of the box office gross after its first $10 million. If the film passed $60 million then he would be entitled to 5 per cent of the gross. Despite his commitment to the film, just a month before filming began he was weighed and found to be too heavy for the role. He dieted severely only to find he had lost too much weight and had to put some back on.

Not for the first time, *The Godfather* would be a Coppola movie that showcased new and emerging talent. With *The Outsiders* and *Rumble Fish* in 1983 and even with a more recent film such as *Bram Stoker's Dracula*, Coppola's casts were comprised mainly of young actors who continue to appear in movies today.

The casting process for *The Godfather* was arduous, committed and varied. Famously, Frank Sinatra was almost cast as Johnny Fontane.

For the role of Kay, Genevieve Bujold, Blythe Danner and Jill Clayburgh were considered. Finally, Coppola cast Diane Keaton in the role. For Michael Corleone, Robert Redford, Ryan O'Neal and a young Tommy Lee Jones were considered as were David Carradine, Dean Stockwell, Martin Sheen, James Caan and Robert De Niro. Ultimately, the role of Michael went to Al Pacino, who had to screen test repeatedly for the part. Coppola's pal Robert Duvall, who appeared in *The Rain People* and George Lucas's *THX-1138* (1971) recommended Pacino, and it was Lucas's wife at the time, Marcia Lucas, who insisted that Pacino's eyes were very dramatic. James Caan (who had also been in *The Rain People*) was cast as Sonny and Duvall as Tom Hagen. None of the actors was paid more than £35,000.

I KNOW THAT FACE: Marlon Brando starred in *On The Waterfront* (Elia Kazan, 1954) and *A Streetcar Named Desire* (Elia Kazan, 1951), films that established his intensity and allure. He also appeared in *Viva Zapata* (Elie Kazan, 1952), *Julius Caesar* (Joseph L Mankiewicz, 1953), *Last Tango in Paris* (Bernardo Bertolucci, 1972), *The Missouri Breaks* (Arthur Penn, 1976), *Superman: The Movie* (Richard Donner, 1978) and, later, *Apocalypse Now*.

Al Pacino, of Sicilian background, remains a major movie star thirty years after *The Godfather*. Prior to *The Godfather* his screen experience had been limited to appearing in *Me Natalie* (Fred Coe, 1969) and *The*

Panic in Needle Park (Jerry Schatzberg, 1971). He has made many films, including *Serpico* (Sidney Lumet, 1973), *Dog Day Afternoon* (Sidney Lumet, 1975), *Scarface* (Brian De Palma, 1983), *Sea of Love* (Harold Becker, 1989), *Frankie and Johnny* (Garry Marshall, 1991), *Scent of a Woman* (Martin Brest, 1992), *Carlito's Way* (Brian De Palma, 1993) and *Insomnia* (Christopher Nolan, 2002).

John Cazale died tragically young in 1978 and featured in just a handful of films, including *Dog Day Afternoon* (Sidney Lumet, 1973), *The Conversation* and *The Deer Hunter* (Michael Cimino, 1978).

Diane Keaton has gone on to become a major American actress, appearing in films that include *Play It Again, Sam* (Woody Allen, 1972), *Sleeper* (Woody Allen, 1974), *Annie Hall* (Woody Allen, 1974), *Manhatten* (Woody Allen, 1975) and *Looking for Mr Goodbar* (Richard Brooks, 1977). She has also worked as a director on the film *Wildflower* (1991).

Talia Shire is Francis Ford Coppola's sister. Her most famous recurring role other than in *The Godfather* series is as the long-suffering Adrienne in the five *Rocky* films.

THE FILMING: A massive studio project, *The Godfather* is now a film-making legend for the intensity of its creation. As with many films, the period spent developing the screenplay is especially intriguing. Mario Puzo wrote the novel in the mid-1960s and the book was optioned by Paramount in 1967, based on just the first sixty pages of Puzo's manuscript. A bidding war then began between Universal and Paramount for the rights to the novel, which was published in 1969. Producer Al Ruddy became attached to the project and, when he had a meeting with Charles Bludhorn, the chief of Gulf and Western – the corporation which owned Paramount – he said he wanted to 'Make an ice blue, terrifying movie about people you love'. In the summer of 1970, Puzo finished a first draft of the screenplay, working from the third floor of Paramount's Marathon Street offices in New York. He worked upstairs from Al Ruddy and would go and confer with him as necessary.

In 1970 Paramount Pictures needed a hit following the commercial failures of *Catch 22* (Mike Nichols, 1970), *Darling Lili* (Blake Edwards, 1970) and *Paint Your Wagon* (Joshua Logan, 1969). They saw *The Godfather* as a very viable commercial project with the inevitable built-in audience derived from the popularity of the novel.

With his producer hat on, Ruddy felt that filming in New York would be too expensive and considered Cleveland, Kansas City and Cincinnati. At this stage there was still no director attached but there were a number of high fliers under consideration: Arthur Penn (*Bonnie and Clyde*, 1969), Peter Yates (*Bullitt, 1968*), Costa-Gavras (*Z*, 1969), Sidney J

Furie (*The Ipcress File*, 1965), Otto Preminger (*Man with the Golden Arm*, 1955, *Cardinal*, 1963), Richard Brooks (*Elmer Gantry*, 1960), Elia Kazan (*On The Waterfront*, 1954), Fred Zinneman (*High Noon*, 1952) and Franklin J Schaffner (*Planet of the Apes*, 1968, *Patton*, 1970). At about this time Sam Peckinpah had expressed an interest in making the film.

It was Paramount Production head Peter Bart who suggested approaching Coppola, who at this time was held in higher esteem as a screenwriter than a director. Indeed, at the time, Coppola was employed mostly as a script doctor, amending material in order to improve its narrative health. Bart took the trip up to northern California to offer Coppola the job and, with some further encouragement from his own father and George Lucas, he accepted the project.

Originally, Kansas City was suggested as a location as it would be cheaper to film there than in New York, but Coppola insisted on shooting in New York so as to invest the film with authenticity. He also wanted to emphasise the story's family saga dimension – its universal dramatic impulse and appeal. Where the original novel flip-flops between past and present, *The Godfather* film was a linear story. The intercutting of time would be the structural basis for *The Godfather Part II*. Coppola sat and worked with Puzo on the screenplay. Their first draft was dated 1 March 1971 and came in at 173 pages. On the 29 March a new draft was submitted.

Paramount Studios head Robert Evans was overseeing the film and there was a degree of conflict and difference of opinion between Coppola and Evans. Evans was keen on keeping directors under his control and supervision while Coppola wanted his creative freedom honoured as the film's director. Evans secured an extra $1 million in order to allow location shooting in New York, especially after the production designer Dean Tavoularis made the case for going there when he said the mock tower block buildings on the Paramount studio lot in Hollywood were not authentically high enough.

With its Mafia setting, the production did have to respectfully negotiate with, and keep informed, the Mafia contacts who were interested in how the film would present their world. *The Godfather*'s producer Al Ruddy attended a series of meetings with Family heads to assure them that the film would not be derogatory or accusatory.

On 29 March 1971, principal photography on the film began. As the early rushes began to come in and be viewed by the studio, some reservations were raised about Coppola's facility with basic film grammar. Whispers were heard that maybe Coppola should be replaced. Peter Bart was pro-Coppola but was not of much use as he was based on the West Coast. Robert Evans's concern was with Brando's performance;

he appeared to be mumbling. Evans bleakly joked that the film might require subtitles. As concern about Coppola's competence as a director grew, the studio approached Elia Kazan as a replacement director. When Brando heard Coppola might be replaced he said that he would walk off the film if this happened.

The film was shot on 120 locations, all in New York. These locations included Penn Central Station, Hotel Edison on 46th Street, Bellevue Morgue and Old St Patrick's Cathedral. Among the wealth of period detail that it was necessary to re-create was the inclusion of vintage De Soto taxis from the 1941–50 period as well as the redecoration of the shop exterior of Best and Co. in Manhattan. The interior, studio-based work was achieved at 127th Street, at Filmway Studios, which is where Don Vito's moody den was built and filmed.

At the end of July 1971, the production shifted to Sicily for two weeks, where the crew shot in Catania rather than the town of Corleone, which lacked the required visual appeal. Forza d'Argo was the location for the wedding of Michael and Apollonia. Coppola's insistence on shooting in Sicily enhances the film's fidelity to the source material.

After an informal screening of the material to date in July 1971, a first assembly of the film was completed in September, which included rough sound effects. The film was edited in San Francisco at Coppola's Zoetrope base on Folsom Street. Paramount's insistence was that the film should not run longer than two hours and fifteen minutes, which was considered a long running time for a movie thirty years ago. Over the years, a two-and-a-half-hour running time is not unusual for many blockbuster movies; sometimes for better, often for worse. It was with the screening of the material and the beginning of post-production that Coppola's relationship with Robert Evans became somewhat tense. When he viewed a cut in December 1971, Evans felt the film, which clocked in at 131 minutes, lacked texture. 'You shot a saga and turned in a trailer,' Evans famously commented. Coppola ultimately agreed to reincorporate another forty minutes of material, which added to the ambience of the film.

Just as Coppola had to battle for casting Brando and filming in New York so too had he to fight his corner when the issue of the film's composer arose. Coppola wanted Italian composer Nino Rota, who had scored many Fellini films, to provide the music. Paramount were unsure and had already begun dealing with Henry Mancini, but Coppola insisted that Rota's music should remain. Only if, at a preview screening, there was a consensus that the film needed a new score would Coppola concede to the studio. Rota's music was well received and so remained in the film.

All of these behind-the-scenes debates and changes on films in the making continue to feed the Hollywood movie press and hype machine –

just look at the column inches devoted to Martin Scorsese's visionary *Gangs of New York* (2002). Ultimately, Rota scored the film and Coppola recruited his own father, Carmine, to compose the tarantella for the wedding scene.

Paramount then screened the film for exhibitors, who feared the material had too much talk and not enough action. Of course, these days it is the film's dialogue that is among its most remembered pleasures.

On 16 April 1972, Paramount Pictures announced that a sequel would be made.

PROMOTION: The film had been due for release at Christmas 1971 but was not at any acceptable stage of completion. *The Godfather* was eventually released on Tuesday 14 March 1972 at New York's Loews State 1 Theatre. When eventually released, the film made more money in six months ($86,250,000) than *Gone with the Wind* (Victor Fleming, 1939) had made in its initial six-month theatrical run ($74,000,000). *The Godfather* set in motion the long run of the blockbuster which continues today with wide releases of films and a recognition of the international market. Hollywood has always adapted hit novels for the screen but *The Godfather* redefined the scale of the commercial potential. In 1975, *Jaws* (Steven Spielberg) was released and achieved great success, which was then superseded by *Star Wars* (George Lucas) in 1977. Both these movies put the commercial success, relatively speaking, in the shade. After nine weeks *The Godfather* had made $53,302,439.

THE OPENING: For such an ultimately expansive, and eventually epic, trilogy, *The Godfather*'s opening image is small and intimate: a close-up of Don Bonasera talking to the Don Vito Corleone in the shadows and secrecy of his office. It suggests nothing less than a meeting with the Pope, a scenario that actually comes into play in *The Godfather Part III*. The film begins with a black screen as Nino Rota's now iconic theme music plays with an air of melancholy. The first words are heard before an image appears: 'I believe in America.' The camera pulls back slowly. Bonasera is lit from above, his eyes cast into shadow. If you cannot see a person's eyes do you ever know what they are really thinking and feeling? (This is a motif that is continued through the series and is especially powerful in the final moment of *The Godfather Part II*.) Eventually the camera stops its slow track back and rests over the shoulder of Don Vito who has his back to us. We see only his shoulder and right hand, his appearance an enigma. Thematically, the social and the personal fuse in Bonasera's dilemma as he and Vito talk about what they see as an absence of justice, which Vito is sure he can redress through his influence and power. A wide shot then reveals the Don in the office, with Sonny and Tom Hagen also present in the shadows. The camera is fixed. In a wider shot, showing Vito standing, a red rose can be seen in the lapel of his tuxedo and this flower is the only vibrant colour amid the shadowy and muted surroundings.

HEROES AND VILLAINS: Though Vito is the Godfather of this film, Michael's journey is the true focus of the story. Michael Corleone begins the film as an innocent. As the film develops, his fall from grace begins, driven as he is by revenge for an attempt to murder his father. Michael is an immensely attractive character: intelligent, emotional and committed. In his body language, Michael is contained and understated. Clean-shaven and bright-eyed at first, Michael becomes unshaven and sullen, his appearance reflecting his darkening soul. Michael moves quickly and precisely and often is shown simply sitting and looking. Michael is more of a throwback to the older world of Vito in the way he dresses. Violence and religion collide in Michael during the close of the film.

Tom Hagen is in a sense the film's best character. He moves and sits quietly and steadily on the fringe of the action, yet always influencing it. Tom is frequently framed in shot in the background as though on the shoulder of Vito, like a protecting angel. In *The Godfather Part II* Coppola frames later scenes with young Vito in a similar way, though in those shots it is a picture of the Virgin Mary that is framed on his shoulder.

Kay is a window for the audience into the clandestine and intricately organised world of the Corleone family. She has strength, but it can only go so far in the face of the family. Nonetheless, she urges Michael to be honest with her, but this proves a huge problem for him and part of his eventual undoing in *The Godfather Part II*.

Connie is a strong character and her strength and resolve grow through the trilogy to the point where her turn to evil is tragic. Not even she escapes the urge to kill by the time of *The Godfather Part III*. She is unquestioningly loyal, which is both the blessing and the curse of the family.

Fredo is the weak brother who we see fumble for his gun when he should readily be able to use it to protect his father under fire. This inefficiency and his absence of macho cool contrast with the confident Sonny. Fredo is on the margin of the family, and this is expressed visually when Vito returns home from hospital. As Vito is carried upstairs, Fredo hangs on the edge of the frame. Fredo's body language is elaborate and slightly goofy.

Vito Corleone is a dying patriarch and in his character Coppola finds something analogous with Shakespeare's *King Lear*. Certainly by *The*

Godfather Part III, Coppola was openly comparing the Corleone patriarch with the king and, interestingly, one of Coppola's film director heroes, Akira Kurosawa, adapted *King Lear* as the epic film *Ran* (1987). For all his power and potential for violence, Brando compels audience sympathy and, ultimately, Vito ends his life as an old man anxious about the security of his dynasty, of his family, apart from the business world he moves in. Vito is the melancholy heart of the film. Coppola has often attested to the film's romantic spirit, and Vito's expressions of family and honour are winningly powerful. When Vito dies at the end he is a frail and lonely man, divested of his power. Vito, like Colonel Kurtz in *Apocalypse Now* (also portrayed by Marlon Brando), is a character who feels an older world code has died away. Throughout *The Godfather*, Vito expresses unease at the incursion of the narcotics trade into the business interests of the Mafia families. Vito feels it is not the right kind of business for his family to enter into, being too much of the modern world. Vito emphasises male strength, the dominance of the man and his necessary sense of responsibility, which is what defines Michael and makes him the worthy successor. Vito says 'women and children can be careless, but not men'. The great achievement of *The Godfather* is the humanity of its killers, staying true to Al Ruddy's pre-production proclamation to Charles Bludhorn.

Sonny and Fredo have something childish about their clumsiness and tendency to anger. Sonny is always on the brink of exploding. Witness the revealing character touch as he anxiously turns a glass in his hand during the meeting with Sollozzo.

Sollozzo and the film's other antagonists are drawn vividly but not to the extent that their losses elicit audience sympathy.

COPPOLA STYLE: Coppola's overriding aesthetic with *The Godfather* was of muted colours and compositional restraint. The theatricality is not in the visuals but rather in the flow of the narrative; that is the film's biggest special effect. *The Godfather* is an elegantly mounted movie. The film's visual power is complemented by the structure of the story and the richness of its characters, which are the most powerful aesthetic elements. Compositionally the film is very simple and direct and Coppola's affinity for the feudal themes and pageantry of Akira Kurosawa's samurai films shines through. Coppola's narrative skills testify to his great capacity as a writer as he intercuts between story threads and various locations. Intercutting brings the movie to a climax as the baptism of Connie's daughter and the killing of the family heads occur simultaneously.

If God is in the details (as the Don would no doubt attest) then *The Godfather* is enriched and elevated to a heavenly degree by attention to

Sicilian dialect, criminal codes and body language. The film uses classical techniques at their most expressive. Coppola's established rapport with actors yields many riches. His use of dissolves and fades in and out emphasises the passing of time. His intercutting harks back to the oldest Hollywood devices and lends a grandeur and sense of impending doom to several key sequences, notably at the crescendo of the film.

IMAGE: *The Godfather* is a hymn to doorways, corridors and rooms, to the stable spaces of a family home around which the chaos of life inevitably swirls. Gordon Willis brings a muted and warm quality to much of the film so that the Corleone home feels warm and inviting in contrast to the coldness of its business and the codes it operates within. Coppola tends not to move the camera much, instead opting for a locked-off form which allows the audience to focus predominantly on the characters. The décor enhances the family theme.

Coppola invests much of the film with a powerful stillness and the film ends on a chilling example of this. At the end the image is a tableau showing Kay in the foreground and Michael leaning against his desk, a statement of their two separate worlds in the one shot.

Coppola and Gordon Willis combine the tableaux form with naturalistic images that immerse the audience in the story world. The distance often put between the camera and the action creates an emotional distancing effect that brings an added chill to many powerful and visceral scenes. The expansive opening movement of the film at Connie's wedding feels almost like a documentary of a family wedding as Coppola often uses long lenses to give a sense of a world observed from a distance.

For the murder of Sollozzo and McCluskey, a subtle and slow track in on Michael as he prepares to leave the table and get the gun with which he will kill them plays up the intensity and unease Michael feels. When he returns with the hidden gun, the camera is behind him as he approaches the table, putting us directly in his position so that we take Michael's side.

In the scene where Sonny beats up Carlo, Coppola emphasises a cold detachment from the action that is free of typical movie thrills. Instead, there is documentary quality to the moment, enhancing the sense of reality and, in this instance, horror of the scene. It captures the ugly chaos of a fight with believability and contrasts with the tendency of films towards spectacle and sensationalism in their presentation of violence. Coppola chooses his moments to control the effects at his disposal, in terms of camera placement and sound effects, wisely. This same distancing and dampening of a potentially melodramatic event is also used for the moment when Michael's car blows up in Sicily.

When *The Godfather* was being made, there was concern that the images were too dark. Yet this emphasis on what cannot be seen is what makes the Corleone clan that much more threatening. At the start of the film, Michael is seen in full light; by the end of the film, he is half in light, half in shadow, as he falls inescapably to a life of violence and anger. The closing part of the film is cooler in its tone, greyer and certainly autumnal.

The film's closing image is as small as its opening image, as we see Kay looking at Michael as he receives people in his office as the Godfather. The door to his office closes in Kay's face excluding her from his world. Michael's posture is one of a prince, of somebody more than human with the ability to curse and bless as necessary.

The film establishes a contrast between the cold and dark of the New York compound and the warm, open, expansive, sunny glare of Sicily.

This morally dark world has characters (nearly all men) continually stepping out of, and retreating into, shadow. Coppola repeats and hones this further in *The Godfather Part II* and also in the playful and more juvenile *The Cotton Club*. In *Apocalypse Now*, the entire final movement of the film plays with faces glimpsed in the near darkness like minotaurs in the labyrinth, emerging for the kill.

Gordon Willis, the director of photography on *The Godfather* trilogy, outlines his aesthetic in *The Godfather* films by saying that his work is a form of 'romantic reality'. Indeed, one of the motivating factors in the lighting design for those scenes in the Don's den, especially in *The Godfather*, was to make Brando's make-up look real. It was only when Willis realised it worked with some power that he extended this style across the rest of the film so that it transcended pragmatism and became far more substantial in expressing character and hence elements of theme. The exterior scenes of the wedding were intentionally overexposed to contrast with the shadow of the inside of the Corleone home. Willis says of his style – and it is certainly evidenced in *The Godfather* trilogy – 'I . . . like using negative space in my compositions. I love anamorphic lenses because you can put a close-up way over on the right side of the screen, leaving the rest of the frame empty; but it's not really empty, it's filled with design.'

SOUND: Walter Murch, sound and editing guru, shifts the audience perspective and sense of space through sound. For the wedding sequence, for example, he combines the sound of the music being played on the loudspeakers, with an original recording of the music. For the murder of Sollozzo, Murch lays in an abnormally loud sound of a subway train, even though we never see such a train and even though a subway train plays no part in the narrative. Instead, the effect is ambient and hints more at a psychological and emotional intensity rather than anything realistic.

The Italian dialogue in the film is not subtitled. Instead, the audience are trusted to interpret the meaning through pitch and intonation. This genuine and respectful approach comes into play in Ken Loach's film *Sweet Sixteen* (2002).

During the film's climax Michael's voice is heard renouncing Satan over images of men being killed on his orders, thereby rendering hollow, and at the very least questionable, his commitment to his Catholicism. He is a liar.

COPPOLA TUNES: Nino Rota composed the film's now legendary and melancholy theme, which speaks nothing of the excitement of gangster life as portrayed by Hollywood.

There is a stylistic device used throughout *The Godfather* wherein the music is used not to underscore and overemphasise a particular moment but instead to guide the audience out of a scene.

The melancholy nature of the film's main subject expresses the dominant theme of the film, which is of time passing and the inevitability of death. It is a tragic theme that thankfully does not take the easy route and convey the gangsterism and violence that forms part of the story. The music helps universalise the true interest of the film and surely accounts for its longevity. Nino Rota's credits include *8½* (Federico Fellini, 1960), *Romeo and Juliet* (Franco Zefferelli, 1972), *Death on the Nile* (John Guillermin, 1978), *La Dolce Vita* (Federico Fellini, 1960), *Roma* (Federico Fellini, 1972). The soundtrack for the film is not in print but many of its themes are reiterated.

HUMOUR: Throughout the film there are traces of humour in terms of behaviour and some blackly comic exchanges. When Sollozzo lets Hagen go he says, 'Blood is a big expense.' Earlier in the film the now legendary phrase 'an offer he couldn't refuse' is related as part of an old family story. Moments later the phrase is used again in a real context and suddenly the humour of it becomes unsettlingly potent.

AWARDS: *The Godfather* instigated Coppola's phenomenal run of awards and accolades that greeted each film he made. At the 1972 National Board of Review awards *The Godfather* won in the category of Best Supporting Actor (Al Pacino). At the 1973 Academy Awards the film won the Best Actor in a leading role award (Brando declined to accept and sent a faux Native American woman in his place), Best Picture and Best Writing (Screenplay based on material from another medium); nominated Best Supporting Actor (James Caan, Al Pacino, Robert Duvall), Best Costume Design, Best Director, Best Film Editing and Best Sound. The 1973 American Cinema Editors awards nominated the film in the Best Edited Feature Film category. In Britain, the applause kept coming. At the 1973 BAFTA ceremony the film won the Anthony Asquith Award for Film Music and also received nominations for Best Actor, Best Costume Design, Best Newcomer (Al Pacino) and Best Supporting Actor. *The Godfather* won the 1973 David di Donatello Award for Best Foreign Film and Coppola was honoured at the 1973 Directors Guild of America awards for Outstanding Directorial Achievement in Motion Pictures. At the 1973 Golden Globes Coppola won Best Director. The film also won for Best Motion Picture Drama, Best Motion Picture Actor (Brando), Best Original Score and Best Screenplay; nominated Best Motion Picture Actor (Al Pacino) and Best Supporting Actor (James Caan). In Germany the film won the Golden Screen and at the Grammy music awards Nino Rota won for Best Original Score. The 1973 National Society of Film Critics Awards gave Al Pacino the Best Actor award. At the 1973 New York Film Critics Circle Awards Robert Duvall won Best Supporting Actor. Coppola's writing won the award at the 1973 Writers Guild of America (Screen) award for Best Drama Adapted from Another Medium. In 1990, *The Godfather* had the distinction of being one of the first 25 films inducted into the National Film Registry 1990 National Film Preservation Board, USA and, in 2002, the film also won the Online Film Critics Society Awards nominated Best Overall DVD.

COPPOLA MAGIC: Hollywood special-effects ace AD Flowers was responsible for the film's practical stunts and effects. Perhaps his finest hour, alongside make-up man Dick Smith, was rigging James Caan with squibs to simulate bullet hits to his entire body, recalling the finale of *Bonnie and Clyde* (Arthur Penn, 1967). The preparations for Sonny's death scene cost $100,000 and took three days to prepare. The shot was made in one take.

MOVIE SPEAK:
Don Vito: 'We're not murderers, despite what this undertaker says.'

Don Vito: 'The man who doesn't spend time with his family can never be a real man.'

Don Vitelli: 'In Sicily, women are more dangerous than shotguns.'

Don Vito: 'I want no acts of vengeance.'

HOME VIEWING: Both Region 1 and Region 2 DVD editions are the same; a stunningly comprehensive package as follows: Director's Commentary on all films, documentaries: *Francis Coppola's Notebook, On Location, The Godfather Family, Behind the Scenes 1971, The Cinematography of The Godfather, Coppola and Puzo on Screenwriting*, two featurettes on music, additional scenes, storyboards for Part II and Part III, character, cast and crew biographies, Academy Award acceptance speeches, photo galleries, theatrical trailers, widescreen 1.85:1. A VHS of the film remains in print and *The Godfather* trilogy is available as a boxed set where the story is arranged chronologically. This was released on video in 1997.

In 1974, NBC television network in the USA agreed to pay $10 million for a single showing of *The Godfather* on television. The network were then able to charge advertisers $225,000 for one minute of air time.

DELETED SCENES: Several scenes were inevitably eliminated from the final film in the interests of clarity and pacing. They included:

- Vito announcing to Sonny that Genco, with whom Vito started out, is dead
- Carlo and Connie quarrelling
- Michael and Kay in bed (this was included in the TV miniseries version of *The Godfather* and *The Godfather Part II*)
- Sonny making sense of the news that Vito has been shot and that he may have to assume control of the family
- A parade of Communists through the Sicilian countryside
- Michael looking for his father's childhood home in Sicily (in *The Godfather Part III* Michael takes Kay to see it)
- Michael telling his father he will avenge the deaths of Sonny and Apollonia

TRIVIA: In 1967 Paramount released a similarly themed film to *The Godfather* called *The Brotherhood*, which had been a box office and critical failure. The success of Puzo's novel *The Godfather* prompted the studio to rethink the prospects of attempting to deal with the subject of the Mafia.

The cat that Brando strokes simply wandered into the scene one day and Coppola encouraged its inclusion as a character trait that would contrast with the intensity of the Don. The screenwriter Robert Towne, whose credits include the script for *Chinatown* (Roman Polanski, 1974) was involved in scripting the scene between Michael and his father towards the end of the film, prior to the Don's death.

Sofia Coppola, Francis's daughter, was born during the shoot on the 14 May which also happens to be George Lucas's birthday. Sofia Coppola went on to play Michael's daughter in *The Godfather Part III* and it is Sofia who is the baby being baptised at the climax of the film.

Plum tomatoes were grown especially for the filming of the Don's death scene.

Oranges are always present prior to a climactic and murderous moment in *The Godfather* series. This was not a designed motif but became apparent to Coppola and Walter Murch during the editing on the film.

On *The Godfather*'s opening Saturday a cinema manager was shot dead and robbed of the day's box office takings, totalling around $13,000.

Coppola anticipated the film would be a disaster upon release. When the film became a commercial and pop-culture phenomenon, Frank Capra wrote to Coppola praising the film's richness. When the film's box office takings surpassed $100 million in August 1972, Francis Ford Coppola and George Lucas, both bearded and dressed in jeans, went into a Mercedes dealership in San Francisco to see the new and very expensive Mercedes 600 model. Custom-made, the car was so exclusive that one owner of this model was the Pope. Coppola and Lucas looked too scruffy for such a purchase and so the seasoned salesmen kept passing the two browsers onto their colleagues. Finally, a young salesman took Coppola's order for a Mercedes 600 and Coppola told the salesman to bill Paramount Pictures.

Coppola's long-standing sound and picture editor colleague and friend, Walter Murch, has noted how Pacino, Duvall, Cazale and Caan, all inspired to act by the example of Marlon Brando, spent much of their energy proving to their actor father that they knew their stuff.

COPPOLA'S VIEW: For all the guns, hats, coats, cars and gangster speak, *The Godfather* testifies to the allure and power of the notion of a family, of a group of people who care and look out for one another. The film is the beginning of a family saga that is far richer than all the violence and vengeance that spins around it. Coppola captures rituals of family and society – baptism, marriage and funeral. Coppola is most at home in the domestic sequences that emphasise the family bond.

The design of the Don's den is the heart of the film, with its warmth and secrecy. In keeping with the Don's status as father confessor and 'miracle-maker' it feels like a confession booth. In his film *The Conversation*, Coppola explicitly dramatises the Catholic obsession with guilt. *The Godfather* explores the religious themes of the fall from grace, forgiveness, redemption, vengeance and temptation. *The Godfather Part II* plays these concepts out with even more vigour and intensity.

People always talk about the place of Catholicism in Scorsese movies. Coppola's work is powerfully underscored by this subject too. The purging of enemies and paying for sin pave the way for much of the film's drama. The film shows that anybody who lives is corrupted. The line between personal emotion and reason is the undoing of Michael and his fall mirrors the biblical Adam and Eve story.

Power is dangerously seductive. *The Godfather* plot is a simple tale of revenge that is enriched by detail of character and their thematic and emotional resonances. *The Godfather* builds its drama on the questioning of fidelity to the family. What gives you life can also kill you.

CRITICAL COPPOLA: In *Sight and Sound* the film was praised thus: 'Many individual vignettes in *The Godfather* are masterly.' In Japan noted critic Tadao Sato wrote: 'Behind the popularity of the movie, I can see Japanese nostalgia for the old family system, which modern Japanese society has lost.' Kim Newman in *Empire* magazine has described the film as 'at once an art movie and a commercial blockbuster . . . this shows it is possible to smash box office records without being mindless.' In *Time Out* Geoff Andrew notes that 'Mario Puzo's novel was brought to the screen on bravura style by Coppola.' *The Virgin Film Guide* calls the film 'One of the central American movies of the last twenty-five years, and one of very few to succeed as both popular entertainment and high art.'

VERDICT: *The Godfather* is an astonishing film. Its simple, pulpy revenge plot is enriched to the point of the classical with its tragic tone and emphasis on the fall of a modern empire. It is the film's structure that is most astonishing. Its performances, from lead roles to supporting characters is remarkably consistent. The film balances generic needs with something more artful. It is the ideal movie. *The Godfather* is undoubtedly an entertainment, showing us a fantasy lifestyle yet rooting it in emotional dilemmas and themes that concern us all. In 2002, Roger Corman, Coppola's first Hollywood employer back in 1962, wrote a glowing appreciation of *The Godfather* as part of *Sight and Sound* magazine's ten-yearly assessment of the so-called Ten Greatest Films of all time. Corman makes the case for *The Godfather* as 'one of the enduring works of American cinema'. He cites the film's artistic and popular success in fusing the popular with the more esoteric, and its expression of immigrant experience in America where the Mafia becomes the only way for an ethnic minority to partake in America's business. Corman also alludes to the gangster film format and how this is one more spin on the ultra-American gerne, the Western. He concludes by describing the film as 'Beautiful, realist, revolutionary.' Coppola is the only American director working today whose work features in the *Sight and Sound* list of critics' top ten films. Lists in other publications bear out the longevity of the film, which regularly makes the top ten. *The Godfather* and *The Godfather Part II* are in at number four, ahead of Stanley Kubrick's *2001: A Space Odyssey* (1969) at number six and behind *Citizen Kane* (1941), directed by one of Coppola's heroes Orson Welles, which remains at number one.

COPPOLA NOW: 'I felt that *Godfather* had never finished; morally, I believed that the Family would be destroyed . . .'

The Conversation (1974)

(Colour – 113 minutes)

Paramount Pictures
Producer: Francis Ford Coppola and Fred Roos (Coppola Company)
Screenplay: Francis Ford Coppola
Cinematographer: Bill Butler
Editor: Richard Chew
Supervising Editor: Walter Murch
Sound Montage and Re-Recording: Walter Murch
Music: David Shire
Production Design: Dean Tavoularis
Set Dresser: Doug Von Koss
Costume Design: Aggie Guerard Rogers

CAST: Gene Hackman (*Harry Caul*), John Cazale (*Stan*), Allen Garfield (*Bernie Moran*), Frederic Forrest (*Mark*), Cindy Williams (*Ann*), Michael Higgins (*Paul*), Elizabeth McRae (*Meredith*), Harrison Ford (*Martin Stett*), Robert Duvall (*The Director*), Mark Wheeler (*Receptionist*), Teri Garr (*Amy*), Robert Shields (*Mime in Union Square*), Phoebe Alexander (*Lurleen*)

BUDGET: $1.9 million

RELEASE DATE: 7 April 1974

MPAA: PG

BBFC: A

TAGLINE: Harry Caul is an invader of privacy. The best in the business. He can record any conversation between two people anywhere. So far, three people are dead because of him.

SUMMARY: The early 1970s, Union Square in San Francisco. A young couple are on their lunch break. They are being monitored by a hidden surveillance team, the leader of whom is a middle-aged man named Harry Caul. The young couple are aware that a man is following them. In the surveillance van, Harry's colleague Stan monitors the sound coming through. With his day's work over, Harry goes home to his apartment where he lives alone, listening to his jazz records and playing the saxophone. The next day, at his immense warehouse studio, Harry plays back the tapes from the previous day. He then makes a call from a phone box to the company employing him on this case. On his way home, Harry stops off to see a woman he knows, called Amy. She asks where Harry works but Harry lies, saying he is a freelance musician.

Harry goes to see the director of the company he is working for to hand over the tapes he has recorded. He is met by a young, cold, creepy assistant named Martin Stett. Stett says he will hand the tapes on but Harry is not happy with this; he usually hands the tapes over personally. Stett threatens him, telling him not to get involved. Harry leaves and sees Ann, the young woman he has been spying on, in the lift. She does not recognise him.

Back at his studio, Harry and Stan go about their work. Stan is a very relaxed and talkative character whom Harry finds difficult to work with. Harry goes to confession and confesses the usual minor indulgences and then something far more serious: the death of two young people several years before, which he considers his fault in his capacity as a spy.

Harry attends a major surveillance and sound convention where his reputation in the field is evident. He sees Stett at the convention but does not talk with him. He meets up with old associates and they all go back to Harry's warehouse for a party and drink. A prostitute, Meredith, talks to Harry and there is an attraction between them. When the party is over she and Harry sleep together in his studio on his makeshift bed.

Harry wants to destroy the tapes he has made because he cannot help but think they will imperil the lives of the couple he has been spying on. He has a dream in which he follows Ann. Meredith takes the tapes before Harry returns home. Stett phones and says that the company has the tapes and that they are watching Harry. Stett asks Harry to bring over the pictures of the couple. Harry goes to the office and the director is there, listening to the tapes. There are pictures of Ann around the office. Harry leaves and goes into a hotel. He tries to access a particular room but has to go with the nearest available one. From the bathroom in his suite, Harry bugs the room next door. He listens and hears people shouting and a fair amount of violence, fighting and anxiety.

Harry returns to the company but is thrown out before he can get upstairs to see the director. He sees Ann in a dark car outside. Harry is trying to unravel the mystery of what has occurred. He pieces it together. The young couple were not going to be killed, they were plotting to kill the director, and they did so. Harry's sense of what has unfolded has become more than he can cope with.

Back in his apartment Harry tears up almost all that he owns, trying to find a bugging device. He finally relents and sits alone playing his saxophone.

COPPOLA'S CONCEPT: *The Conversation* is considered one of Coppola's most personal and certainly one of his greatest films, though it is one of his small movies and tends to get lost in the shuffle of *The Godfather*, *The Godfather Part II* and *Apocalypse Now*. The film beautifully fuses mainstream narrative demands with more esoteric, psychological and philosophical elements, which are the film's points of real interest. Coppola wrote the screenplay in the late 1960s and the script is a rich treat of ideas and emotions, reflecting Coppola's self-perception as a writer first and a director second. Coppola developed the screenplay over a six-year period and, in his fidelity to a necessary realism, he attended conventions for surveillance professionals so as to immerse himself in the mindset and culture of that world. Given Coppola's own lifelong interest in technology, the project was an ideal marriage between a writer and his subject. Coppola's interest in creating the screenplay was sparked by fellow-director Irvin Kershner (*The Flim Flam Man*, 1967; *Loving*, 1970 and *The Empire Strikes Back*, 1980), who had shown Coppola a *Life* magazine article about a man named Hal Lipset, a surveillance technician in San Francisco.

The film was released post-Watergate[1] and so was regarded as especially, and eerily, prescient. Coppola's acknowledged love of technology partly fuels the premise. Indicative of the personal significance of the project to Coppola, and equally telling of his industry standing in the context of the massive success of *The Godfather*, Coppola insisted the film be released on his birthday 7 April 1974.

---

[1] Supporters of Republican president Richard Nixon broke into the offices of the Democratic National Committee in the Watergate building in Washington DC in 1972 in the hope of bugging the telephones there. A night watchman caught them and the police were called in, unleashing a torrent of scandal and pessimism about the state of American democracy.

Reflecting his love of literature, Coppola's screenplay for *The Conversation* was inspired heavily by Herman Hesse's novel *Steppenwolf* (1921) regarded as a key text of the 1960s counterculture. That novel's protagonist is named Harry Haller, and he moves with existential angst through the modern world and its shadows. Haller battles to make sense of the world around him based on his own perception and value of it, rather than simply acquiescing to an accepted notion of how the world works. In crafting the material, Coppola's narrative design was built around the idea of the film functioning like a piece of music – there is a repetition of certain key moments taking on different meanings each time. In turn this compels the audience to some degree to put the meaning of the story together.

The Conversation remains Coppola's most European-like film and maybe hints at the kind of films he would have liked to continue making. In *The Conversation*, Coppola's concept hinges on the moral aspects of the story rather than the mechanics of a whodunit. In *Cinema Journal*, Dennis Turner wrote that the film is 'one of a series of early 1970s crime movies which, in presenting their protagonists with "unreadable" mysteries which defy solution, seem to out-noir the classic film noir.'

For Coppola one of the intrigues of the concept was Harry's becoming more morally conscious but in the process finding that new-found integrity undermined.

INFLUENCES: The idea of an event being seen and assessed from different points of view suggests the influence of one of Coppola's heroes, Japanese director Akira Kurosawa. Kurosawa's film *Rashômon* (1950) is a key frame of reference for *The Conversation*. In Kurosawa's film four points of view are offered on an incident in which a woman is raped and her husband is killed in the forest. The most obvious cinematic influence on *The Conversation* is the film *Blow Up* (Michaelangelo Antonioni, 1966) which has become a cult classic. Its premise is that a photographer unwittingly photographs a murder. A third, distinct influence on the *The Conversation* is that of Catholicism. For Harry Caul his Catholic faith is not a source of hope but rather a source of shame. Coppola drew on his own childhood experiences, especially memories of feeling guilty, to inform elements of the story. When Coppola was a child he punched a boy and soon after the boy died. Coppola's father always said it was because Coppola threw the punch.

Finally, Coppola's dream-life informed the development of the story. In an interview given around the time of *The Conversation*'s DVD release in North America, Coppola explained how Harry's low-key liaisons with Amy was inspired by a recurring dream of the director's in which he would meet with a woman in a South American country.

COSTUME: Aggie Guerard Rogers designed the costumes for *The Conversation*. Harry wears the same outfit all through the film, an utterly plain and nondescript jacket and tie, typically covered by a transluscent raincoat which assumes symbolic value. He is a man whose inability to relax finds expression in the monotony of his clothing.

When Harrison Ford attired himself in a green suit for his role as Martin Stett, Coppola initially objected quite vocally to its flamboyance. Production designer Dean Tavoularis thought Ford's choice was good and designed the set for Stett's office based on Stett's suit.

TEAM COPPOLA: As with *The Godfather*, Coppola brought production designer Dean Tavoularis and producer Fred Roos on board. *The Conversation* galvanised Coppola's core collaborative team that would stay with him for virtually the rest of his career, and who remain associates thirty years later. Bill Butler the cinematographer on *The Rain People* was the cinematographer on *The Conversation*. Haskell Wexler had originally been the cinematographer but differences of opinion about the choice of location prompted Wexler to leave the project and be replaced by Bill Butler who would go on to shoot *Jaws* (Steven Spielberg, 1975).

Walter Murch, who had been involved with Coppola's work since *The Rain People,* worked on *The Conversation* as sound designer. Murch had also been sound designer and co writer on *THX-1138* (George Lucas, 1971) and sound designer on *American Graffiti* (George Lucas, 1973). He would go on to work on *The Godfather Part II* and *Apocalypse Now* in the same capacities.

CASTING: Way back in 1969 Coppola had originally wanted to cast Marlon Brando as Harry Caul but Brando turned him down. By the early 1970s a new generation of actors (very much inspired by Brando's legacy) were proving themselves and one of these performers was Gene Hackman, who had recently broken through with his portrayal of Popeye Doyle in *The French Connection* (William Friedkin, 1972). Hackman was now in a position to capitalise on the success of that film and a collaboration with the director of *The Godfather* was an ideal opportunity to do so. Of his work with Hackman Coppola has commented: 'I tried to obtain emotions from Gene Hackman that would have been passed over if the picture had been done in the usual manner of thrillers.' Many years later, Coppola considered directing the western *Unforgiven*, which eventually was directed to great effect by Clint Eastwood in 1992 and co-starred Gene Hackman.

A regular face from Coppola's repertory of actors, Robert Duvall (*The Rain People, The Godfather*) returned and appears briefly and mysteriously as The Director.

Typically, Coppola rehearsed *The Conversation* thoroughly prior to
filming. He promised Hackman that they would rehearse the screenplay
as though it were a play. For example, the entire warehouse scene was
rehearsed as though a play in itself. The actors pantomimed all the props
used in the scene. So intense and productive was the rehearsal process
that if Hackman mimed hanging up on the phone, then minutes later he
would mime stepping over an imaginary phone cord on the floor. This
dedication to emotional authenticity is one of the elevating features of
The Conversation and is a touchstone of Coppola's work as a director
(see **The Godfather Part II** and **Rumble Fish**, two especially strong
displays of this quality).

I KNOW THAT FACE: Gene Hackman became a name actor with his
starring, Oscar-winning role in *The French Connection* (William
Friedkin, 1972). He has also appeared in *Bonnie and Clyde* (Arthur
Penn, 1969) and, since the early 1970s, has starred in a vast range of
films; highlights include *The Poseidon Adventure* (Irwin Allen, 1973),
Young Frankenstein (Mel Brooks, 1974), *A Bridge Too Far* (Richard
Attenborough, 1977), *Superman: The Movie* (Richard Donner, 1978),
Hoosiers (David Anspaugh, 1986), *Unforgiven* (Clint Eastwood, 1992),
Geronimo: An American Legend (Walter Hill, 1993), *Get Shorty* (Barry
Sonnenfeld, 1995), *The Royal Tenenbaums* (Wes Anderson, 2001) and
Heist (David Mamet, 2002).

Cindy Williams, fresh from her success in *American Graffiti* (George
Lucas, 1973), on which Coppola was executive producer, was cast in the
role of Ann. Williams went on to star in the hit sitcom *Laverne and
Shirley* alongside Penny Marshall, who went on to direct *Big* (1988) and
Awakenings (1991).

With his role as Mark in *The Conversation*, Frederic Forrest began a
career-long association with Coppola which continued into *Apocalypse
Now*, *One From The Heart* and *Tucker: The Man and His Dream*.
Forrest also starred in the little seen Zoetrope production, *Hammett*
(Wim Wenders, 1983) in the role of crime writer Dashiell Hammett.
Other appearances include *The Missouri Breaks* (Arthur Penn, 1976),
The Rose (Mark Rydell, 1979), *Music Box* (Costa Gavras, 1989), *Falling
Down* (Joel Schumacher, 1993) and the epic Western TV series
Lonesome Dove (Simon Wincer, 1989), based on Larry McMurtry's
novel.

Teri Garr went on to star in *Close Encounters of the Third Kind*
(Steven Spielberg, 1977), and also starred in Coppola's *One From the
Heart* as the dreamy, overgrown kid Frannie. As a child Garr appeared
as a dancer in countless Elvis Presley movies and can also be seen in *The
Black Stallion* (Carroll Ballard, 1979), *The Escape Artist* (Caleb

Deschanel, 1982), *The Player* (Robert Altman, 1992) and *Michael* (Nora Ephron, 1996).

Famously, *The Conversation* showcases a supporting role for an actor, unknown at the time, called Harrison Ford. Ford had recently appeared in *American Graffiti* (George Lucas, 1973) but had a couple of years to go until breaking through with *Star Wars* (George Lucas, 1977) and *Raiders of the Lost Ark* (Steven Spielberg, 1981). From there came a range of rich and memorable performances in *Witness* (Peter Weir, 1985), *The Mosquito Coast* (Peter Weir, 1986), *Frantic* (Roman Polanski, 1988), *Working Girl* (Mike Nichols, 1988), *Presumed Innocent* (Alan J Pakula, 1990), *Sabrina* (Sydney Pollack, 1995), *Six Days, Seven Nights* (Sydney Pollack, 1999), *What Lies Beneath* (Robert Zemeckis, 2000), *K19: The Widowmaker* (Kathryn Bigelow, 2002) and *Hollywood Homicide* (Ron Shelton, 2003).

THE FILMING: Shooting began on *The Conversation* on 26 November 1972. To save money, the film was shot entirely on location in San Francisco where American Zoetrope was, and continues, to be based. Two unrelated but hard-to-ignore events conspired to bring the shoot to an abrupt end, ultimately impacting on the film's eventual structure and thematic and dramatic intrigue. Coppola actually ran out of money during the shoot, which meant that ten pages of script were never filmed, an issue rectified during the edit. He also got fed up with the filming and just called it to an end when the effort to conjure the illusion of San Francisco fog, for what became the dream scene, got too frustrating. Originally, this was an ending for the film.

During work on *The Conversation* Coppola quickly went into pre-production on *The Godfather Part II*, appointing Walter Murch to supervise post-production on *The Conversation*. Murch edited *The Conversation* by day and mixed *American Graffiti* by night.

PROMOTION: Test screenings revealed (somewhat amazingly) that audiences were unsure what Harry did for a job. In response to the fantastic reviews the film garnered, a new poster was laden with excerpts and quotes. The German poster for the film was comprised of an illustration of the moment in the story when Harry curls up in the bathroom to bug the hotel room next door. More arrestingly, the Polish release poster showed a cross section of the human head in the manner of a medical diagram, emphasising the psychological thrust of the story.

THE OPENING: Just one of *The Conversation*'s many amazing and precise elements is its opening shot. It begins as a wide shot from the top of a tower block overlooking Union Square. Very slowly, the camera zooms in on a figure in the lunchtime crowd below. The sense is of surveillance and the deliberate, precise and slow quality of this opening camera move immediately clues us in to the tone and pace of the film. The action then switches to crowd level as a series of long-lens shots track the movement of a young couple as they move through the crowd. Through this device the film plays on the role of the viewer in building the meaning of the film. The couple are also shown being trailed by two men, Harry Caul and a colleague. People cross frame and we lose sight of characters for a moment which emphasises the believability of the sequence. The opening is a very real scene, devoid of gimmickry or even music. Instead the combination of image and thoughtful soundtrack suggests something eerie and unsettling, and this creates tones which will build and intensify throughout the film.

HEROES AND VILLAINS: *The Conversation* concentrates all of its preoccupations and themes into one character, Harry Caul. Coppola is very much at home lingering on Harry's character and the film is far more engaged by this than by the thriller element. *The Conversation* has a strong interior quality and, for Walter Murch, so vital to Coppola's 1970s output, Harry Caul's name has a metaphorical connotation in the sense of a caul being something that is wrapped around a body. Harry craves protection and this meaning is enriched by his membrane-like translucent raincoat. Throughout the film Harry retreats behind surfaces whenever he comes under threat, either real or imagined.

For Coppola the centrality of sin features heavily in the character of Harry Caul and the film assumes a metaphorical weight that goes beyond what audiences might expect of a thriller. In his notes for the film Coppola wrote: 'There is always the idea that the sins a man performs are not the same as the ones he thinks he has performed.' Harry's Catholic upbringing (he destroys his statue of the Virgin Mary at the end of the film) means that guilt is a big part of his life and we see him at confession, the creepiness of that experience perhaps all too powerfully expressed for those Catholics watching the film. As Harry kneels and confesses, the camera pulls focus onto the grille of mesh behind which the unseen, but very present, priest is listening. Coppola was intrigued by the notion of confession and that Harry's Catholicism informed all his actions. In an interview with Marjorie Rosen in *Film Comment* he said, 'Confession, at first, was something I thought related to the central theme.' Harry even chastises his assistant Stan for blaspheming. For all his professional success and respect Harry's private and personal life is more difficult. Screenwriter and director Lawrence Kasdan once acutely and memorably described American movie heroes as attractive people accomplishing things. Harry Caul is the complete

COPPOLA The Conversation

antithesis of this. In *The Conversation*, he is nondescript, inarticulate, guilt-ridden and afraid. He cocoons himself in a world of sound (in his work) at the expense of any meaningful relationship, and this is his undoing. His work causes him to literally tear his life apart in the climax of the film.

Harry is a metaphor for any creative person who observes life rather than participating in it. Harry lives at a remove from life, keeping his telephone in a drawer and saying to Amy, 'I don't have any secrets.' Of course, it emerges that he does. In an amusing scene, his intense sense of privacy is expressed when he discovers a birthday gift from a neighbour waiting for him inside his apartment. It concerns Harry that the neighbour has been able to access his apartment. Just how efficient is Harry really? Somewhat ridiculously, Harry tells the neighbour on the phone that 'I don't have anything personal except my keys.' Harry is at his most lively and impassioned when talking about his work. The moment conversation turns to the more personal and meaningful, Harry is a lost man unable to express himself or show vulnerability. Meredith tells him that work doesn't have to be felt it just has to be done. Of course, for the artist (which in part is how Coppola has drawn Harry) feeling and a more personal attachment are precisely what transform work into something more than 'just work'. Harry's work ethic is further complicated as he wants to destroy the tapes, not wishing to be responsible for anybody's death again. Harry's nervousness manifests itself in the way he is constantly looking around in a furtive way.

Like Willard in *Apocalypse Now*, Harry has a mission and his sense of reality and self is exploded by his entry into a morally uncertain world. There is the potential for Harry to be corrupted and the dilemma he confronts is where to draw the line in atoning for past moral failure.

Harry's control obsession recalls the control of Michael Corleone (*Godfather* trilogy) and, by the end of *The Conversation*, perhaps Harry has been liberated, his home torn to pieces just as his sense of self has been undone. As to his sense of 'happiness' at the end of the film, that is ambiguous; he still sits playing the saxophone just as he always has done. Like Corleone and Kurtz (*Apocalypse Now*), Harry has built his own reality into which he can retreat and from where he can control the world. Ultimately, though, this detachment is his undoing. Only at the end of the film, as Harry self-destructs, does the action explode, all perception altered and distorted. Harry has not been able to survey the situation with detachment. Like Michael Corleone he has let the line between his personal and his business life become blurred and dangerous.

Moran is a surveillance kit retailer who has known Harry a long time. Unlike Harry, he is a man who talks too much; upbeat and wisecracking, he keeps reminding Harry of his 'secret' past where Harry's surveillance work resulted in the death of two young people.

Amy, with whom Harry has some kind of relationship, is warm and loving, her apartment warm and cosy in contrast to the open space that Harry has to sometimes work in, and certainly far removed from the alien environment of the company.

The character of The Director, referred to but rarely seen, is rather like Kurtz in *Apocalypse Now*, his presence hanging over the main action, manipulating it from a hidden lair rather like Michael and Vito Corleone do from their compound. The Director and the company are a faceless and dangerous entity. The Director is never seen in close up, but instead as a silhouette against a big window overlooking San Francisco.

Martin Stett, with his slightly high-pitched voice, is a menacing presence who seems to come and go in an otherworldly manner. When Harry first leaves the building, we see Stett against a red wall at the end of a long corridor, watching until Harry leaves. Stett's creepiness and air of mystery is never more apparent than when Harry is unable to track him with the surveillance camera on show at the convention. It is as though Stett is an apparition.

COPPOLA STYLE: The great elegance of *The Godfather* is refined in *The Conversation*, an utterly beautiful film in its deployment of cinema technique. There is a stillness to much of the film. Just as Harry is a calm and passive character, at least on the surface, so too the element of surveillance that is central to the story. It finds expression in certain slow and smooth camera movements or absences of movement which render the camera eerily still and inconspicuous. Throughout *The Conversation* characters come in and out of a static frame as though the camera is immobile in its secret hiding place. 'The film is doing to him everything he's done to everyone else,' Coppola explained in an interview with online magazine *Scenario*, and this description of Coppola's is consistent with the biblical resonances of Coppola's cinema generally.

In the film's choice of locations, Coppola gives Harry a feeling of security at home and equally so in his workspace, both of them at a remove from the rest of society. From above, Harry can see without being seen.

Coppola's affinity for understatement dominates *The Conversation*. There are no angst-ridden tracking shots, no triumphal epiphanies marked by a glorious booming camera shot over the brow of a hill, no superfast edits underpinning an entire narrative. Coppola and Bill Butler's images are unforced. From its essentially naturalistic base, the film climaxes with an overtly psychological sequence as a flurry of images reveal the truth of the murder that the young couple mention at the start of the film. Only at this point does the film's overriding style fracture, and this stylistic break is achieved just about perfectly.

IMAGE: The film hinges many of its key moments on visuals that suggest a documentary approach, particularly in the use of a long lens for a range of shots. Much of *The Conversation*'s action has a very naturalistic look. It is this emphasis on realism, partly achieved by location filming, that connects the film to the European tradition of the 1960s when more portable cameras made crews more readily mobile.

Décor plays a key role in the visual scheme of the film, and this is powerfully expressed in the scene where Harry flushes the toilet in the hotel suite. As the blood rises up over the bowl, the violence and horror of the moment is intensified by the contrast between the red of the blood and the cleanliness of the white tiles. It is the film's most florid moment and it anticipates the equally over-the-top, though less psychologically powerful, floods of blood in *The Shining* (Stanley Kubrick, 1980) and Coppola's *Bram Stoker's Dracula*.

When Harry is first shown at home, the camera is fixed and somewhat detached from the action. There are no close-ups as Harry enters the apartment and sits on his sofa. To some degree this very cool and quiet approach recalls the framing of domestic rooms in the work of director Yasujiro Ozu in films such as *Late Spring* (1949), *Autumn Afternoon* (1962) and his most celebrated movie, *Tokyo Story* (1953).

By contrast with the locked-off images of Harry at home, the camera moves far more fluidly for the party at Harry's studio, most notably in the scene when Harry and Meredith talk. The camera tracks slowly around them as their conversation centres on the difficult personal issues for Harry. This unease with the more complex emotions and insecurities is also expressed in the confession scene. For this scene, shadow dominates the moment. As with Michael in his den in *The Godfather* and Kurtz in his compound in *Apocalypse Now*, the film shows Harry's face in the partial light of the confession box, a place that is far from comforting.

More emphatically dramatic shots frame Harry's approach to the company, the camera's low height making the building overpowering and certainly imposing.

By contrast with the essentially low-key, sombre look of the film, the convention sequence and subsequent party are brightly lit sequences that offer some welcome relief from the contained approach used for most of the story.

The Conversation's visual design is further enhanced by a judicious use of slow-moving zoom shots and pans. In the scene where Harry sets up a bugging device in the hotel bathroom, the camera's slow zoom in makes the audience complicit in Harry's work and also suggests the film, and by extension the audience, is monitoring Harry. Slow camera pans reveal information and communicate a sense of loneliness and tedium for the character such as when Harry is revealed lying on the hotel bed.

A hand-held camera is also used occasionally in the film and there are several atmospheric shots of San Francisco, including images of Harry on the tram and crossing the tramlines to get to work.

Though the film's visual compositions are strong, the editing is deliberately paced. Only in the explosive discovery in the hotel suite does the editing pattern of the film change to a series of frenzied edits almost too quick to grasp completely, thereby plunging the audience into Harry's confused sense of what is happening.

In *The Godfather* and in *The Conversation*, Coppola presents church interiors in glorious wide shots. Churches are places to be revered, their spectacle to be revelled in, while at the same time they are harbingers of sin and shadow. In contrast to the unwelcoming church and the exposure of public spaces, Harry creates very cosy places: his apartment and, even more so, his studio. His studio is presented as a cathedral of sound, a sacred place, with its pillars and shadows. At the other end of the spectrum The Director's office is a room of hard, vertical lines and silhouettes, and has a real coldness to it.

For the dream sequence, mist engulfs Harry as he follows Ann. There are no post-production image effects. The scene has a dead, grey pallor to it as Harry works through his fear of dying.

The film's opening shot finds its visual rhyme in the closing image where the camera pans slowly and menacingly back and forth across Harry's ravaged apartment. Is he now being spied upon by a camera he has not yet found?

SOUND: Coppola's movies have always maximised the potential of sound to be not just representational but also symbolic and psychologically affecting. Thus, there is a deadened quality to the Director's office that reflects the uneasy feeling the location generates in Harry. The building seems removed from reality and the familiar sights and sounds of San Francisco, and there is something science-fiction-like about it, as though it has been pulled from the reality of the American Zoetrope production *THX-1138* (George Lucas, 1971).

The Conversation's sound designer and post-production supervisor Walter Murch plays up sonic distortion and noise, enveloping key scenes with an intense wall of sound. When Harry goes to see the Director, the sound of the tapes playing encompass the whole room, no longer in a completely realistic way. This device of having the audio tape material so much in the foreground that it overwhelms the image is also used after the party scene when Harry lies down to sleep. The tape plays, the loudness of the recording intensifying as Harry's thoughts are occupied ever more by what he has recorded.

For the dream sequence a simple, slight echo effect enhances the sense of the unreal so evident in the image.

COPPOLA TUNES: Coppola's composer on *The Conversation* was David Shire. Whereas a composer will typically view an edited version of the film in order to time and synchronise their music to the rhythm of the movie, on *The Conversation* Coppola and Shire collaborated prior to beginning filming when Coppola showed Shire the screenplay long before the film was shot. Shire composed themes based on the screenplay and recorded these. During the shoot some of Shire's music was played on set to help evoke an appropriate mood. Other directors such as Peter Weir (*Gallipoli*, 1981; *Witness*, 1985; *Dead Poets Society*, 1989 and *The Truman Show*, 1997) and Cameron Crowe (*Singles*, 1992; *Jerry Maguire*, 1996; *Almost Famous*, 2000 and *Vanilla Sky*, 2001) also adopt this technique. Shire's music for *The Conversation* is occasionally jazzy in keeping with Harry's musical taste but an appealing melancholy is what defines the film's music score. For the murder scene, a strident piano accompanies the action. In keeping with Alfred Hitchcock's dictum that silence is sometimes the strongest musical statement a composer can make at a key point in the film, there is no music where one might expect it – in the shock moment where blood spills from the toilet bowl – proving the concept that less is more.

HUMOUR: For all its austerity and psychological seriousness the film contains a seam of comedy. This is mostly found in the convention sequence and the party scene afterwards. The other comic element is Harry's colleague Stan, who serves partly as a comic foil to superserious Harry. The first scene of Harry at home is also funny as he speaks on the phone with a neighbour.

AWARDS: *The Conversation* represents a moment of critical mass in Coppola's career, proving to audiences and the film industry that Coppola was not a one-hit wonder and realising the promise of his artistic and commercial success with *The Godfather*. *The Conversation* received three major nominations at the 1975 Academy Awards: for Best Picture, Best Sound and Best Writing (Original Screenplay). At the 1975 BAFTAs the film won for Best Film Editing (Walter Murch and Richard Chew) and Best Soundtrack and was nominated for Best Actor (Gene Hackman), Best Direction and Best Screenplay. The 1974 National Board of Review awards honoured the film in the categories of Best

Actor (Gene Hackman), Best Director and Best Picture (English Language). At the 1974 Cannes Film Festival the film won the Palme D'Or (Francis Ford Coppola), and the Prize of the Ecumenical Jury, Special Mention. At the 1975 Directors Guild of America, Coppola was nominated for Outstanding Directorial Achievement. The 1975 Edgar Allan Poe Awards nominated the film for an Edgar, in the category of Best Motion Picture, and the 1975 Golden Globes festooned the film with nominations for Best Director, Best Motion Picture Drama, Best Motion Picture Drama Actor (Gene Hackman) and Best Screenplay. Coppola was nominated at the 1975 Writers Guild of America awards in the category of Best Drama written directly for the screen and in 1995 the National Film Preservation Board, USA, inducted *The Conversation* onto the National Film Registry.

COPPOLA MAGIC: Coppola's confidence and command of the medium is perfectly showcased in *The Conversation*. Editing and sound fuse at the climax of the narrative in a powerful display of the magic these devices are capable of. They both confirm what is shown on screen in terms of character expression and their perception of events, but also contradict it. The film's crescendo echoes with equivalent power the endings of *The Godfather*, *Apocalypse Now* and *The Godfather Part II*, all of them apocalyptic in spirit.

MOVIE SPEAK:
Harry: 'I don't know anything about human nature. I don't know anything about curiosity . . .'

HOME VIEWING: *The Conversation* is available as a Region 1 DVD and includes a featurette, *Close Up on The Conversation*, an audio commentary by Francis Ford Coppola, an audio commentary by film editor Walter Murch, the theatrical trailer, interactive menu and scene access. The film has been presented in widescreen 1.85:1.

There is no Region 2 DVD of the film available and on VHS the film has limited availability.

TRIVIA: For the opening shot of *The Conversation*, the camera crew really did have to find the actors in the crowd below and follow them, adding to the sense of real surveillance that permeates the entire film. As filming proceeded Coppola realised how much of a parallel there was between the movie and the unfolding Watergate scandal.

When *The Conversation* was nominated for Best Director at the Oscars it marked the first time a director was in competition with himself, as Coppola was also up for Best Director with *The Godfather Part II*.

Coppola's restless energy and new-found success courtesy of *The Godfather* meant that, prior to directing *The Conversation*, he directed the Gottfried von Einem opera *The Visit of the Old Lady* for The San Francisco Opera. Coppola also wrote the screenplay for *The Great Gatsby* (1974), which was directed by Jack Clayton.

In keeping with Coppola's very personal connection to *The Conversation* he has recounted how as a child he bugged the bathroom of his house at a party so that he and his pals could hear what the girls were talking about.

The scene where Harry takes his trousers off, and he is unaware of something at the window that we can see, was a real event that Coppola integrated into the film. The building across the way was being torn down. Coppola chose the apartment across the road from the building that he knew was going to be demolished. Is it a construction worker at the window?

In the screenplay, but not the finished film, Harry goes to Amy's apartment and she is not there. He stands in the empty room and in his head hears the tapes and Mark and Ann's goodbye. It is as though this is the kind of goodbye he was never able to effect with Amy.

COPPOLA'S VIEW: *The Conversation* powerfully explores themes of guilt and forgiveness, cornerstones of any Catholic's emotional life by choice or as an unwanted tattoo from childhood. Like *The Godfather* trilogy, *The Conversation* builds its drama around moments of guilt and the exercise of power, giving the film an almost ancient quality.

This is a spiritual film about a modern man in crisis. Whether he is redeemed or not by his choices and actions is unclear.

The film is far more concerned with Harry's crisis of conscience and heart, and Coppola exposes the danger of letting work become too much a part of one's life.

Professionalism is a key motif of *The Conversation*. Harry's colleague, Stan, describes Harry's bugging of the young couple in the square as 'a work of art'.

Alongside *Apocalypse Now, The Conversation* is Coppola's most open presentation of ideas and philosophies that have interested him. The film is perhaps all the stronger for being a small, concentrated piece of work – something the sprawling Vietnam adventure could never be.

CRITICAL COPPOLA: David Denby in *Sight and Sound* called the film 'remarkably ambitious and serious . . . a Dickensian richness of eccentricity, an extension of spiritual condition into physical metaphor.' In *Time Out* it was described as 'A bleak and devastatingly brilliant film.' On the film's re-release, the *Guardian* described it as 'Coppola's cerebral classic of paranoia and surveillance . . .'

VERDICT: This is a phenomenal film and undeniably one of Coppola's greatest. It feels so crafted and elegant and is a relief from the expansive sprawl of *The Godfather* and *The Godfather Part II*, the films immediately preceding and succeeding this movie. Intriguingly it is a thriller with a minimum of obvious thrills. Instead, the film dramatises one man's sense of failure and emotional inarticulacy. It is a real character movie.

COPPOLA NOW: 'I'm interested in films where the audience visits its own emotions and really becomes a participant in the film. *The Conversation* is an experiment in that.'

The Godfather Part II (1974)

(Colour – 200 minutes)

Paramount Pictures
Producer: Francis Ford Coppola
Co-Producers: Gray Frederickson and Fred Roos
Associate Producer: Mona Skager
Screenplay: Francis Ford Coppola and Mario Puzo, from
Puzo's novel
Cinematographer: Gordon Willis
Editor: Peter Zinner and Barry Malkin
Music: Nino Rota (conducted by Carmine Coppola)
Sound Montage and Re-Recording: Walter Murch
Production Design: Dean Tavoularis
Costume Design: Theodora van Runkle
Make-up: Dick Smith

CAST: Al Pacino (*Michael Corleone*), Robert Duvall (*Tom Hagen*), Diane Keaton (*Kay Adams*), Robert De Niro (*Vito Corleone*), John Cazale (*Fredo Corleone*), Talia Shire (*Connie Corleone*), Lee Strasberg (*Hyman Roth*), Michael V Gazzo (*Frankie Pentangeli*), GD Spradlin (*Senator Pat Geary*), Richard Bright (*Al Neri*), Gaston Moschin (*Fanucci*), Tom Rosqui (*Rocco Lampone*), B Kirby Jr (*Young Clemenza*), Frank Sivero (*Genco*), Francesca De Sapio (*Young Mama Corleone*), Morgana King (*Mama Corleone*), Mariana Hill (*Deanna Corleone*), Leopoldo Trieste (*Signor Roberto*), Dominic Chianese (*Johnny Ola*), Amerigo Tot (*Michael's bodyguard*), Troy Donahue (*Merle Johnson*), John Aprea (*Young Tessio*), Joe Spinell (*Willi Cicci*)

BUDGET: $13 million

THE BOX OFFICE: $57.3 million

RELEASE DATE: 12 December 1974

MPAA: R

BBFC: X

TAGLINE: None, since the film's title was so familiar and descriptive.

SUMMARY: The black screen fades up to reveal Michael Corleone, as last seen at the end of *The Godfather*. He is receiving associates and subordinates who kiss his hand in deference to him.

Sicily, 1901. A boy named Vito Corleone and his mother lead a funeral procession for Vito's father who has been killed for offending local crimelord Don Ciccio. Suddenly, gunfire rings out. Vito's brother Paolo has been killed having gone into hiding in the woods. After the funeral, Vito and his mother go to Don Ciccio, the murderer of her husband, and she attempts to kill Ciccio. She is gunned down by Ciccio's men and Vito runs. Vito leaves Sicily for New York. He is health-checked and then put into quarantine.

Lake Tahoe, Nevada, 1958. It is the first Holy Communion of Anthony Corleone, Michael's son. After the ceremony there is a lavish party at the new Corleone home at Lake Tahoe. Michael, Kay, Fredo, Connie and her new husband are all present. Senator Pat Geary addresses the audience and thanks the Corleone family for their financial gift to the state university. Inside the den, Geary meets with Michael. Tom Hagen is quietly ever-present in his trusted capacity as consigliere. Geary says he wants nothing to do with the Corleone family and spits out racial invective when Michael suggests Geary can help the Corleone business secure a gaming licence to operate in Las Vegas. Geary leaves the den.

Michael receives Johnny Ola and associates and they talk about gang boss Hyman Roth, who is based in Miami. Michael is interested in a Miami hotel and wants to get in on the business there.

Connie finally comes in to see Michael and asks him for financial support. Michael chastises her and suggests that she come and live on the estate.

Later, Michael and Kay dance and talk about the baby they are expecting. Kay complains that it is taking Michael too long to make the Corleone family business legitimate. Michael later says to Tom that he fears Fredo is too weak to be valuable to the business. Michael wants Tom to run things while he is away on business in Miami and Havana.

Soon after, an assassination attempt is made on Michael as he prepares for bed.

New York, 1917. Vito, now in his 20s, learns about Don Fanucci, the Black Hand, the progenitor of the Mafia. Fanucci exercises fear and control over the local community, offering paid protection. One night Vito is asked a favour – to look after some guns for a few days for a tenement neighbour named Clemenza. Vito does so and a few days later meets up with Clemenza. As a payment, Clemenza procures an expensive rug for Vito and so the transition of favours being exchanged becomes part of Vito's life and his beginnings as a Don are clear to see.

1958. Michael arrives in Miami and goes to see Hyman Roth. They talk about the bloodshed that will ensue between the families as they prepare a series of audacious deals. Frank Pentangeli, a Corleone associate of old, now living in Michael's former New York compound, is imprisoned by the FBI. In Nevada, Tom Hagen and Fredo visit Senator Geary who has been found in a compromising position. Hagen tells Geary that the incident will be 'erased' in turn for Geary's support as needed.

In Havana Michael meets Roth and other investors as they form an alliance with the government there. Fredo arrives in Havana, bringing with him the $2 million that Michael needs to become a partner in Roth's enterprise. Michael tells Fredo he plans to kill Roth. Michael then realises that Fredo has unwittingly jeopardised the family through his association with Johnny Ola, a Corleone enemy. Roth is finally shot dead as he returns to the USA. Michael is informed by Tom that Kay has had a miscarriage.

1917. Vito is very much the family man with crying baby Fredo on his lap. Don Fanucci then catches up with Vito on the busy streets of New York. Vito and his friends talk about Fanucci's hold over people and they agree that Fanucci should not be running everything. Vito and his friends make a plan and later Vito kills Fanucci, clearing the way for him to become the eventual Godfather. Vito holds court in his apartment as an elderly woman asks Vito for help in making sure she is not evicted from her apartment.

1958. Michael and Kay's marriage is fracturing. Michael attends HUAC hearings about the Corleone business and he denies accusations of illegitmate business practice and that he ever killed anybody.

The HUAC hearings continue and the compromised Senator Geary speaks up for the integrity of the Corleone family and Italian Americans everywhere. Michael confronts Fredo because Fredo knew Roth had attempted to kill him. Michael disowns Fredo. Kay confronts Michael saying she is not going back to Nevada. She tells Michael that it was not a miscarriage she had but an abortion.

1919. Young Vito arrives in Sicily with his young family. Vito kills Don Ciccio to avenge his own mother's and father's deaths at Don Ciccio's hands.

1958. Back at Lake Tahoe, Connie sees Michael and says she should look after him. Kay leaves Michael, who closes the door on her once more (see **The Godfather**). On Lake Tahoe, Fredo is shot dead by one of Michael's men. Frank Pentangeli commits suicide. The whole Corleone empire seems to be falling fast. Michael is alone.

A brief flashback shows Vito's sons as younger men at the moment when Michael announces he has enlisted to fight in World War Two. The film's final image is of Michael looking out at the lake in his loneliness under intensely bleak skies.

COPPOLA'S CONCEPT: For the most part, movie sequels (whether adaptations of sequel source material or not) tend only to repeat rather than to expand on the original's concept. It's a rare follow-up that has the capacity to enrich a dazzling original, but there are examples of this in the work of screenwriters Robert Zemeckis and Bob Gale who did it in *Back to the Future Part II* (Robert Zemeckis, 1989). Also with *Star Wars: The Empire Strikes Back* (Irvin Kershner, 1980) and *Star Wars: Attack of the Clones* (George Lucas, 2002), the emotional investment of the opening episodes of that double trilogy is deepened. Even *Superman II* (Richard Lester, 1980) gives audiences a Clark Kent willing to sacrifice his native, Kryptonian powers in order to fall in love with Lois Lane.

The Godfather Part II remains the granddaddy of all sequels, however, showing that a follow-up can be an entity in itself which can still significantly and meaningfully build on the foundation of the original. The emotional stakes, which is what it is all about, get higher and is surely the primary creative reason to go with a follow-up, other than the obvious commercial allure. Coppola believes the power of the story of *The Godfather Part II* derives from the interrelation of father and son stories, which ultimately function as parallel storylines rather than flashbacks. Through this device the tragedy that is so evident in the Corleone family history is accentuated and also made universal – history repeats itself.

Given the great artistic success of *The Godfather Part II*, it is important to recognise that initially Coppola did not have any interest in a sequel. He aimed to use the critical and commercial success of *The Godfather* as a springboard from which to return to his initial love of small, personal films, an ambition he achieved with *The Conversation*.

In picking up the gauntlet of *The Godfather Part II*, Coppola made the emotional impact of this story deeper by finding a way to make a highly expressive film from a mass-market formula.

After the intensity of making *The Godfather* Coppola anticipated a certain level of freedom in making the sequel. Paramount Pictures production head Robert Evans offered Coppola $1 million to direct *The Godfather Part II*. Coppola had suggested that Martin Scorsese direct the movie but Evans wanted Coppola. Coppola was unsure but eventually agreed based on several conditions that ensured his concept of the film would remain as undiluted as possible. He insisted on complete creative freedom in scripting, casting and all other elements. Coppola wanted the film simply to be called *The Godfather Part II*, emphasising unity with the original. Paramount were uneasy with this title but Coppola persisted – a display of creative integrity that makes the film so special.

Like *The Godfather*, the development of the screenplay for *The Godfather Part II* was a rich and involved process, reflecting Coppola's deep affinity for writing and his desire to create the best film possible. To his delight, Coppola was able to immerse himself in researching the period and settings of the film. Such detailed research was also part of development on *Apocalypse Now* and, to some extent, *The Cotton Club*.

To build a sense of the world of *The Godfather Part II*, Coppola investigated architecture, health, poverty and many other social and historical contexts. Through late 1972 and most of 1973, Coppola and Mario Puzo worked on the screenplay. Puzo's first draft is dated 5 May 1972 (just one month after Paramount announced that a sequel would be made) and Coppola's first draft is dated 4 July 1972. For Coppola, chapter fourteen of Puzo's novel was key to the development of the screenplay as it illustrated Don Vito's early life.

As with *The Godfather*, the emphasis was on the family dynamic, set against the backdrop of violence and lawbreaking. When Coppola suggested that Michael kill Fredo, Mario Puzo was unsure, though he went on to suggest the killing happened after the death of their mother and he acknowledged how much more of a emotional charge this brought to the funeral scene.

One of Coppola's key concepts was to have a final scene which was a flashback to the 1940s showing Don Vito, portrayed by Brando, surrounded by his family. However, when Brando was not prepared to return for this one scene, it was cut from the screenplay and, as has been suggested, perhaps this absence only emphasised more the spectre of old Vito on the scene.

INFLUENCES: The most obvious influence on *The Godfather Part II* is the original film. Other points of references include the film *America,*

America (Elia Kazan, 1963), which is about the experience of nineteenth-century immigrants arriving in the United States. Certain films by early Hollywood director DW Griffith, who masterminded and refined so many mainstream film forms in films like *Way Down East* (1920) and *Birth of a Nation* (1915), seem likely influences on the aesthetic of certain parts of the film. The silent film era generally informs the spirit of *The Godfather Part II* in its sequences centring on young Vito.

The other influence on the look of the film is considered to be the paintings of celebrated late-nineteenth-century painter John Singer Sargeant, who was noted for the concentrated use of shadow, silhouettes and a restricted colour scheme in much of his work.

COSTUME: *The Godfather Part II* intriguingly charts the development of clothing across the period and uses it primarily to express character. Michael's sombre dress code is akin to his father's clothing and reinforces the sense of Michael's comfort with the old ways of doing things. His cravat suggests not just his practical side but also his eye for fashion. Hyman Roth is always clothed very anonymously, suggesting nothing of the power and violent influence he holds. He's just an old man in simple slacks – proving how deceptive appearances can be.

The sequences set in the early years of the twentieth century are replete with detailed costume. The most striking of these is the white suit and hat of evil worn by Don Fanucci. His elegant dress sense disguises his brutality and it makes him stand out very boldly against the muted colours of the immigrant streets he moves through. This ultimately leads to his undoing – he becomes an easy target.

Young Vito's clothes are simple, almost rustic, but as he develops a foothold his attire becomes more sophisticated.

TEAM COPPOLA: As with *The Godfather* and *The Conversation* Coppola surrounded himself with colleagues and trusted friends on *The Godfather Part II*. Gray Frederickson and Fred Roos co-produced the film and once more the production-design genius Dean Tavoularis came on board to design the film and overhaul certain parts of the real world. Gordon Willis, who had been cinematographer on *The Godfather*, returned for the second instalment and would return for *The Godfather Part III*. Make-up wizard Dick Smith, progenitor of Rick Baker and Stan Winston, returned also. Gray Frederickson and Fred Roos served as producers and went on to manage the expansive and exhausting *Apocalypse Now* shoot. Roos remained with Coppola on almost all of his other films.

CASTING: Both *The Godfather Part II* and *The Godfather Part III* are notable for the consistency of their casting (with the sad exception of Robert Duvall's absence in the third instalment). The acting bloodline to the original movie remained strong as many of *The Godfather*'s actors returned. Al Pacino reprised his star-making role as Michael Corleone, and others who returned were Diane Keaton as Kay Adams, Robert Duvall as Tom Hagen and Johnny Cazale as Fredo.

The major addition to the cast was Robert De Niro, portraying Don Vito as a young man. De Niro had originally been cast as one of the buttonmen in *The Godfather* but had been unable to appear because of scheduling conflicts. The film's principal villain, Hyman Roth, was played by Method actor guru Lee Strasberg, most famous for running the Actors' Studio in New York. His nervous coughing during filming (apparently symptomatic of his lack of actual film-acting experience) was incorporated into his character. Hyman Roth was inspired by real-life gangster Myer Lansky. When Strasberg first began working on the film, Coppola's concern about whether he had made the right choice was such that he contacted aging film director Elia Kazan and asked him to consider stepping in to portray Roth. Kazan was unable to commit as he was busy writing.

Martin Scorsese auditioned for the role of Genco and Roger Corman appears as a Senator.

Where appropriate some of the cast took lessons in speaking Sicilian and Robert De Niro was flown to Sicily for three weeks' research for which Paramount paid him $1500 in living expenses for the time he was there.

I KNOW THAT FACE: Robert De Niro spent the early part of the 1970s establishing himself as one of America's premier actors, alongside Al Pacino. De Niro has starred in *Mean Streets* (Martin Scorsese, 1973), *Taxi Driver* (Martin Scorsese, 1976), *1900* (Bernardo Bertolucci, 1976), *The Deer Hunter* (Michael Cimino, 1978), *Raging Bull* (Martin Scorsese, 1980), *The King of Comedy* (Martin Scorsese, 1982), *Once Upon a Time in America* (Sergio Leone, 1984), *Brazil* (Terry Gilliam, 1985), *The Untouchables* (Brian De Palma, 1987), *GoodFellas* (Martin Scorsese, 1990), *Casino* (Martin Scorsese, 1995), *Heat* (Michael Mann, 1995), *Ronin* (John Frankenheimer, 1998) and *Meet the Parents* (Jay Roach, 2000).

The Godfather Part II has, in small roles, Danny Aiello as the guy who attempts to kill Frank Pentangeli in the bar, and Harry Dean Stanton, visible at the HUAC hearings. Aiello went on to star in *Do The Right Thing* (Spike Lee, 1989) and Harry Dean Stanton is one of America's finest character actors, appearing in *Alien* (Ridley Scott, 1979), *Paris,*

Texas (Wim Wenders, 1982) and *The Straight Story* (David Lynch, 1999) among many other films.

THE FILMING: Filming began on *The Godfather Part II* on 1 October 1973 and wrapped on 19 June 1974. The film's budget expanded noticeably, finishing up at $13,600,837.

One of the great design challenges of *The Godfather Part II* was the 'rebuilding' of a street in New York to resemble the year 1917, or thereabouts. This reimagining of the street took around six months of work, including putting gravel across the tarmac and changing all the street lights. The intensely detailed commitment to realism contributes greatly to the drama, which is often rooted in larger-than-life action.

As it had on *The Godfather* and would do on *The Godfather Part III*, the filming focused on New York's Lower East Side, around Mott Street. The shoot also returned to Sicily, a tradition that is part of all three *Godfather* movies.

PROMOTION: The anticipation in 1974 for *The Godfather Part II* was huge. However, because of the film's long running time only 160 first-run cinemas across North America showed the 200-minute version. All other cinemas showed the 180-minute version.

Whatever the concerns were about its length, cinema exhibitors were only too happy to book the film. 340 cinemas had advanced $26 million for the right to show the film. Certainly, the title of the film dominated the film's theatrical release poster, telling audiences all they needed to know. The sole image on the poster was of Michael in his long coat and hat, white against the black poster, emerging like a ghost.

THE OPENING: Although a sequel was not originally part of *The Godfather*'s conception as a film, its commercial and critical success made a follow-up almost inevitable. Maintaining stylistic consistency, the film begins with the mournful musical theme over a black screen which then fades up. The image ties *Parts I* and *II* together without any ambiguity. At the end of *The Godfather* Michael is shown receiving people in his den in his new persona of Godfather. *Part II* begins with that same moment and it assumes a symbolic resonance as his hand is kissed. Michael assumes the aura of a god and his assumption to the throne is emphasised by the shot of the leather chair in which his father had once sat. The chair is lit just enough to reveal the impression made in it by Vito.

From this dark interior the film goes back to 1901 and the bright sun of Sicily to establish the film's narrative strand that charts the early years of Vito Corleone. A wide, sunbaked shot reveals a funeral procession that seems to be melting in the heat as the black-clad mourners cross the sand and rock. Gunfire shatters the tranquillity. Vito's mother runs to her dead son and slumps over him protectively, their black clothes starkly contrasted with the sand in a briefly held tableau of misery and unbreakable unity.

There is then a cut to Don Ciccio's home. The moment of Vito's mother's death is shown in a wide shot, startling in its detachment. The film does not make the death melodramatic, instead capturing its brutality with a documentary quality. Vito runs.

HEROES AND VILLAINS: As with *The Godfather* there is a boldly drawn conflict between the Corleone family and their enemies. Compounding this is the essential villainy present within the heroes of the story. It is a remarkable achievement that the audience always roots for the Corleones when we know their moral code is so corrupt. Central to the hero and villain intrigues is the relationship between Michael and his older brother Fredo, which evokes the Old Testament conflict between the brothers Cain and Abel. Allegiances shift and swirl and Michael can trust nobody, not even his brother Fredo.

Michael Corleone continues his tragic descent into anger and vengeance, allowing these issues to bring about the apparent downfall of his blood family. He alienates his wife and murders his older brother. Michael's struggle to live up to his father's example is enriched by the parallel structure of the film, which delineates the genesis of the Corleone family in New York and plays to the full the idea of the sins of the father being visited on the son.

Mothers are important to many of Coppola's films and *The Godfather Part II* makes this a critical part of the drama and moral code of the film, building on the maternal figures from *The Godfather*. At an especially low point, and in his desperation to understand what is happening, Michael finds solace in his aging mother. Who hasn't turned to their mother in a time of need for that one word of wisdom? Michael talks about how his father, Vito, held the family together and was always strong in his support for it. While Mama Corleone only features occasionally in the story she is a key presence and she occupies a place that ties into the Catholic iconography of the young Vito sequences. On several occasions in these scenes Vito is framed with a picture of the Virgin Mary in the background, resting protectively nearby, as though on his shoulder. The film posits America as a mother figure through its early emphasis on, and romanticisation of, the first sight the immigrants get of the Statue of Liberty. The Statue assumes an almost religious significance like the Holy Mary, nurturing and protective. When young Vito goes to the theatre, the Statue of Liberty is painted on the stage curtain and the statue is ringed with a halo as though investing the landmark with religious power.

Michael's retreat into deeper darkness and increasing violence is expressed through décor – the stone of the den walls give it the allure of a cave and Michael's desk is a barricade between him and the pains and complications of the world beyond. The film repeatedly emphasises his silent stare as he studies those around him, never giving anything away himself. Any trace of Michael's boyishness as seen in *The Godfather* is gone and this is amplified during the film's closing flashback. It is when the film divests Michael of his business dealings and shows him simply as a man with the same problems and insecurities as anyone else that the film excels. Michael's descent into inhumanity dominates the closing moments of the film. As he sits looking out at bloodied Lake Tahoe his eyes appear utterly dark, as though only the eye sockets remain, his face more like a skull than anything warmly human. If the eyes are the windows of the soul then where is Michael's soul?

Tom Hagen is Michael's only confidant and, in one of the film's outstanding scenes, Michael says, 'Tom, you're my brother.' Tom looks touched by this honest moment. They are ten years older than they were in *The Godfather* and they look wearier and more anxious.

Young Vito Corleone is first seen as a little boy in the film, alone in the New World sitting at his quarantine ward window in an image of loneliness. When Vito is introduced as a young man he is a dashing, confident character, and his commitment to family is evident from the start, it is the bedrock of his life. Just consider the shot of him looking on very pensively as baby Fredo lies sick on the bed.

Connie's most notable contribution to the story is the scene towards the end of the film where she pledges her allegiance to Michael, a bond that is fully played out in *The Godfather Part III* where she becomes a very sinister presence.

The film's secondary villain is the oily Senator, Pat Geary, who is racist and morally dubious. Early in the film he lambasts Italian Americans, earning the ire of Michael Corleone. Later in the film Geary is eating out of Corleone's hand and is essentially working for him. Geary emerges as a buffoon.

The principal antagonist and threat is the low-key, apparently harmless, but ultimately deadly, Hyman Roth, an old and frail man with the heart of a young killer. The theatrical Don Fanucci speaks with a rasp which compounds the evil of his actions. He acts like a monster and sounds like one. Vito heroically kills Fanucci, casting out the evil, but over time Vito himself will assume Fanucci's position but on an even grander scale.

COPPOLA STYLE: Not as commercially popular as *The Godfather*, *The Godfather Part II* may have confused some audiences with its structure. The film is, however, even more of an accomplishment than the original movie. Coppola's dexterity in building tension within scenes and across sequences is as sure as ever and he amplifies the muted emotional palette of the story. The original film's style is maintained and enriched in *The Godfather Part II* so that ways of framing the action are repeated, and the overall colour scheme and visual tone of the film remain consistent with the original instalment. The other sequence of films to work this consistently is George Lucas's *Star Wars* serial, which bears many resemblances to the concerns of *The Godfather* story albeit wrapped up in a very different format.

IMAGE: As with *The Godfather*, image and décor reinforce the solidity of family through the emphasis on domestic décor, doorways, doorframes, tables. Space is used to emphasise emotional distance, never more powerfully than late in the film when Michael and Kay argue in the aftermath of the revelation that Kay had an abortion. They stand on opposite sides of the room, the distance between them saying as much as the dialogue.

In contrast to the shadow world of the Corleone compound, the sequences featuring young Vito possess a burnished, golden quality, a nostalgia that reflects the optimism the immigrants may have held towards the possibilities America held.

In *The Godfather Part II* even the weather emphasises the mood of loss and death, being either snowy and cold at the Lake Tahoe compound or more autumnal when Michael sits looking out over the lake. The violence and loss of the film's final moments is moodily and memorably expressed. Michael is shown sitting alone outside the family home. A shot then follows in which the camera tilts up from the fallen leaves blowing towards the empty Corleone house.

As in *The Godfather* and *Apocalypse Now*, Coppola culminates with the intercutting of several climaxes all unified by music.

Silhouettes are a frequent visual element of the film and this device is never more powerful than in the scene in the lounge at Lake Tahoe, where Michael confronts Fredo. Michael is silhouetted against the window and the snow outside, and the frame is divided by the window frames. It is an emotionally cold scene which draws the net of treachery together. The silhouette of Michael strips him of any warmth as he condemns Fredo. The dead world outside foreshadows the emotional death between the brothers and the literal death soon to come.

In an early scene in the film, and certainly one of the most generically exciting, Coppola uses a wide shot to undercut the sense of impending menace so that the eventual highpoint of the scene is ultra-threatening and charged. As Michael and Kay prepare for bed, Kay nonchalantly notices their bedroom curtains have not been pulled. Michael approaches the window and there is a cut to a wide shot as he nears the glass. Suddenly, the windows explode with gunfire. This way of unleashing violence so starkly recalls the scene where Vito's mother is killed at the beginning of the film.

In contrast to the brutality of both these scenes, the lead-up to the murder of Don Fanucci, as Vito races along the rooftops, is lent a romantic energy by the elegantly gliding camera tracking alongside him, lending the pursuit energy and excitement. When young Vito crosses the road with a box of groceries, the camera tracks behind him and then crosses with him, passing a wealth of stalls and people and immersing the audience in the world of immigrant New York with documentary-like grace. This approach is elegantly embedded in some of the more composed and stately images, none more so than the virtually still shot of Vito sitting on the steps of the town house with his young family. The image is more a still photograph, encapsulating the film's emphasis on tableau images.

Whereas the young Vito sequences ooze nostalgia and feel like sepia photographs writ large, the 1950s part of the story in Cuba feels as though it was shot at that time; there is a certain flatness. The entire trilogy emerges in part as a document of certain aspects of American culture, particularly its dress, automobiles and architecture.

SOUND: The film's naturalistic sound dominates the action and occasionally dialogue bridges over separate locations to clarify a link between them in terms of plot or theme. Near the end, when Fredo says a Hail Mary on the boat, we cut back to Michael so that some of the prayer is heard as his face is shown.

For the Cuban revolution scene, crowd sounds expand the sense of scale and emphasise the contrast between the noise of New York and the graveyard silence of the Corleone compound.

COPPOLA TUNES: Carmine Coppola conducted Nino Rota's score and supplied a range of source music for the film. Nino Rota composed some new thematic material and reprised several key themes from the original film, thereby maintaining the continuity of the story and making it an organic whole. As with *The Godfather* the richly drawn music is judiciously and sparingly placed.

The soundtrack listing for the *The Godfather Part II* by Nino Rota/Carmine Coppola is: 'Main Title/The Immigrant', 'New Carpet', 'Kay' (Beres Hammond), 'Every Time I Look In Your Eyes/After the

Party', 'Vito and Abbandando', 'Senza Mamma/Dinri-Cini/Napule Ve Salute', 'Godfathers at Home' (Beres Hammond), 'Remember Vito Andolini', 'Michael Comes Home', 'Marcia Stilo Italiano' (Carmine Coppola), 'Ninna Nanna a Michele', 'Brothers Maim', 'Murder of Don Fanucci' (Carmine Coppola), 'End Title'.

HUMOUR: The most humorous elements of the film are located in the young Vito story where we see him befriending Clemenza. The carpet-stealing scene has the quality of a silent film comedy in its pace and framing and contains hardly any dialogue. The other humorous segment revolves around Vito getting the local landlord to comply with him and allow the old woman to stay in her apartment.

AWARDS: Coppola won the Best Director Oscar for *The Godfather Part II. The Conversation* was also in the running. At the 1975 Academy Awards the film won Best Actor in a Supporting Role (Robert De Niro), Best Art Direction/Set Decoration, Best Director, Best Music (Original Dramatic Score), Best Picture, Best Writing (Screenplay adapted from other material). The film was also nominated for Academy Awards in the categories of Best Actor in a Leading Role (Al Pacino), Best Actor in a Supporting Role (Michael V Gazzo), Best Actor in a Supporting Role (Lee Strasberg), Best Actress in a Supporting Role (Talia Shire) and Best Costume Design (Theodora van Runkle). At the 1975 BAFTAs the film won Best Actor (Al Pacino), Anthony Asquith Award for Film Music (Nino Rota), Best Film Editing and Best Newcomer (Lee Strasberg). The winning streak continued to dazzle at the 1975 Directors Guild of America awards where Coppola won for Outstanding Directorial Achievement. The film was nominated for a range of awards at the 1975 Golden Globes in the categories of Best Director, Best Motion Picture Drama, Best Motion Picture Actor Drama, Best Original Score, Best Screenplay and Most Promising Newcomer (Lee Strasberg). The 1975 National Society of Film Critics, USA awards honoured the film for Best Cinematography (Gordon Willis) and Best Director, and Coppola won at the 1975 Writers Guild of America awards for Best Drama adapted from another medium. In 1993, the National Film Preservation Board USA inducted *The Godfather Part II* onto the National Film Registry.

COPPOLA MAGIC: Intercutting has a magic all its own in this film. It is the film's big special effect. The other striking piece of movie magic is the phenomenal re-creation of an entire street in its early-twentieth-century guise. It is so detailed and textured, and immerses the audience in its energy and crowds (see **SOUND**). In today's digital era, this transformation would no doubt be created in the computer. The scale of the endeavour in the early 1970s was entirely real and physical and is a testament to the vision of production designer Dean Tavoularis.

MOVIE SPEAK:
Mama Corleone (reminding Michael at a critical moment): 'You can never lose your family.'

Michael: 'Times are changing.'

HOME VIEWING: Both Region 1 and Region 2 DVD editions of the film are available and are the same, the film being part of the trilogy boxed set whose stunningly comprehensive package is as follows: Director's Commentary on all films, documentaries: *Francis Coppola's Notebook, On Location, The Godfather Family, Behind the Scenes 1971, The Cinematography of The Godfather, Coppola and Puzo on Screenwriting*, two featurettes on music, additional scenes, storyboards for *Part II and Part III*, character, cast and crew biographies, Academy Award acceptance speeches, photo galleries, theatrical trailers, widescreen 1.85:1.

In both Britan and North America the film is available on VHS. Note that only the VHS *Godfather* trilogy boxed set arranges the story of the entire trilogy in chronological order across the three films.

In 1975, NBC announced they would screen *The Godfather* and *The Godfather Part II* in four separate segments, arranged chronologically by Coppola. Barry Malkin edited the TV version from a suite inside The Brill Building.

The TV version was subsequently titled *Mario Puzo's The Godfather: The Complete Novel for Television*. This mega event was screened each day from 12 to 15 November 1977. It was the most widely viewed feature film on television, garnering 100 million viewers. In this TV edition, Sonny's death is less bloody and the Italian and Sicilian dialogue incorporates more English phrases than in the theatrical release.

DELETED SCENES: Inevitably, certain scenes are eliminated in the composing of a film at the edit stage. The following is a list of some of the scenes excised for the 1974 theatrical release of the film (though included on the DVD):

• Don Ciccio's men searching for young Vito after the death of Vito's brother Paolo
• Don Fanucci being attacked by thugs as Vito watches
• Young Clemenza impressing young Vito
• Young Vito going to a local gunsmith and seeing his flute-playing son (a tribute to Carmine Coppola, a flautist)

- Vito and the landlord Signor Roberto talking for longer
- A scene where young Vito is called Don Vito Corleone by Signor Roberto
- Young Vito meeting a young Hyman Roth
- Vito murdering two of Don Ciccio's guards prior to murdering Don Ciccio

TRIVIA: Coppola edited *The Conversation* over the weekends during production on *The Godfather Part II* at this high point in his career. The original edit of *The Godfather Part II* intercut too fast and furiously between Michael and Vito's stories and was deemed too confusing for audiences, so the material was changed to bigger blocks.

To create the explosion of blood for the death of Fanucci, a condom was filled with blood and attached to actor Gaston Moschin's neck.

John Cazale experienced minor gunshot burns in his left armpit when filming his death scene.

Carroll Ballard shot footage of the run-down Kaiser Estate at Lake Tahoe. The footage was not included in *The Godfather Part II*. Remarkably, Walter Murch discovered the footage while working on the edit of *The Godfather Part III* in 1990 and used it in that film, proving that nothing creative is wasted.

For the festa sequence, the windows on one side of the street were covered over to stop sunlight bouncing back onto the filmed action, thereby keeping the image flat. The moment when the towel covering the gun used by Vito Corleone catches fire was not an accident – it had been in Coppola and Puzo's script. That particular image is one of a number now synonymous with the *Godfather* trilogy, showing up repeatedly in film magazines and in books.

In March 2003 American movie magazine *Premiere* ran a fun listing of the 100 greatest movie moments. At number one was the moment when Michael kisses Fredo in Cuba, realising that Fredo has betrayed him. It is a very resonant moment, on New Year's Eve, as Batista flees Cuba and Castro seizes power. Coppola did only three takes of the scene.

COPPOLA'S VIEW: Coppola's interest in heritage and history manifests itself throughout *The Godfather Part II*.

The motif of time passing (and hence, of death) in *The Godfather* is made stronger still in *The Godfather Part II* as Michael watches things change radically and frighteningly. The need for the stabilising influence of family is a favourite Coppola theme. Ultimately, though, greed undoes the family bond and is the source of great damnation. In stylistic contrast, but in thematic unity, Coppola's film *Bram Stoker's Dracula* also dramatises the fall from favour of a dazzling young man and how he must then find a way to redeem himself. His sense of love and commitment is so strong it both emboldens him and tears him apart, just as it does with Michael Corleone.

There is a biblical quality to *The Godfather Part II*, inevitably realised through its family dynamic and a sense of the allure of power. This biblical tone is also embedded in some of the language at specific points. Having disowned Fredo, Michael says, 'You're nothing to me now.' When Kay confronts Michael near the end of the film she tells him, 'I wouldn't bring another one of your sons into this world . . . this must end.'

Coppola's much quoted commitment to drawing the story along the lines of the Roman Empire is made explicit during an exchange between Pentangeli and Hagen, and the last image of Pentangeli is of him dead in his own bath. At the close of *The Godfather Part II*, Tom Hagen visits Frank Pentangeli and they talk explicitly about how the family tradition was arranged along the lines of the Roman army. Pentangeli even goes so far as to compare the Corleone family to the Roman Empire. Hagen ruefully replies that 'It was once.'

For Coppola, the fall from grace that is central to the story is far more engaging and meaningful than the crime angle. The spiritual resonances are what make this sequel so special.

CRITICAL COPPOLA: *Sight and Sound* talked about the film's 'converging and diverging purposes that can only register on the screen as ambiguity about the relative importance accorded to meanings and effects, the "personal" statement versus the more impersonal blockbuster', while *Empire* magazine simply said, 'this is nothing short of magisterial.' and a BBCi Online review said 'masterful . . . a telling metaphor for America's immigrant experience'. For *Time Out*, the film is 'far superior to *The Godfather* . . . Coppola, so impressed by the rituals of the Corleone clan, still fails to actually show the Mafia's pernicious effect on society at large . . .'

VERDICT: *The Godfather Part II* is astonishing. As sturdy as *The Godfather* was, this sequel is stronger and more emotionally powerful. The simplicity of the film is a great strength, allowing space for mood and theme to emerge with a real universality. As in *The Conversation*, the thriller element is much less exciting and engaging than the spiritual implications of the drama.

COPPOLA NOW: 'They were siblings. One film hangs over the other like a ghost.'

Apocalypse Now (1979)

(Colour – 141 minutes, *Apocalypse Now Redux* version: 195 minutes)

Omni Zoetrope
Producer: Francis Coppola
Co-Producers: Gray Frederickson and Fred Roos
Associate Producer: Mona Skager
Screenplay: John Milius and Francis Coppola
Cinematographer: Vittorio Storaro
Editor: Walter Murch, Gerald B Greenberg, Lisa Fruchtman
Music: Carmine Coppola
Sound Montage/Design: Walter Murch
Supervisory Sound Editing: Richard Cirincione
Production Design: Dean Tavoularis
Art Direction: Angelo Graham
Second Unit Photography: Stephen H Burum
Costume Design: Charles E James
Visual Effects: Joe Lombardi, AD Flowers

CAST: Marlon Brando (*Colonel Walter E Kurtz*), Robert Duvall (*Lt Col. Bill Kilgore*), Martin Sheen (*Captain Benjamin L Willard*), Frederic Forrest ('*Chef* Hicks'), Albert Hall (*Chief Phillips*), Sam Bottoms (*Lance B Johnson*), Larry Fishburne ('*Clean*'), Dennis Hopper (*Photo Journalist*), GD Spradlin (*General Corman*), Harrison Ford (*Colonel Lucas*), Jerry Ziesmer (*Civilian*), Scott Glenn (*Captain Richard Colby*)

BUDGET: $31.5 million

THE BOX OFFICE: $78.8 million (original release), *Redux* release $4.61million

RELEASE DATE: 15 August 1979, *Redux* release date May 2001

MPAA: R

BBFC: 18

TAGLINE: Francis Ford Coppola presents *Apocalypse Now*.

SUMMARY: Captain Benjamin Willard is in Saigon, his tour of Vietnam duty over. He has been waiting a week for details of his mission. He is called in by intelligence to undertake a mission to go upriver into the deep jungle of Cambodia (where America has no reason to be). Once there he must terminate a renegade American colonel named Kurtz.

Willard is escorted to intelligence and handed a dossier on Kurtz, which includes correspondence and images; a tape is played of what is believed to be Kurtz's voice. Willard accepts the mission and boards a Patrol Boatriver (PBR) crewed by four men: Chief, Clean, Chef and Johnson. During the early part of the journey the Air Cavalry, commanded by Captain Kilgore, escort Willard upriver. Kilgore calls up an air attack on a village; Willard and his men take a ride in one of the helicopters. The village is destroyed and Willard and his crew continue their journey, away from the last vestiges of the American military.

Willard keeps his mission a secret from the PBR crew. The men bond as they make the river trip. En route Willard spends time trying to understand what kind of character Kurtz is by reading through the dossier. One night, the PBR comes across a US supply station where a United Services Organisation (USO) event is being prepared. Willard and his men stay overnight and attend a Playboy bunny show. The river narrows and the PBR arrives at the last American line, the Do Long bridge. The battle scene is chaotic and Willard speaks to some of the dazed and confused troops in an effort to get some idea about what is going on.

Willard learns that several months previously another soldier had been sent on the same mission as Willard and had not returned, instead staying at Kurtz's camp. The PBR comes under fire and Clean is killed and buried.

Willard finally tells Chief the specifics of the mission. Lance, meanwhile, is becoming increasingly primal from exhaustion and drugs while Chef becomes increasingly worried and uneasy. Chief is then killed when the boat comes under fire and his dead body is carried away by the river.

Of the PBR crew, only Johnson and Chef remain, neither one knowing the nature of the mission. Willard finally reaches the riverbank where Kurtz's compound is located amid an ancient temple. Hundreds of indigenous Ifuago people are there and Montagnard soldiers line the riverbank. Willard is met by a talkative photographer and then taken to Kurtz, who imprisons him in a bamboo cage and then in a container. Chef is killed by Kurtz. Finally, Willard is taken into Kurtz's inner sanctum and is confronted by the Colonel, who talks about his disillusionment with the world and the military. Willard listens patiently and finally prepares to kill him. Wielding a machete, Willard slays Kurtz and then emerges into the night where he is greeted by the soldiers as the new leader. Willard returns to the boat with Johnson. The boat pulls away from the temple and Kurtz's face is shown for the last time. Willard starts the journey back to the known world and the film fades to black.

An extensive sequence in the *Apocalyspe Now Redux* version (2001) shows Willard and his crew arriving at a French plantation house, where they dine and stay overnight. The French explain their resolve to stay there. This sequence is the most significant restored material to the edit and occurs in the film after the death of Clean.

COPPOLA'S CONCEPT: Coppola's energy and imagination are not to be disputed, and *Apocalypse Now* is one of the boldest films of the 1970s – a reminder of just how powerfully quest narratives can speak to an audience. There is something of the Boys' Own adventure about the film, but Coppola and his creative team ally this with a genuine desire to invest the adventure genre with a philosophical soul.

Apocalypse Now is one of the few films – and Coppola has directed a couple of the others – whose title and concept has transcended the immediate realm of film and become a major part of contemporary pop culture. Like only a handful of other adventure films (including *The Wizard of Oz* (Victor Fleming, 1939) and *Star Wars*, George Lucas, 1977) *Apocalypse Now* has taken on a life of its own. As with the best and most resonant stories, this film is many different things to many different people, thereby ensuring its longevity and status as a classic. Generating its own mini-media empire of books, articles and documentaries, it frequently makes it on to an assortment of 'Best Of' lists in magazines and other journals.

Even people who have not seen the entire film may be familiar with images from it, such as Willard rising from the water, Kurtz's bald head in the shadows, and the American helicopters riding in to the strains of Wagner's 'Ride of the Valkyries'. Perhaps the elemental simplicity of these images is why they have tattooed themselves on a collective movie-going consciousness. The film presents a torrent of images of man and nature, of light and darkness. The all-consuming nature of the film's purpose and the obsessional nature of the quest undertaken, eerily, powerfully and excitingly mirror one another and have plugged into our pop-culture psyche. With the world today still confronting a regular display of first world military might, the film continues to carry a strain of social significance and protest.

The film is by turns crazed and thoughtfully poetic, and undoubtedly appeals to the adolescent male fantasy of heroism. Generally, it is regarded as Coppola's mad obsession, the film from which he may never have returned artistically. Coppola's commercial and artistic standing at the time was such that he was able to sell the movie to a distributor before shooting any material.

Vital to the eventual conception of *Apocalypse Now* was the fact that at release America had only very recently finished its disastrous intervention in Vietnam, for which bullishness they were punished. During the conflict John Wayne had directed the tub-thumping, pro-American movie *The Green Berets* (1968), which was designed to explain to movie audiences why American troops had to be in Vietnam. Wayne even wrote a letter to Lyndon B Johnson in December 1965 expressing his intention with regard to the film.

In 1977 a TV movie called *Limbo* had been aired in America. It focused on the wives of American POWs and how their husbands' fates impacted on life at home. Coppola's later film *Gardens of Stone* would deal with this very subject. *Heroes* (Jeremy Paul Kagan, 1977) starring Henry Winkler, Sally Field and Harrison Ford had failed to make much impact and *Coming Home* (Hal Ashby, 1978) dramatised the experience of the Vietnam veteran back home with far more success. *The Boys in Company C* (Sidney J Furie, 1978) was another film that centred on the soldiers in the battlefield of Vietnam. However, it was *The Deer Hunter* (Michael Cimino, 1978) that made the biggest impact on audiences in the late 1970s and which predated *Apocalypse Now* by one year. In 1986 director and screenwriter Oliver Stone began work on an informal trilogy of Vietnam movies, starting with *Platoon* (1986) detailing life in Vietnam for a young American soldier. In *Born on the Fourth of July* (1989) Stone dramatised the experience of Vietnam veteran Ron Kovic and finally with *Heaven and Earth* (1993) explored the relationship between a Vietnamese woman and an American soldier. In 1987, Stanley Kubrick released *Full Metal Jacket*. But the grandiose *Apocalypse Now* continues to throw its shadow over all films set during the Vietnam war.

When *Apocalypse Now* was released there was the sense that it might play its cultural part in purging recent history. Maybe even more important was the recognition that a Vietnam movie could not claim to be some version of the truth if it portrayed the American experience there as victorious.

When Coppola took on the challenge of making *Apocalypse Now* he was well aware of the problems and tensions inherent in the task. At the time of completing work on *The Godfather Part II*, Coppola commented: 'I'll be venturing into an area that is laden with so many implications that if I select some aspects and ignore others, I may be doing something irresponsible.'

Famously, the origins of *Apocalypse Now* lay in the late 1960s when George Lucas concocted the idea of a Vietnam movie shot on 16mm in the rice fields of northern California. He spoke about the project with his friend and fellow film student, John Milius, and he began work on a screenplay which at one point had been called *Psychedelic Soldier*. Milius's screenplay conjures a sense of just how much combat will warp a soldier's sense of reality. Coppola's old colleague Carroll Ballard had also wanted to make a movie based on Joseph Conrad's novella *Heart of Darkness*. Screenwriter and Zoetrope founder member John Milius had a keen interest in the military and was an aspiring screenwriter. It was he who responded to a badge popular at the time which was emblazoned with the legend 'Nirvana Now'. Milius dipped into the Bible and recalled the phrase 'apocalypse now'. For Milius, *Heart of Darkness* suggested itself as a powerful framework and metaphor that would enhance the basic concept.

Eventually, the narrative of the film's developing screenplay would be clarified by journalist Michael Herr's war reports in *Esquire* magazine. These pieces went on to form the basis of Herr's celebrated book *Despatches*. His most notable *Esquire* piece was an article entitled 'The Battle for Khe Sanh', which certainly inspired the Do Long bridge sequence in the film.

One of the central concepts of *Apocalypse Now* is of civilisation vying with the primitive, and in terms of the wider American narrative culture *Apocalypse Now* feeds into the stream of native consciousness and of the frontier and wilderness mythology. This cultural progression is stunningly mapped out in Richard Slotkin's book *Regeneration Through Violence*.

The film also has sociopolitical interest. *Apocalypse Now* strives to express the media presentation of the war and also the mindset of imperialist cultures. For the *Redux* version, Coppola reinstates the French plantation sequence (see **SUMMARY**) that runs about twenty minutes and articulates the issue of colonialism, so much a part of Western intervention in the non-Western world.

Coppola gave Milius $15,000 to write the script when Milius told him that was how much he needed to live on for a year. Coppola said that if the film ever got made then Milius would be paid another $10,000.

Milius' first draft of the script was dated 15 December 1969. One of the major questions has always been Milius' identification with the maverick, martial, primordial Kurtz character. In an interview with *Film Comment* in the July–August 1976 issue (volume 12, no. 4) John Milius tells interviewer Richard Thompson that he regards Willard's trip upriver as akin to Homer's *Odyssey* narrative, with the character of Kilgore being nothing less than the Cyclops. For Milius, had he been director, the film's inspiration would have been *The Bridge on the River Kwai* (David Lean, 1957), suggesting the more explicitly adventure-based narrative that the screenplay originally took;

unsurprising perhaps given George Lucas's initial involvement in the concept.

Given George Lucas's huge impact on American popular cinema, it is intriguing to think that initially he was to have directed *Apocalypse Now*. The involvement of George Lucas in the project eventually lessened and he became busy with *American Graffiti* (1973). By this time, Lucas had also begun developing what would become *Star Wars* which, in the opinion of editor and sound man Walter Murch, is a transposition of the essence of *Apocalypse Now* – namely, that a primitive race, working on invention and great courage, could overcome the challenge of a mighty empire of machines. It remains a central motif in Lucas's prequel trilogy nearly thirty years later.

During the shoot of *Apocalypse Now*, when Coppola was at an especially low point, he confided in John Milius that if he died making the film then Milius should take over. If Milius did not complete it then George Lucas would replace Milius.

It has been reported that when Lucas and Milius saw the film several years later, in 1979, they were uneasy with the way in which Coppola had transformed the material. It seemed as though Coppola had transcended the concept and taken it away from a pulpy sense of adventure to something more rooted in mythology and symbolism.

So, having taken on the job of developing *Apocalypse Now* in the early 1970s, Coppola finished a rewrite of Milius's script in late 1975. Famously, Coppola would rewrite the screenplay endlessly through the seemingly interminable filming period of 1976–77.

One early draft of the screenplay began with Willard back in America working as a bodyguard to a businessman on a boat. Willard begins to tell a woman on board about the trial of being in Vietnam. The film was originally to have concluded with Kurtz and Willard fighting alongside one another against the Viet Cong and succeeding. When a helicopter comes in to fly them out, Kurtz guns the chopper down. Coppola discarded this conclusion in favour of the scenes in Kurtz's compound.

As with any movie adaptation of a source text, it can be fun to note what has been transformed or eliminated in the process. In the movie, the shower of arrows that strike the PBR just before it arrives at Kurtz's compound recalls the arrows that rain down on Marlowe's boat in *Heart of Darkness*. 'Exterminate all the brutes' is a line in Conrad's novel which has an echo in the movie line 'Drop the bombs, exterminate them all.' In the film, Willard calls himself 'caretaker of Kurtz's memory'. In Conrad's text, Marlowe says, 'I was to have the care of his memory.' In both the film and the book, Kurtz's last words are the same, 'The horror, the horror' – a line which inspired TS Eliot's poem *The Waste Land*, which is suggested in the film as being part of Kurtz's reading.

Gardens of Stone is Coppola's later film about the impact of the Vietnam war and it makes a fascinating contrast to *Apocalypse Now* in every respect. In a sense it is a more potent expression of the cost of war.

INLUENCES: Joseph Conrad's novella *Heart of Darkness* was the film's most prominent influence, and as Coppola ventured towards shaping the conclusion of the film, he paid more attention to Conrad's text than to the screenplay, drawing from the prose a sense of the primitive and the savage. The film makes a quantum leap from notionally being a war movie to being an exploration of the wildness in man.

For cinematographer Vittorio Storaro, one of the principal influences was French painter Eugene Henri Paul Gauguin's work, especially his painting *Where Do We Come From? What Are We? Where Are We Going?* Coppola also referred to Gauguin in explaining the character of Kurtz to Brando.

For the end of the film, Coppola sought much inspiration in TS Eliot's *The Waste Land*. Eliot's landmark poem explores the world after the First World War and, like *Apocalypse Now* alludes to a range of tensions and associations between the modern and the ancient.

Cinematically, an informing source for Coppola was the work of Werner Herzog, a German director and contemporary he very much admired, and who had directed *Aguirre, Wrath of God* (1972), a story about a Peruvian expedition into the jungle in 1560 to search for El Dorado. Herzog's later film *Fitzcarraldo* (1982) repays the compliment to Coppola in the imagining of the clash between the civilised and the wild. In that film the drama turns on efforts to bring opera to the jungle.

The other key influence on the film is James Frazer's book *The Golden Bough* (1887). This was a nineteenth-century work of multiple volumes (the final one published in 1915), detailing and comparing world rituals and mythic narratives.

Frazer published a supplement to *The Golden Bough* in 1936 called *Aftermath*. John Milius has said that the inspiration for the title *The Golden Bough*, was Virgil's poem *Aeneid,* which in turn influenced elements of the narrative of *Apocalypse Now*. In Virgil's story, Troy has been destroyed and Aeneas's father, Anchises, heads off to found Rome. He dies en route and Aeneas, wanting to see his father one last time, consults the Sybil, who instructs him on how to enter the Underworld. Willard's journey takes him into a kind of Underworld where he experiences a death and a resurrection. The mythological associations and influences on the film manifest themselves further in shots of Kurtz's library that show Jessie L Weston's *From Ritual to Romance*, a study that is concerned with Grail mythology, one of whose most prominent narratives is the myth of The Fisher King. There is an appeal in knowing that the journey Willard takes into a mythic zone was matched by Coppola's own creative entanglements with mythic tropes. Just as Willard is tested by a mission to enter an unknown world, only to re-emerge transformed and enlightened, so too it seems that Coppola also found himself plunging into a kind of creative darkness. He re-emerged with a potent sense of the strain of film making and the intensity a film can generate. The production of *Apocalypse Now* seems to confirm the value of a creative battle. Would it have been as emotionally vivid and memorable had the quest to make the film lacked the challenges, confusions, frustrations and doubts that were part of the adventure of making it?

Coppola and John Milius dominate the conceptual proceedings in most accounts of the creation of *Apocalypse Now*. Dennis Jakob, a longtime Coppola associate, emerges from the film's production history as a vital creative source, aiding Coppola in fashioning the mythological resonance of the climax to the narrative. He was on the *Apocalypse Now* set much of the time, particularly during the filming of Kurtz's scenes and, with his interest in mythology, Jakob was able to advise Coppola on how the film could best incorporate and allude to ancient narratives and motifs. Indeed, it was Jakob who suggested the Fisher King narrative reference to Coppola in his refinement of the screenplay. Several years later, in the film *Rumble Fish*, Coppola would replay the Fisher King allusion to equally powerful effect.

COSTUME: *Apocalypse Now* adheres to Hollywood's long-standing commitment to descriptive realism in terms of military clothing. For the final phase of the film, the material becomes more symbolic and abstract. Willard dresses very conventionally befitting his straight arrow status within the film. Like Dorothy Gale in *The Wizard of Oz* (Victor Fleming, 1939) and Luke Skywalker in *Star Wars* (George Lucas, 1977), he is the connective tissue between the movie world and the audience. For the confrontation with Kurtz, Willard's emotional transformation is mirrored by his mud-caked, shirtless body. He has divested himself of civilisation completely. As the film progresses, Coppola's symbolic ambitions and metaphor overwhelm all. Johnson liberates himself from his army outfit and paints his face, and even Chef gets into the spirit of things wearing a hat made of immense leaves. The film's primal theme finds expression across the spectrum of effects. Kurtz's costume is simple and unfussy and is almost monastic in its simplicity. In huge contrast, Captain Kilgore's affinity for the romantic notion of the American Cavalry sees him strutting around with an old time Cavalry hat, a very bright satin scarf and a pearl-handled gun. The Air Cavalry regarded themselves as the best of the best and in the film trade on a sense of the American West.

TEAM COPPOLA: *Apocalypse Now* consolidated the team that Coppola had built, starting with *The Rain People*, through *The Godfather*, *The Conversation* and *The Godfather Part II*. Returning to Coppola's movie-making fold were Gray Frederickson and Fred Roos, fresh from the success of *The Godfather Part II*. Frederickson was responsible for the locations of *Apocalypse Now* and Roos for the logistical issues that were massive and many.

Once again, Dean Tavoularis reprised his duties as production designer, a monumental task in this instance. Walter Murch headed up the post-production effort.

Screenwriter John Milius was one of the Movie Brat gang, as they were dubbed by the press in the early 1970s. These were the wave of new film directors and writers who revitalised Hollywood film making, often recharging stale genres with a personal strain of cinema. The so-called Movie Brats were marked by their youth and determination and their names are now all enshrined as movie-making legends. Francis Ford Coppola led the way and Martin Scorsese, Steven Spielberg, John Milius, Brian De Palma and George Lucas all followed. Milius also wrote *Dirty Harry* (Don Siegel, 1972), *Jeremiah Johnson* (Sydney Pollack, 1973), *Judge Roy Bean* (John Huston, 1970) and *The Wind and the Lion* (John Milius, 1975). He had also written and directed *Dillinger* (1973) for Roger Corman and went on to direct intermittently through the 1980s and 1990s with the brilliant surfing epic *Big Wednesday* (1978), the adventure *Conan The Barbarian* (1982), *Red Dawn* (1984), *Farewell to the King* (1989) and two TV movies *Motorcycle Gang* (1994) and *Rough Riders* (1997). Milius may yet team up with the Wachowski Brothers (*Bound*, 1996; *The Matrix Trilogy*, 1999, 2003) to make another Conan movie. Milius has also written the screenplay for *Geronimo: An American Legend* (Walter Hill, 1993).

Apocalypse Now marked Coppola's first collaboration with Vittorio Storaro whose work Coppola had been impressed by on *The Conformist* (Bernardo Bertolucci, 1970). Storaro had originally been unsure about committing to an American film where he had no obvious personal connection or 'interest' in the subject, but his mind was changed when he read the *Apocalypse Now* screenplay on a flight to Australia to seek out locations for the film. Storaro's other credits as cinematographer include Bernardo Bertolucci's *The Spider's Stratagem* (1969), *Last Tango in Paris* (1972), *1900* (1976), *The Last Emperor* (1987), *The Sheltering Sky* (1990) and *Little Buddha* (1993), and *Agatha* (Michael Apted, 1979), *Reds* (Warren Beatty, 1981), *Ladyhawke* (Richard Donner, 1985) and *Bulworth* (Warren Beatty, 1998). Storaro was the youngest fully ranked cinematogrpaher in Italian film history, achieving this position by the age of twenty-six. Storaro's intensity and intellectual integrity enrich his work.

As happened on *The Conversation* and *The Godfather Part II*, Coppola was committed to an intense period of research which, for *Apocalypse Now*, was undertaken and led by Deborah Fine. Research ran from the spring of 1975 until the summer of 1977. Information about the North Vietnamese army, Cambodian ruins, China Beach, PBRs and USO shows, among many other minutiae, was part of Deborah Fine's fact-finding mission.

CASTING: Most famously, Coppola teamed up again with Marlon Brando, whose role is essentially an extended cameo during the end sequence of the film. Brando had been contracted for fifteen days work over a three-week period. However, when he arrived on set, the first three days were spent huddled with Coppola going through the script. Brando had not realised that the screenplay was not a direct adaptation of *Heart of Darkness*. Everything Coppola and Milius's script laid out was clarified for him when he read the book and allowed him to move ahead with his performance.

Steve McQueen had been first choice for the role of Willard, but declined. His take on the character was that he should essentially be cool, but this did not sit well with Coppola. Furthermore, McQueen did not want to be away from his family for an extended period of time. Coppola, in his keenness to work with McQueen, said that the production would let him bring his family to location. McQueen was then offered the role of Kurtz and declined that too. Keith Carradine, Tommy Lee Jones, Nick Nolte and Frederic Forrest were all candidates for Willard. Clint Eastwood had also been considered for the role of Willard as had Yves Montand.

After McQueen pulled out of the project, Coppola went to Al Pacino, Jack Nicholson, Robert Redford and James Caan before finally casting Harvey Keitel. This decision proved to be something of a misjudgement. After a few weeks' filming Keitel's style of performance, for which he is recognised as one of the modern greats, as a film such as the astonishing *Ulysses Gaze* (Theo Angelopoulos, 1995) demonstrates, was considered not quite what the film needed. Coppola felt that Willard needed to be a more passive entity than Keitel was portraying him as, so Martin Sheen was cast and was working on the movie by 26 April 1976. Sheen had auditioned for the role of Michael Corleone in *The Godfather*.

As with so many Coppola films, familiar faces reappear in *Apocalypse Now*, notably Robert Duvall in a very showy and loud role as Kilgore, quite in variance to the thoughtful quietness of his Tom Hagen character in *The Godfather*.

Frederic Forrest also reprised his relationship with Coppola after the success of *The Conversation*.

Laurence Fishburne, back then Larry Fishburne, appears as the young soldier Clean, the youngest soldier on the boat that Willard takes upriver.

Harrison Ford, on the cusp of breaking through as a leading man, was cast in a small role as Colonel G Lucas, an affectionate homage to George Lucas with whom Ford had recently finished working on *Star Wars: A New Hope* (1977). Ford looks very young and bookish in the film's briefing scene with his thickset glasses and clean-cut hair.

Dennis Hopper was cast in the summer of 1976 during Coppola's return to America, and for him the role was something of a redux, no less, restoring his profile with both the industry and audiences. On location, Hopper was taken to heart by the Ifugao tribe who made him a badge of honour from pine needles.

I KNOW THAT FACE: Martin Sheen was a star with a strong run in television shows. His credits have included: *Badlands* (Terrence Malick, 1973), *Gandhi* (Richard Attenborough, 1982), the TV miniseries *Kennedy, The Dead Zone* (David Cronenberg, 1983), *Wall Street* (Oliver Stone, 1987), *Da* (Matt Clark, 1988), as narrator in *JFK* (Oliver Stone, 1991), *Catch Me If You Can* (Steven Spielberg, 2002) and a starring role as Josiah Bartlet, the President of the United States in the TV series *The West Wing*.

Larry Fishburne changed his name to Laurence Fishburne and has lit up the screen in *Death Wish 2* (Michael Winner, 1982), *The Cotton Club, The Color Purple* (Steven Spielberg, 1985), *A Nightmare On Elm Street 3: Dream Warrior* (Chuck Russell, 1986), *Gardens of Stone, Boyz N the Hood* (John Singleton, 1991), *Searching for Bobby Fischer* (Steven Zaillian, 1993), *Higher Learning* (John Singleton, 1993), *What's Love Got To Do With It?* (Brian Gibson, 1993) and *The Matrix* movies (The Wachowski Brothers, 1999 and 2003).

Dennis Hopper has had an immensely long career that has included *Johnny Guitar* (Nicholas Ray, 1954), *Rebel Without a Cause* (Nicholas Ray, 1956), *Hang 'Em High* (1967), *Easy Rider* (Peter Fonda, 1969), *The Last Movie* (1971) which he also directed, *River's Edge* (Tim Hunter, 1986), *Hoosiers* (David Anspaugh, 1986), *The Indian Runner* (Sean Penn, 1991), *True Romance* (Tony Scott, 1993) and *Speed* (Jan DeBont, 1994).

THE FILMING: The making of the film, fraught with struggle, has assumed a legendary status and, in the process, Coppola became a real movie-making legend, his name (even today) immediately conjuring images of the brave and grandiose. For many observers, the film marked a cruel watershed in Coppola's creative output and in his standing in the industry. It was like he had gone upriver himself and never returned with the same vigour.

The shoot was anticipated to last around four months. It went thirty-seven weeks over schedule, and filmed over a fifteen-month period. Coppola referred to the film as the 'idiodyssey'.

To say that Coppola faced challenges and setbacks with the production of *Apocalypse Now* is one of the great understatements. The shoot fused financial, personal and even spiritual concerns as Coppola struggled to make a movie that would make sense to him and the world. The course the production of the movie took was the same as the course the story took.

Unsurprisingly, one of the first hurdles was the attempt to secure the support of the American military. This was not forthcoming as the screenplay was regarded as ultimately unpatriotic. This may have been why the Australian military was not keen to support the movie either. Coppola had considered basing the movie in Cairns on the northeast coast of Australia but, following the objection of the military, another location needed to be chosen and so the Philippines became the production's base. Famously, Coppola convinced President Marcos of the Phillippines to loan the shoot a number of its helicopters. When assistant director Jerry Ziesmer arrived on set the first conversation he had with Coppola concerned the number of helicopters available as Coppola had not been told how many he would have. US insignia would be painted on them and if necessary the Philippine airforce logos would be repainted at the end of the shooting day.

For the film's finance, the Bank of America lent $7,000,000 to Coppola Cinema Seven, the company Coppola had formed after the initial 'failure' of the first incarnation of American Zoetrope. This money was forthcoming because United Artists had agreed to distribute the film. Coppola was the Spielberg of the era.

In a neat parallel, Coppola began shooting *Apocalypse Now* on the same day that George Lucas began filming in the Tunisian desert on *Star Wars: A New Hope* (1977). Throughout its production, the *Apocalypse Now* crew were challenged by the problems of shooting in such a remote location with little infrastructure. The project was affected particularly badly when Typhoon Ruby demolished the set for the Playboy Bunny scenes leaving it twisted and broken. Two PBRs were left utterly destroyed. The typhoon cost the production $1,185,000 and the film shut down in early July to recover from the impact. Coppola returned to his northern California base to think things through and was back on location on 25 July. In August the Saigon hotel scenes were shot.

As on *The Godfather* films, Coppola challenged the creativity and pragmatism of production designer Dean Tavoularis. His tasks included overseeing the construction of an immense Cambodian temple complex at the Pagsanjan riverbank location. In all, Tavoularis had the task of creating the sets for 292 scenes.

For the intense Saigon Hotel scene that opens the film, Coppola encouraged Sheen to improvise. According to Jerry Ziesmer, Sheen got too near to the mirror when he miscounted his steps; when he lashed out he connected and smashed it. Coppola encouraged Sheen to continue when he registered no dismay at cutting his hand. 'I felt as if Francis was pulling Marty inside out,' Ziesmer comments in his book *Ready When You Are, Mr Coppola, Mr Spielberg, Mr Crowe*.

For the Kurtz compound scenes, two hundred extras were required on the set every day, and on one occasion there were 900.

The Ifuago natives would work as crew on the production, carving props and totems and building the cages that Willard and his crew were imprisoned in.

It proved a happy accident that it was Eleanor Coppola (shooting the 16mm footage of the production that became the foundation footage for *Hearts of Darkness*, the 1991 documentary about the filming of *Apocalypse Now*) who saw the Ifuago slaughtering a water buffalo, an action that sparked concepts in Coppola's mind for the primal finale.

One of the biggest logistical problems in staging the battle scenes was that some of the American soldiers acting as extras were indeed Vietnam veterans. When the helicopters flew in for the shot the veterans would become very intense and almost manic, and then, when the brief moment of filming was over, a sort of depression would kick in.

It was post-typhoon, during the summer of 1976, that the shoot became more chaotic than anybody could have predicted. Sometimes, though, it is the films made under great duress and tension that often seem to yield astonishing results. Coppola began doubting his ability to deal with the material adequately and felt that he was cheapening the subject. Symptomatic of this were his constant rewrites as he wrestled with the problem of how best to suggest that Willard's trek upriver takes him and the crew effectively into the past and into something primal and disturbing; something that civilisation had covered over.

Coppola found the French plantation sequence especially vexing and the production spent two weeks shooting it, as it became weighed down by an obsession with detail, right down to the inclusion of a 1954 bottle of Latour wine that was shipped in from Coppola's own home in California.

On the 15 September 1976, Coppola considered calling everything to an end and returning to California. Storaro encouraged him to continue and to keep pushing the symbolism of Kurtz's character and situation.

As December 1976 approached Coppola felt studio pressure to complete the shooting. He had just shot the USO concert sequence, which included 1500 extras. Coppola wanted to signal that the shoot had made him a new entity and insisted United Artists drop his middle name Ford from any of their advertising on the movie.

Over Christmas 1976, Coppola returned to northern California and viewed five hours of footage. The film was already way over budget but Coppola still needed to shoot images of the boat going upriver and the destruction of Kurtz's compound. The film was evidently going to finish up costing about $25 million. On 5 March 1977, after he had been out jogging, Martin Sheen suffered a heart attack and was given the last rites. The event was initially denied by the film's publicity so as not to cause investors any alarm and was described as heat exhaustion. The last day of March was the 100th day of shooting. The sequence of the destruction of Kurtz's compound was shot over nine nights using ten cameras, some of which used infrared film to lend the images a surreal quality.

The location shoot finished on 21 May 1977, just four days before George Lucas's *Star Wars* was released.

In the spring and early summer of 1978, pick-up filming was done in northern California around Sacramento along the Napa River, including a scene of Chef and one of the Bunny girls (Colleen Camp) inside a helicopter. Insert shots of Willard going through his pouch were also shot at this time.

PROMOTION: There had initially been plans to premiere the film in December 1977 but this plan was soon unachievable. A revised premiere date of 17 May 1978 was pencilled in. Coppola prevailed on United Artists to give him more time, until October 1978.

In May 1978 Coppola announced the film would not be ready until May 1979 and his sense of failure continued to mount.

A preview of the movie, as a work in progress, was presented in May and June 1978.

A sneak preview was held at the Uptown Theatre, Minneapolis, and then in Atlanta, Georgia. Coppola, Murch, Tom Sternberg and Fred Roos attended. In Atlanta the audience reaction suggested that, at around two-and-three-quarter hours, the film was running too long. Inspired, Murch accessed a Moviola editing machine in Atlanta and edited five minutes out of the movie there and then. In due course, the French plantation sequence would be edited out for being too slow though it was reinstated for the *Redux* version.

Jimmy Carter invited Coppola to show the movie at the White House on 19 May 1979 and the administration responded positively. On 11 May 1979 at the Bruin Theatre in Los Angeles there was another sneak preview and to Coppola's great relief word began to spread that the film was a great success and *Variety* gave it a very positive review. There was concern, though, that the more surreal elements of the story would turn off some audiences expecting a straightforward war film. At Cannes, the film was incredibly well received when screened as a work in progress. The film won the Palme d'Or, sharing it with Volker Schlondorff's film of the Günter Grass novel *The Tin Drum.*

For the movie's poster, legendary poster artist Bob Peak was brought in. The simple, moody image he created showed helicopters over a sunset-red river and jungle. The film's logo had a tatty, ruined quality to it and also resembled a painted bit of sloganeering. Another poster had a more lurid, horror-movie quality to it showing Kurtz's blood-red face dominating (almost as though it is melting) and in the background is Willard's face, and below them is seen an image of the Do Long bridge aflame. This image expresses the more symbolic aspect of the film and emphasises Brando's presence.

For *Apocalypse Now Redux,* the original image was used with the names of Harrison Ford and Laurence Fishburne as prominent on the poster as those of Brando, Sheen and Duvall. The only other text simply stated: 'Francis Ford Coppola presents an all new version of his groundbreaking masterpiece.' When the film was originally released in Poland it was accompanied by an especially vivid poster which featured just a painting of Kurtz that accurately suggested his emotional torment rather than the fact that Marlon Brando was portraying him.

On the 15 August 1979, *Apocalypse Now* was released in North America, three years after filming had begun. The audience at the 70mm screenings of the film (a few such venues) received a special booklet explaining the film's production and listing the cast and crew. The booklet included a note from Coppola. The 70mm version included no opening text credits. Just the image.

In 1982, *Apocalypse Now* was sold to ABC for 2 TV screenings at a price of $4 million.

THE OPENING: The beginning of *Apocalypse Now* functions like a musical overture introducing and associating a range of diverse themes and settings. All the core concepts of the film fuse in this dreamy and nightmarish opening sequence, which functions as a miniature of the entire film, a symbolic device. There are sounds before there is an image. The sound of helicopters begins the film and the first image is a long-lens, locked-off shot of a portion of the Vietnamese jungle. The choppers swoop across frame, initially out of focus. They move closer to the jungle and are seen in full. The forest erupts in a fireball, establishing clearly the sense of apocalypse, right now and for the next three hours. There is then a dissolve to a close-up on the face of Willard. This inverted image dissolves to show a ceiling fan whose movement and sound rhymes with that of the chopper blades, and then another dissolve to a blood-red sky behind a silhouette of trees. Another dissolve brings in the element of an ancient jungle statue. The camera revolves as we watch Willard on a bed with letters at his bedside and a picture of his ex-wife. He sleeps and the camera reveals a glass of whiskey. Another dissolve shows a gun lying next to Willard and we see his face in near darkness. He goes to the window and a point of view shot through the blind shows a street and we hear Willard's weary voice: 'Saigon. Shit. I'm still only in Saigon. Every time I think I'm going to wake up back in the jungle.' The scene continues, plunging the action further into the angst of Willard. There is a dissolve to Willard on the floor and he looks at the camera directly. A dissolve to flames is then followed by an image of Willard executing several drunken karate moves and he smashes his hand in the mirror. He smears his face with the blood and a jumpcut shows him naked on the floor crying.

He has been reduced to an animal state; by the end of the film he will have come full circle.

HEROES AND VILLAINS: The heroes of *Apocalypse Now* are the young men on the PBR escorting Willard upriver. They do their job without questioning its integrity or worth. As one character says in Coppola's later film *Gardens of Stone*, the army is not the place for an opinion. In the same breath, though, this sense of duty is presented as honourable and responsible. Willard, of course, is the film's protagonist, the one who endures the adventure and emerges from its crucible of trial and terror. He spends much of the time observing the craziness around him, only coming into his own in the last phase of the film, when the film 'asks' its audience to consider who the villain is. It is an indefinite, ever shifting line as uncertain as the many faces in the shadows. Like Michael Corleone, Willard is an emotionally contained young man focused on his goal, not given to wild displays of emotion, unlike the other men on the boat. By the end of the film Willard has divested himself of the trappings of his civilisation and become utterly primal, he becomes what had once scared him, he has become wild. Willard enters a corrupt world and becomes corrupted by it.

With Kurtz dead, Willard, in broad daylight for most of the film, stands in half light, half shadow. Finally, he walks with Johnson towards a literal and symbolic light on the riverbank, returning to the world after his adventure and test.

The characters of the men on the PBR are economically sketched out in simple shots showing them doing things, not saying things. Verbal characterisation comes a little later. Chef reads, Johnson suns himself, Clean brushes his teeth and Chief is at the helm. Clean and Johnson represent the unquestioning, uninformed young soliders drafted for the war as canon fodder. Johnson is the surfer dude kid whose ignorance is maybe what keeps him sane, a point made especially clearly when he stands on the PBR deck, with a purple flare blazing and says 'This is better than Disneyland.'

Chef is the older, more cynical and realistic of the group. He is the soldier who seems to least want to be in the jungle.

Inevitably it is the spectre of Colonel Kurtz that hangs over the action and the journey of the heroes, although he is not revealed until the final part of the film, true to the way in which Kurtz is revealed in Conrad's novel. Once Willard arrives, Kurtz is able to define his motives, actions and outlook. Kurtz is somebody for whom power has become all-consuming, but he does believe he is acting out of genuine disillusionment with the American military. Kurtz may be brilliant but brilliance is only valuable when used compassionately. Michael Corleone is a smart man in *The Godfather* movies but his intelligence is directed towards the shadows and not the light. In *Apocalypse Now* the duality of dark and light is explicitly expressed by the French woman when, talking to Willard, she says, 'There are two of you, one that kills, one that loves.' In some sense, Kurtz is less a character and more a vessel that contains a wealth of ideas, and he may even be the film's moral compass, offering up two lines that would not be out of place coming from Vito Corleone in *The Godfather*: 'You have to have men who are moral.' And, 'It's judgement that defeats us.'

The other force that engulfs the film is that of imperialism and in the French plantation sequence it is the basis of a major dinner discussion. The Frenchman talks in a way that echoes the Corleone line, 'This piece of Earth, we keep it!' He then goes on to say they want to stay in Vietnam because being there 'keeps our family together'. At other points in the film, imperialism and American intervention are alluded to. The political and social dynamic of imperialist activity is made understandable by having it personalised.

Kilgore is based on Colonel John B Stockton – a real-life military man. Kilgore serves as a key stage and guide in the adventure of Willard. He is cynical and saddened by the American military, but is the wisdom-giver who begins the process of illuminating Willard about the journey ahead.

Finally, the jungle itself is a character in the story. The wilderness of that place is both threatening and beautiful and, for all the pain it contains, it is the means of salvation for the hero of the film.

COPPOLA STYLE: *Apocalypse Now* is celebrated for its interplay of extremely theatrical images, its spectacle linked with intense human conflict, its naturalistically drawn characters, and the anxiety being played out amid the chaos. The characters often look directly at camera, which can have a slightly unsettling effect in a form of cinema that is so dependent on transparency as part of its storytelling. We feel as if we are simply watching another world that is unaware of being observed. Complementing the unforgettable visual design is Coppola's ability to draw out a range of finely etched performances with, at key points, actors looking directly at the camera to strengthen the rapport between the audience and the character. Ultimately, the entire journey that Willard undertakes possesses the quality of a dream.

IMAGE: Vittorio Storaro, the cinematographer on the film, invested his work with a visual plan very different from that which is usually seen in a war film. The psychedelic emphasis on surreal images and the juxtapositions of unexpected images run through *Apocalypse Now*. Storaro has spoken of three phases to his career: the first investigated the properties of light, the second the properties of colour and the third the properties of earth, water, air and fire. *Apocalypse Now* places itself neatly in this final phase of his work. For Storaro, *Apocalypse Now* represented the culmination of a phase in his career focusing on the earth and natural forms. Furthermore, Storaro regarded darkness not as an absence of light but the antithesis of light. The final sequence of the film dramatises the interplay of darkness and light: Willard is illuminated by his experience in the darkness of Kurtz's compound.

Storaro said that 'The original idea was to depict the impact of one culture which had been superimposed over another culture.' The film disturbs our perception and juxtaposes contradictory elements, such as surfing in the jungle waters. Countless images suggest a world gone utterly mad, tipping frequently towards the surreal. Late in the film the image of the tail of an American plane jutting out of the river suggests a high-tech ruin.

In the scene where Willard and Chef go mango-hunting, Storaro constructs a majestic and terrifying shot of the two men, tiny against the immense, primordial roots of a tree. It is evident that the men, and the military generally, are strangers in a land that is gradually consuming them.

Contrasting with the expansive and chaotic vistas of the riverboat journey that comprises most of the film, there are scenes near the beginning of the film that exist on a much smaller scale, but which are no less quirky. For the briefing scene, Coppola instructed his camera operator to pan whenever he felt bored, in order to give some sense of Willard's disorientation at being badly hungover.

Key to the interest of the *Apocalypse Now Redux* edit is the inclusion of the long-discussed French plantation sequence. The sequence begins with the PBR arriving at the site on the riverbank, engulfed in deathly smoke. Once inside the property it is a very different and far more opulent world than Willard might have imagined. The dinner scene is lit with a golden light, partly to suggest the setting sun (symbolic of the sun setting on the French empire) and also to bathe the meal (decorous and delicate) in a sense of old world glory.

The duality of the jungle's beauty and danger runs right through the visuals. Indeed, this aesthetic, which partly recalls some of the paintings of Henri Rousseau, can also be seen in *The Thin Red Line* (Terrence Malick, 1998). The PBR is often shown cutting through the golden, sunlit water. Contrasting with the stillness and calm of the river (a far safer place than the jungle around it) are the immense battle scenes, which are at their most intense when the camera tracks at speed through the carnage and confusion, dragging the audience right into the chaos.

As a film with a distinctly episodic structure born of the adventure format, its culmination point in Kurtz's temple becomes virtually a film of its own. The sequence emphasises the central conflict between, and closeness of, dark and light. Kurtz ducks in and out of the shadow like the Minotaur in the labyrinth. Coppola's penchant for tableaux shows Kurtz in silhouette in the doorway to his inner sanctum, which is a portal to another world, another way of thinking, just like the doorway into the Corleone den in *The Godfather*.

For the sequence that brings the film to its climax, Coppola refrains from using his intercutting crescendo technique (famously wrapping each episode of *The Godfather* trilogy), so that as Willard hacks into Kurtz we see the Indians hacking into a water buffalo. The build-up to Kurtz's death employs the same narrative tricks that Coppola uses for the killing of gangsters in *The Godfather*, and music is central to this design (see also **COPPOLA TUNES**). As Willard moves in for the kill, cast in silhouette, divested of anything recognisably human, the song 'The End', by The Doors, plays on the soundtrack. Kurtz is then seen in silhouette and the mute intercutting lends the scene a nightmarish, unreal quality.

When *Apocalypse Now* comes to its exhausted close it repeats the dissolves that began the film, associating apparently disparate elements, the meaning of which is now more vivid. The fade out ends the film with a sense of uncertainty and ambiguity about the fate of Willard. There is not a typical sense of victory but, instead, one of relief that the journey is over.

SOUND: The film is a strong example of an effort to elevate the role, and indeed the density, of sound, combining the demands of realism with the allure of more symbolic uses of sound. Coppola's brief to Walter

Murch was to make the sound quintaphonic, authentic and psychedelic. Interestingly, though, Walter Murch has described how Coppola was not that involved in the mix and other elements of post-production. The reasoning behind this was that Coppola could view the film in the edit in the mindset of an audience member rather than a film maker.

A powerful but not necessarily obvious example of the considered use of sound occurs when Willard looks out onto the streets of Saigon. The sound of a policeman's whistle subtly transforms into the sound of birdsong and the sound of motorcycles becomes the hum of insects. The sound is working to express the theme of the civilised world gradually consumed by the natural order and chaos.

The film has enormous rigour and vitality in its sound recording and sound design. *Apocalypse Now* was one of the first films with split stereo sound. For the *Redux* release, several of the actors were called back into the studio to re-record certain lines of dialogue being included in the film for the first time. The narration that accompanies the on-screen action is one of the film's highlights and this material was written by Michael Herr. The film is very much like a silent film and it is the voice-over that contributes much of the film's metaphorical weight and expands on the symbolic power of the images. To get the narration just perfect, between 35 and 40 voice-over sessions were conducted.

A lot of work went into creating the intensity of the film's frequently naturalistic sound effects. For the sound of a helicopter crew in transit, four veteran pilots were brought into a studio where a mute image of the scene was played. The veterans were asked to improvise their wild chatter in flight while at the same time on speakers the loud sound effect of chopper wings in motion added to the ambience.

As in *The Conversation*, where voices that have been recorded are replayed by the characters and seem to be all-consuming, in *Apocalypse Now* the intelligence officers play a tape of Kurtz's voice and it dominates the sound texture, as though Kurtz is present like an all-seeing, all-knowing phantom.

After the visual explosiveness of the film's final minutes, *Apocalypse Now* concludes very quietly and restfully with the sound of rain over a black screen. The sound effect communicates the jungle environment but also has a symbolic value. It is the sound of the natural world and not of man that has the last say, staying true to the film's expression of the wild and natural being far stronger and enduring than humanity. The rainfall may also suggest cleansing in the sense that Willard's journey has cleansed him and reawoken him to life.

COPPOLA TUNES: Carmine Coppola's score is a synthesiser piece that emphasises the dissonant, the ambient, the hallucinatory and the eerie, suggesting the nightmare that Willard is caught in. At no point is the music triumphalist or sentimental. Most famously, the film features Wagner's 'Ride of the Valkyries', an inclusion audiences can thank John Milius for. The music – taken from a version with Georg Solti as conductor – was played on set for that scene. Securing the rights to this piece of music was difficult and resulted in Walter Murch buying up eighteen other versions in an effort to find one that tied the image and sound together perfectly. However, Murch found that no recording was as appropriate as the Solti one. Murch even noticed how, in one shot of the ocean, the blue of the water, in his mind, seemed to rhyme with the sound of the brass being played. Eventually, the Solti version was acquired. When the music hits its crescendo, this is matched by a cut to a wide shot of the helicopters swooping in.

Music helps establish the time period so that the soundtrack includes The Rolling Stones' classic 'Satisfaction' played on the PBR radio. Most famously, The Doors' song 'The End' opens and closes the film. The song's opening lines run over the start of the film and its concluding lines close the movie.

The film's drumming music was provided by Mickey Hart, a percussionist for the Grateful Dead (the San Francisco band) and he put together a group called The Rhythm Devils. Coppola got them to provide percussion for the entire film, which they improvised as the film was running for them.

The soundtrack release for *Apocalypse Now Redux* is the same as for the original release of the film with the inclusion of two excavated tracks, namely 'Clean's Funeral' and 'Love Theme'. By Carmine Coppola: Opening – 'The End' (The Doors), 'Delta Dossier', 'Orange Light', 'Ride of the Valkyries' (Vienna Philharmonic Orchestra), 'Nung River' (Mickey Hart), 'Do Lung' (Randy Hansen), 'Letters from Home', 'Clean's Death' (Mickey Hart), 'Clean's Funeral', 'Love Theme', 'Chief's Death', 'Voyage', 'Chef's Head', 'Kurtz Chorale', Finale.

HUMOUR: Perhaps surprisingly for its seriousness and intense title, there is a lot of humour in *Apocalypse Now*. Much of it is rooted in details of character behaviour. Kilgore's obsession with surfing in the battle zones, for example, and also his placing of a deck of playing cards on dead Vietnamese bodies.

There is also humour in the film's criticism of media intervention on the battlefield when Willard rushes through an attack on a village and is instructed not to look at a documentary camera and the film crew, in fact portrayed by Coppola and Storaro. War has become entertainment.

There is even time and space for some slapstick when Chef and Willard meet a tiger while out looking for mangoes.

AWARDS: At the 1980 Academy Awards the film won for Best Cinematography (Vittorio Storaro) and Best Sound (Walter Murch, Mark Berger, Richard Beggs, Nathan Boxer). It was nominated for Best Actor in a Supporting Role (Robert Duvall), Best Art Direction and Set Decoration (Dean Tavoularis, Angelo P Graham, George R Nelson); Best Director; Best Film Editor (Richard Marks, Walter Murch, Gerald B Greenberg, Lisa Fruchtman); Best Picture (Francis Ford Coppola, Fred Roos, Gray Frederickson, Tom Sternberg); Best Written Screenplay (John Milius and Francis Ford Coppola). The film won the 1980 Golden Screen award in Germany and in 1981 took home the London Critics' Circle Film Awards Film of the Year award. Frederic Forrest won the Best Supporting Actor award from the 1980 National Society of Film Critics. 1980 Writers Guild of America nominated the film for Best Drama Written directly for the Screen (John Milius and Francis Ford Coppola) and the American Cinema Editors, USA 1980, nominated it for Best Edited Feature Film (Lisa Fruchtman, Gerald B Greenberg, Richard Marks and Walter Murch); at the 1980 American Movie Awards it won Marquee for Best Supporting Actor (Robert Duvall) and was nominated for Best Actor (Martin Sheen) and Best Film.

At the 1980 BAFTAs the film won for Best Director and Best Supporting Actor (Robert Duvall) and was nominated for the Anthony Asquith Award for Film Music (Carmine Coppola, Francis Coppola), Best Actor (Martin Sheen), Best Cinematography (Vittorio Storaro), Best Editing (Richard Marks, Walter Murch, Gerald B Greenberg, Lisa Fruchtman), Best Film, Best Production Design and Best Soundtrack (Nathan Boxer, Richard P Cirincione, Walter Murch). At the 1979 British Society of Cinematographers Awards the film was nominated but did not win and at the 1979 Cannes Film Festival the film was submitted as a work in progress and went on to win the Palme D'Or. The film was nominated for Best Foreign Film at the 1980 Cesar awards and won the 1980 David di Donatello Award for Best Director Foreign Film. At the 1980 Golden Globes awards the film won for Best Director, Best Motion Picture Actor in a Supporting Role (Robert Duvall) and Best Original Score (Carmine Coppola and Francis Coppola). It was nominated for a Golden Globe in the category of Best Motion Picture. In 2000 the National Film Preservation Board (USA) placed the film on the National Film Registry and in 2001 the Boston Society of Film Critics Awards acknowledged the *Redux* version.

COPPOLA MAGIC: Alongside *Bram Stoker's Dracula*, *Apocalypse Now* is Coppola's most effects-heavy film, though mainly it is the effects of practical set-ups and pyrotechnics rather than miniatures and optical effects applied in post-production. AD Flowers and Joe Lombardi dug a trench at the tree line and filled it with twelve hundred gallons of gasoline. When the jets fly over and drop fake napalm bombs, Flowers and Lombardi, lying in bunkers on the beach, ignited the gasoline, the heat of which could be felt across the river.

For the scene showing the destruction of the Do Long Bridge, 500 smoke bombs, 100 phosphorous sticks and 1200 gallons of gasoline were combined. There were 2,000 rockets and 5,000 feet of detonating cord. Pyromania Now.

The severed heads that are seen in Kurtz's compound were the heads of extras sitting in boxes that had been buried below the ground.

MOVIE SPEAK:

Colonel Lucas (on Willard's mission instructions): 'terminate with extreme prejudice'.

Willard: 'kids, rock and rollers with one foot in the grave'.

Willard (about the river, at the start of his mission): 'a circuit cable plugged straight into Kurtz'.

Kilgore: 'Charlie don't surf.'

Willard: 'we'd cut 'em in half with a machine gun and give 'em a Band Aid'.

The Photographer: 'You don't talk to Kurtz, you listen to him.'

HOME VIEWING: Both the Region 1 and Region 2 DVDs of *Apocalypse Now Redux* are the same. There are no featurettes though the disc includes a booklet that outlines Coppola's decision in creating the *Redux* edition and also lists all the scenes reinstated. The disc has an interactive menu, scene access, and has been formatted in widescreen 2.10:1 (The VHS of *Apocalypse Now Redux* is also available.)

Key to the long-standing cult following of *Apocalypse Now* and possibly accountable for renewed interest in the film in the early 1990s is the documentary *Hearts of Darkness: A Filmmaker's Apocalypse*. This is a stunning documentary by Fax Bahr and George Hickenlooper which was released in 1991. It combines the wealth of footage shot by Eleanor Coppola on location with clips from the film and more recent, retrospective interviews with many of the film's principal players. The documentary serves to support the claims made over the years that the film was a tidal wave of creativity for Coppola and also a mega-draining experience in all respects. Segments of the plantation scene that eventually made it into the *Apocalypse Now Redux* version are included, as are outtakes of Kurtz talking. *Hearts of Darkness* is available on VHS though not yet on DVD.

TRIVIA: The word redux refers to the process an organ has gone through in order to bring it back to good health.

Coppola began discussing the film as a production with Gray Frederickson in the spring of 1974, at which time *The Conversation* was being released in cinemas.

Coppola's Golden Age role model, Orson Welles, had attempted his own version of *Heart of Darkness* as early as 1939 at RKO Pictures, but Welles would not comply with budgetary cuts that the studio wanted to make.

When Coppola was at UCLA film school, a classmate called Jack Hill (who went on to be a low-budget movie producer) made a short called *The Host* which was inspired by *The Golden Bough* (see **INFLUENCES**).

It told of a young man taking refuge in an Aztec temple. Coppola has joked that *Apocalypse Now* was a splashy remake of the same concept.

During filming, Marlon Brando allegedly told Assistant Director Jerry Ziesmer that the reason he mumbled his lines was so that he would have the final performance, many months later, in re-recording dialogue. He also said that the reason he did not learn his lines and therefore had huge boards dotted around the set with his lines on them was to allow for a stronger sense of spontaneity. Brando reasoned that nobody knows what they are going to say until they say it.

Coppola once told Brando that one day actors would only be required in a limited way as their image could be stored on a computer file and used whenever necessary.

By the time Coppola came to shoot wide shots of Kurtz in the background of the temple, Brando had already left the project, and so a crew member called Pete Cooper had his head shaved and stood in for Brando.

During his briefing scene, Kurtz is referred to as Leighley, as the name had not yet been changed to Kurtz during the shooting schedule.

The water buffalo really was killed on camera and had not originally been intended as part of the film's finale, yet it seemed very appropriate as Coppola struggled to resolve the drama at the end of the screenplay.

Because the film repeatedly missed proposed release dates, journalists dubbed the film *Apocalypse When?*

In 1999, *American Cinematographer* readers voted *Apocalypse Now* the sixth best film of the 60s, 70s, 80s and 90s.

Scott Glenn had been in Vietnam, paid his own fare to the Philippines for filming, and was 'just' a background soldier. However, Coppola pumped up his limited screen time and we see Glenn glaring at Willard when Willard lands at Kurtz's compound. When a typhoon hit the shoot in May 1976, Glenn rescued several Filipinos from the jungle.

Montagnards were Cambodians living in the Vietnamese mountains.

Brando was paid $3 million for his work, though he was asked to come back for one more day immediately after his location work was over. Gray Frederickson hotfooted it to Manila airport before Brando left and Brando agreed, charging $75,000 for the day's work.

The film's intense detail extended to the creation of fake letters for use as props. Milius penned the original letters (from Kurtz's wife to Kurtz), which were enveloped and stamped La Jolla, CA. These letters are some of the documents that Willard is given at the start of his mission. Also, fifteen boxes of Wrigley's gum were shipped to the location in 1968-style wrappers.

Two hundred thousand feet of film was shot of the Air Cavalry raid on the village.

There was no Sampan massacre in the screenplay. Walter Murch had suggested the My Lai massacre scene for the start of the film.

Fifty-four takes were shot of Dennis Hopper welcoming Willard and the crew.

Coppola was given a bodyguard by President Marcos on his arrival in the Phillipines.

There were three military advisers on the project: Pete Kama, Paul Hender and Doug Ryan. Some American soldiers in the film were portrayed by aspiring American doctors whose grades were not good enough to work in North America, but this was not an issue in the Phillipines.

Terrence Malick had almost come on board the movie to direct some second-unit footage of a guy selling rivets upriver. This was never shot.

Several years later, in a real life spin on the film's 'Ride of the Valkyries' scene, General Noriega, hiding out in a Vatican Consulate in Nicaragua was flushed out by American forces playing very loud rock and roll.

Apocalypse Now and *The Mission* (Roland Joffé, 1986) are the only feature films to have been entered in The Cannes Film Festival as works in progress. Both are set in jungles.

Creating the *Apocalypse Now Redux* edit from the original negative means that the original negative, in its original form, no longer exists.

The in-joke of the two briefing colonels is that one is named Colonel Lucas and the other General Corman.

Legendary comic magazine *MAD* spooled the film in vintage style courtesy of the great Mort Drucker and Larry Siegel in their version of the movie, *A Crock O'Blip, Now*.

The film once clocked in at around seven and a half hours. Three and a half of these hours covered the journey upriver and the remaining four were at Kurtz's compound.

On one day, no filming was accomplished at all until everyone was almost ready to call it quits. Then Vittorio Storaro and his crew, filming the troops early in the film, shot twelve set-ups in thirty minutes, racing on foot through the jungle because the twilight was just right. They would basically set up, shoot and then run a few yards before repeating the endeavour again.

The scene of Chef confronting a tiger was shot in two parts, each part separated by a year in the schedule.

COPPOLA'S VIEW: Ernest Hemingway once noted that all of American literature flows from Mark Twain's landmark novel *Huckleberry Finn*. In turn, a number of films have been buoyed along by that great novella, *Heart of Darkness*. *Apocalypse Now* is one of them.

An incredibly simple adventure narrative serves as a way to express a deluge of ideas. Throughout storytelling history the adventure format of a journey has served as a rich mine for metaphor. The linear nature of a quest means that it tends not to get too sidetracked by plot complication and exposition. Instead, the central characters find themselves reacting to the events that go on around them and which shape their sense of self and the world. *Apocalypse Now* is one of many in a long line of American adventures that goes back to the country's frontier mythology. It is not just about the Vietnam war but also about America on home turf. The other narrative that grapples with similar issues is the film *Deliverance* (John Boorman, 1972) based on the novel of the same name by James Dickie.

Coppola goes for philosophical and metaphorical integrity in *Apocalypse Now* as the story charts the fall of two men: one from a position of grace; the other from a position of humility. As the primal instinct overwhelms both of them, their spirits are consumed by the unconscious forces of the jungle. Hearts of darkness is absolutely the concern.

The war element and critique of the American miliary in Vietnam seem secondary, regardless of intent. It is there but it is overwhelmed by the personal drama. This is very much a hero's journey with the film taking its protagonists through the highs and lows of defining themselves so that they return to the world, bruised, broken and illuminated yet stronger. It is a spiritual film with a social inflection.

Like *The Godfather* and *The Conversation*, there is a Catholic sense of sin and the fall of Eden at work through *Apocalypse Now*. Duty is what 'kills' many a Coppola character, either literally or metaphorically. Kurtz is the most severely lonely of Coppola's thematically richest characters, more so than Michael Corleone or Harry Caul.

CRITICAL COPPOLA: *Empire* magazine said the film presented 'Vietnam as an epic, psychotic nightmare . . . with almost every line in the script sounding like a classic quote.' *Time Out* considered the film as 'brilliant as movie-making, but it turns Vietnam into a vast trip, into a War of the Imagination.'

VERDICT: Both the original *Apocalypse Now* and *Apocalypse Now Redux* remain intense and arresting experiences. For some the film is no more than a trashy adventure set against war. For others it hints at the miasma of madness that the American intervention in Vietnam became. In an age where the cinema of spectacle dominates the mainstream movie world, *Apocalypse Now* stands tall, combining big pictures and adventure as its engine fuelled by powerful ideas and associations.

Though a landmark film of 1970s cinema, to these eyes the film lacks the elegance and emotional resonance of *The Godfather*, but compensates for that in its bravado and resolute determination to give expression to age-old dualities.

As America moves further away from the Vietnam War, it is hard for us to register the impact that the film's implicit criticism of the conflict must have caused. As a film making an antiwar statement and, as Coppola always said, an anti-lie statement, *Apocalypse Now* will probably always have a currency. It remains most powerful, though, at the personal level, dramatising one man's fall and possible resurrection through going into his own heart of darkness.

COPPOLA NOW: (original film) 'We had access to too much money, too much equipment and little by little we went insane.'

(redux version) 'This new, complete and definitive version extends this idea (of the lie) to all young people, boys and girls, who are sent out to function in an established immoral world expected to function in a moral way.'

One From The Heart (1982)

(Colour – 103 minutes)

American Zoetrope/Columbia
Producer: Francis Ford Coppola, Gray Frederickson and Fred Roos
Associate Producer: Mona Skager
Executive Producer: Bernard Gersten

Co-Producer: Armyan Bernstein
Screenplay: Armyan Bernstein and Francis Ford Coppola,
from the original screenplay by Armyan Bernstein
Cinematographer: Vittorio Storaro
Editor: Anne Goursaud
Music: Tom Waits, sung by Crystal Gayle and Tom Waits
Production Design: Dean Tavoularis
Costume Design: Ruth Morley
Sound Design: Richard Beggs
Art Direction: Angelo Graham
Visual Effects: Robert Swarthe
Choreography: Kenny Ortega
Electronic Cinema: Thomas Brown, Murdo Laird, Anthony St
John, Michael Lehmann in co-operation with the Sony
Corporation

CAST: Frederic Forrest (*Hank*), Teri Garr (*Frannie*), Raul Julia (*Ray*), Nastassja Kinski (*Leila*), Lainie Kazan (*Maggie*), Harry Dean Stanton (*Moe*), Allen Goorwitz (*Garfield*), Jeff Hamlin (*Airline Ticket Agent*), Italia Coppola, Carmine Coppola (*Couple in Elevator*), Edward Blackoff, James Dean, Rebecca De Mornay, Javier Grajeda, Cynthia Kania, Monica Scattini.

BUDGET: $23 million

THE BOX OFFICE: $2.5 million

RELEASE DATE: 11 February 1982

MPAA: R

BBFC: A

TAGLINE: When Francis Ford Coppola makes a love story . . . don't expect hearts and flowers. From the director of *The Godfather I* and *II* and *Apocalypse Now* . . . a unique vision of love.'

SUMMARY: Las Vegas, Fourth of July weekend, early 1980s. Frannie is putting up another travel shop window display in the glare of the lights of night-time Las Vegas. She talks with her friend Maggie about getting away on her own.

Across town, Frannie's partner Hank works with his friend and business partner Moe at Reality Wrecking. The weekend marks Frannie and Hank's fifth anniversary together. Hank has purchased the deeds to the house as a gift and Frannie has purchased two tickets for them to Bora Bora. Frannie wants to go out and she and Hank argue.

Frannie is at work again and at her window stands Ray, a dashing Latino figure. He asks her to meet up with him later at a hotel where he sings. Frannie heads out into Las Vegas to join the party. Hank also heads into the lights and the night with Moe. Hank and Moe wander the busy streets and Hank is entranced by a circus performer, a young woman named Leila. Moe encourages Hank to speak to her and Leila tells Hank to meet her later. Moe takes Hank to get a haircut and to smarten up for his date.

At home, Frannie gets dressed up for her date with Ray – they meet and dance. Hank meets up with Leila and she begins to seduce him. Hank bumps into Frannie dancing on the strip with Ray and a lot of other revellers, so Hank and Leila go back to the Reality Wrecking yard and they spend the night together. Frannie spends the night with Ray in his apartment.

The next morning Leila leaves; Hank goes to find Frannie. She is not at Maggie's. Hank drives on to find Frannie who, Maggie says, is still with Ray. Hank drives to Ray's motel apartment and drags Frannie out. Back at their home Frannie packs her bags and heads for the airport to fly with Ray for Bora Bora. Hank races to the airport in a frantic attempt to win back the love of his life; Frannie boards the plane.

Hank sits alone; Frannie returns. They kiss as the sun rises on Las Vegas once more.

COPPOLA'S CONCEPT: *One From the Heart* has two concepts beating and pulsing their way through Coppola's movie-making imagination. First, there is the sweet and intimate creation of a modern-day love story that recalls an older sensibility of Hollywood film making in the 1930s and 1940s. Second, there is the goal to create a fluid and efficient film-making process that will allow for more creativity. The film's reputation and existence in the collective movie memory has suffered in part because of Coppola being synonymous with the tough guy action of *The Godfather* films and *Apocalypse Now*.

By 1980, Coppola's career was at an all-time high. After the trauma of location filming on *Apocalypse Now*, Coppola's new project would unfold within the controlled space of a new studio. MGM invested in the film and, on the back of that investment, Coppola was able to take a personal loan from Security Pacific Bank to supplement the budget: for eight weeks, Coppola took out a $1 million loan each week to cover the film's budgetary shortfall of $8 million. A further $2.5 million dollars from the TV sales of *Apocalypse Now* helped resource Coppola's lavish storytelling and movie-making experiment.

The American Zoetrope studio covered a ten and a half acre lot on the corner of Santa Monica and Las Palmas. For some who had started out with Coppola in San Francisco in the late 1960s the relocation of his enterprise to Los Angeles was hard to take.

Coppola started the 1980s by creating his own studio, this time called Zoetrope Studios. As he had done in the late 1960s, he was looking to secure a certain level of independence from the Hollywood machine. He had bought the General Studios in Los Angeles in March 1980 for $6.7 million – money earned from *Apocalypse Now*. He set about modernising the studio. In his enthusiasm and sense of play, Coppola gave the streets on the lot names like 'Akira Kurosawa Avenue' and 'Sergei Eisenstein Park'.

Coppola's great technical and technological watershed with *One From the Heart* was to devise a system called Electronic Cinema. Today the term would be digital cinema, and it is being taken up by more and more directors, certainly those in prominent positions as directors such as George Lucas, Steven Soderbergh, Robert Rodriguez and Lars Von Trier. The digital cinema process is essentially a system of streamlining and making the process of film making more cost effective by incorporating video into the process at the planning stage to design sequences and lay out the movie. The term digital cinema now also applies to the creation of visual effects and also the use of high-definition cameras on which to shoot movies. Coppola had considered shooting *One From the Heart* on video but Vittorio Storaro convinced him that the quality of video was not yet defined enough for a feature.

One From the Heart is a grand experiment in both storytelling and storymaking. It is typical to equate the sombre and serious with something that has integrity and resonance. Lighter-toned material tends to be misunderstood as somehow lacking that kind of engagement. Clearly, this is not always the case. Comedy (in the broadest sense) can be as revealing and expressive of human dilemma as the most serious tragedy.

Coppola first proposed and heralded electronic cinema at the 51st Oscar TV broadcast saying, 'We're on the eve of something that's going to make the Industrial Revolution look like a small out-of-town tryout.'

It is fascinating to look back through the January 1982 issue of *American Cinematographer* magazine and derive some sense of the excitement at what Coppola was attempting with video's integration into film making. There truly was an excitement in the industry which was only matched more recently when computer-generated visual effects really began to break through in *Terminator 2: Judgment Day* (James Cameron, 1991) and *Jurassic Park* (Steven Spielberg, 1993).

Aesthetically, at a time when street realism was a part of film-making style, Coppola decided to turn to the past for inspiration and conceived a movie where the overwhelming artifice was a character within the film.

In Coppola's imagination the film was a small-scale love story but watching the film one sees a far larger-scale piece of work. *One From the Heart* was Zoetrope Studios' first movie. In part, it was a love letter project from Coppola to his childhood when musical comedy was part of the backdrop of family life.

From a production angle Coppola's concept was to use video to achieve a rough version of the movie before any film was shot. Coppola used a Betacam to record actors reading their lines and then combined these with extensive storyboards to create a massive moving sketch of the finished film. During the filming Coppola would refer to this video material from within his now-legendary Silverfish production trailer. He had had this mobile trailer fitted out with monitors and video editing equipment as well as an espresso machine. The Silverfish has remained a mainstay of Coppola's productions since its inaugural use on *One From the Heart*.

When Coppola announced production on *One From the Heart* in April 1980, he explained the premise and then expanded on this saying that for the rest of the 1980s he was going to write and direct a series of movies about men and women, exploring the subject from many different angles rather like a novelist might across a series of books.

The screenplay for *One From the Heart* was originally set in Chicago, but it was Coppola who made the change to Las Vegas. For Coppola, Las Vegas functioned as a metaphor of America because of its emphasis on money and artifice and the fact that, as an oasis in the American desert, it was the impossible made real.

Coppola's approach to the story was to treat it like a grown-up Disney film. The scale of the film was big and it came in the immediate aftermath and shadow of *Heaven's Gate* (Michael Cimino, 1980), a similarly expensive film that failed at the box office and which brought an end to the studio United Artists. For all their early 1970s glory, the new generation of Hollywood directors, who had become 'movie stars' in their own right, were beginning to be regarded as overindulgent. By 1980, Coppola was regarded as visionary but prone to allowing productions get out of control and, regardless of artistic integrity and his excellence as a writer, he was not as commercially surefire as other directors.

INFLUENCES: *One From the Heart* is inspired by Hollywood musicals of the 1930s and 1940s when a director such as Vincente Minelli was invigorating the form with films such as *Meet Me in St Louis* (1944) and *The Pirate* (1948). Like the latter film, *One From the Heart* centres on a woman who is dissatisfied and wants more from life. The other influences on the film were Coppola's affinity for the carnivalesque and the films of Federico Fellini, notably *La Strada* (1954), which centres on two travelling performers and a circus.

COSTUME: The costumes in *One From the Heart* are contemporaneous with the early 1980s, rooting the fantasy in a familiar reality. The clothes for Frannie at the start of the film reflect the sense of a mundane life as she dresses simply, practically and plainly. As her weekend unfolds Frannie's clothes become more fanciful. Hank's T-shirt and jeans are similarly cast aside for a smart suit as the weekend potential for fantasy develops.

The performer Leila wears a circus outfit throughout the film so that the real life and fantasy that she represents are fused. She is a real life Tinkerbell. Similarly, Ray has an unreal quality and he is cast as a fantasy figure from the start of the story when he steps into Frannie's humdrum life.

TEAM COPPOLA: Building on the success of his collaboration on *Apocalypse Now*, Coppola once more worked with cinematographer Vittorio Storaro on *One From the Heart* and for Storaro the project was an energising challenge. They would collaborate again some years later on the space-adventure musical short, *Captain Eo*, the overly whimsical short, *Life Without Zoe*, and the upbeat biopic *Tucker: The Man and His Dream*.

As with every film since *The Godfather*, Coppola worked with production designer Dean Tavoularis to create an entire world in the shape of Las Vegas and the Vegas strip on the Zoetrope soundstages. Coppola was thrilled to have his own studio and to be making an old-fashioned Hollywood film; he enlisted dancing genius and Hollywood legend Gene Kelly as an adviser on the project. Kelly had been a star of movie musicals and had directed features too. His credits include *The Pirate* (Vincente Minelli, 1948), *An American In Paris* (Vincente Minelli, 1951) and *Singin' in the Rain* (Stanley Donen and Gene Kelly, 1952). Kelly had also worked as an adviser in the 1970s when Coppola was working on his concept for what would become *Tucker: The Man and His Dream*, and on an idea for a film called *Sex and Violence* which Cindy Williams was due to star in. Kelly was a big fan of Coppola's ambitious plans. To choreograph *One From the Heart*, Kenny Ortega was hired. Ortega choreographed *Xanadu* (Robert Greenwald, 1980), *Pretty in Pink* (Howard Deutch, 1986) and *Dirty Dancing* (Emlie Ardolino, 1987).

Armyan Bernstein, the co-screenwriter of the film, has gone on to be a successful Hollywood producer. He wrote the screenplay for disco movie

Thank God It's Friday (Robert Klane, 1978). As a producer his credits include *The Commitments* (Alan Parker, 1991), action movie *Air Force One* (Wolfgang Petersen, 1997), the autumnal *For Love of the Game* (Sam Raimi, 1999) and *Thirteen Days* (Roger Donaldson, 2000).

In making *One From the Heart*, Coppola revived the old studio format – in the manner of old Hollywood, Zoetrope was a self-contained studio environment where there was a full-time staff of technicians and artists. By 1980 Dean Tavoularis was head of art and design; Jennifer Shull head of casting; Raymond Fielding head of special effects; Walter Murch head of sound; and Dennis O'Flaherty, Dennis Klein and Bill Bowers, staff writers. Coppola even established a roster of contract actors, signing up Teri Garr, Raul Julia, Frederic Forrest, Laurence Fishburne and Albert Hall.

CASTING: Coppola's affinity for the repertory acting company has been present throughout his career and *One From the Heart* features familiar faces, including Frederic Forrest and Teri Garr (The Conversation). The film also highlights Raul Julia, an emerging actor at the time.

I KNOW THAT FACE: Raul Julia went on to star in *Kiss of the Spider Woman* (Hector Babenco, 1985) and also *The Addams Family* (Barry Sonnenfeld, 1991) and *Addams Family Values* (Barry Sonnenfeld, 1993). Julia also starred in *Presumed Innocent* (Alan J Pakula, 1990).

THE FILMING: There is something both thrilling and, ultimately, saddening about the dream that was *One From the Heart*.

Filming began on 2 February 1981. To test run his electronic cinema concept during post-production on *Apocalypse Now*, Coppola had run a small off-line editing system to see what was possible. A fan of video, Coppola shot a rough version of *One From the Heart* during the rehearsal period on the streets of the real Las Vegas. This footage would then be available on set for the production rather like a sketch. Even though this package of technology had been designed to make film making more efficient and budget friendly, *One From the Heart* soon fell behind schedule and the budget grew.

The first phase in Coppola's electronic cinema process was to make an audio recording of the screenplay being performed. This soundtrack was then married to storyboards for the film which were mounted on an animation stand. Coppola listened to the audio reading and called out illustration numbers to accompany the dialogue. This material then formed a reference tool for rehearsals. Polaroids were taken during rehearsals and, where appropriate, these replaced the drawn images in the evolving storyboard.

Coppola ran technical rehearsals over a three-week period, combining two elements, namely the stage electronics package and the Image and Sound Control Vehicle. According to Vittorio Storaro, 'we tried to use the best ideas from radio, from the theatre, from television, from the cinema'. The Stage Electronics Package comprised Sony Betacam recorders, monitors, speakers, switching networks and an intercom. The Image and Sound Control Vehicle (29 feet long) housed this equipment. Over the years some actors have maintained Coppola directed them over a PA system hooked up to the Silverfish where he would monitor the action. From most accounts, however, Coppola did not simply retreat to the trailer for the entire shoot but would go there mostly to review a take. Coppola did make the very fair observation that watching the actors on monitors from the trailer allowed him to see the performers as the eventual movie audience would. Before every take Coppola would give instructions to his actors over the studio PA and, during a take, Storaro would watch on a monitor.

Once Coppola was satisfied with a take it would be transferred to Beta tape and timecode would be added to it and then it might even be edited into a rough video cut while the movie was being shot. Thus, at the start of each shooting day, Coppola could watch an assembly of the previous day's material.

For technical rehearsals the film cameras did not contain any film. Instead they were hooked up to the stage package which video recorded what the camera was seeing. This material was then edited on video as the tightest sketch version of the film to be made. Vittorio Storaro became an enthusiastic user of a Sony Handicam, using it as a viewfinder.

In 1979, Stanley Kubrick directed *The Shining* and one of his principal collaborators on that film was cameraman and engineer Garret Brown, inventor and operator of the Steadicam. The Steadicam is a rig on which a film camera is mounted which facilitates very smooth hand-held, mobile shots. The Steadicam has become a feature of many major films, notably being used for the opening sequence of *Bonfire of the Vanities* (Brian De Palma, 1990) and for a nightclub sequence in *GoodFellas* (Martin Scorsese, 1990). *One From the Heart* was Garret Brown's other early-days movie for proving the value of the Steadicam. Remarking on Coppola's affinity for employing new devices to expand the possibility of cinema, Brown wrote, 'He is gifted (or cursed) with the ambition to innovate, to advance the art and science of filmmaking into the 21st century.'

One take in *One From the Heart* ran for ten minutes and involved thirty different camera positions being taken up and hit precisely during the ten minutes of Steadicam shooting. To add to the complexity of staging action, certain sets comprised moving walls and, for scenes of Hank and Frannie in their house – often going up and down stairs – the production used a device called The Elevator. This allowed the Steadicam to film parallel to the actors as they ran up and down stairs. The Elevator was designed to move up and down but rarely functioned smoothly, often being too slow and therefore missing the action. One of Brown's favourite shots is at the end of the film when Hank and Frannie reconcile. As the Steadicam pulls away Brown has to step onto a crane which then booms up and moves back to the farthest end of the set as the sun is seen rising over Las Vegas. Far from being chaotic and tense, Brown recalls how the set was always a positive place to be, everybody rooting for Coppola's Zoetrope dream of a studio at its best.

As the film's production rolled along, the mainstream press began circling, aware that there might be a story to be made around a fraught production, in a sense extending the trauma of shooting *Apocalypse Now*.

Compounding the intensity of a complex and large-scale shoot were Coppola's financial obligations and concerns. A Canadian real estate mogul, Jack Singer, called in a loan that he had given Coppola several years before and it was this that really did damage to Coppola's finances. In the aftermath of *Apocalypse Now*, which had gone over budget, Coppola had shouldered the burden of money owed to Chase Manhattan Bank.

One From the Heart was intended as the Zoetrope flagship project. The studio had a payrolled staff but, as the movie became increasingly expensive, the staff found themselves being laid off. At one point union technicians voted to continue working on the film in support of Coppola on the understanding that their fees would be deferred. Coppola had sold the TV rights to *Apocalypse Now* and Paramount had bought a Zoetrope-owned script; Barry Diller and Michael Eisner at Paramount Pictures offered Coppola a $1/2 million interest-free loan and TV mogul Norman Lear put in half a million. However, on 28 April 1982, just a short while after the release of *One From the Heart*, Coppola filed for bankruptcy and Zoetrope studios was offered to the highest bidder.

PROMOTION: On 18 August 1981, with the film still in post-production, Coppola screened *One From the Heart* for potential exhibitors (cinema owners) but he got a negative response. There were also critics at the screening and word got out that the film, still unfinished, was not working. In pre-Internet days this kind of practice was not as familiar and widespread as it is today. Paramount made up 600 prints and spent $4 million on advertising and offered to help Coppola with completion funds in exchange for a distribution fee.

Paramount wanted the film off their books and they said Coppola had gone against his contract by shooting more material in the light of the exhibitor screening. Coppola even considered distributing the film himself. His one ardent mainstream supporter was Sheila Benson of the *Los Angeles Times*. Coppola continued to refine the film and early the next year he felt it was ready for the world.

On 15 January 1982, Coppola, the showman supreme, screened the film at Radio City Hall in New York, bypassing the studio and setting up the screening himself. Invited guests at the premiere of the film included Martin Scorsese, Andy Warhol and Norman Mailer. Mailer would go on to direct a feature for Zoetrope called *Tough Guys Don't Dance*, based on his novel of the same title and starring Ryan O'Neal. There were two screenings, one at 7 p.m. and one at 10 p.m. Paramount were furious that Coppola had arranged this screening without their input or consent and pulled out. The screening was a sellout and the audience enjoyed the movie. Coppola even put out soup for people queueing in the winter cold.

However, as the film garnered increasingly bad reviews, no studio wanted to distribute the film. Subsequently, American Zoetrope distributed the film to 25 cinemas in eight cities. Finally, Columbia agreed to release the film on 29 January 1982. There was a gala premiere on 10 February at Plitt's Century Plaza Theatre in LA and, in a severe case of audiences typecasting a director, a lot of the audience were not aware Coppola had directed it.

Columbia showed the film in eight cinemas in eight cities, but the film did not fare well commercially. After twenty days it had taken just $804, 518. By 1 April one cinema was showing the movie – the Guild in New York.

Intriguingly, the poster for the Japanese release has the character of Leila in the foreground, in a dreamy profile, while Frannie and Hank are relegated to small images at the bottom amid the throng of Las Vegas street dancers.

THE OPENING: Confirming *One From the Heart*'s fidelity and homage to the 1940s musicals of Golden Age Hollywood, and its sense of life as a show, the film begins with its titles appearing against a blue curtain onto which shines a spotlight. The curtains open to reveal the moon and the film's title in pink neon shines across it. The camera drifts down magically through the clouds to reveal Las Vegas below. As the camera moves with a graceful, gliding energy between, and up and around buildings and neon lights, the film's credits are incorporated into the signage. Finally the camera arrives at street level and drifts above car rooftops to find, amid the crowds and neon, a plain and simple shopfront window and, on the other side of it, Frannie.

HEROES AND VILLAINS: Far from the Sturm und Drang of *The Godfather* and *Apocalypse Now*, *One From the Heart* is one of several Coppola films defined by a very vibrant energy and optimism and, in keeping with the playful tone, the film does not really feature any movie-style villains. For all its artifice the film is built on a real emotional framework as a young couple struggle to maintain their relationship and recognise how deep their love for one another really is.

In the opening scenes Coppola explores the various pains and joys of a relationship. Frannie, her name childlike – recalling JD Salinger's novel *Franny and Zooey* – wants more from life.[2] Like Judy Garland's character in the musical *The Pirate* (Vincente Minnelli, 1948), Frannie dreams of a bigger life, of escaping. It is no accident that Frannie works for a holiday travel company, and she is first seen building a shop window display selling the fantasy of a holiday resort. One of the first things Frannie says in the film, to her friend Maggie, is 'wish I was going someplace really wonderful'. Frannie yearns to break out of her everyday world and her story arc shows her doing this, in emotional terms, before finally returning to the world she knows, with a new, unspoken understanding. Frannie and Hank's youthfulness and Frannie's sense of romance are supported by the production design. She has a heart-shaped mirror; she is cute and, like Vera Cicero in *The Cotton Club*, is like a little girl doing all she can to be an adult. Frannie says to Hank, 'Life has to be more than this.' Frannie's most gauche, and completely winning, comment is when she sees Ray and shouts across the street to him, 'I'm Frannie. I like to dance!' In meeting Ray, Frannie has her 'getaway' of the heart, as Ray represents a fantasy figure, as though from a movie. This reaches its climax when she and Ray dance across a blatantly artificial balcony on an artificial coastline with a very artificial boat moored just beyond the beach. The realism here is not that of a physical environment but of Frannie's state of heart and mind.

Contrasting with fizzy Frannie is low-key Hank, a man of simple needs. He is a boyish man, clearly confused and uneasy with maintaining a relationship. Hank finds expression difficult, but through his weekend journey away from the routine and familiar he revives himself, his emotional arc matching Frannie's. In *One From the Heart,* the power of fantasy steps in and helps out with reality, just like films sometimes can. Hank prides himself on being grounded and he feels that Frannie should appreciate this more. Hank might be lost but he has a helping hand in the shape of his older friend Moe, a naturally charismatic figure with an

---

[2] In Salinger's novel, Franny is a thoughtful teenager who sees the world as merely superficial. To cope with her sense of being intellectually marrooned, Franny endlessly recites the 'Jesus prayer'. It takes Franny's brother Zooey to point out that she is as self-involved as the rest of the world.

amazing head of hair. Whereas Hank is too much in thrall to everyday things (as his gift to Frannie at the start of the film shows), Moe knows about romance, telling Hank that 'Love is a high wire act.' By the end of his nocturnal adventure Hank has let something more playful enter his life. In a very quirky but cute moment he conducts the lights of the cars in his Reality Wrecking yard.

The journeys undertaken by Hank and Frannie see reality wrecked and put back together again. Hank recognises that he has to let himself go a little and, at the end of the film, knowing he is a bad singer, he sings 'You are my Sunshine' to Frannie as she boards a plane. Hank's artfulness and boldness ultimately win the day. Art soothes the pain in life. In *One From the Heart* dance and playfulness help the confused, melancholy central characters see a better way to live. Art allows the characters to look at themselves with fresh eyes. In the musical movie *The Pirate* (Vincente Minnelli, 1948), the character of Sarafin (portrayed by Gene Kelly) sings 'Be A Clown', a feelgood song testifying to the power of laughter in winning people's hearts. At the end of *One From the Heart*, Hank wins back Franny's heart by singing shamelessly to her at the airport in a last attempt to save their relationship.

Ray is a fantasy figure, representing the dash and verve that Frannie feels is missing in Hank. Dash and verve, though, are shown only to go so far.

Similarly Leila is a fantasy figure for Hank; she flits around like a fairy, reminding Hank of the gentility that should be part of romance.

Leila and Ray help Hank and Frannie confront their problems both within themselves and between themselves and then exit from their lives having worked their magic.

COPPOLA STYLE: There is a theatrical pulse to much of *One From the Heart*, as fantasy, artifice and emotion collide. Sadly, we live in an era where naturalism holds sway over fantasy and anything tending towards a sense of heightened reality does not sit comfortably with many people. How could a musical possibly be called realistic? When do people ever stop and sing in real life? That is precisely the point. That is *why* characters burst into song; it is the only way they can express certain emotions that normal conversation would make difficult if not impossible. The artifice of *One From the Heart* allows for the characters to play out their emotional fantasies.

At a realistic level *One from the Heart* re-creates the streets of Las Vegas and uses lighting, camera movement and set design to comment on the characters. By setting the action over one night, the film removes the action from a certain kind of everyday quality, and Las Vegas itself carries hints of a fantasy environment which allows the story to play out with some credibility.

IMAGE: The film begins by elegantly descending into the world of the story and concludes by drawing us up and out of it, leaving the fantasy world behind; the equivalent of the opening and closing of a book. For cinematographer Vittorio Storaro, Coppola's overall aesthetic plan for the movie, emphasising artifice over any kind of naturalism, was a rich opportunity. At the time of the film's release Storaro had published a 'manifesto' of sorts explaining his approach to the film; he felt sure he could express the power and intensity of love through his visual design and use of colour. For him it was a 'physiology of colour' concept that he was developing in the film. '. . . The unlimited desire of love that exists in mankind leads this togetherness of emotions – radiations to a union in a light that comprises them all, and of which all are a part . . .' The impact of light and colour on human behaviour was the source of Storaro's work during this period and *One From the Heart* shows that in a clear and intriguing way. Perhaps the film had some influence on Baz Luhrmann's *Moulin Rouge* (2001).

Storaro's lighting effects embolden the spoken word. Aside from the more naturalistic effects, such as the re-creation of sunlight cutting through window blinds, the most interesting effect is when the lighting theatrically and self-consciously fades up and down within a scene. There is a very strong use of this early in the film at Frannie and Hank's home. Coppola intercuts between Hank cleaning the dishes and Frannie getting dressed up, an intense red light on the scene – red having an association with passion and high emotion. As Frannie and Hank talk in the late afternoon light, the highs and lows of their relationship are expressed in the half light of the room. Shadow suggests unease. Another scene follows shortly after where they kiss and make up. Frannie and Hank undress and embrace. A red light illuminates the shot as the camera pulls away from the mattress. Frannie leaves the room for a moment and the red light fades out. Hank pulls up a little lamp and only this illuminates the room as he makes a little den for them. There is a tableau quality to the shot. The camera then gently pushes back in towards the mattress as Hank and Frannie get under the covers and the scene fades to black.

For Hank's encounter with Leila, set against the night sky of the Nevada desert (suggested by a wilfully artificial backdrop painting), blue light predominates, giving the action a mysterious, otherworldly quality. The fantasy of Hank's encounter plays out at Reality Wrecking as his sense of self is wrecked and rebuilt. The swan statue and the broken neon starfall that dominate the yard raise the location above its mundane everyday quality. Props also enhance the sense of magic as when Leila spies the ruby ring lying in the sand. Leila calls it the all-seeing eye and a visual effect suggests this power as Hank and Leila look into the ring and Hank sees Frannie and Ray.

As in *Tucker: The Man and His Dream*, Coppola playfully, inventively and artificially moves between locations in an effort to suggest the connections between characters separated by distances of land and emotion. As in *Apocalypse Now*, the film overlays images, but with a very different motive. To suggest the ultimately unbreakable bond between Frannie and Hank, close-ups of them are overlaid so that they appear to be in the same space. In a scene after they argue, Frannie and Hank feel downbeat and unsure. There is a dissolve to Frannie at her friend Maggie's. She calls Hank and the lighting reveals that what looks like a solid wall is in fact gauze. Frannie goes into silhouette and a light comes up on the other side of the gauze to reveal Hank on the phone. The scene then cuts to Hank at the wrecking yard. He walks through the half light and finally the light cuts out, casting him into moody silhouette. In *One From the Heart*, character and meaning are expressed naturalistically through dialogue but enriched through heightened visuals.

Another strong example of the interplay between what is spoken and what is shown is the scene where Ray chats up Frannie as she works. Coppola and Storaro go against the notion of mainstream cinema being 'transparent' and not calling the audience's attention to its devices. The camera glides happily back and forth from either side of the window.

Complementing the intricate and thoughtful use of camera movement and lighting are simpler compositions. In one such image the theme of escape is suggested in a series of shots that always include a billboard showing a plane against a golden sky.

As with *Apocalypse Now*, Storaro uses light and shadow for the moodier scenes to convey uncertainty and an emotional void. Contrasting with the vibrant yellows, reds, greens and blues of most of *One From the Heart*, silhouette and shadow dominate the scene when Hank returns home from the airport without Frannie. He walks in silhouette through the silent house. A shot with some early morning light pouring in through a window reveals Frannie in silhouette. She has returned. The light on the set comes up and Hank and Frannie are reunited.

SOUND: Given the arsenal of resources available to Coppola and his team, the sound of *One From the Heart* is typically thorough and detailed. When Hank returns home from the airport, the sound of thunder plays on the track, suggesting the doom he feels has fallen on him. Coppola has used the good old-fashioned thunder rumble in other movies too, notably in *The Godfather Part III*, where it denotes impending doom.

Comical sound effects accompany Hank's sneak across the motel roof through which he drops in on Ray and Frannie. As in *The Godfather Part II*, the sense of a large crowd is expanded through the use of sound.

125

COPPOLA TUNES: As with all the elements of *One From the Heart*, the music is thoughtfully integrated with the main narrative, and functions as a chorus. Coppola's interest in an organic creative process with the music is evidenced in his collaboration with David Shire on *The Conversation*. In *One From the Heart,* Coppola repeated the process.

In pre-production, Coppola screened for musician Tom Waits a wealth of previsualised material (storyboards, a reading of the script) so that Waits and his producer Bones Howe could begin developing music prior to filming.

The songs function to make the film feel like a musical, commenting on the action, underscoring it, unifying characters and undeniably contributing to the underlying highs and lows of Hank and Frannie.

One From the Heart is by Tom Waits and Crystal Gale. The soundtrack listing is as follows: 'Opening Montage/Tom's Piano Intro/Once Upon a Town', 'Is There Any Way Out Of This Dream?', 'Picking Up After You', 'Old Boyfriends', 'Broken Bicycles', 'I Beg Your Pardon', 'Little Boy Blue', 'Instrumental Montage/The Tango/Circus Girl', 'You Can't Unring a Bell', 'This One's From the Heart', 'Take Me Home', 'Presents'.

HUMOUR: *One From the Heart* is a very playful film, quite in contrast with the apparent grown-up seriousness of *The Godfather* films, *Gardens of Stone* and *Bram Stoker's Dracula*. The film has a lightness to it and also a real sadness as we watch a relationship break up and restore itself by the end in keeping with the happy endings of most romantic comedies. The funniest scene has a lot at stake emotionally in the moment when Hank sings to Frannie at the airport.

AWARDS: The lack of public enthusiasm for *One From the Heart* followed it everywhere. Its only nomination was at the 1983 Academy Awards in the category of Best Music (Original Song/Score).

COPPOLA MAGIC: *One From the Heart* is Coppola's most visual-effects-driven film, alongside *Bram Stoker's Dracula*, which similarly delights in the artifice of cinema. *One From the Heart* is exemplary in Coppola's body of work for the extent to which special effects contribute to the believability of the illusion. Made at a time when visual effects were experiencing a renaissance, in what would be the last gasp for optical effects (rather than digital), Coppola utilised effects resources not to create aliens and far-off planets, but to re-create Las Vegas, while lending it an air of definite magic and real-world fantasy. To achieve this, Coppola assembled an army of model makers, camera operators, matte painters and compositors. Several of these crew members continue to lead the visual effects field.

Coppola's overall aesthetic for the visual effects was that they should exist somewhere between the real and the not too real, combining the impressionistic and the surreal.

Model-making genius Greg Jein, a young man who had worked on the stunning miniatures for *1941* (Steven Spielberg, 1979), served in the same capacity on *One From the Heart* and it is a miniature set of Las Vegas that is seen at the beginning of the film. In order to allow the camera to photograph the Las Vegas miniature in great detail a camera was mounted on the end of a crane and pointed straight down at the model. A pitching-lens assembly at the end of the optical system redirected the field of view along the line of the set, which simulated a height above the pavement of just six feet. Coppola wanted the camera to be able to move through the streets of the miniature city model.

Ten months were spent preparing the special effects, with three months to construct the film's miniatures, and this work was supervised by Wally Gentleman, Bob Swarthe, Ray Fielding and Don Weed. Other, younger special effects crew, included 'graduates' of *Close Encounters of the Third Kind* (Steven Spielberg, 1977) and *Star Trek: The Motion Picture* (Robert Wise, 1979), such as visual effects editor Kathryn Campbell and Scott Squires, in the earliest days of his career. More recently Squires was a visual effects supervisor on *Star Wars: Episode 1: The Phantom* Menace (George Lucas, 1999).

Rather akin to Lucas and the Industrial Light and Magic Company that Lucas established in 1975, Coppola named a division of his new studio Zoetrope Images, which also spent time and money in research and development. On the Zoetrope Images stage a 95-foot platform, six feet wide, had several miniature buildings constructed on it made at a scale of a quarter inch to the foot. However, this resulted in depth-of-field problems that could not be resolved easily. The ideal scale would have been a half inch to the foot but this would have resulted in the need for a 200-foot-long soundstage, which was unavailable.

Matte paintings were also created to give the illusion of different times of day. In pursuit of a certain kind of physical realism, the camera speed duplicated the motorcar speed of 10–60 mph for those scenes where the characters are in cars. Again, in offering a certain perceptual realism, the special effects crew reproduced the optical phenomenon that occurs for anyone who travels down a road in a car and notices that distant objects do not seem to move.

In the film's 'Little Boy Blue' sequence where Hank sadly walks up to the Blue Lady neon sign, he looks up and sees the Lady turn into Leila and sing the Tom Waits song 'Little Boy Blue'. As the song unfolds Hank and the Lady appear within the Las Vegas sets. The actors were superimposed onto the background. While Coppola was shooting the actors on one stage, the visual effects crew were shooting backgrounds on a stage next door and, when needed, Forrest and Kinski would rush across to the effects stage.

One From the Heart is as dependent on visual effects to build its reality as were other films of the era, such as *Blade Runner* (Ridley Scott, 1982).

MOVIE SPEAK:
Hank: 'You're always talking about Paradise. And it'll be you and all of your shit walking along the beach.'

Leila: 'If you want to get rid of a circus girl, you close your eyes.'

Hank: 'I didn't come here to lose you to some Rudolph Vaselino guy!'

HOME VIEWING: Tragically, *One From the Heart* is unavailable in the UK on either VHS or DVD. It has been screened on television but its lack of a high profile suggests that it will not find its way onto these formats anytime soon. In America the film is available on VHS but not on DVD.

TRIVIA: The scale of *One From the Heart* resulted in craftsmen building sets months before filming commenced. In reproducing parts of Las Vegas the set used ten miles of flashing neon. A model of the Dunes Hotel sign used 1600 neon light bulbs and cost $11,000.

In a theatrical display of occasion, when Coppola's Silverfish editing suite trailer first rolled onto the Zoetrope lot one December evening in 1980, the sound of Wagner's 'Ride of the Valkyries' played over the studio PA system.

Amazingly, the great French director Jean-Luc Godard, who had been in talks with American Zoetrope about a feature project, assisted Coppola by shooting background plates for the film.

A newly restored print of *One From the Heart* was screened at the Academy of Motion Picture Arts and Sciences in Los Angeles on 18 July 2003.

COPPOLA'S VIEW: This is not a deep, complex film but it does address real issues through a fairy-tale kind of narrative. Just as *Apocalypse Now* cascaded with ideas about violence and the primordial, so *One From the Heart* cascades with notions about romance in terms of love and, more broadly, in terms of something bigger and better elsewhere beyond the everyday. Like its movie-musical progenitors, *One From the Heart* celebrates the interplay of fantasy and dreams with reality. It is clear that the film is attempting to map out the contradictions and frustrations of relationships and their joys, within a highly generic form. *One From the*

Heart was originally considered to be the first of a series of films Coppola wanted to make about aspects of the relationships between men and women.

CRITICAL COPPOLA: Pauline Kael wrote of the film that it was 'like a jewelled version of a film student's experimental pastiche – the kind set in a magical junkyard.' The *Los Angeles Times* felt that 'the picture comes from the same artistic impulse that inspires airbrush art', while the *Village Voice* wrote, 'Coppola has thrown out the baby and photographed the bath water.' *Time Out* called it 'a likeable, idiosyncratic musical, its few remaining pretensions so bare-faced they're almost winning . . . the saving grace is a light heart.'

VERDICT: Vastly underrated and one of Coppola's most intriguing films alongside *The Godfather Part II, The Conversation, Apocalypse Now, The Outsiders* and *Rumble Fish*. At the time, the film received mixed reviews but is surely ripe for rediscovery especially as musicals have seen their profile rise with the success of *Moulin Rouge* (Baz Luhrmann, 2001) and *Chicago* (Rob Marshall, 2002). The film is emotionally honest, balancing that with fantasy and a fairy-tale sensibility. It makes a neat counterpart to the theatricality and artifice of *Bram Stoker's Dracula*. Like many directors, Coppola has his preoccupations but can work consistently and inventively across a range of formats and styles.

Sadly, a film like *One From the Heart*, so replete with good vibrations and fanciful ambitions, stands little chance of being taken with the same seriousness as some of Coppola's other, more intense, films.

One From the Heart is widely regarded as Coppola's grand folly, and its eventual commercial failure contributed to an ensuing decade of financial headaches (and jobs for hire) as Coppola tried to recover his losses. To concentrate on those financial woes is to ignore the film's allure as a narrative rather than as a money pit. *One From the Heart* stands as a key moment in modern film-making processes as Coppola strove to bring a new level of control and planning to directing.

Whereas *Apocalypse Now* was a series of vignettes about war and our interpretation of it, *One From the Heart* is an equally vivid series of vignettes about love and the fragility of relationships.

COPPOLA NOW: When the film was made, Coppola said, 'I'm on the side of the audience. I want to make a film about love that feels like it . . . The sets themselves will be emotions.'

The Outsiders (1983)

(Colour – 91 minutes)

Columbia
Producer: Fred Roos and Gray Frederickson
Associate Producer: Gian-Carlo Coppola
Screenplay: Kathleen Knutsen Rowell, from the novel by SE
Hinton
Cinematographer: Stephen H Burum
Editor: Anne Goursaud
Music: Carmine Coppola
Production Design: Richard Beggs
Costume Design: Marge Bowers

CAST: Matt Dillon (*Dallas Winston*), Ralph Macchio (*Johnny Cade*), C Thomas Howell (*Ponyboy Curtis*), Patrick Swayze (*Darrel Curtis*), Rob Lowe (*Sodapop Curtis*), Emilio Estevez (*Two-Bit Matthews*), Tom Cruise (*Steve Randle*), Glenn Withrow (*Tim Shepherd*), Diane Lane (*Cherry Valance*), Leif Garrett (*Bob Sheldon*), Darren Dalton (*Randy Anderson*), Michelle Meyrink (*Marcia*), Gailard Sartain (*Jerry*), Tom Waits (*Buck Merrill*), William Smith (*Store Clerk*), Tony Hillman (*Greaser*), Hugh Walkinshaw (*Soc*), Domino (*Little Girl*), Teresa Wilkerson Hunt (*Woman at fire*), Linda Nystedt (*Nurse*), SE Hinton (*Nurse*), Brent Beesley (*Suburb Guy*), John C Meier (*Paul*), Ed Jackson (*Motorcycle Cop*), Dan Suhart (*Orderly*), Steve M Davison, Reid Rondell, Scott Wilder

BUDGET: $10 million

THE BOX OFFICE: $25.6 million

RELEASE DATE: March 1983

MPAA: PG

BBFC: PG

TAGLINE: They grew up on the outside of society. They weren't looking for a fight. They were looking to belong.

SUMMARY: Tulsa, the early 1960s. Ponyboy Curtis and his friend Johnny hang around town with their older friend, Dallas. A flick-knife fight ensues between the boys, who belong to a wrong-side-of-the-tracks gang called the Greasers. Their rivals are the well-to-do Socs (short for socialites). Later, Ponyboy, Johnny and Dallas break into a drive-in and chat up a few girls. One of them, Cherry Valance, strikes up a conversation with Ponyboy and Johnny after Dallas has gone elsewhere. A little later Cherry's Soc friends confront Ponyboy and Johnny. Cherry gets into the car with the Socs and they drive off. Soon after Ponyboy and Johnny are confronted in the park by the Socs and Johnny kills one of them. They go to Dallas for help and he tells them of an abandoned church in the country where they can hide out. Dallas gives the boys some money and they head for the country. Dallas eventually drives out to see them and takes them for some food. Returning to the hideaway, they find the church is on fire and a group of schoolchildren are caught inside it. Ponyboy and Johnny rescue a few children from the fire and Johnny is seriously injured. Returning to town, Johnny and Ponyboy are treated as heroes. Johnny is hospitalised and told he will not walk again. Ponyboy is reunited with his brothers, Darrel and Sodapop, and their friends, Steve and Two-Bit.

However, the Socs still want to fight the Greasers. Dallas shows up for the rumble, in which the Greasers are victorious. Dallas takes the injured Ponyboy home and a motorcycle cop sees them and says he will escort them to hospital.

Johnny dies and Dallas cannot contain his anger. He is carrying an unloaded gun. In town he threatens a shopkeeper and is then pursued by the police. Thinking Dallas has an armed weapon, they gun him down.

The film's coda shows Ponyboy sitting in a diner composing a piece about the friends he knew for his school homework. He titles the composition 'The Outsiders'.

COPPOLA'S CONCEPT: There were two choices for Coppola after the critical and commercial failure of *One From the Heart*. He could stop making films or find a way to make them with less anxiety. Like Scorsese, Coppola was having to reinvent himself, not so much aesthetically, but in terms of the industry's perception of him. Scorsese had been bruised and nearly broken doing *New York, New York* (1977), *Raging Bull* (1980) and *King of Comedy* (1983). After the expansive story scale and super-intense shooting periods of *The Godfather*, *The Godfather Part II*, *Apocalypse Now* and *One From the Heart*, Coppola downsized and along the way made one of his most charming films.

SE Hinton's novel *The Outsiders* had a big teen readership following, as required school reading, far and wide in North America. Hinton had been approached about a film version of the material in the 1970s but had declined. Fate eventually stepped in a few years later in the form of a

librarian called Jo Ellen Misakian. She lived in Fresno California and had
seen the Coppola-produced *The Black Stallion* (Carroll Ballard, 1979)
and felt that Coppola and his company would be perfect to realise the
novel. She wrote Coppola a letter encouraging him to make the film
version. The letter was undersigned by thirty students and sent to
Paramount's offices in New York. Coppola happened to be in New York
when the letter arrived. Fred Roos read the letter and was not sure about
the wisdom of Coppola considering it. Nonetheless, he showed Coppola
the correspondence and Roos read the novel, sure enough recognising
that, yes, it could make a very good film, and so he recommended it to
Coppola.

Coppola wrote fourteen drafts of the screenplay while the financial
outcome of *One From the Heart* swirled around him. The scriptwriting
on *The Outsiders* was welcome relief. The Writers Guild of America,
however, decided, after arbitration that because Kathleen Knutsen
Rowell had written the first two drafts she should receive the writing
credit.

The film is soaked in the tone of 1950s movies and, like several other
Coppola movies, is a celebration of youth. All through his career
Coppola has expressed his affinity with young people and *The Outsiders*
certainly expresses that sense of teenage years when emotion and
possibility are especially intense.

INFLUENCES: Surely one of the key cinematic influences on *The
Outsiders* must be Nicholas Ray's film *Rebel Without a Cause* (1955) and
also Elia Kazan's adaptation of the first half of John Steinbeck's vintage
novel, *East of Eden* (1955). The flick-knife fight at the start of the film
feels, almost shot for shot, like a similar fight in *Rebel Without A Cause*.

Coppola's literary sensibility sees him place the reference to Robert
Frost's poem 'Nothing Gold Can Stay' in the foreground as its
sentiments lie at the heart of the film. In many ways this one scene
represents much of Coppola's sensibility.

COSTUME: The film faithfully immerses itself in the jeans and T-shirt
culture of the iconic 1950s teenager. The Greasers represent the James
Dean end of the spectrum, contrasting with the easy-listening stylings of
The Socs sporting their chinos and sweaters.

TEAM COPPOLA: Faithful to the collaborators who had helped
Coppola ensure such creatively strong films in the past, the director
continued with his tried and trusted band of brothers, who, by this time,
had been through a lot of film-making challenges. *The Outsiders* also
returned Coppola to the location-based work that marked his most

celebrated films. *One From the Heart* had been shot entirely on a soundstage, a considered choice that contemporary critics felt deprived the film of any sense of reality. Coppola's son, Gio, worked as associate producer. He had written to his father asking his permission to drop out of high school and be an apprentice to his father. Roman Coppola worked as a production assistant. Dean Tavoularis served as production designer. Returning from *One From the Heart* was Robert Swarthe as special effects supervisor. A new collaborator Stephen H Burum joined the fold. He had shot *The Escape Artist* (Caleb Deschanel, 1982) for Zoetrope and his other credits include a notable collaboration with Brian De Palma on films such as *Casualties of War* (1989) and *Mission: Impossible* (1996). Fred Roos served as producer, having done so on *The Godfather Part II* and *Apocalypse Now*.

CASTING: As with so many Coppola films, *The Outsiders* showcases an ensemble of emerging acting talent and this helps to make it a key film of the early 1980s. While some of the actors are less high profile twenty years on, the film launched some successful film careers and one of its smaller roles was taken by Tom Cruise, someone who became one of the biggest box office draws of all time, and whose appeal as an actor continues to strengthen the older he gets. Cruise and his agent Paula Wagner lobbied hard for the young actor to be cast in the film. At the time Cruise was aware he lacked the experience to portray one of the leading characters but was simply happy to be working on a film directed by Coppola who, on set, was dubbed 'Father Film'.

True to his theatre roots, Coppola held acting workshops in order to encourage a Method-style depth of thought and feeling in the actors' approach to their work. In pursuit of realism and authentic emotion, the reality of the movie was extended into the time spent off set and, between takes, the actors were treated as if they were still in character in the world of the film. Consequently, those actors playing Socs were far better treated than those playing Greasers. Soc actors had the best hotel rooms on location and bigger expenses.

Coppola considered Matt Dillon one of the best actors since the Brando/Dean years – the very period that *The Outsiders* taps into. Dillon's character, Dallas, is a punk rebel consistent with the young tough males portrayed by Marlon Brando in *A Streetcar Named Desire* (Elia Kazan, 1951) and *On The Waterfront* (Elia Kazan, 1954), and by James Dean in *Rebel Without A Cause* (Nicholas Ray, 1956).

I KNOW THAT FACE: *The Outsiders* stars Emilio Estevez (his father, Martin Sheen, starred in *Apocalypse Now*), Rob Lowe, Ralph Macchio, C Thomas Howell, Patrick Swayze and Tom Cruise.

Diane Lane went on to appear in *Rumble Fish*, *The Cotton Club* and *Jack*. She has also been in *Chaplin* (Richard Attenborough, 1992), *Judge Dredd* (Danny Cannon, 1995), *The Perfect Storm* (Wolfgang Petersen, 2000) and *Unfaithful* (Adrian Lyne, 2002). In the April 2003 Hollywood issue of *Vanity Fair* she is finally called a star, twenty years after starting out. Emilio Estevez went on to star in *Young Guns* (Christopher Cain, 1988).

Rob Lowe became an 80s movie star and later landed a recurring role in the hit US TV series, *The West Wing*. Lowe's feature-movie credits include *The Hotel New Hampshire* (Tony Richardson, 1984), *St Elmo's Fire* (Joel Schumacher, 1985), *Bad Influence* (Curtis Hanson, 1990) and *Wayne's World* (Penelope Spheens, 1992).

C Thomas Howell had been one of Elliot and Michael's friends in *ET: The Extra Terrestrial* (Steven Spielberg, 1982) and went on to star in *Soul Man* (Steve Miner, 1986). Patrick Swayze starred in *Uncommon Valor* (Ted Kotcheff, 1983), *Red Dawn* (John Milius, 1984), *Youngblood* (Peter Markle, 1986), *Dirty Dancing* (Emilio Ardolino, 1987), *Road House* (Rowdy Herrington, 1988), *Ghost* (Jerry Zucker, 1990) and *Point Break* (Kathryn Bigelow, 1991). Ralph Macchio starred in *The Karate Kid* (John G Avilsden, 1984) and *Crossroads* (Walter Hill, 1986).

Matt Dillon also starred in *Rumble Fish* and in *Tex* (Tim Hunter, 1982), *The Flamingo Kid* (Garry Marshall, 1984), *Drugstore Cowboy* (Gus van Sant, 1989), *Malcolm X* (Spike Lee, 1992), *The Saint of Fort Washington* (Tim Hunter, 1993), *To Die For* (Gus van Sant, 1995) and *There's Something About Mary* (The Farrelly Brothers, 1999).

THE FILMING: On 1 March 1982, Coppola went to Tulsa to start work on *The Outsiders*. Production began in March 1982 with Coppola's Silverfish production trailer/electronic cinema in place. On *The Outsiders*, any technological complications experienced on the set of *One From the Heart* were ironed out and the shoot went to schedule. The previsualisation process worked perfectly. Rehearsals were videotaped against a blue screen and the actors' rehearsal performances superimposed onto stills of the locations. To enhance the richness of the actors' performances, SE Hinton wrote up character biographies in an effort (ultimately successful) to keep each character distinctive and to stop them blurring into unhealthy stereotype.

Warner Brothers agreed to distribute the film, and production financing came from Chemical Bank and a completion guarantee from the National Film Finance Corporation in England.

As the final rumble scene testifies, Tom Cruise approached the action with real enthusiasm, even to the extent that he broke his thumb. During rehearsals Estevez cut a lip and Howell bruised his eye.

During production Coppola told the press how some day soon films would be made without sets, simply on stages with the backgrounds being added later. In effect what Coppola was talking about was the digital backlot idea made so popular and cost-efficient by George Lucas in his fantasy films.

PROMOTION: Initially, *The Outsiders* was to have been released in the autumn of 1982 but Coppola had to edit the film down to around ninety minutes in accordance with the wishes of the movie studio. The film's promotion focused on Coppola and SE Hinton's involvement, and the faces of the film's stars were also central to the advertising campaign. The film was originally due for release in October 1982 but this was postponed until the spring of 1983. The film remains one of Coppola's most profitable, and one of his best.

THE OPENING: The film is marked by a lush opening title sequence that is likely to bring tears to the eyes before the film has even really begun. Over a series of sunset-splashed images of the small town in which *The Outsiders* is set Stevie Wonder is heard singing the hugely sentimental *Stay Gold*. Against this sunset-red image the film's title crosses the screen in huge gold letters, redolent of the opening title sequence for the film *Gone with the Wind* (Victor Fleming, 1939). The image then fades into a shot of Ponyboy Curtis sitting at a diner table, the wall behind him streaked with golden sunset light slashed by the window blind. The camera tracks in slowly on Ponyboy. A point of view shot then shows the empty page of Ponyboy's school composition book. He has written a title: *The Outsiders*. As he begins writing the camera zooms in slowly on his words, lending them significance. The image fades out and then fades up to the events that Ponyboy is recalling. This opening scene is melancholy, and Ponyboy's concerned expression indicates difficult times ahead.

HEROES AND VILLAINS: The film's heroes are the boys who belong to the Greasers' gang and the villains are the Soc gang members – they represent the status quo.

Dallas is the leader of the Greasers' gang, the oldest, coolest and the real rebel without a cause. Dallas is patriarchal, helping his younger 'brothers' Johnny and Ponyboy escape from the public eye. Dallas's loyalty to these younger boys proves to be his undoing just as Michael Corleone's loyalty leads to his damnation in the *Godfather* series. Dallas finds the world a hard place to understand when things go wrong and loss plays its part in life. He feels a responsibility towards his family and gives advice to Ponyboy and Johnny – just like Vito and Michael, in the *Godfather* series, give advice to their families.

Ponyboy is a contained young man, thoughtful and certainly sensitive. He questions things, just like Willard questions Kurtz in *Apocalypse Now*, Michael questions Vito in *The Godfather*, Clell questions Vietnam in *Gardens of Stone* and Harry questions himself in *The Conversation*. Ponyboy is almost too fragile for the world. He is the classic sensitive dreamer and typical of all creative types, who tend to be seen in that way.

The film's coda is a very moving encapsulation of what Ponyboy and the film as a whole stand for. As Ponyboy sits reading Johnny's letter, its romantic sensibility (in the broadest sense) is celebrated. It is no surprise that it is thoughtful Ponyboy, and not cocky Dallas, who strikes up a friendship with Cherry Valance. Ponyboy sees another world beyond the one he is in, which is clear from the opening of his composition: 'When I stepped out into the bright sunlight . . .' Ponyboy is the one whose sense of self and of the world is illuminated through his experience. When Johnny and Ponyboy watch the sunset during their time in hiding, it is a life-affirming moment, not just for the boys but for the audience too, about the need to remain sensitive to the true beauties of life. Ponyboy and Johnny are gentle-hearted and caring and their sense of duty that underpins their gang loyalty extends to saving the children in the burning church. When Randy the Soc speaks to Ponyboy and says he finds their action surprising for Greasers, Ponyboy says it had nothing to do with being a Greaser. When Two-Bit asks what he and Randy were talking about, Ponyboy says, 'He ain't a Soc, just a guy that wanted a talk. That's all.' Ponyboy has the maturity to see the stupidity of gang culture and thus has a connection with the older character of The Motorcycle Boy in *Rumble Fish*.

Johnny is a more intense character than his great friend Ponyboy. He is angrier, always carrying a flick knife. For Johnny the world is often too much to take and he has even considered suicide. The melodrama of being a teenager suffuses the entire film. The pathos of Johnny's fate emphasises his goodness and, especially, his sense of how quickly and sudddenly life can be snatched away. In this way he is a soul brother to Jack Powell in *Jack*.

The supporting characters of Steve, Two-Bit and Darrel serve as big brothers to Ponyboy and, indeed, Johnny. Steve and Two-Bit particularly give the impression they will never grow out of brawling, eating chocolate cake and wearing Mickey Mouse T-shirts.

Cherry Valance is the kind of beautiful young woman seen in many Coppola films. She is smart, diplomatic and strong-willed, and saves the boys when she tells them not to fight one another. Cherry is a nurturing young woman and is idealised by the teenage boys. Like Ponyboy and Johnny there is a lasting sadness in her eyes.

COPPOLA STYLE: *The Outsiders* revels in romantic image-making, very true to Coppola's self-confessed predilection for romanticism. In this film the camera is often at a low height looking up at the action, aggrandising the kids in their world.

Coppola alternates between naturalistic settings and images, such as the car lots and diners, but it is the more flamboyant sequences and images which really resonate and charge the drama. The film's aesthetic debt to *Gone with the Wind* (Victor Fleming, 1939) is huge. In the film's central scene Ponyboy and Johnny marvel at a sunset, and the theatricality of the scene's execution is brilliant, the sky a super-rich background, studio-bound and with no effort made to conceal that fact. The scene is super-real and so expresses the vivid state of the boys' emotional response to the world which the film claims is one of the great things about being a kid.

When Johnny and Ponyboy are by their campfire early in the film, one shot from slightly overhead binds them together as they sit with their heads against one another.

The rumble contrasts with the gentle tone of much of the film; the edits are fast and the sense of the primal emphasised by the rain and fire in shot. This connects us to *Apocalypse Now* and the Greasers' collective primal scream in their moment of victory is entirely valid.

Towards the end of the film Cherry speaks to Ponyboy against the background of a sunset; they are framed in silhouette against the gold and blood-red sky. In the over-the-shoulder shots, their faces are lit with golden rim lighting and, for a moment, the world is as perfect as can be.

IMAGE: *The Outsiders* is marked by a series of intense close-ups of anxious, angry teenage faces and an emphasis on wide shots that melodramatically frame the world as threatening and ragged. Coppola and Burum's camera captures pop-culture artefacts such as the local Dairy Queen, the drive-in and the sweets for sale. Counterbalancing this documentary-like approach is the florid and intensely bucolic imagery of the nature scenes. The film's coda, with its images of Ponyboy reading Johnny's letter and Johnny reading aloud some of the letter, recalls the layered images of *Apocalypse Now* and is tinged with a golden sheen.

In the scene where the church is burning, some of the flames have evidently been superimposed, but rather than this denying the scene intensity and believability, it only adds to it, giving it an appropriately theatrical, larger-than-life tone. Coppola uses a montage to compress

Johnny and Ponyboy's time in hiding. Several shots of Johnny in hospital emphasise the strangeness of his life, the images as disorientating as his predicament.

The film's investment in melodrama is apparent in the night-time attack on Johnny and Ponyboy in the park. As their sense of safety slips rapidly away, the camera is canted to emphasise Johnny and Ponyboy's sense of their world about to slip out of control. When Ponyboy is being 'drowned' by the Socs the image is suddenly washed with a splash of lurid, superimposed blood, as though from a horror movie. Not until the next scene is it clear whose blood it is. The rumble is as smalltown-operatic as all the smoke and colour of certain scenes in *Apocalypse Now*.

In the scene where Johnny and Ponyboy sneak out of town on a train at night, the image has a chilling deep blue tone to it that soon contrasts with the welcoming sunlight that engulfs their country hideaway.

Coppola's love of the tableau shot is most evident and effective where the older Curtis brothers embrace Ponyboy when they are reunited with him in the hospital.

Against the stillness of certain key moments in the film, Coppola and Burum pump up the energy for the scene where Dallas attempts to flee from the police. The moment's severity is marked by a shot of the shadow of his feet pounding on the tarmac. When Dallas is shot by the police the street swirls with smoke and moonlight, and when Ponyboy and the others rush to Dallas's side, saying the gun is not loaded, it recalls the climax to *Rebel Without A Cause* (Nicholas Ray, 1955), with a hint of the theatricality found in *Apocalypse Now*.

SOUND: Sound is deployed naturalistically in *The Outsiders*. For the rumble at the end of the film, the sound's fidelity to realism is heightened so that it reinforces the sense of the world gone wild.

COPPOLA TUNES: Carmine Coppola's score is highly evocative of a mid- to late 50s Hollywood film score sound, notably the work of Elmer Bernstein and Leonard Rosenman. Rosenman scored *Rebel Without A Cause* and *East of Eden* (Elia Kazan, 1955). It is sweet music that charges and pumps the already melodramatic images. When Dallas runs for his life the music accentuates driving, anxious strings; when the Curtis brothers embrace in the hospital the music fills with warmth. The music is as bold and clearly drawn as the emotions on screen.

The Outsiders by Carmine Coppola: 'Stay Gold' (sung by Stevie Wonder), 'Fate Theme' (Dallas Tragic Music), 'Country Theme – Brothers Theme' (Reunion), 'Cherry Says Goodbye – Ponyboy and Brothers', 'Dallas Death Scene', 'Fire in the Deserted Church', 'Sunrise – Stay Gold' (Instrumental), 'Flight and Fight in the Park', 'Bob is Dead',

'Train to Deserted Church – Passing Time', 'Go to Rumble – Rumble' (Gang Fistfight), 'The Outside In' (vocal version).

HUMOUR: *The Outsiders* gets a lot of laughs out of Dallas's comic bravura as he attempts to chat up Cherry Valance. Coppola also goes for some cute animal humour, as though from a Disney film, showing us a rabbit who seems intrigued by the presence of Johnny and Ponyboy in the church.

AWARDS: Even though it was a commercial success *The Outsiders* failed to be recognised for any major awards. It did receive a few acknowledgements, though. At the 1983 Moscow International Film Festival the film was nominated for the Golden Prize (Francis Ford Coppola), and at the 1984 Young Artist Awards the film won the Young Artist Award Best Young Motion Picture Actor in a Feature Film (C Thomas Howell) and secured a nomination for Diane Lane in the category of Best Young Supporting Actor in a Feature Film.

COPPOLA MAGIC: Coppola's theatrical approach to certain moments has great emotional impact. The most evident optical effects are the superimposed wash of blood in the fountain scene and the flames of the burning church. In Coppola's movies he has the judgement to ensure that visual effects balance emotional effects.

MOVIE SPEAK:
Ponyboy Curtis: 'My father was an original person.'

Johnny: 'You're gold when you're a kid.'

Johnny: 'When you get sunsets, that's gold. Keep it that way. It's a good way to be.'

Dallas: 'Look after yourself and no one can touch you.'

HOME VIEWING: *The Outsiders* is available on VHS in the US and as a Region 1 DVD, and includes an interactive menu and scene access. The film is unavailable on Region 2 DVD and out of print on VHS in the UK.
   When the film was shown on American television in 1985, five and a half minutes were added. This extra material comprised a courtroom flashback where Cherry says she could have prevented the closing rumble. There was also a scene showing the Greasers who survived.

TRIVIA: In the wake of the commercial success of the film a short-lived TV series was produced. As she has done in some of her father's other films, Coppola's daughter Sofia made a cameo appearance – this time as a young girl who approaches Dallas in his car.

The film is dedicated to the librarian and schoolchildren who wrote to Francis Coppola suggesting he turn *The Outsiders* into a movie.

The supermarket that Dallas goes into is the same supermarket that Rusty James holds up in *Rumble Fish*, the film Coppola directed immediately after finishing work on *The Outsiders*. *Rumble Fish* is also an SE Hinton novel.

COPPOLA'S VIEW: With *The Outsiders*, Coppola makes one of his boldest statements about the privileges of youth and how they should be cherished and never forgotten no matter how old you are.

The film also offers the Coppola motif of characters creating safe havens. Like the den that Michael and Vito Corleone create for themselves and the apartment that Harry Caul has, Ponyboy and Johnny make a cosy hideaway home in the abandoned church where they are safe and away from the pressures of the world that besieges them. Kent Jones calls it Coppola's characters' interest in nesting (see **Introduction**). *The Outsiders* has a common bond with *Peggy Sue Got Married*, *Gardens of Stone*, *Jack* and *The Godfather* trilogy in its emphasis on the precious, fleeting nature of life.

Like *The Godfather* series and *Rumble Fish*, the film celebrates fraternity and family (natural or adopted) and, like Hinton's source novel, the film owes a debt to Mark Twain's *The Adventures of Huckleberry Finn*.

The Outsiders is a romantic evocation of youth and Coppola delineates the universal frustrations of growing up.

The Greasers are the embodiment of Coppola's idealism. In his comments about his long-planned movie *Megalopolis*, Coppola has talked about the idea of a Utopia. So many films about kids end with a kind of meltdown and apocalypse. Teenagehood is both change and the end of a chapter in life. Coppola's film *Jack* (a film for young children rather than teens) ends with a ceremony marking the end of youth, and Jack's closing speech has a kinship with Johnny's at the end of *The Outsiders*.

CRITICAL COPPOLA: *Time Out* said that 'Surprisingly for Coppola, it's a modest, prosaic, rather puritan drama, with a moral . . .' and John Engstrom in the *Boston Globe* described it as a 'small, sincere and nearly perfectly realised film about adolescence'. *The Virgin Film Guide* states that 'The fault lies in Coppola's unduly reverent interpretation of the story, which resulted in a film steeped in artistic pretension.'

VERDICT: *The Outsiders* is one of three beautiful films that Coppola made in one burst of underappreciated creative flow in the early 1980s

(See **One From the Heart** and **Rumble Fish**). This mid-career period is fascinating and the films deserve to be pulled out of the shadow of his bigger, wider-known films. Coppola moves between the visually overstated and melodramatic and the naturalistic, synthesising the sensibilities of the 1950s and the 1980s. *The Outsiders,* along with *Rumble Fish*, *Peggy Sue Got Married* and *Jack*, is one of Coppola's 'young' films. It is a major contribution to the teen-movie subgenre that was revived in the 1980s, especially by John Hughes, and which lives again in the early twenty-first century.

COPPOLA NOW: 'One of the central concepts was the idea of time running out and young people not understanding that time is running out.'

'I got so saccharine and sweet natured with *The Outsiders* . . .'

Rumble Fish (1983)

(Black and white/Colour – 94 minutes)

Zoetrope Studios
Producers: Fred Roos and Doug Claybourne
Executive Producer: Francis Ford Coppola
Associate Producers: Gian-Carlo Coppola and Roman
Coppola
Screenplay: SE Hinton and Francis Ford Coppola, based on
the novel by SE Hinton
Cinematographer: Stephen H Burum
Editor: Barry Malkin
Music: Stewart Copeland
Production Design: Dean Tavoularis
Costume Design: Marge Bowers
Sound Design: Richard Beggs

CAST: Matt Dillon (*Rusty James*), Mickey Rourke (*The Motorcycle Boy*), Diane Lane (*Patty*), Dennis Hopper (*Father*), Diane Scarwid (*Cassandra*), Vincent Spano (*Steve*), Nicolas Cage (*Smokey*), Christopher Penn (*BJ Jackson*), Larry Fishburne (*Midget*), William Smith (*Patterson the Cop*), Michael Higgins (*Mr Harrigan*), Glenn Withrow (*Biff Wilcox*), Tom Waits (*Benny*), Herb Rice (*Black pool-player*), Maybelle Wallace (*Late Pass Clerk*), Nona Manning (*Patty's Mom*), Domino (*Patty's Sister*), Gio (*Cousin James*), SE Hinton (*Hooker on Strip*), Emmett

Brown, Tracey Walter, Lance Guecia, Bob Maras, JT Turner, Keeva
Clayton, Kirsten Hayden, Karen Parker, Susannah Darcy, Buddy Joe
Hooker, Bill Hooker, Tim Davison, Fred Hice, Dick Ziker

BUDGET: $10 million

THE BOX OFFICE: $2.5 million

RELEASE DATE: October 1983

MPAA: PG 13

BBFC: A

TAGLINE: Rusty James can't live up to his brother's reputation. His
brother can't live it down.

SUMMARY: Set in Tulsa at some unspecified time that could be
anywhere between the early 1960s and early 1980s, the story focuses on
seventeen-year-old Rusty James.

At Benny's Billiards, Rusty hangs out with his friends. Kicking around,
Rusty sees his girlfriend Patty (from the good side of the tracks). Local
gang rival Biff Watson is looking for Rusty James and his gang for a
rumble. The sun sets on the town and a fight has been set for ten o'clock
that night.

Rusty goes over to Patty's but just in time remembers the proposed
rumble and he leaves Patty behind. Rusty and his gang go to a ragged
warehouse alongside a railroad track and Biff's gang show up. A savage
fight ensues until it is brought to a close by the arrival of the legendary
Motorcycle Boy, who has been out of town for two months – the
Motorcycle Boy is Rusty's 21-year-old brother.

In the aftermath of the fight, the local ironjaw cop turns up and is
unhappy to see The Motorcycle Boy back in town. Rusty has been
injured in the fight and the Motorcycle Boy takes care of him. The
Motorcycle Boy explains that he has been to California then sits reading
quietly at Rusty's side.

Rusty recovers and goes over to Patty's during the day. On his way
back to their dad's run-down apartment, Rusty bumps into Cassandra,
an old flame of The Motorcycle Boy. Rusty berates her for not
acknowledging him on her way out of school, and she leaves. When
Rusty's dad comes home he is drunk and worn down but Rusty, his
brother and their father enjoy some time together.

Rusty, Smokey and friends go to a party that Patty has not been
invited to. When word of this gets out, Patty is not pleased and Rusty's

friend Smokey cuts in. Rusty is more interested in his brother's
reappearance than Patty; he arrives at school late again and is suspended.

In a local shop, Rusty finds The Motorcycle Boy, who shows Rusty a
picture of himself in a magazine, taken while he was in California. Out
on the street, Rusty and The Motorcycle Boy encounter the tough cop
again. At night Rusty and The Motorcycle Boy walk through town and
talk about their family. Rusty and his brother split up and, as he crosses
town, Rusty is beaten up by two guys and left for dead. For a moment,
Rusty has an out-of-body experience and floats through the town
observing everything from above. The Motorcycle Boy turns up and sees
off the thugs and once again tends to his brother.

The next morning, Rusty, The Motorcycle Boy and Steve hang out
under a flyover and The Motorcycle Boy says how worthless the gang
culture is. Later, Rusty and The Motorcycle Boy go into the local pet
store just before closing time and The Motorcycle Boy shows his brother
two beautiful rumble fish in their tank. The Motorcycle Boy explains
how they would attempt to fight their reflection. The cop turns up again.
Leaving the pet shop, Rusty and his brother go into a run-down bar
where their father is drinking. They talk and then their father leaves.
Rusty and The Motorcycle Boy return to the pet store and The
Motorcycle Boy breaks in. He liberates some of the animals and then
takes the tank with the rumble fish down to the river. Before he can get
there he is shot dead by the ironjaw cop. As a crowd gather, Rusty exits,
taking his brother's motorcycle and riding out to the coast of California.

COPPOLA'S CONCEPT: It was during the filming of *The Outsiders*
(1983), that Coppola read one of SE Hinton's other novels, *Rumble Fish*.
So excited was he by the material, that he set about making it
immediately after finishing *The Outsiders* and retained much of the cast
and crew in Tulsa. Much was made when *Back to the Future Part II* and
Part III (Robert Zemeckis, 1989 and 1990) were shot back to back or
The Matrix sequels (Andy and Larry Wachowski, 2003) or *Lord of the
Rings* (Peter Jackson, 2001, 2002 and 2003), but Coppola was first to
film movies from the same stable. One problem that Coppola did face in
approaching Warner Brothers to finance the film was that the studio had
not been a huge fan of *The Outsiders* at the rough-cut stage and so were
reluctant to see *Rumble Fish* go into production. They turned the project
down. It was only once shooting began that Coppola got Universal
Pictures on board as a distributor.

In broadly aesthetic terms, Coppola regarded *Rumble Fish* as an
antidote to *The Outsiders*. *Rumble Fish* demonstrates the significance of
style and content, reminding audiences of how tightly bound they are.
The difference in approach also testifies to Coppola's thoughtfulness

about striking the right tone and meaning, proof of his sensitivity and facility.

Coppola has always been loved by filmgoers for the fusion of the personal with the generic and *Rumble Fish* is no exception. Coppola takes the teen rebel without a cause image and playfully and powerfully charges it with a philosophical dynamic that recalls his genre-splicing with *Apocalypse Now* where the war movie and the so-called art film memorably combusted. As Coppola has acknowledged, *Rumble Fish* is inflected with his own, well-documented memories of his older brother, August, whom Coppola idolised.

The novel *Rumble Fish* is a direct source for much of the film's dialogue. True to the detail of the novel Coppola succeeds in expressing the heightened sense of things that Rusty James experiences during fights. Everything has a clarity to Rusty in the book and he confesses to the reader that he feels as though he can fly when he is in the middle of a rumble. Sure enough, in the film, Rusty's athleticism lets him take flight amid the punches and knife-blade swings in the fight with Biff's gang.

As with *One From the Heart* and *The Outsiders*, Coppola's pre-visualisation approach again came into play and there were two weeks of videotaped rehearsal prior to filming.

INFLUENCES: The most obvious film influence on *Rumble Fish*, with its ultra-American setting, is German Expressionism, with its tradition of working with extreme contrasts between light and shadow creates an intense visual scope that matches the intense sense of the world experienced by the main characters. The other key cinematic reference was *The Outsiders*, the film he made prior to *Rumble Fish*. While keen to make a film that was, stylistically, its polar opposite, Coppola was aware of a continuing fidelity to certain shared issues. In terms of visual language, though, the two films are very different; rather like brothers tend to be.

In keeping with Coppola's love of literature and its impact on all his work, he gave Mickey Rourke some of Albert Camus's writing, and also a biography of Napoleon, as an aid in thinking through his performance as The Motorcycle Boy.

Camus's two principal novels are *The Outsider* (1942) and *The Plague* (1947). Albert Camus's fiction exists within the broad scope of existentialism – the concept that the sense of the world is absolutely to be determined by an individual's experience of it – it is not about overarching theories of living. Jean Paul Sartre, however, claimed that existentialism is yours to make sense of. The individual confers meaning on events and things. It is a very pro-individualistic stance and one can see its appeal to any teenager as they battle to define themselves in that self-conscious, self-interested way that is such a part of being a teen. For the existentialist, to be conscious of your individual freedom to assign value to things is the indicator of an authentic existence, where sincerity and creativity are clues as to how to lead a moral life. With this basic outline in mind, it becomes clear to see how *Rumble Fish* does adhere to the fundamentals of the existentialist spirit, and the film encourages the audience to think this way too and, perhaps, take off on their own quests.

COSTUME: As part of the film's timeless feel the costumes synthesise a range of styles and time periods. Rusty James dresses in a T-shirt, jeans and sneakers and his headband suggests something tribal, befitting his obsession with the gang culture. The older, more travelled Motorcycle Boy dresses in a more urbane, mature way, with his dark jacket, dark T-shirt, dark trousers and cowboy boots. He is both more European and also very Californian. In contrast, the character of Midget dresses in a sharp suit and hat at all times, and Steve is more preppy. Nicolas Cage, with his bouffant hair and bomber jacket, emblazoned with the legend Wild Deuces on the back, suggests something more conventionally teenage and Chris Penn has something of the biker-boy about him.

TEAM COPPOLA: By the time of *Rumble Fish*, Dean Tavoularis had worked with Coppola as production designer on every film. Tavoularis creates a shadowy run-down world of broken homes, streets and alleyways, all of them as battered as the people who inhabit them. The pet store is more of a fantasy world consistent with it becoming a refuge in its short time on screen.

Stephen H Burum served as cinematographer and his other credits include *St Elmo's Fire* (Joel Schumacher, 1985) and a string of films in one of the major director-cinematographer collaborations of recent years with Brian De Palma. Their work together includes *Body Double* (1984), *Casualties of War* (1989), *Raising Cain* (1992), *Carlito's Way* (1993), *Mission: Impossible* (1996), *Snake Eyes* (1999) and *Mission to Mars* (2000).

Fred Roos returned as producer. It had been his reading of *The Outsiders* that had sparked Coppola's collaboration with SE Hinton on *The Outsiders* and *Rumble Fish*.

CASTING: Several of the cast from *The Outsiders* including Diane Lane and Matt Dillon returned for *Rumble Fish* and again Coppola put his rehearsal period to good use. As with *Apocalypse Now*, Coppola made great use of Dennis Hopper's capacity for portraying a warm quirkiness and a gentle quality, casting him as the father of Rusty and The

Motorcycle Boy. Laurence Fishburne also returned from *Apocalypse Now*.

I KNOW THAT FACE: Tom Waits also appears briefly in *The Cotton Club* and *Bram Stoker's Dracula*. In the mid-1980s, Mickey Rourke was just beginning his acting career, which saw him in a range of movies in the 1980s including *The Pope of Greenwich Village* (Stuart Rosenberg, 1984), *9½ Weeks* (Adrian Lyne, 1986), *Angel Heart* (Alan Parker, 1987) and *Johnny Handsome* (Walter Hill, 1989). His career tailed off somewhat during the 1990s but he seems ready to return to the movie arena. He teamed up again with Coppola on *The Rainmaker*.

Nicolas Cage, a nephew of Coppola's, became a major movie star and appeared in films that include *Peggy Sue Got Married*, *Wild at Heart* (David Lynch, 1990), *Bringing out the Dead* (Martin Scorsese, 1999) and *Windtalkers* (John Woo, 2002).

Vincent Spano has also appeared in *The Black Stallion Returns* (Roert Dalva, 1983), *Good Morning, Babylon* (Paolo and Vittorio Taviani, 1987) and *City of Hope* (John Sayles, 1990). Chris Penn can also be seen in *All The Right Moves* (Paul Brickman, 1981), *Pale Rider* (Clint Eastwood, 1985), *Reservoir Dogs* (Quentin Tarantino, 1992), *True Romance* (Tony Scott, 1993) and *The Funeral* (Abel Ferrara, 1996).

THE FILMING: Filming began on 12 July 1982, in Tulsa, straight after filming on *The Outsiders* had been completed. Filming on *Rumble Fish* concluded in mid-October 1982. Much of the filming took place at night in the heat of summer.

PROMOTION: *Rumble Fish* debuted at the New York Film Festival in October 1983. It was released in the same month but failed at the box office, perhaps being too quirky and almost certainly because it had been shot in black and white, with the exception of several shots towards the end of the film which combine colour with black and white. Furthermore, the film's title, though identical to that of the source novel, says little about the plot and must have been hard to market to an audience unfamiliar with Hinton's novel. In France, the film was justly celebrated and *Cahiers du Cinema*, the legendary film magazine, praised the movie. The film's release poster in North America was a black and white still of Rusty James and The Motorcycle Boy leaning against the clock without hands. The Motorcycle Boy leans coolly against the clock while Rusty James mouths off at the world – the brothers' essential difference and one of the film's principal concerns all rolled up in one gorgeous black-and-white image.

THE OPENING: The film's interest in mythologising a character is present from the first image. Clouds race by and a direction sign is emblazoned with the graffiti legend telling all the world that the mysterious Motorcycle Boy lives.

HEROES AND VILLAINS: The characters of *Rumble Fish*, like so many strong and sure-footed dramas about, and aimed at, young people (especially) draw on archetypes. Rusty James is the young boy who is learning to understand what the world is about. His mentor is his older brother, the legendary Motorcycle Boy. As a tale of two brothers, the film plugs right into the thematic pulse of much of Coppola's work, especially, and most obviously, *The Godfather* saga, but the brotherly bond is also seen in *The Outsiders*. In all respects, *Rumble Fish* makes a fascinating companion piece to that film.

Rusty James is in complete thrall to his older brother, as is the rest of the town. For Rusty, his older brother represents the best kind of person. Rusty, however, is the classic rebel without a cause, always in trouble with authority figures and striving to be cool. Rusty wants to be tough and memorable like his brother and so he puts on a front. Tellingly, Patty says to Rusty 'You're better than cool, you're warm.'

Typically he is misunderstood; his anger is a product of wanting more from life than his current situation can provide, rather like Frannie in *One From the Heart*. Rusty is from a broken home and the film charts his struggle to pull something together before he self-destructs. When Rusty rides off on his brother's bike we see him in silhouette, himself mythologised. Like his brother, Rusty is finally associated with the natural world and, in the film's closing image, we realise that Rusty finishes the dream his brother never could – to see the coast.

The Motorcycle Boy says little and is marked by an enigmatic silence. He is a classic American figure: a terse man of action. Twice he rescues Rusty, and in the larger context of the film, and most importantly, he rescues Rusty at an emotional and spiritual level. The Motorcycle Boy is associated with the rumble fish and occupies the position of classic, teen rebel burnt by a self-destructive impulse; it is a character that Hollywood movies have always loved. The tie between the code of the gangs in *Rumble Fish* is akin to the code of the gangs and families in *The Godfather* series. The Motorcycle Boy presides patriarchally over the heated younger men just as Don Vito does in *The Godfather* and Dallas does in *The Outsiders*. The Motorcycle Boy is the contained man, often holding one arm across the other, as though he has been wounded.

The Motorcycle Boy is the embodiment of the cool adult young kids aspire to emulate. His death is almost sacrificial for the larger community of kids. He is akin to Kurtz in *Apocalypse Now*, a figure of the unknown, well read and outside the understanding of most people. Like the Don in *The Godfather*, The Motorcycle Boy has a sense of how time has passed and things have inevitably changed. Just as Don Vito is uneasy with the place of drugs in the Mafia businesses so too The Motorcycle Boy, who regrets the role of drugs, saying it 'Ruined the gangs. Ruined everything.' The Motorcycle Boy does not romanticise the gangs nor does he romanticise himself through what he does. He is doing all he can to stay low-key and he says he came back because he got homesick.

Beneath his cult status he is just a humble man, just as Michael Corleone, for all his power and influence, is a man dying alone in a chair at the end of *The Godfather Part III*. The Motorcycle Boy is different, and it takes his father to spell out the importance of this to a confused Rusty: 'every now and then a person comes along who has a different view of the world than the usual person. Doesn't make 'em crazy ... an acute perception, man, doesn't make you crazy, sometimes drives you crazy.'

The Motorcycle Boy represents an engagement with life, an ability to seize hold of it and not to get wrapped up in the violence and anger of it. His gentle nature is his downfall, as though he is too good for this world. Like Jimmie in *The Rain People* he liberates animals from their cages.

For Coppola, The Motorcycle Boy was akin to the kind of characters in the plays of Tennessee Williams or the novels of Carson McCullers. In Williams's work *A Streetcar Named Desire* Stanley Kowalski is also a primal force of young masculinity. In McCullers'work the characters are spiritually isolated in a similar sense. For McCullers this was the heart of her protagonists' concerns and certainly The Motorcycle Boy is intellectually and emotionally marooned throughout *Rumble Fish*. Coppola made The Motorcycle Boy colour-blind because Coppola's opinion was that the character was only able to see situations in black and white, without compromise.

Dennis Hopper as the father is a quieter version of the photographer he portrays in *Apocalypse Now*, in a sense clarifying Rusty's understanding of his brother, just as the photographer helps Willard understand Kurtz.

The character of Patty is not so different to that of Cherry Valance in *The Outsiders,* though in *Rumble Fish* she is a little more idealised, in keeping with the archetypal themes and images.

The cop who is on Rusty and The Motorcycle Boy's case is marked by the fact that his eyes are never shown, so there is a monstrous, soulless quality to him. He represents malicious authority.

In the character of Benny, the owner of the billiard hall, an adult is in tune with the town's teenagers. He serves as a chorus, dispensing cool and melancholy aphorisms, none more memorable than 'I got thirty-five summers left.' It does not take much to imagine Benny has a copy of a Kerouac novel somewhere behind the bar.

The film's characters grapple with what it is to be different and, in Coppola's movies, difference is to be embraced and celebrated. In his much later film *Jack,* the title character learns to delight in his being different. In *The Outsiders* the boys are defined by not being like everyone else, and Ponyboy recalls fondly the fact that his dad gave his sons such original names. In *Apocalypse Now* Kurtz risks termination because he acts originally, stepping outside the code of the American army because he is disillusioned with it.

COPPOLA STYLE: Coppola and his creative team hang a sequence of dreamy images onto a very simple story with mythological associations. The film is expressionistic and there is a dreamy haze to the action, an idealised memory of being a teen. *Rumble Fish* is structured around a series of set pieces expressing teenage confusions and volatility, rather like *One From the Heart* is a sequence of riffs on romance, and *Apocalypse Now* a sequence of visual essays about the primal urge that still remains in the world no matter how modern it becomes.

IMAGE: Stephen H Burum's cinematography emphasises the interplay of shadow and light, and the time lapse images, particularly, express the drama's emphasis on the passing of time and how precious the realisation of that is. Coppola uses an emphasis on the sunset to communicate the same idea in *The Outsiders*, which is explored further in *Jack* through the inclusion of a butterfly motif.

Frequently, a wide-angle lens is used to distort action in *Rumble Fish*, as in the high shot looking down past the clock ticking ominously above the bar where Benny stands. The rumble that occurs near the start of the film is energised by tracking shots at ground level and a swashbuckling, highly romanticised sense of violence equating with the boys' sense of their heroism. It is when Rusty swings around on a chain, when a dove flashes across screen, when the Wilson gang emerge against a backdrop of train-blasted steam and when a flick-knife glistens in the light that the film pitches the audience into an operatic arena, part pirate movie, part *Rebel Without a Cause* revisited, part tribal rite. (*The Outsiders* rumble is presented in a different kind of way.)

Throughout the film The Motorcycle Boy is the focus of peoples' conversations. As Steve and Rusty talk about him, The Motorcycle Boy stands on the other side of the room and the camera pushes in slowly on the back of him. The voices of Rusty and Steve can be heard over the shot commenting on how old he looks. The camera is often uncomfortably close to The Motorcycle Boy, a character who likes his space but who is so often under the scrutiny and awe of the young people around him.

Alongside these more intimate ways of building the meaning of the movie there are more elaborate displays of style. In a wilful disregard for any sense of naturalism, smoke billows across a suburban street in the scene where Rusty and Patty talk after she gets off a bus. The plumes of smoke turn the quiet street into something resembling a war zone in which Rusty fights so many battles.

Key to the visual design of the film is the use of colour. The placement of blue and red for the rumble fish scene suggests The Motorcycle Boy's colour-blindness that has been referred to earlier in the film. The colours also link the symbolic value of the fish to the concept of the story. Late in the film there is an equally smart use of metaphor derived from nature images. It is when The Motorcycle Boy frees the birds from the pet shop that there is a brief shot of the liberated birds flying past a painting of a desert. The issue of freedom and space is encapsulated in this one, briefly held image which combines the real (the birds) with the fantastic (the sweep of the desert in the painting) that fills the frame.

Finally, there is the symbolic shot of the clock without hands as The Motorcycle Boy and Rusty speak to the cop. This clock recalls the image of a clock in *Wild Strawberries* (Ingmar Bergman, 1957), a film like *Rumble Fish* that highlights how time changes so much.

Rumble Fish ends with a classic Coppola tableau of Rusty on his dead brother's bike, seagulls sweeping around him as he looks at the sunlit sea. He is in silhouette, the universal beyond the specific, the film nudging the viewer never to forget the importance of keeping some part of their being free and forever young.

SOUND: *Rumble Fish* is notable for the eerie, otherwordly softness of its sound, which distances the dialogue and the events as though just out of reach in a dream. Almost all the dialogue was looped in post-production, meaning that it could be extensively manipulated. More specifically, The Motorcycle Boy's hearing deficiency is evoked by putting a slight echo on conversations around him, notably as he, Rusty and Steve walk through the town at night. Coppola's thoughtful sound design on the film proves again that form and content are one and the same.

COPPOLA TUNES: Coppola initially worked on the score for *Rumble Fish* himself and then brought on board ex-Police drummer Stewart Copeland, who went on to score other movies such as *Silent Fall* (Bruce Beresford, 1994), *Wall Street* (Oliver Stone, 1987), *Leopard Son* (Hugo Van Lawick, 1996), *Rapa Nui* (Kevin Reynolds, 1994), *Talk Radio*

Above: *You're A Big Boy Now* – Bernard Chanticleer finally discovers girls in the form of sensitive young beauty Amy

Right: In *Finian's Rainbow* Finian delights in the sunshine glow of family and community

Below: Jimmy and Natalie on the road in *The Rain People*

Left: Vito Corleone, a frail, lonely man for whom the passing of time is the greatest enemy, in the first part of Coppola's seminal *Godfather* trilogy

Below: Fredo and Michael Corleone – the weak and the strong, the powerless and the all-powerful in the second *Godfather* instalment

Left: *The Conversation* –
Harry Caul and his
dangerous obsession

Above: Hank starts out on
his search for love in *One
From The Heart*

Right: Kurtz emerges from
the darkness to illuminate
Willard in *Apocalypse Now*

Above: Rusty James rages at authority while his brother, The Motorcycle Boy, is passively lost in thought in *Rumble Fish*

Left: *The Outsiders* – Ponyboy Curtis and Johnny stay gold in the warmth of the setting sun

Above: In *The Cotton Club*, Dixie and Vera fall in love and deeper into the corruption of the criminal underworld

Left: Peggy Sue prepares for the reunion ball and an unexpected trip into her past

Below: Clell Hazard and young Willow, adoptive father and son, in *Gardens of Stone*

Above: A dreamer, Preston Tucker, and his dream

Right: In *Bram Stoker's Dracula*, the passion of Prince Vlad consumes both him and Mina

Below: The eyes are the window of the soul: Michael Corleone and his power-hungry nephew, Vincent, in the final part of the *Godfather* trilogy

Above: *The Rainmaker*: Rudy and Kelly – young hearts in a tough world

Below left: 'How sweet it is!' Jack enjoys life beyond the confines of his bedroom

Below right: Captain Eo leads the dance against the forces of darkness

Above: Zoe and her father enjoy a quiet moment away from their social whirl in Coppola's contribution to *New York Stories*

Left: Francis Ford Coppola: young film maker at heart

(Oliver Stone, 1988) and *Simpatico* (Matthew Warchus, 1999). There is a ticktock quality to the score that taps directly into the concept of time passing. Copeland's score is upbeat, funky, cocky and, at the end, in its more tonal form, suggests something more emotionally epic.

Rumble Fish by Stewart Copeland: 'Don't Box Me In', 'Tulsa Tango', 'Our Mother Is Alive', 'Party at Someone Else's Place', 'Biff Gets Stamped by Rusty James', 'Brothers on Wheels', 'West Tulsa Story', 'Tulsa Rags', 'Father on the Stairs', 'Hostile Bridge to Benny's', 'Your Mother is not Crazy', 'Personal Midget/Cain's Ballroom', 'Motorboy's Fate'.

HUMOUR: *Rumble Fish* is an intense drama where the humour is fleeting. Benny is certainly a lighter character amid the teen angst and Rusty's own strutting style is amusing in its seriousness. The scene where Rusty and The Motorcyle Boy's father talks to them with a crazed energy is a comic counterpoint to the seriousness of the young men fighting to find their place.

AWARDS: At the 1984 Golden Globes the film was nominated for Best Original Score (Stewart Copeland) and at the 1984 San Sebastian International Film Festival it won the FIPRESCI award (Francis Ford Coppola). In the same year, Diane Lane was nominated for a Young Artist Award.

COPPOLA MAGIC: Evidently the biggest piece of magic and novelty in the film is its black-and-white photography and then the integration of colour into several shots towards the end, quite a sophisticated conceit to achieve in 1983. Maybe the least obvious but most amusing visual trick is a shot where Rusty and Smokey stand talking outside Benny's. In the reflection of the window the clouds race by at high speed when everything else in the frame is in real time.

Rusty's out-of-body flight is a mechanical effect, not a digital or optical one. This keeps the fantasy more real than an effect achieved in post-production. The flight is lent some menace by the sea of smoke rolling across Patty's porch as Rusty floats by.

MOVIE SPEAK:
Benny: 'Time is a very peculiar item.'

Rusty: 'I love you but I gotta run.'

Rusty: 'I feel like I'm wasting my life waiting for something.'

HOME VIEWING: *Rumble Fish* is available as Region 1 DVD and the disc includes production notes, cast and film makers' biographies, film highlights, the film's trailer, an interactive menu and scene access, and is presented in the widescreen format at 1.85:1. There is also a Region 2 DVD available, and the film can be found on VHS.

TRIVIA: The author of *Rumble Fish*, SE Hinton, portrays a hooker who speaks to Rusty as he wanders around town with his brother.

Coppola dedicates the film to his older brother, August, calling him his 'first and best teacher'. The Wild Deuces was August Coppola's old club.

COPPOLA'S VIEW: *Rumble Fish* is undiluted Coppola, rather like *The Conversation*. The film's focus on the bond between blood brothers is classic Coppola material and suggests both the good and the bad in idolising a sibling. As with *The Outsiders*, *Rumble Fish* dramatises one character's recognition of a larger world and a certain way of thinking. This awareness is the gift that The Motorcycle Boy leaves to Rusty and that the film leaves the audience.

Some of the dialogue is as arch as the images, so that when The Motorcycle Boy makes his grand entrance at the end of the rumble he says, 'What is this? Another glorious battle for the kingdom?' Lines like this suggest Coppola's interest in the ancient world. A major part of Coppola's thematic work in *Rumble Fish* is the inclusion, consciously or not, of the Fisher King myth as part of the story's associations. In the Grail legends and stories the Fisher King is the king whose land has fallen into ruin. Injured in battle, the King can no longer ride his horse and goes fishing instead. The drama and resonance of the Fisher King story lies in the young hero's quest to relieve the King of his wound in such a way as to inherit the King's role but without the wound. The wound in Christ's side is akin to the wound sustained by the Fisher King in battle.

Through his work on *Apocalypse Now*, Coppola had wrestled with the resonance of the Fisher King myth. In light of Coppola's work with his colleague Dennis Jakob in developing the mythological resonances at the close of *Apocalypse Now*, it's not much of a leap of faith to think some of that powerful material remained with the director. When Rusty is wounded it is not simply a cut to the arm but something with more of a biblical connotation, namely a wound in the side. *Rumble Fish* is a spiritually minded teen movie.

The religious sensibility of the film registers in its presentation of a fallen kingdom, and this is the starting point for The Fisher King allusion. When one bar-room patron calls The Motorcycle Boy 'royalty in exile. Is there anything he can't do?' we know the kids of Tulsa feel they are in the presence of a king. Maybe a Fisher King. Thus, The

Motorcycle Boy transfers his glory to his younger brother, who takes the motorcycle and accomplishes what his wounded brother could not.

CRITICAL COPPOLA: *Empire* complained of the film that 'Coppola seemed to trade in plot for style . . .' and *Time Out* calls the film 'Camus for kids . . . a startling Expressionist style, which is very arresting but hardly appropriate to the matter at hand.' *The Virgin Film Guide* describes it as 'an unabashed art film . . . Coppola has never made a more beautiful film.'

VERDICT: This film is gorgeous, visually and emotionally. It works almost as a silent film, but its beauty is not just in its surfaces but also in its sympathy for the frustration of being a teenager and wanting to see the world. *Rumble Fish* feels like the work of a new film maker, not someone who had already been directing feature films for over a decade. *Rumble Fish* has invention, playfulness and an 'experimental' vibe to it that stands it head and shoulders above other more conventionally styled teen movies of the 1980s. It is a masterpiece of the teen movie genre and, possibly, Coppola's last great movie.

  Rumble Fish is 94 minutes of dreamy movie joy for anyone who has been a kid and needed a hero. It is one of Coppola's richest movies in the range of its themes, its mood and good old-fashioned emotional truth, grappling as it does with the way young minds find their sense of place in the world when everything around and within them seems shot to bits.

COPPOLA NOW: '*Rumble Fish* was (more) existential and dreamy. I like *Rumble Fish* a lot. It's one of my favourite movies.'

The Cotton Club (1984)

(Colour – 128 minutes)

Orion
Producer: Robert Evans
Co-Producers: Silvio Tabet and Fred Roos
Line Producers: Barrie M Osborne, Joseph Cusumano
Executive Producer: Dyson Lovell
Screenplay: William Kennedy, Francis Ford Coppola, from a
story by William Kennedy, Francis Ford Coppola and Mario
Puzo
Cinematographer: Stephen Goldblatt
Editor: Barry Malkin

Music: John Barry, Bob Wilber
Production Design: Richard Sylbert
Principal Choreographer: Michael Smuin
Tap Choreographer: Henry Le Tang
Montage and Second Unit Director: Gian-Carlo Coppola
Costume Design: Milena Canonero

CAST: Richard Gere (*Dixie Dwyer*), Gregory Hines (*Sandman Williams*), Diane Lane (*Vera Cicero*), Lonette McKee (*Lila Rose Oliver*), Bob Hoskins (*Owney Madden*), James Remar (*Dutch Shultz*), Nicolas Cage (*Vincent Dwyer*), Allen Garfield (*Abbadabba Berman*), Fred Gwynne (*Frenchy*), Gwen Verdon (*Tish Dwyer*), Lisa Jane Persky (*Frances Flegenheimer*), Maurice Hines (*Clay Williams*), Julian Beck (*Sol Weinstein*), Novella Nelson (*Madame St Claire*), Larry Fishburne (*Bumpy Rhodes*), John Ryan (*Joe Flynn*), Tom Waits (*Irving Stark*)

BUDGET: $47 million

THE BOX OFFICE: $25.9 million

RELEASE DATE: December 1984

MPAA: R

BBFC: A

TAGLINE: Where crime lords rub elbows with the rich and famous.

SUMMARY: Harlem, 1928. In the low rent Banville Club, Dixie Dwyer plays the cornet with panache. Delbert Williams dances on stage. The show is suddenly interrupted by gunfire inside the club, the result of a tangled web of Harlem gangsterism. After the interruption, Dixie speaks to Vera Cicero, one of the young women who has been watching him. Vera is drunk and Dixie takes her back to her hotel room. When asked to stay he sleeps next to her bed on the chaise longue.

Delbert Williams and his brother Clay go for an audition at The Cotton Club and they get a slot.

Dixie Dwyer has a wild card of a brother, Vince, who works for crimelord Dutch Schultz and who is keen to make his own way in the gangster underworld. One night Dixie is playing at the Banville when he is approached by an associate of Schultz – Schultz wants Dixie to play immediately at a party. Dixie cuts short his club performance to go to Schultz's party. The party is sedate compared to the smoky, raucous club that Dixie has been working, but Schultz's racist tendencies provoke anger. Guests at the party include Owney Madden, owner of The Cotton Club and Vera Cicero. Vera sees Dixie playing piano and speaks with him again.

Owney Madden, Flynn and Schultz leave the party for another room where they talk business. Madden says the fighting has to stop. The party comes to an abrupt end when Schultz loses his temper and murders someone on the spot for slighting Jews.

Dixie drops Vera off at her home. She invites him inside but he declines.

At The Cotton Club, the Williams brothers arrive for their performance and do a dazzling dance routine. Dixie, his brother and mother are all in the audience. Owney is impressed by Dixie and wonders if he could handle operations on the west coast, though his sidekick, Frenchy, is less sure. Schultz offers Dixie a job – escorting Vera around. Although Dixie says he does not want to get involved, he finally goes to work for Schultz. Vera is loyal to Schultz because she wants her own club. Schultz wants to take over the Harlem numbers racket, so there is a rising tension between the white gangsters and their black counterparts.

Schultz is angered by Dixie and Vera's developing relationship. Dixie has been spotted by Gloria Swanson at The Cotton Club; she remarks on his handsome face, saying he should be in films. He therefore takes her comment to heart and heads for Hollywood where he develops a successful career in films. Owney then proposes to Dixie that he front operations in Los Angeles; in return Owney will keep Schultz off Dixie's back.

At The Cotton Club, Delbert has been asked to perform a solo act. When Clay finds out, he is rightly incensed at his brother's betrayal of their shared dream. Eventually, they reconcile. Across town, Dixie meets with his brother, Vince, who has been injured by Schultz. Dixie then has a successful Hollywood screen test and heads west; Vince intensifies his turf war with Schultz.

The black crime bosses in Harlem recognise the need to fight back at the white gangsters cutting in on their business. A montage of newspaper headlines clarifies the point.

In 1929 the Wall Street Crash kicks in and Prohibition fuels the criminal underworld. It is the opening night at Vera's club and Dixie, back from Hollywood, goes there with Owney Madden. Vera sings and Dixie plays cornet. Dutch Schultz is also present and soon he is confronted by Vince who wants a slice of the numbers racket.

On the streets one of Vince's associates is killed by Schultz's men and Vince retaliates by shooting Schultz's associate Saul. Owney's partner

Frenchy is then taken by Vince and held. Dixie ensures the safe return of Frenchy but Vince is then killed by Schultz's men.

It is 1931. Dixie stars in the film *Mob Boss*; his relationship with Vera continues. Cab Calloway is performing at The Cotton Club and finally black people are allowed in the audience; Dutch Schultz is wiped out by his enemies.

Owney goes back to jail to complete a sentence; Delbert and his love Lila Rose Oliver are married. Dixie decides to take off for Hollywood but Vera will not go west with him. Dixie heads for the station. As he stands on the platform Vera joins him and they take the train to Hollywood together.

COPPOLA'S CONCEPT: *The Cotton Club* began as a project that producer Robert Evans hoped to make on a lavish and thrilling scale as his first movie as an independent producer. The film was marked by an intense creative and production management process that was fraught and reminiscent of the angst Coppola had experienced on *The Godfather*, *Apocalypse Now* and *One From the Heart*.

Evans had overseen the production of *The Godfather* and *The Godfather Part II* during his successful tenure at Paramount in the 1970s. *The Cotton Club* was to be a spectacular movie set against the Prohibiton era in New York that in some ways traded on the success of *The Godfather* films. Evans paid Mario Puzo (who had co-written the screenplay for *The Godfather* with Coppola, from his own novel) $1 million to write the screenplay.

However, as *The Cotton Club* developed Evans became concerned about the script that he and Mario Puzo had drafted based on the James Haskins book, *The Cotton Club*. Evans had paid $350,000 for the film rights to the book. In an effort to begin fixing the script as soon as he could, Evans contacted Coppola for feedback on the material. Evans was anxious for a hit film to follow up his run of success with the films *The Odd Couple* (Gene Saks, 1968), *Rosemary's Baby* (Roman Polanski, 1968), *Love Story* (Arthur Hiller, 1970) and *Chinatown* (Roman Polanski, 1974). However, there was concern that a film with an African–American setting might not be especially popular in the early 1980s, and Evans found it difficult to secure the backing of any of the major studios. He turned instead to private investors to enable him to make the film independently. Evans brought foreign distributors on board and, in October 1982, secured the backing of the Doumani brothers, who had property in Las Vegas and who had also brought in a Denver businessman, Victor Sayyah.

At this time, Evans planned to direct the film, which had a budget of $18–20 million, himself. Critically, the Doumani brothers almost pulled out of the movie after reading Puzo's script. By this time, Evans had gained the interest of rising star Richard Gere, but he too was uneasy with the screenplay.

Coppola offered his writing services free of charge as a favour to Evans. Coppola said the script required a lot of attention and his first step was to corral Evans, Gere, Gregory Hines – a top-flight Broadway dancer for whom *The Cotton Club* was his big break into films – and producer Dyson Lovell, at Coppola's Napa base. They brainstormed a reworking of the screenplay and Coppola then shared his idea for the movie with them. It was to frame the rise and fall of The Cotton Club through the eyes of two minor characters. At this point, Evans offered Coppola $250,000 to rewrite the screenplay and Coppola accepted.

Unfamiliar with the setting and history of The Cotton Club and the Harlem Renaissance (a massive wave of African–American culture, including the writers Langston Hughes and Jean Toomer), Coppola headed to New York to research the project.

On 5 April 1983, Coppola submitted his screenplay. Evans found it too thoughtful and not thrilling or exciting enough – there was too much social history and not enough shoot-outs. Coppola's screenplay was rich with detail about the Harlem Renaissance and the character of Dixie Dwyer had been made less central than in Evans and Puzo's earlier versions. Coppola rewrote his material for another $250,000.

Sets for the film were being constructed and the production was running at a cost of $140,000 per week before even a foot of film had been shot. Among a string of problems, the Doumani brothers would not pay for Coppola's rewrite, so Evans paid out of his own funds. The Doumani brothers were content with Evans and Puzo's material and less keen on Coppola's draft. Orion Pictures, however, wanted Coppola's script used so that they could sell the movie as being from the three talents behind *The Godfather*.

In continuing to develop the screenplay, Evans hired an African–American actress named Marilyn Matthews to work on the screenplay with Coppola. Coppola felt that Matthews was only there to communicate Evans's vision. Coppola complied with Evans's suggestions, however, and reduced the Harlem Renaissance component of the script and built up Dixie Dwyer's role again and the easy thrills of gunplay. Evans was satisfied and offered Coppola the chance to direct the film when the main players reconvened in Napa. Coppola initially resisted and then agreed. Evans paid him $2.5 million to direct the film, including a share in the gross profit. Coppola also retained complete creative control, as he had done with *The Godfather Part II*.

As pre-production on *The Cotton Club* rolled on, Evans felt his authority on the project lessening as Coppola asserted his creative control. Coppola told Evans that if he challenged his decisions he would leave the project. To refine the film's dialogue Coppola hired novelist William Kennedy, who revelled in his collaboration with Coppola. Kennedy had written the novel *Ironweed* which had won the Pulitzer Prize. On one occasion, Coppola and Kennedy worked a straight 34 hours on the screenplay. A further 48-hour session ensued and five scripts were generated. There were between 30 and 40 drafts of the screenplay for *The Cotton Club* before shooting began. Coppola worked hard to make the script fit the budget they had available.

Sure enough much of the material filmed was cut from the final edit.

Coppola's experience on *The Cotton Club* was traumatic and it became another massive movie that was more consuming than any film production should be.

INFLUENCES: *The Cotton Club*'s most obvious cinematic inspiration is *The Godfather* and other Hollywood gangster films of old such as *Scarface* (Howard Hawks, 1932) and *Angels with Dirty Faces* (Michael Curtiz, 1938). Interestingly, at around the same time Sergio Leone was making his similarly scaled gangster epic *Once Upon a Time in America* (1984).

COSTUME: The film's detailed costumes contribute much to the atmosphere. Dixie's rise to stardom is marked by changes and upgrades in his attire. When first seen, Dixie is dressed rough and ready but, as his experiences around the Cotton Club expose him to new opportunities, his attire becomes more sophisticated. As a point of film history interest, some of the costumes worn by Diane Lane had once been worn in films starring Jean Harlow.

TEAM COPPOLA: *The Cotton Club* represents a break in the collaborative work with his regular producing team and heads of department that Coppola had become accustomed to since *The Godfather*. Unsurprisingly, Coppola had wanted Dean Tavoularis to work as production designer, but he was unavailable, so hotshot designer Richard Sylbert came on board. Sylbert's other production design credits include several major Hollywood movies such as *The Graduate* (Mike Nichols, 1967), *Chinatown* (Roman Polanski, 1974), *Shampoo* (Hal Ashby, 1975), *Reds* (Warren Beatty, 1981), and the more recent *Unconditional Love* (PJ Hogan, 2001).

Coppola also exercised directorial authority in selecting and revising key personnel on the film. Jerry Wexler, who was the film's musical director, was replaced under Coppola's aegis; the job was given to jazz clarinettist Bob Wilber. He also replaced cinematographer John Alonzo.

Coppola wanted to recruit Gordon Willis in Alonzo's place but Willis rejected his offer. Coppola then thought of hiring Stephen H Burum with whom he had successfully worked on *The Outsiders* and *Rumble Fish* just prior to *The Cotton Club*, but Evans talked Coppola out of that idea. Ultimately, Stephen Goldblatt was hired. Goldblatt was also the cinematographer on *Breaking Glass* (Brian Gibson, 1980), *Outland* (Peter Hyams, 1981), *The Hunger* (Tony Scott, 1983), *Young Sherlock Holmes* (Barry Levinson, 1985), *Lethal Weapon* (Richard Donner, 1987) and *Joe Versus the Volcano* (John Patrick Shanley, 1990).

CASTING: Early in the film's development process, Evans had hoped to secure Sylvester Stallone in the starring role alongside Richard Pryor. When Pryor pulled out, Gregory Hines signed on (see **COPPOLA'S CONCEPT**). Richard Gere came on board to replace Stallone. Gere had had a hit with *An Officer and a Gentleman* (Taylor Hackford, 1982) and had made a good impression in the beautiful *Days of Heaven* (Terrence Malick, 1979). Gere insisted on script approval and that he should be permitted to play the cornet in the movie. Maintaining his fidelity to his research, Coppola informed Gere that white people did not perform at *The Cotton Club*.

Coppola, against Evans's objections, cast Fred Gwynne as Frenchy. Evans thought audiences would see Gwynne and immediately think of *The Munsters*, the spooky 60s sitcom (see **I KNOW THAT FACE**).

Diane Lane (*The Outsiders*, *Rumble Fish*) and Laurence Fishburne (*Apocalypse Now* and *Rumble Fish*) were also cast.

I KNOW THAT FACE: Richard Gere had already emerged as a major movie star when he agreed to star in *The Cotton Club*. He had been seen in *Yanks* (John Schlesinger, 1978), Terrence Malick's beautiful and sombre *Days of Heaven* (1979) and had starred in *American Gigolo* (Paul Schrader, 1980) and *An Officer and a Gentleman* (Taylor Hackford, 1982). Gere went on to star in *King David* (Bruce Beresford, 1985), *No Mercy* (Richard Pearce, 1986), *Internal Affairs* (Mike Figgis, 1990), *Pretty Woman* (Garry Marshall, 1990), *Rhapsody in August* (Akira Kurosawa, 1990), *Sommersby* (John Amiel, 1993), *Chicago* (Rob Marshall, 2002) and *Unfaithful*, with Diane Lane (Adrian Lyne, 2002).

Bob Hoskins has starred in *Mona Lisa* (Neil Jordan, 1986), *Who Framed Roger Rabbit* (Robert Zemeckis, 1988) and *24/7* (Shane Meadows, 1999). Gregory Hines has appeared in *The Muppets Take Manhattan* (Frank Oz, 1984), *White Nights* (Taylor Hackford, 1985), *Running Scared* (Peter Hyams, 1986), *Waiting to Exhale* (Forest Whitaker, 1995) and *The Preacher's Wife* (Penny Marshall, 1996). Nicolas Cage went on to become a major mid- and late 1990s movie star appearing in *Wild At Heart* (David Lynch, 1990), *Honeymoon in Vegas* (Andrew Bergman, 1992), *Bringing Out the Dead* (Martin Scorsese, 1999) and *Adaptation* (Spike Jonze, 2002).

THE FILMING: The film began shooting on 22 August 1983, a little later than expected, after the wrangles over script and casting (see **COPPOLA'S CONCEPT** and **CASTING**). Around three-quarters of the budget had been spent before the film had even begun shooting. It is unlikely that Coppola was at fault – the film was already in serious need of rethinking in all respects when he came on board. When filming began there was no final script in place. Coppola liked his actors to improvise but Gere was not a big fan of this approach and there was some tension between them. Gere even had his contract redrafted so that it shifted from his being paid paid $1.5 million plus 10 per cent of the adjusted gross to being paid a flat fee of $3 million, a fee which boosted his industry standing.

As shooting continued, new trouble kicked in when a variety show promoter named Bud Diamond claimed he owned the rights to the name *The Cotton Club*. The film was costing $300 per minute to film and there were frequently up to nine takes of a shot. Ed Doumani could clearly see that the budget was not enough. Orion invested $15 million for completion financing providing Evans ceded all control to Coppola. The shoot had a deadline of 23 December 1983 and the budget ballooned to $47 million with $1.5 million available for pick-up footage. During the filming American Zoetrope was bought by Jack Singer for $12.3 million.

Shooting on *The Cotton Club* finally ended on 31 March 1984 and 500,000 feet of film had been exposed.

PROMOTION: At a San Diego sneak preview of *The Cotton Club* Robert Evans attended as a paying customer and was disappointed by what he saw. As with *The Godfather*, he felt a lot of strong material had been wrongly edited out of the film. In response to the screening Evans spent 14 hours writing a 31-page memo of notes which Ed Doumani then delivered to Coppola at his Napa home. Coppola took on board none of Evans's notes for the release version of the film.

The film premiered on 2 December 1984 at a gala charity event in Albany, New York. Coppola did not attend as he was in Los Angeles working for Shelley Duvall on an episode of *Faerie Tale Theatre* (see **Short Film Projects**).

The film received mixed reviews and did not generate much box-office business. An announcement was made that a four-hour version of the film would be screened as a miniseries. Prospective customers must have asked why they needed to pay to see a movie when it would soon be available in a longer form, for free, on television.

THE OPENING: The film's opening titles are retro-styled, as though taken straight from the late 1920s, the silvery letters against a dark background sliced through with a sliver of light. The titles are intercut with fast-paced images of a dance number in full swing at The Cotton Club, suggesting the energy of the film to come.

HEROES AND VILLAINS: Dixie Dwyer is a charming young man, playful and boyish, who finds himself being drawn, against his will, into a corrupt world from which he fights to break free. His dilemma echoes that of Michael Corleone in *The Godfather*.

In *The Godfather* and *The Godfather Part II*, the mother figure is a presence in the borders of the main storyline; in *The Cotton Club* Dixie's mother is one of the last characters to occupy the screen as she says goodbye to her son.

The villains of *The Cotton Club* are boldly drawn. Key among these is Dutch Schultz, who lacks the subtlety of villains in *The Godfather* but remains a potent threat. Schultz exhibits the same racism that Senator Geary does in *The Godfather Part II*.

Vera Cicero drifts back and forth between being on the side of the heroes and, apparently, siding with the villains, but finally she takes sides with Dixie. The relationship between Dixie and Vera self-consciously mimics the patter of Golden Age Hollywood with some sharp talking and cute lines. Dixie and Vera are like two children trying to find their way through a very corrupt world. When they meet one another for the second time at Schultz's party, Vera calls Dixie 'the altar boy' and Dixie calls Vera 'the little girl'. As the film progresses their relationship matures and develops. Vera is gorgeous, like all women in Coppola's films, and she is confident if a little frail beneath.

The characters of Del and Clay Williams reflect, in a very light-hearted way, the relationship between Michael and Fredo in *The Godfather*, where the one brother is seen to betray the other. In *The Cotton Club*, though, the differences are forgiven and in a touching moment the brothers reunite. The character of Delbert Williams is that of a cocky, can-do American whose ambition partly undoes him until he is rescued by a deeper sense of family. Clay warns Del of the danger in satisfying the needs of the white audience when he says 'give white people what you think they want and soon you got no blood left'.

The other black characters, notably Bumpy Rhodes, suggest a different kind of film that Coppola had perhaps hoped to make had there not been the push for girls, guns and fast cars. All through the film is a very clear subtext about race relations in Harlem and Bumpy makes a comment that defines this tension between black and white cultures in that part of New York when he says 'two things I have to do – one is stay black, the other is die'. This seems to be the aspect of the drama that most intrigues Coppola yet he has to keep up the gunfire quotient to the film's detriment.

The real hero of the film is the sense of community that underscores the drama. A key scene, and a highlight of the film, is when Del takes Angelina to meet his friends at The Hoofer Club. They all take turns dancing, the camera tracking lovingly along the floor as the feet tap away.

COPPOLA STYLE: *The Cotton Club* fizzes with a postmodern playfulness, but it is perhaps the most anonymous film Coppola has made, both in dramatic and thematic terms and hence in terms of imposing a recognisable and consistent visual identity. It is a little more openly knowing about its roots in Hollywood gangster films than the far straighter and far more melancholy *Godfather* films. *The Cotton Club* still adheres to a familiar Coppola style of elegantly composed shots and a fusion of music and editing to build tension, but feels too cartoony and fun; the killings don't carry the moral ramifications of those in *The Godfather*. The film's performances are strong and detail enhances many scenes. Maybe the most Coppola-like moment amid the sprawl is the tiniest moment of menace when a drop of blood falls from a chandelier onto Vera Cicero.

IMAGE: The shadowy morals of the world the movie is set in finds expression in the low-key, high-contrast lighting.
For the love scene between Dixie and Vera, back at his family apartment, there is a gentility and familiar Coppola romanticism as a kaleidoscope of colours cross Dixie's face. Dixie and Vera lie in bed, their bodies seemingly wrapped in the delicate shadow of a net curtain. Another shot in this scene simply shows the silhouette of Dixie and Vera.

Dixie's home recalls the warmth of the Corleone home and the one scene at the Williams brothers' apartment is equally cosy. Home is a vital location in Coppola's films and is typically a source of security and retreat from the chaos of the world outside.

Contrasting with the quiet warmth of the few domestically based scenes is the snap and energy of The Cotton Club. The film's dance numbers are shot very much in the manner of a musical, although in an early number when Dixie and his mother are at the club, he opts for a hand-held camera to take the movie audience into the heart of the dance. The hand-held camera is also used with a documentary impulse for action backstage.

As with *The Godfather*, the climax of the *The Cotton Club* is based around intercutting different pieces of apparently unconnected action which, when associated in this way, have a new power. As Del dances wildly on stage at The Cotton Club his staccato dance steps underscore the killing of Dutch Schultz and the rat-a-tat-tat of gunfire. There is then another phase of intercutting which unifies the different story strands, as we watch Del and Angelina being married and Dixie and Vera heading off west.

The film's sense of good-humoured play extends to one of the final images, which attests to the street influence on American dance. Having said goodbye to her son, Dixie's mother dances a while with a kid at the railway station. The train's departure has some of the same playful artifice that is present all the way through *One From the Heart*.

SOUND: This is a very traditionally and grandly conceived film where sound is applied and built naturalistically. The film's violent climax juxtaposes sounds and images in a way familiar from *The Godfather*.

COPPOLA TUNES: Much of the film's music is sourced from the time of the late 1920s. Supplementing these tunes, though, is an orchestral score by John Barry, who provides a sweet theme for Dixie and Vera's relationship in particular. Barry's other credits include *Thunderball* (Terence Young, 1965), *The Lion in Winter* (Anthony Harvey, 1968), *Chaplin* (Richard Attenborough, 1992), *Dances with Wolves* (Kevin Costner, 1990), *Out of Africa* (Sydney Pollack, 1985), *Goldfinger* (Guy Hamilton, 1969), *Somewhere in Time* (Jeannot Szwarc, 1980), *Enigma* (Michael Apted, 2001), *Midnight Cowboy* (John Schlesinger, 1969) and *Zulu* (Cy Endfield, 1964).

The Cotton Club by John Barry (including source music): 'The Mooche', 'Cotton Club Stomp #2', 'Drop Me Off In Harlem', 'Creole Love Call', 'Ring Dem Bells', 'East St Louis Toodle-O, Truckin',' 'Ill Wind', 'Cotton Club Stomp #1', 'Mood Indigo', 'Minnie the Moocher', 'Copper Colored Gal', 'Dixie Kidnaps Vera', 'The Depression Hits/Best Beats Sandman', 'Daybreak Express Medley'.

HUMOUR: *The Cotton Club* has a strong line of humour running through it, notably in the relationship between Owney Madden and his partner, Frenchy. Part of the humour is visual; where Owney is short and stocky, Frenchy is very tall. Some of the self-consciously old-style dialogue, which surely is taken from movies more than everyday life, also amuses.

The film's acknowledgement of the famous guests at *The Cotton Club* is also amusing: Gloria Swanson, James Cagney and Charlie Chaplin are 're-created'.

AWARDS: *The Cotton Club* secured a clutch of nominations but it lacked the artistic coherence that might have led to more nominations.

The film was nominated at the 1985 Academy Awards for Best Art Direction and Set Decoration, and Best Film Editing. At the 1985 Golden Globes Coppola was nominated for Best Director and Robert Evans for Best Motion Picture Drama. At the 1985 Motion Picture Sound Editors awards the film was nominated for Best Sound Editing in a Feature Film. The 1986 BAFTA awards honoured the film with the award for Best Costume Design, and the film was nominated for Best Sound.

COPPOLA MAGIC: The film is at its most zestful in the song and dance numbers and it recalls the energy that Coppola was able to bring to the somewhat leaden *Finian's Rainbow*. In his short film, *Captain Eo*, dance is also an important element of the story. The montage sequences of *The Cotton Club* bring to mind those of *The Godfather* when newspaper headlines telescope and compact a range of events over time, but in this film there is a more playful, parodic tone to this effect. Clearly, the film's biggest visual effect is the set that re-creates the interior of *The Cotton Club*. There is no sense that this is anything but the real place.

MOVIE SPEAK:

Dixie: 'give me a chance to dazzle you, take your breath away'.

Dixie: 'I can save you.'

Vera (to Dixie): 'Kiss me on my lips and don't say anything.'

HOME VIEWING: *The Cotton Club* is readily available on Region 1 DVD and the disc includes the original theatrical trailer, interactive menu and scene access, and is formatted in widescreen 1.85:1. There is no Region 2 DVD of the film available though it is in print on VHS.

TRIVIA: Nicolas Cage apparently got so bored by the slow speed of the shoot that he trashed his trailer in frustration.

Production Designer Richard Sylbert made such detailed sets that he even duplicated the menus that were available at the real Cotton Club.

When technicians became hypercritical of Coppola's directing he fired them and producer Dyson Lovell as well.

Unions shut the production down when they found out that no pay cheques were being issued.

COPPOLA'S VIEW: *The Cotton Club* is quite a juvenile film which nonetheless does contain a sketchy version of Coppola's recurrent themes of family and blood brotherhood. *The Cotton Club* does not provide an especially compelling take on this subject, but it is just about discernible. What seems to interest Coppola more is the cultural mix in Harlem, but it does not get much story space. One can imagine that a film that was more his own would have explored the dramatic dynamic of racial integration and segregation across crime and culture.

Familiar themes of corruption, racial tensions and the place of history and community all come into play in *The Cotton Club* but not in any really coherent way. Like Coppola's early feature *Finian's Rainbow*, *The Cotton Club* suggests an integration of black and white cultures in America.

CRITICAL COPPOLA: *Empire* describes the film as 'Another of Francis Coppola's runaway productions, this fails to hang together . . . but has some terrific things in it . . .' Pauline Kael wrote that 'Francis Coppola . . . seems to have skimmed the tops off every twenty–thirties picture he has seen, added seltzer, stirred it up with a swizzlestick, and called it a movie.' *Time Out* assesses the film saying, 'The misconception that sinks this often handsome confection is that revivalism will spread over separate cultures.' *The Virgin Film Guide* calls the film 'Lavish, interesting, evocative but strained and self-conscious.'

VERDICT: *The Cotton Club* is a relatively anonymous Coppola movie and perhaps the great anomaly of his career. It just lacks any real focus and emotional staying power. This was also a criticism made about *One From the Heart*, but time has been much kinder to that far more singular film. *The Cotton Club* is lovely to look at, and it certainly exhibits moments where Coppola's flourish enlivens the proceedings. The film is very buoyant and playful but ultimately lacks the emotional richness of many of his other films.

The performances are strong if a little one-dimensional. The film cannot be faulted for attention to detail and it is a real shame that more of the drama could not have been played out around the racial angle. Laurence Fishburne, in the short time he is on screen, is a real highlight of the film, lending it an intensity that might perhaps have been realised had Coppola been able to pursue his conception of the project as discussed in script meetings with Evans. The film must be regarded as a missed opportunity to create an emotionally rich spectacle. Instead, it comes across as a grown-up version of *Bugsy Malone* and, from all accounts, one has to conclude that Coppola's heart was never really in the project.

COPPOLA NOW: 'It's not even a movie I particularly wanted to do.'

Peggy Sue Got Married (1986)

(Colour – 103 minutes)

TriStar
Producer: Paul R Gurian
Executive Producer: Barrie M Osborne
Screenplay: Jerry Leichting and Arlene Sarner
Cinematographer: Jordan Cronenweth
Editor: Barry Malkin
Music: John Barry
Production Design: Dean Tavoularis
Art Direction: Alex Tavoularis
Costume Design: Theadora van Runkle
Electronic Cinema: Murdo Laird, Ted Mackland, Ron Mooreland

CAST: Kathleen Turner (*Peggy Sue Kelcher/Bodell*), Nicolas Cage (*Charlie Bodell*), Barry Miller (*Richard Norvik*), Catherine Hicks (*Carol Heath*), Joan Allen (*Maddie Neagle*), Kevin J O'Connor (*Michael Fitzsimmons*), Jim Carrey (*Walter Getz*), Lisa Jane Persky (*Delores Dodge*), Lucinda Jenney (*Rosalie Testa*), Will Shriner (*Arthur Nagle*), Barbara Harris (*Evelyn Kelcher*), Don Murray (*Jack Kelcher*), Sofia Coppola (*Nancy Kelcher*), Maureen O'Sullivan (*Elizabeth Alvorg*), Leon Ames (*Barney Alvorg*), Helen Hunt

BUDGET: $18 million

THE BOX OFFICE: $41.38 million

RELEASE DATE: May 1986

MPAA: PG13

BBFC: 15

TAGLINE: Knowing what you know, what would you do differently?

SUMMARY: It is 1985 and Peggy Sue Bodell is preparing, with some unease, for her high school reunion. Peggy has separated from her husband Charlie. At the reunion, Peggy meets four old classmates she has not seen in twenty-five years, notably Richard Norvik, the former maths whiz of the school, and now a successful businessman, and her old pals Carol, Maddie and Walter. Richard is nominated high school king, as he's been the most successful ex-pupil since they left, and Peggy is high school queen. Into the school hall comes Charlie. As Peggy Sue is crowned, her unease and anxiety mount and she faints.

When she awakes, a moment later, she finds herself back in 1960, and to all the world, Peggy Sue looks eighteen. Peggy is lying on a hospital bed in a hall having participated in a blood donation day. Charlie, also eighteen, sits by Peggy's bedside as she stirs. Peggy is not feeling well at all and is driven home by her friends, Carol and Maddie. At home, Peggy sees her mother and sister, Nancy. Overwhelmed by the realisation that she has somehow travelled back in time, Peggy Sue sneaks a couple of drinks then goes to her room to sleep. The next morning, she goes back to school and fits in straightaway. She sees Charlie and Walter and then meets Richard Norvick whom she asks to meet after school.

Peggy asks Richard if he believes time travel is possible and he says yes. Peggy overcomes Richard's scepticism when she says she is from the future and tells him all she can about the world twenty-five years hence. Peggy and Richard even attempt to cheat history by inventing microchips. Peggy goes to a party with Charlie where he and his four-part harmony group sing. Charlie has dreams of hitting the music big time. After the party, Peggy and Charlie talk in his car and Peggy suggest they have sex which shocks Charlie. Peggy is dropped off at home by Charlie, but rather than go in, she takes a walk to a rowdy diner where she meets the high school hunk and English star, Michael Fitzsimmons. They talk and drive to a hilltop that overlooks the town. Michael tells her of his plans to be a writer and Peggy encourages his ambition.

At night, Charlie sneaks into Peggy's bedroom and goes into the basement with her to talk about their relationship. Peggy has been seen with Michael, and Charlie wants to know what is going on. She tells Charlie their relationship is over. Charlie's pursuit of musical success fails when a talent scout is not sufficiently impressed. Peggy desperately wants to go back to 1985 and says goodbye to Richard. He wants to go with her but she feels that would be wrong.

Peggy visits her grandparents and says goodbye to them. Her grandfather knows how to send Peggy back to the future. He takes her to his Masonic lodge to perform a ritual, but Peggy is kidnapped by Charlie. Charlie and Peggy talk again and reconcile. He announces that he has quit his teen dream of a musical career.

Peggy wakes up in hospital in 1985. She is told that she had a heart tremor and passed out. At her bedside is Charlie, and their daughter Beth joins them.

COPPOLA'S CONCEPT: Just as the George Lucas-directed, and Coppola-produced, *American Graffiti* (1973) had been a love letter to the 1950s, *Peggy Sue Got Married* was also a nostalgic movie, the film taking its title from the Buddy Holly song.

When Coppola was hired to direct the film, brought in by producer Ray Stark (with whom Coppola, as a writer, had worked in 1967 on *Reflections of a Golden Eye*) at TriStar, his initial response was that the script was more suited to television than a big-screen format. Coppola emphasised what he saw as the film's possibility for melancholy. To allow more space for this kind of material, he reduced the amount of comedy and fantasy elements that had been in the original screenplay, but certainly did not erase them completely. Coppola wanted to play up the sense of time passed, of its transience, just as his movie *The Outsiders* had explored this time in its setting of teenage boys in trouble who are struggling to understand the world they find themselves in, and how it works.

Notions of mortality and regret underlie the drama. Looking back on the movie in 1997, Coppola commented that '. . . I decided the secret to *Peggy Sue* was real love for the people you've lost.'

INFLUENCES: With its small-town American setting, *Peggy Sue Got Married* recalls one of Coppola's key sources of inspiration for the film, Thornton Wilder's play *Our Town*, specifically its last third. Cinematically, the key informing sources are some of the films of Frank Capra, known for his small-town settings and strain of optimism in such films as *It's A Wonderful Life* (1946). The other influence on the look of the film must have been, almost unavoidably, the paintings that artist Norman Rockwell regularly produced for the *Saturday Evening Post* in the United States in the 1940s and 1950s, his images playing a major part in the mythology of the American small-town.

COSTUME: The film's costumes remain faithful to the era but also enhance character. Charlie's gauche yellow jumper and bouffant hair lend him a slightly ridiculous quality. Overall, the pastel shades of the clothes complement the bright and airy look of the visuals and are a strong influence in creating the mood.

TEAM COPPOLA: Coppola's hired status on *Peggy Sue Got Married* meant that he followed the lead of the studio in contrast with his earlier career when he often valiantly challenged the opinions of the studio system in creative matters. Nonetheless, Dean Tavoularis, in his fourteenth year of collaboration with Coppola, served as production designer. Theodora van Runkle teamed up again with Coppola for the first time since *The Godfather Part II* to design the costumes. Once again, Coppola looked to Barry Malkin to edit the picture. The film was photographed by Jordan Cronenweth, whose credits include *Altered States* (Ken Russell, 1980), *Cutter's Way* (Ivan Passer, 1981), *Blade Runner* (Ridley Scott, 1982), *Stop Making Sense* (Jonathan Demme, 1984), *U2: Rattle and Hum* (Phil Jouanou, 1988), *State of Grace* (Phil Jouanou, 1990) and *Final Analysis* (Phil Jouanou, 1992). Immediately after teaming up on *Peggy Sue Got Married* Coppola and Cronenweth worked together on *Gardens of Stone*.

CASTING: Hollywood is full of stories of actors who almost took roles and then were unable to at the last moment. Debra Winger had originally been due to star as Peggy Sue. In the mid-1980s Winger was a big star, having appeared in *An Officer and a Gentleman* (Taylor Hackford, 1982) and *Terms of Endearment* (James L Brocks, 1983). However, ill-health meant that Winger had to pull out. By the end of 1984, Kathleen Turner had assumed the status of movie star and so became the obvious replacement. She had starred in the brilliant *Body Heat* (Lawrence Kasdan, 1982) and also *Romancing the Stone* (Robert Zemeckis, 1984). Turner loved the notion of working on a Coppola movie but then production troubles loomed when Turner's commitment to a sequel to *Romancing the Stone*, the impoverished *Jewel of the Nile* (Lewis Teague, 1985) had to take precedence. Turner went off to make that movie and, in the interim, Coppola refined the screenplay and pre-production chores.

I KNOW THAT FACE: Kathleen Turner has appeared in *Crimes of Passion* (Ken Russell, 1985), *Prizzi's Honor* (John Huston, 1985), *Switching Channels* (Ted Kotcheff, 1987), *Who Framed Roger Rabbit?* (Robert Zemeckis, 1988), *Wars of the Roses* (Danny De Vito, 1989) and has also appeared in the sitcom *Friends*. Nicolas Cage has gone on to movies such as *Bringing Out the Dead* (Martin Scorsese, 2000) and *Con Air* (Simon West, 1998).

Jim Carrey puts in an appearance before hitting the big time with *The Mask* (Chuck Russell, 1994), *Dumb and Dumber* (The Farrelly Brothers, 1995), *The Grinch* (Ron Howard, 2001) and *The Majestic* (Frank Darabont, 2001).

Helen Hunt also appears in the movie, many years before starring in *As Good as it Gets* (James Bridges, 1998), *CastAway* (Robert Zemeckis, 2000) and *What Women Want* (Nancy Meyers, 2000).

Joan Allen stars in Coppola's movie *Tucker: The Man and His Dream* and has also appeared in *Nixon* (Oliver Stone, 1995) and *The Ice Storm* (Ang Lee, 1997).

THE FILMING: *Peggy Sue Got Married* began filming in Santa Rosa in the summer of 1985, the very summer that *Back to the Future* (Robert Zemeckis) was released. Both had a time-travel premise in which a hero from the mid-1980s went back to the late 1950s. Dean Tavoularis, working on a scale akin to *The Outsiders* and *Rumble Fish* recreated Santa Rosa around about 1960. The shoot moved efficiently, Coppola to some degree having to repeat his mission (following *One From the Heart*) of proving that he could shoot a film on time and budget after the longeurs of *The Cotton Club*. A few sets were built, notably Peggy Sue's childhood bedroom and a Masonic hall, which was constructed inside an existing building. To enhance the sense of fantasy, sidewalks were given a fresh lick of yellow paint on the kerbs and some of the fences were painted red. The shoot was completed by the end of October 1985 and a new ending for the film was shot in March 1986. The two endings were essentially the same, but Coppola wanted the chance to focus and strengthen the performances in the reshoot and to add one shot that brought the film full circle. That shot was of the family and the mirror.

PROMOTION: *Peggy Sue Got Married* was released in May 1986 and its poster emphasised the time-frame of the film and the overriding gentility rather than the time-travel aspect, offering a strong contrast with the kinetic energy of the similarly inspired *Back to the Future*.

THE OPENING: The opening credits establish the light and airy nostalgia of the film. The first image is of Peggy Sue looking in her mirror as she prepares for the high school reunion. She will spend her time back in the 1950s reflecting on the life she has led in adulthood. The scene economically establishes Peggy's situation and character and the drama to come.

HEROES AND VILLAINS: Peggy Sue is sketched as a typical suburban, middle-American woman whose sense of self is challenged and exploded by her fantastic voyage back in time. By going back to her life when she was an eighteen-year-old with all the world before her, Peggy Sue is able to use her adult wisdom to see the mistakes she made and even challenge the class bullies. Her sense of failure is also manifested, notably in her thoughts about married life. At the start of the film she talks to her daughter about her 'unresolved feelings about your father' referring to his going off with a woman named Janet.

Peggy Sue's husband Charlie is a warm-hearted, initially buffoonish character, who elicits growing sympathy as he sees his music ambitions fade away.

Typically, Peggy Sue has her chatty best friends, Carol and Maddie, who are archetypal teenagers, one outgoing, the other a little more restrained. Charlie, too, has his friends, notably the whacky Walter Getz.

The film's roster of classroom archetypes is rounded out in the character of Richard Norvick, a shy and academic young man (who becomes a success). Then there is the class rebel and brooding hero, Michael Fitzsimmons, who is a Beat-style aspiring writer who would be at home in the more angst-ridden world of *Rumble Fish*, though in this film his self-consciously bohemian manner carries comic value. All the characters in the film are elements found in many teenagers as they struggle to come to terms with who they might be, while clinging to some of the securities of home.

The parent figures in the film are comically drawn, notably the men. Peggy Sue's father is a figure of fun and the film also gently mocks the men who attend the masonic lodge. The one male parental figure who is drawn without irony is Peggy's grandfather, who is a man of folksy wisdom. Peggy Sue's mother is rock solid and her grandparents are the most savvy adults of the film. As in *The Godfather* there is a place for the wisdom of old age when Peggy Sue visits her grandparents, seemingly the only adults who can connect with her. Only they have no fear of dying and they offer the comfort Peggy Sue needs.

COPPOLA STYLE: The overall visual design of the film is based on a sense of warmth and innocence. The images glow and the pastel colours of costumes, sets and vehicles, matched with an emphasis on sunlight, make the film an embodiment of youthful optimism. This is a very gentle film, bright and playful, like a more contained version of *One From the Heart*.

IMAGE: Much of the film was shot on actual locations near and around Santa Rosa, California, lending it a real believability against which the fantasy can unfold. For Jordan Cronenweth, the cinematographer, the challenge was one of working in spaces not designed for movie crews. For example, in one scene where Peggy Sue is an eighteen-year-old in her family cellar looking for a secret stash of cigarettes, the only light source emanates through a small window so that the scene is essentially lit by one key light with barely any fill light to supplement it.

This crucial scene, where Peggy Sue and young Charlie argue, is conducted in light and shadow with only moonlight blasting in through a window, the characters moving in and out of the light as they grapple with failure, rejection and regret, much like Hank and Frannie do in *One From the Heart*.

The game plan for Jordan Cronenweth and his lighting crew was to render the images somewhat surreal in places, enhancing the fantastic, real-world situation Peggy Sue finds herself caught in.

Contrasting with the suburban pop colour-scheme, there is a segment of the film where Peggy Sue visits her grandparents in the country. The establishing wide shot of the sequence is a vintage piece of American pastoral as Peggy Sue approaches the building in an exquisite sunset, the house (more of a cabin) nestled among the silhouette of trees.

The character of Michael Fitzsimmons is associated with shadows and a darker lighting scheme befitting his moodier nature.

For the scene where Peggy Sue and Richard first talk about the future in an after-school classroom, the shot is left wide enough to show the mural of the universe on the classroom wall tying in with the cosmic nature of their conversation. This one shot neatly places the film back into film history by recalling the planetarium scene in *Rebel Without a Cause* (Nicholas Ray, 1955), another film in which teenagers grapple with their place in the world and, by extension, the cosmos.

Peggy Sue Got Married is warmth and softness all the way through. When Peggy Sue awakes at the end of the movie, the hospital room is warmly coloured and softly lit. The closing shot is in tune with the opening of the movie, as the camera pulls away from a hospital mirror to reveal Peggy Sue, Charlie and their daughter Beth in a tableau together. The film's opening and its close emphasise the mirror as part of the décor as Peggy Sue's whole adventure prompts her to reflect on her life.

SOUND: Even though the film is built around a fantastic premise, the sound work is low-key and naturalistic. The one exception is the arrangement of sound for the moment when Peggy Sue passes out. To create a sense of disorientation and unease there is a discordant fusion of clapping and music which dominates the action, accompanied by flashing lights across the stage.

Music from the era is used to define the time period just as the source music is in *Apocalypse Now*.

COPPOLA TUNES: John Barry renewed his collaboration with Coppola having worked with him on *The Cotton Club*. Barry has scored many major Hollywood movies including *Out of Africa* (Sydney Pollack, 1985), *Dances with Wolves* (Kevin Costner, 1990) and *Chaplin* (Richard Attenborough, 1992). Barry's soundtrack for *Peggy Sue Got Married* is appropriately wistful, being used sparingly but powerfully.

Peggy Sue Got Married by John Barry: 'Peggy Sue Homecoming', 'Charlie's Unplayed Guitar', 'Did We Break Up?', 'Charlie', 'I Had the Strangest Experience', 'Peggy Sue Got Married' (Buddy Holly), 'I Wonder Why' (The Belmonts), 'He Don't Love You' (Nicolas Cage), 'Teenager In Love' (The Belmonts), 'You Belong to Me'.

HUMOUR: *Peggy Sue Got Married* was Coppola's first all-out comedy since *You're a Big Boy Now*. His previous films had contained traces of humour and *Peggy Sue*, like *Back to the Future*, finds a wellspring of humour in Peggy Sue's future knowledge gone back in time. She comments on her sister Nancy's diet and tells Richard about all the inventions to come and the moon landing. The prudery of the young women regarding sexuality is also a source of some humour. Adult characters in the film tend to be annoying in the eyes of their children and Peggy's clean-cut father is mocked gently in the scene where he proudly shows his family the new car – Peggy Sue can only laugh. Coppola also derives a few chuckles from the masonic lodge scene and also from the affectionate tribute to four-part harmony singing in the shape of Charlie's band, which owes a debt to the Four Freshmen, the group whose music largely inspired the Beach Boys.

AWARDS: An unassuming film, *Peggy Sue Got Married* was recognised at the 1987 Academy Awards with nominations for Best Actress in a Leading Role (Kathleen Turner), Best Cinematography (Jordan Cronenweth) and Best Costume Design (Theodora van Runkle).

COPPOLA MAGIC: Although a time-travel film and hence, very generally, a piece of science fiction, the story is not especially concerned with the mechanics and possible spectacle involved in time travel.

MOVIE SPEAK:

Peggy Sue: 'We just got married too young.'

Beth: 'You look like you stepped out of *Life* magazine.'

Peggy Sue: 'I have too many unresolved relationships in my life.'

Charlie: 'Nothing else matters. That's the great thing about love.'

Peggy Sue: 'I am a walking anachronism.'

Peggy Sue: 'I may be crazy, but I'm not crazy enough to marry you twice.'

HOME VIEWING: The film is available on Region 1 DVD and the disc includes the theatrical trailer, interactive menu and scene selection, and is formatted in widescreen 1.85:1 There is no Region 2 DVD of the film but it is available on VHS.

TRIVIA: Prior to Coppola's involvement, two younger directors had been in contention for the job. One was Penny Marshall who went on to direct *Big* (1988) and *Awakenings* (1991) and the other was Jonathan Demme who directed *Something Wild* (1984), *Married to the Mob* (1989), *Silence of the Lambs* (1992), *Philadelphia* (1993) and *Beloved* (1999).

Coppola's daughter Sofia puts in an appearance as Peggy Sue's sister, Nancy.

One of Coppola's movie-making heroes is Orson Welles, with whom he has often been compared. Welles died during the period that *Peggy Sue Got Married* was being filmed. To commemorate Welles, Coppola stopped the shoot and played a record on which Welles featured. The song was called 'I Know What It Is To Be Young, But You Don't Know What It Is To Be Old'.

COPPOLA'S VIEW: Whereas his youth movies *The Outsiders*, *Rumble Fish* and *Jack* all concern themselves with thoughts of the future and the painful reality of how quickly life passes by, *Peggy Sue Got Married* uses youth to emphasise the regrets of adulthood. Peggy Sue recognises the fragility of time when she realises the mistakes and misjudgements she feels she has made. Whereas The Motorcycle Boy opened up Rusty's sense of the wider world in *Rumble Fish*, in *Peggy Sue Got Married*, Peggy tastes the wider world but retreats from it to the security of home.

CRITICAL COPPOLA: Pauline Kael said of the film, 'it has a golden, romantic look . . . Coppola seems to be trying to get back to something more solid, something that the audience can connect with.' *Time Out* felt it was 'More relaxed – sloppy even – than any of Coppola's usual busy films.' For Roger Ebert in the *Chicago Sun-Times*, though, it was 'a human comedy . . . there are times when it is just plain creepy, because it awakens such vivid memories in us.' *Sight and Sound* said that the film contained 'some fuzzy Capraesque homilies about how everything is for the best in the best of all possible neighbourhoods.'

VERDICT: *Peggy Sue Got Married* is a minor Coppola movie that reminds audiences of Coppola's flair for easygoing comedy. The film is distinctive from the similarly designed *Back to the Future*. Where that film explored possibility, this film is far more about regret and so, for all its fanciful set up, is a more adult film. The film feels like a sigh of relief after the massive *The Cotton Club* and the intense romanticism of *The Outsiders* and *Rumble Fish*.

Kathleen Turner holds the film together, communicating both youthful zest and adult regret. Jim Carrey explodes on screen and gives us a very clear glimpse of what was in store several years later (see **I KNOW THAT FACE**).

The film exhibits Coppola's familiar elegance and warmth and demonsrates how comedy can be as emotionally true and painful as all the angst that can be hurled at the movie camera.

COPPOLA NOW: 'My model was the last act of Thornton Wilder's *Our Town* . . . I was looking for more of that kind of small-town charm and emotion than for jokes or effects.'

Gardens of Stone (1987)

(Colour – 111 minutes)

TriStar
Producer: Michael J Levy and Francis Ford Coppola
Executive Producer: Stan Weston, Jay Emmett and Fred
Roos; David Valdes (co-executive)
Screenplay: Ronald Bass, based on the novel by Nicholas
Proffitt
Cinematographer: Jordan Cronenweth
Editor: Barry Malkin
Music: Carmine Coppola
Production Design: Dean Tavoularis
Art Direction: Alex Tavoularis
Sound Designer: Richard Beggs
Costume Design: Willa Kim, Judianna Makosky

CAST: James Caan (*Clell Hazard*), Anjelica Huston (*Samantha Davis*), James Earl Jones (*Goody Nelson*), DB Sweeney (*Jackie Willow*), Dean Stockwell (*Homer Thomas*), Mary Stuart Masterson (*Rachel Feld*), Dick Anthony Williams (*Slasher Williams*), Lonette McKee (*Betty Rae*), Sam Bottoms (*Lt Webber*), Elias Koteas (*Pete Deveber*), Larry Fishburne (*Flanagan*), Casey Siemaszko (*Wildman*), Peter Masterson (*Colonel Feld*), Carlin Glynn (*Mrs Feld*), Erik Holland (*Colonel Godwin*), Bill Graham (*Don Brubaker*)

BUDGET: $12 million

THE BOX OFFICE: $4,358,779

RELEASE DATE: May 1987

MPAA: R

BBFC: 15

TAGLINE: 'It was a dangerous time to be young. An impossible time to be a hero.'

SUMMARY: 1969. A funeral is underway at Arlington National Cemetery in Washington. A soldier killed in Vietnam is being given the final salute, his loved ones present at the graveside.

1968, Fort Myer, Virginia. A young man, Willow, arrives to begin working as a volunteer soldier for The Old Guard. Clell Hazard, a veteran soldier who fought alongside Willow's father, has reservations about the Vietnam war, while Willow is keen to go and fight. Clell meets a neighbour, Samantha. He flirts with her, then invites her to come to a meal he is hosting for his friend and colleague, Goody Nelson. The evening is a success and the relationship between Clell and Sam develops.

In the barracks, Willow comes to the aid of a less confident soldier, Wildman, and so begins his climb up the military ladder, with some backing and encouragement from Clell and Nelson, with whom Willow develops a warm bond. Willow is given the news that his father has died and is discharged for a week on compassionate leave.

Clell's relationship with his superior deteriorates as Clell has been voicing his opinions about the Vietnam war around the barracks. At a function, Clell's frustrations boil over and he beats up an anti-war protester.

On duty at a ceremony in Washington, Willow spots his ex-girlfriend, Rachel, taking photographs. Willow speaks to her and then takes her out for a meal. They attempt to reconcile their differences. Clell has agreed to give Willow his apartment for the night but when Willow and Rachel go back to it, Clell is still there.

Willow's plans are cut short for training manoeuvres. This is Clell's chance to show his young charges the tough side of being a soldier and he decides to break his unit away – effectively going AWOL – in order to train them in a way that he feels would really prepare them for action in Vietnam. Clell is making a stand against the level of officially available training. Clell's maverick decision is a gesture of real concern for the fate of the young men he is responsible for, but it is Nelson who finally brings him back in. Clell's commander is infuriated and says he still will not transfer Clell to a training fort.

Willow and Rachel get engaged, though her father objects.

Willow is transferred to Officer Candidate School and, beyond that, a year-long tour of duty in Vietnam. A year passes and then news is received that he has died in battle.

Clell wants to go back to Vietnam and fight but he asks if Sam will marry him first. She says she will. Clell, Nelson, Rachel and Sam stand at Willow's graveside at his funeral.

COPPOLA'S CONCEPT: At variance with *Apocalypse Now*, *Gardens of Stone* is a sedate and quiet reflection on the price of war, this time inflecting the drama back home. The film is probably more successful than *Apocalypse Now* as a reminder of the futility of war.

Coppola was approached in early 1985, prior to work starting on *Peggy Sue Got Married*, to direct the film, by Victor Kaufman, who was head of TriStar Pictures. Coppola was keen to express the harmony of a regiment like the army's The Old Guard.

Tragically, during the making of the film, Coppola's son Gian-Carlo died in a boating accident and for some observers his death powerfully informed the tone of this piece. *Gardens of Stone* very simply lays out the complex opposing views towards the Vietnam war (indeed, any war) and the Vietnamese soldiers. Clell regards the Vietnamese as 'farmers' with no moral code of combat that can be respected.

INFLUENCES: *Gardens of Stone* is based on the 1983 novel of the same name by Nicholas Proffitt, and told the story of the army's Old Guard. As with *Apocalypse Now*, *Gardens of Stone* was also partly inspired by pieces of journalism. Nicholas Proffitt had been a correspondent for *Newsweek* just as Michael Kerr had written pieces for *Esquire* which informed the *Apocalypse Now* screenplay.

Coppola had been to military school as a boy and so was used to a certain level of regimentation. Despite its very different scale and intent, and the influence *Apocalypse Now* had on this film, *Gardens of Stone* is its total opposite. Where *Apocalypse Now* had criticised American attitudes to the war and the sense that the military was out of control, in *Gardens of Stone* the critique of the war is balanced by real respect for the American military process or, more accurately, military codes.

COSTUME: *Gardens of Stone* emphasises the detail of military uniform. However, in its concern with the effect of war on personal lives, much of the film is played out away from the barracks. Frequently Clell is shown in his apartment. His typical attire is a plaid shirt, suggesting a sense of the traditional and folksy. As such he contrasts with the more flamboyant Goody Nelson and certainly Sam with her urbane dress sense.

TEAM COPPOLA: Coppola teamed up again with Dean Tavoularis in his capacity as production designer, working in one of their most naturalistic palettes yet, in contrast to their collaborations on *Apocalypse Now* and on *One From the Heart* particularly. Also working with Coppola again, straight from the success of *Peggy Sue Got Married*, was the cinematographer Jordan Cronenweth, whose credits have included *Blade Runner* (Ridley Scott, 1982), *U2: Rattle and Hum* (Phil Jouanou, 1992) and *Final Analysis* (Phil Jouanou, 1992).

Again, Fred Roos, a collaborator of Coppola's since the early 1970s returned as a producer on the project. Roos had worked as a producer on *The Godfather Part II*, *Apocalypse Now*, *The Outsiders*, *Rumble Fish* and would get on to *Tucker: The Man and His Dream*.

CASTING: In the mid-1980s James Caan's standing as an actor was low – unfairly so – and *Gardens of Stone* reminded audiences of his great skill as a screen actor. The film was the first time he had worked with Francis Coppola since *The Godfather* (1972); he had also worked with the director on *The Rain People*. Coppola also cast Larry Fishburne again (*Apocalypse Now*, *Rumble Fish*, *The Cotton Club*).

As with so many of his films (*The Godfather*, *The Outsiders*, *Rumble Fish*, *Bram Stoker's Dracula* and *The Rainmaker*), Coppola finds a place for emerging young acting talent, in this case DB Sweeney and Mary Stuart Masterson.

Coppola's knack for casting emerging stars was again evident: Anjelica Huston had emerged as a star actress of the highest calibre in the mid-1980s.

As always, the casting process for *Gardens of Stone* was rounded off by two weeks of videotaped rehearsal in which the screenplay evolved and developed.

I KNOW THAT FACE: Anjelica Huston starred in *The Dead* (John Huston, 1987), *The Grifters* (Stephen Frears, 1990) and *The Addams Family* (Barry Sonnenfeld, 1991). Dean Stockwell has starred in *The Boy with Green Hair* (Joseph Losey, 1948), *Dune* (David Lynch, 1984), *Blue Velvet* (David Lynch, 1986) and *Tucker: The Man and His Dream* as well as the science fiction TV series *Quantum Leap*. Mary Stuart Masterson has appeared in *Some Kind of Wonderful* (Howard Deutch, 1987), *Fried Green Tomatoes at the Whistlestop Café* (John Avnet, 1991), *Benny and Joon* (Jeremiah Chechik, 1993) and *Radioland Murders* (Mel Smith, 1994). James Earl Jones is famously the voice of Darth Vader in *Star Wars: A New Hope* (George Lucas, 1977) and has also appeared in *Conan The Barbarian* (John Milius, 1982), *Matewan* (John Sayles, 1987), *Field of Dreams* (Phil Alden Robinson, 1989), *Patriot Games* (Philip Noyce, 1992) and *Clear and Present Danger* (Philip Noyce, 1994).

THE FILMING: *Gardens of Stone* began filming in May 1986 and concluded in August of that year. The film received army backing, unlike Coppola's *Apocalypse Now*, which, apparently, had military support turned down by none other than Donald Rumsfeld. For *Gardens of Stone*, the army provided technical support, advice, equipment and personnel. Four hundred and fifty soldiers were seen in the troop review scene. The film shot on location at Fort Myer and Fort Belvoir and at Arlington National Cemetery, which also featured in *JFK* (Oliver Stone, 1991). For production designer, Dean Tavoularis, the neoclassical architecture so prominent throughout the film lends it a timelessness and affinity for the traditional that the Old Guard represent. Six hundred soldiers were on hand as extras in the film.

PROMOTION: *Gardens of Stone* received a fairly narrow release, going out on only sixty screens across North America. After three weeks the film had grossed just $4.35 million.

The film was the first Coppola film in over twelve years not to use his name in the advertising. It was not presented as a 'Francis Ford Coppola' film. Perhaps another reason for the film's failure was that audiences had become used to the cry and holler of films like *Platoon* (Oliver Stone, 1986), *Heartbreak Ridge* (Clint Eastwood, 1986) and *Full Metal Jacket* (Stanley Kubrick, 1987). *Gardens of Stone* is very much a whisper in a subgenre known for its bellicose style.

THE OPENING: *Gardens of Stone* begins silently and incredibly mournfully. A camera tracks deliberately and slowly past countless graves at Arlington Cemetery, the gardens of stone of the film's title, finally coming to a stop on the edge of a rise, where gravestones stretch forever, as a horse and carriage cross the frame. Like many graveyards, the cemetery, with its old-world atmosphere, seems removed from the rush and mania of the twentieth century, which is consistent with the film's affinity for the order of the past into which the chaos of war and death has been placed.

HEROES AND VILLAINS: The innocent, young Willow wants to fight in Vietnam, having volunteered to serve in the Old Guard to begin his career, following his father's own military career. Willow becomes a surrogate son to the older men of the story. He wants to grow up and go out into the world – just like other young Coppola heroes do in the films *Rumble Fish* and *Jack*.

Clell Hazard is a contained, thoughtful man given to outbursts of anger when that is the only form of expression available to him. Rather like Michael Corleone, he is afraid of being alone. Touchingly, Clell takes Willow into his care as a son of sorts. Clell's affinity for the old ways connects him to Michael and Vito Corleone. He also possesses a cultural interest in Persian rugs and classical music. Some of Schubert's music is to be heard being played in his apartment on the stereo. His anger about the conduct of the American military in Vietnam connects him to the spirit of *Apocalypse Now*. Like Kurtz, Clell is a man of principal and again like Kurtz, at one point in the film, Clell goes AWOL in a 'jungle' training scenario. Clell talks about the military being his 'family' and says to Sam that 'This is not a very good business for hanging on to a woman.' The same could be said for the life Michael Corleone leads. In Coppola's films there is sometimes a real price to be paid for an unhealthy obsession with work.

Whereas *Apocalypse Now* thunderously and memorably dramatised and visualised America's crazed intervention in Vietnam, in *Gardens of Stone* criticism is once again articulated, but through Clell, and with more reserve. He describes the war as 'a funny little war' where there is apparently nothing to win and not even a front line. Clell cannot accept how things have changed and he and his closest friend, Goody Nelson, have a phrase they repeat throughout the film, and which Willow adopts: 'Here's to us and those like us.' The implication that Clell and Goody represent a dying breed is readily apparent. In Proffitt's original novel, the effusive Goody quotes Othello, himself a military man for whom honour and codes of conduct form the basis of his tragic downfall.

Goody Nelson is like a brother to the sombre Clell. Together they form a strong bond and reflect the film's focus on male military codes; they refer to one another as 'bears'.

Sam is another in a long line of beautiful and strong women in Coppola's films, and she is certainly one of the best defined, confident in expressing her objection to the war while in a relationship with a soldier.

There is a great sadness to the characters in this film. Rachel struggles with Willow's military life and the price that must be paid. She is a Coppola woman, beautiful and independent and also struggling to understand the codes of a male-centred world. She is like Kay in *The Godfather*, attempting to understand the world her husband keeps very separate from her.

COPPOLA STYLE: In a refreshing change from the expansive *Godfather* trilogy and the fizzy energy of movies like *Peggy Sue Got Married*, *Tucker: The Man and His Dream* and *Jack*, *Gardens of Stone* is Coppola's most restrained film both visually and in terms of the actors' performances. The muted visuals and performances serve one another well and the film's largely springtime setting contrasts with the autumnal emotions of the drama.

IMAGE: For Jordan Cronenweth, the cinematographer, the appeal was in working with Coppola again and in portraying the pageantry of The Old Guard. As with *Peggy Sue Got Married*, *Gardens of Stone* utilised many real locations which posed various lighting challenges. The barracks was lit through the windows in the daytime and fluorescent lights were used at night where the crosslight pattern was the dominant visual design. For the wide shots the colour-controlled fluorescents were used, but not for the close shots. The film's overall look is clean and precise, reflecting the discipline of the world being shown. At the time of the film's release, Jordan Cronenweth praised Coppola's directing technique for the freedom he gave Cronenweth.

Like the movements and uniforms of the soldiers, the film's look is crisp and precise. The film favours locked-off shots, which give it a static and quiet quality. The camera rarely moves. The images emphasise order and control with a further emphasis on straight lines and door frames, so that the often static camera has a solidity that recalls the design of *The Godfather*.

Towards the end of the film its texture changes as Coppola intercuts 16mm documentary footage of the Vietnam war, contrasting the reality of exhausted and shellshocked American faces with the clean, smiling face of Willow.

The images are pristine and, as always, Coppola goes for a tableau effect, notably towards the end when a bugler plays amid the gravestones and, in a wide shot, the camera holds on him for some time. There is also an arrestingly precise and contained image of Clell standing in front of Willow's coffin in the chapel. The stillness of the film connects it with *The Conversation*.

SOUND: The film finds several opportunities to puncture its naturalistic design. At the wedding, the sound of celebration is replaced by the sounds of the battlefield, very clearly expressing the horror in which Willow is so eager to participate. This juxtaposition lends the wedding a sadness, making its celebration of life seem somewhat futile.

At the end of the film as the credits come to a close there is the sound of a soldier calling out a march.

COPPOLA TUNES: For the first time since *The Outsiders*, Francis and Carmine Coppola were reunited on *Gardens of Stone*. The music is very low-key but tends to avoid anything excessively sentimental, in keeping with the film's understated tone.

HUMOUR: The father–son relationship between Clell and Willow has ample space for humour. For example Willow has to borrow Clell's car, apartment and a fifty dollar bill to take his ex-girlfrend out.

The film endlessly expresses the male camaraderie in the barracks. A memorable example of this is when Nelson inspects a barracks; in a later scene, when Willow receives his sergeant's stripes, there is humour in the tough male posturing that ensues.

AWARDS: *Gardens of Stone* was shown at the Moscow International Film Festival and nominated for The Golden Prize. The American Political Film Society nominated the film for the Peace category. The film found no further accolade or acknowledgement at any of the high-profile awards ceremonies.

COPPOLA MAGIC: The film's biggest special effect is the brilliant integration of 16mm documentary footage of the Vietnam war with the drama, clarifying the anomaly between a young man's heroic dreams of military service and the bloody chaos of the reality.

MOVIE SPEAK:

Clell: 'I care about the United States Army. That's my family.'

Clell: 'I am not a peacenik, captain!'

Willow: 'A soldier in the right place at the right time can change the world.'

Sam (when Clell says he may return to Vietnam): 'I don't ride off into the sunset. I sit alone in this apartment scared to death and wait.'

HOME VIEWING: *Gardens of Stone* is available on both Region 1 and Region 2 DVD, formatted in widescreen 1.85:1, but without any extras. The VHS of the film is also in print.

TRIVIA: The film is dedicated to the 3rd US Infantry, The Old Guard of the Army, Fort Myer, Virginia.

A scene showing some kind of split between Sam and Clell appears not to have been included in the final cut.

COPPOLA'S VIEW: As with *The Godfather* series and *Peggy Sue Got Married* there is a commitment to dramatising the effect on the individual of time's passing. Age and youth collide in this film and nurture one another. As with other Coppola films a family unit forms between people experiencing adversity.

A complaint levelled at the film is that it does not even allude to anti-war protests or any wider social engagement with the Vietnam war.

This can be challenged, however, by the fact that the film does refer to anti-war protesters (see **SUMMARY**).

As always with Coppola there is an attention to details of process, such as the way the soldiers line up the peaks of their caps just perfectly. *Gardens of Stone* has much in common with *The Godfather*, embodying in its characters a sense of loss and uneasiness with the passing of time. Honour between men is one of the film's key concerns. The Old Guard unit is presented in a very warm and positive way. Clell knew Willow's father, and when Willow leaves for his father's funeral, Clell gives Willow a pin as a gesture of remembrance. The Coppola interest in stories about fathers and sons is central to the interest of *Gardens of Stone* within Coppola's larger body of work.

CRITICAL COPPOLA: *Empire* magazine called the film 'Francis Coppola's soulful, elegiac film . . . heavily symbolic . . . A wistful lament.' For Pauline Kael, '*Gardens of Stone* is far from being a seamless work of art, but it probably comes closer to the confused attitudes that Americans had towards the Vietnam war than any other film has come.' *Time Out* described the film as 'Coppola's oblique, muted and curiously revisionist drama of life on the home front during the Vietnam War . . . some exceptional acting (especially from Caan)'. 'The movie creates its characters with realism, love and detail,' wrote Roger Ebert in the *Chicago Sun-Times*. *Sight and Sound* is more reserved in its assessment saying 'Functioning like a well-made play . . . *Gardens of Stone* seems somehow abject in its careful pussyfooting through the already charted reefs of Vietnam.'

VERDICT: *Gardens of Stone* is one of the finest films Francis Coppola has ever made; its emotional range is perfectly calibrated. Of the cluster of films Coppola made after the greatness of *Rumble Fish* and before the return to the surer waters of *The Godfather Part III*, *Gardens of Stone* is the best. The emotional reserve the film has been criticised for is its great strength. After the surreal war-movie roar of *Apocalypse Now*, *Gardens of Stone* is like a whisper, sombrely presenting a mature story of loss.

COPPOLA NOW: 'I've always been fascinated by the role of ritual in the military, particularly the code of honour.'

Tucker: The Man and His Dream (1988)

(Colour – 111 minutes)

A Lucasfilm Ltd Production released through Paramount
Producer: Fred Roos and Fred Fuchs
Executive Producer: George Lucas
Screenplay: Arnold Schulman and David Seidler
Cinematographer: Vittorio Storaro
Editor: Priscilla Nedd
Music: Joe Jackson
Production Design: Dean Tavoularis
Costume Design: Milena Canonero
Visual Effects: Industrial Light and Magic

CAST: Jeff Bridges (*Preston Tucker*), Joan Allen (*Vera Tucker*), Martin Landau (*Abe Karatz*), Frederic Forrest (*Eddie*), Mako (*Jimmy*), Elias Koteas (*Alex*), Christian Slater (*Junior*), Nina Siemaszko (*Marilyn Lee*), Anders Johnson (*Johnny*), Corky Nemec (*Noble*), Marshall Bell (*Frank*), Jay O Sanders (*Kirby*), Peter Donat (*Kerner*), Lloyd Bridges (*Senator Ferguson, uncredited*), Dean Goodman (*Bennington*), John X Heart (*Ferguson's Aide*), Don Novello (*Stan*), Patti Austin (*Millie*), Sandy Bull (*Stan's Assistant*), Joseph Miksak (*Judge*), Scott Beach (*Floyd Cerf*), Roland Scrivener (*Oscar Beasley*), Dean Stockwell (*Howard Hughes*), Bob Safford (*Narrator*), Larry Menkin (*Doc*), Ron Close (*Fritz*), Joe Flood (*Dutch*)

BUDGET: $25 million

THE BOX OFFICE: $19.65 million

RELEASE DATE: 12 August 1988

MPAA: PG

BBFC: PG

TAGLINE: When they tried to buy him, he refused. When they tried to bully him, he resisted. When they tried to break him, he became an American legend. The true story of Preston Tucker.

SUMMARY: The 1940s, Ypsilanti, Michigan. Tucker pulls up excitedly outside his family home with plans for a new, safer car that he has designed and wants to build. Inside, Tucker goes through his plans with his family and colleagues and later an investor named Abe Karatz arrives to speak with Tucker about the project. Karatz is sceptical about Tucker's plan. To develop interest in his concept, Tucker gets an article published about his dream car and swiftly receives 150,000 letters from people who want to buy a Tucker car. The problem is there is not yet one to buy. Karatz goes to see an investor who says they will need the backing of one of the Big Three automobile companies because Tucker is an unknown commodity. A young man called Alex has read about Tucker's plans and been so inspired that he turns up at Tucker's house one morning having made the journey to Michigan to work on the project. This display of faith prompts Tucker to hire Alex there and then.

Tucker, his wife Vera and Karatz have a meeting about a factory base. Tucker then speaks with representatives of the Big Three companies but fails to make a positive impression. However, one man, Beesley, asks Tucker to return the next day. He does so and is given a vacant Chicago factory. Part of the deal is that Tucker produces fifty cars in the first year. All he needs now is $15 million and a car. Karatz is in shock: there is as yet no money to build cars. He says he will give $6,000 to Tucker so that can get started on building his first car – he has sixty days to make it. With the car in production, Karatz hits the road and begins selling the car to dealerships.

Karatz and Tucker go to see the Chairman of the Board, Bennington, and he arranges for Tucker to see Senator Ferguson. The Senator speaks obliquely and in riddles and is opposed to Tucker's independent challenge to the Big Three car manufacturers. Ferguson wants to put Tucker off through intimidation.

Tension mounts among the engineers as the clock ticks away. The car is completed and launched at Tucker's Chicago factory. Bennington and Beesley attend the event. Soon enough The Big Three conspire for Tucker to go on a promotion tour that will leave them able to oversee the manufacturer of the cars to their own design. Bennington begins to instigate engineering changes and Vera goes to see the board to object to their interference. Vera contacts Tucker and tells him of their proposed changes to the car's colour and cost to the paying public. Tucker confronts Bennington who says he is head of the company, as per the contract. Tucker then receives a call from a mysterious, and interested, party, Howard Hughes. Tucker visits Hughes, who tells him about a source of steel that Tucker needs in order to do his work.

Karatz informs Tucker that the Big Three are tightening their grip and that Tucker only has a few weeks until the deadline. It then emerges that

Karatz has a bad history. He was imprisoned for two years for bank fraud. This is all that Ferguson needs to shut down the Tucker operation. Tucker is then put on trial for fraud and conspiracy. If convicted he will be imprisoned for life. Tucker wins the day and gives a tub-thumping speech about the little guy in American business. Outside, fifty Tucker Torpedo cars roll past the courthouse and Tucker watches with satisfaction, the dream made real.

COPPOLA'S CONCEPT: Preston Tucker (1903–1956) was an engineer and inventor. In the late 1940s he came up with an innovative new car design, The Tucker, which had an emphasis on safety and performance features. But his dream to bring the car to the commercial market was never to reach fruition. One of his more successful ideas had been to design a combat car during World War Two, but the American military felt that it was too fast.

Tucker is widely regarded as one of the most overlooked American mainstream movies of the 1980s. Since the early 1970s (between *The Conversation* and *Apocalypse Now*) Coppola had wanted to make a film about the car designer and dreamer, partly, as modern movie lore states, because in Tucker's brio, pluck and plan of a better way of making cars Coppola saw himself and his American Zoetrope studio. Coppola had been aware of the inventor for some time – he was a child when his father bought a Tucker car – but it was at the 4 July 1985 parade in the small town of Calistoga near Coppola's Napa Valley home that his son, Gio, suggested that his father finally make the film. They were riding in Coppola's Tucker car at the time.

Though it had been just over ten years since his last collaboration with George Lucas, one of his oldest friends, Coppola had spent two weeks in the summer of 1985 shooting a short space fantasy musical for Disney called *Captain Eo*, on which George Lucas had been executive producer; Coppola wondered if this would be the right feature project for a further collaboration with Lucas.

The real-life character of Tucker was seen as something of a kindred spirit to Coppola, and indeed to Lucas. Having considered making the movie as a musical at one point, even bringing on board Leonard Bernstein, and songwriters Betty Comden and Adolph Green of *Singin' in the Rain* (Stanley Donen, 1956) fame, Coppola finally made it as a straight dramatic piece with the backing and encouragement of George Lucas. Prior to Lucas's involvement as executive producer, Coppola had approached Frank Capra – *Tucker: The Man and His Dream* was drawn in the spirit of much of Capra's work.

Late in 1986, Lucas offered his support for the project having heard Coppola's stories about Tucker's life for many years. When Coppola and

Lucas touted the project to Universal, Paramount, TriStar and Disney, all were reluctant to fund it. Lucas eventually funded the film himself, Lucasfilm with Paramount studios agreeing to distribute it. Lucas's commitment to the film was based on a strong interest and belief in the concept and not on whether it would go out and make, as he phrased it, 'a hundred zillion dollars'.

At the time of making *Tucker,* Coppola felt some loss of confidence concerning his ability to connect with audiences, and by teaming up with fellow maverick movie maker George Lucas one assumes that his popular touch gave Coppola a sense of storytelling security. Lucas's main contribution was in keeping Coppola focused on the essentials of the story, the 'ballbearings' as Coppola has termed them. Lucas clarified the position the screenplay should take, which was to focus on the concept of what it means to have a dream. The philosophical aspect of Tucker's life was what was stimulating, not so much the fact that he only manufactured fifty cars.

Coppola and Lucas hired Arnold Schulman to write the screenplay. Schulman had written Capra's movie *A Hole in the Head* (1959), *Love With a Proper Stranger* (Robert Mulligan, 1963) and also *Goodbye, Columbus* (Larry Peerce, 1969), based on Philip Roth's debut novel. For Preston Tucker's family, it was understandable that they wanted their father's life and endeavours to be dramatised positively. For Coppola, part of the concept was to make the film feel a little wacky and certainly to assume the quality of a contraption rather like Tucker's car design.

For Coppola, the film was designed to be upbeat and inspiring. On the DVD of the film, he states, 'I have a personal connection to Tucker.' In the same mini-documentary supplement Martin Landau talks about Karatz coming to life through the film as he 'finds he can dream again'. Lucas also stated that 'Tucker addresses that very subject. About bringing your dreams to reality.'

INFLUENCES: The films of Frank Capra, with their espousal of American can-do spirit, are among the principal influences on *Tucker.* The warmth of the film is also an extension of the period whimsy seen in *Peggy Sue Got Married* and owes something to Coppola's affectionate recreation of late 50s and early 60s America in *The Outsiders.*

Real life was also an influence on the film as Coppola had access to still and moving pictures from the Tucker archive so that in certain instances he was able to replicate what had actually occurred, as at the unveiling of the Tucker car at the plant in Chicago.

COSTUME: In designing the costumes, there were many photos of Tucker available for reference. Tucker's boyishness and irrepressible character is reflected in his sharp suits. These contrast with the stark, sombre and funereal suits of the quiet and deliberate Abe Karatz.

TEAM COPPOLA: *Tucker* is one of Coppola's surest film-making family affairs, with Dean Tavoularis designing the movie, Vittorio Storaro as the cinematographer, Fred Roos (*The Godfather Part II, Apocalypse Now, One From the Heart, The Outsiders, Rumble Fish*) producing and George Lucas overseeing the project. Lucas had begun his career, in the late 1960s, working as an assistant to Coppola on *The Rain People*. It was Coppola's American Zoetrope company that financed Lucas's debut feature, *THX-1138*, and it was Coppola who was executive producer on Lucas's second feature as a director, *American Graffiti* (1973). In 1986 Lucas had been executive producer on Coppola's short theme-park movie *Captain Eo* (see **COPPOLA'S CONCEPT** and **Short Film Projects**). With *Tucker: The Man and His Dream*, Lucas returned the favour, and Coppola availed himself of Lucas's extensive post-production facilities.

CASTING: One of the great contemporary American actors, Jeff Bridges, was cast as Preston Tucker. Joan Allen who co-stars as Preston's wife, Vera, had appeared in *Peggy Sue Got Married*; she began her notable career as a stage actress with *Steppenwolf Theatre Company* in Chicago and prior to her work on *Tucker* had been awarded a Tony for her role in the Broadway play, *Burn This*.

Frederic Forrest returned from *One From the Heart*, *Apocalypse Now* and *The Conversation*. Dean Stockwell returned from *Gardens of Stone*.

I KNOW THAT FACE: Jeff Bridges has been a Hollywood face since the early 1970s in films such as the funny *The Last Picture Show* (Peter Bogdanovich, 1971), *Bad Company* (Robert Benton, 1973), *Thunderbolt and Lightfoot* (Michael Cimino, 1975), *Against All Odds* (Taylor Hackford, 1984), the brilliant *Starman* (John Carpenter, 1984), *The Fisher King* (Terry Gilliam, 1991), *American Heart* (1991), the beautiful *Fearless* (Peter Weir, 1993) and *The Big Lebowski* (Joel Coen, 1997).

Martin Landau played a heavy in James Mason's gang in *North by Northwest* (Alfred Hitchcock, 1956) and starred in the TV series *Space: 1999*. Since his high-profile performance in *Tucker*, Landau has been seen in *Ed Wood* (Tim Burton, 1994) where he portrayed Bela Lugosi. Landau also puts in a cameo appearance in *Sleepy Hollow* (Tim Burton, 1999) until being decapitated early in the film.

Christian Slater portrays Tucker's son in the film and he went on to a leading role in cult teen drama *Heathers* (Michael Lehmann, 1989) and *True Romance* (Tony Scott, 1993). Joan Allen appeared in *Peggy Sue*

Got Married (1986) and *Manhunter* (Michael Mann, 1986). Many years later she starred in *The Ice Storm* (Ang Lee, 1997). Mako appeared in *Magnum P.I.* (TV series), *Hawaii Five-O* (TV series) and *I, Spy* (TV series). He had also been Oscar nominated for his role in *The Sand Pebbles* (Robert Wise, 1966).

Jeff Bridges' father Lloyd Bridges takes an unbilled role as Senator Ferguson. Lloyd Bridges is a Hollywood veteran appearing in *High Noon* (Fred Zinnemann, 1952), *Joe Versus the Volcano* (John Patrick Shanley, 1990) and *Hot Shots* (Jim Abrahams, 1991). Elias Koteas as Alex can be seen in *The Thin Red Line* (Terrence Malick, 1998).

THE FILMING: Coppola and Lucas brought *Tucker* in on time and budget. In pre-production, Coppola spent eighteen-hour days going through the film's visual design and, according to reports, 90 per cent of this game plan was adhered to during shooting.

Filming began on 17 April 1987 in northern California. Tucker's family were on set much of the time and were able to aid Bridges in the fidelity of his performance as Preston Tucker. They would advise him on gestures, turns of phrase and stance.

Over 100 vehicles from the 1930s and 1940s were rounded up for the filming. Two of the original Tuckers seen in the film belonged to Francis Coppola and a third to George Lucas; other Tucker car collectors loaned their cars to the production. One of Coppola's cars was used as the basis for the dozens of replica Tuckers that were made. The original was taken apart and each piece moulded for the fake Tucker Torpedos which, for the film, were made from plastic, fibreglass and metal.

Locations for the film included northern California and the San Francisco Opera House exterior, which stood in for a Chicago court house. The interior of the court house was shot at the Oakland Hotel, complete with a full-scale Lady Justice statue. For the Tucker home, actually in Ypsilanti, Michigan, Coppola and his production designer Dean Tavoularis decided on a mansion in Sonoma county, northern California. The old Ford car plant in Richmond also served as a key location.

PROMOTION: *Tucker: The Man and His Dream* was one of two George Lucas-produced movies released in 1988; the other was *Willow* directed by Ron Howard. Despite a slick campaign and the promise of Lucas and Coppola joining forces, *Tucker* did not connect with audiences and quickly left cinemas.

The film's poster was a glitzy shot of Tucker in a tuxedo, leaning against a maroon Tucker car, encircled by a gold neon arch in the background. Perhaps the film was too nostalgic and old world. In France and Japan, though, the film was very well received.

THE OPENING: The film begins with a faux promo film, which establishes the life of Preston Tucker. The tone of the opening establishes the tone of the film, overall an energetic and upbeat story. The Tucker company badge appears and then we see Tucker at the window of his factory. A series of family photos outline the life of Tucker, including his success designing the bubbles for American fighter-plane gun turrets.

HEROES AND VILLAINS: Like so many Coppola heroes, Preston Tucker is a family man. He is certainly one of Coppola's cheeriest heroes, and it was Tucker's sense of life and his fallibility that appealed to the director. Tucker is confronted by a corrupt world of business and control that he resists rather than allowing himself to become tainted by it. Coppola's film *The Rainmaker* features the same resistance to corruption on the part of its young hero, Rudy Baylor. Tucker's courtroom speech converts the character to an icon and a spokesman for American invention and commitment to forward thinking. Preston is a dreamer. He could also be regarded as a control freak, and there are certain moments where his megalomania is expressed. Tucker is a boyish character who, even at the end, cannot stop dreaming up another project.

Vera is Tucker's strong-willed wife, as beautiful as many other Coppola women on screen. She is blessed with the confidence to confront Tucker's bureaucratic enemies.

Contrasting with the frenetic boyish energy of Tucker is Abe Karatz, who functions partly as a father figure to Tucker, cautioning and guiding him. This father–son relationship is a feature of other Coppola films such as *The Godfather*, *Gardens of Stone*, *Jack* and *The Rainmaker*.

Like Willard, in his journey upriver in *Apocalypse Now*, Tucker has a team of men who join in his journey into corporate darkness. The character of Eddie Dean was a composite one based on real-life Eddie Offutt, who worked with Tucker.

The powers of evil are, in classic Coppola fashion, defined as people of the shadows, committed only to profit rather than the smartness of a new idea, even if it represents a risk.

COPPOLA STYLE: *Tucker* is a zestful, fun, peppy movie that takes on the spirit of its protagonist. It's a novelty kind of film informed by the promo films of the 1940s.

The film is very nostalgic, and while smaller in scale than Coppola's 1970s films, it is as heartfelt and rich in atmosphere. Coppola's notion was for the style of the film to feel like a contraption: itself an invention. As in *The Godfather* and *The Cotton Club*, the home is a vital location, and its stability is reinforced through framing shots in doorways and on stairways. For the scenes in the city the camera is often at a low height, emphasising the overbearing power of the architecture and, by association, the might of the corporate world.

IMAGE: Again working with cinematographer Vittorio Storaro, Coppola bathes *Tucker: The Man and His Dream* in a warm golden light of nostalgia and rural idyll, particularly for Tucker's family home in the country. In his home, Tucker is often lit in close-up by golden rim lighting, and the camera lovingly rises and drops past the tree in front of the family house. Tucker's association with heroic warm light continues in the courtroom scene where he speaks to the jury about the place of the entrepreneur and dreamer.

By contrast, for a scene where Karatz and Tucker talk at night, the entire scene is drenched in a deep blue moonlight richer and more vivid than reality would ever allow. Whereas colour and brightness denote the world that Tucker lives and works in, the administrators and politicos in Chicago inhabit a shadow world that owes something to *The Godfather*.

For phone conversations in *Tucker*, Coppola and Storaro, in a reflection of the devices of *One From the Heart*, use deep focus to unite characters distanced by geography, but very much in one another's hearts and thoughts. When Tucker calls home from Chicago he is in the background, and in the foreground, in sharp focus and profile is Vera. At several points, the camera tracks across two different sets or shows characters on either side of a wall.

Perhaps the darkest scene of the film in terms of the emphasis on shadow is the one where Tucker visits Howard Hughes. Tucker enters Hughes's otherworldly domain and the meeting between the men is lit almost monochromatically. Even Hughes's entrance suggests his unearthliness. He simply drifts into shot as Tucker stands with his back to him, so that one minute Hughes is absent and then suddenly and mysteriously he is present.

Tucker makes it hard to ignore the impact of Norman Rockwell's paintings on the popular conception of American domestic life in the middle years of the twentieth century (see also **Peggy Sue Got Married**).

Coppola's facility for elegantly simple images peppers the film and never more so than in a lovely silhouette shot of the car team working on a problem in the backyard at the family home, their black shapes set against the green of the trees.

SOUND: The film contrasts between the restful silence of the country and the noise of the city factory. The most memorable use of sound to suggest mood is in the scene where Tucker visits Howard Hughes in his hangar: the dissonant, uneasy sounds are quite otherworldly.

COPPOLA TUNES: As with the score for *Rumble Fish*, Coppola turned to a pop musician for the score to *Tucker*. Joe Jackson provided the film's energetic, 40s-sounding score, which is buoyant, jaunty, sultry and jubilant, a fine analogue to the protagonist of the movie.

Tucker: The Man and His Dream by Joe Jackson: 'Captain of Industry' (Overture), 'The Car of Tomorrow – Today', 'No Chance Blues', '(He's A) Shape in a Drape', 'Factory', 'Vera, It Pays to Advertise', 'Tiger Rag', 'Showtime in Chicago', 'Lone Bank Loan Blues', 'Speedway', 'Marilee', 'Hanging in Howard Hughes' Hangar', 'Toast of the Town', 'Abe's Blues', 'The Trial', 'Freedom Swing/Tucker Jingle', 'Rhythm Delivery'.

HUMOUR: Tucker is an upbeat, cocky character, so much of the humour comes from his interplay with the downbeat Karatz.

AWARDS: The 1988 National Society of Film Critics Awards – Dean Stockwell for Best Supporting Actor, while at the 1989 Academy Awards the film secured nominations for Best Supporting Actor (Martin Landau), Best Art Direction/Set Decoration and Best Costume Design. The 1989 Golden Globes – Martin Landau for Best Performance by an Actor in a Supporting Role. 1989 New York Film Critics Circle Awards – Best Supporting Actor (Dean Stockwell). At the 1989 BAFTAs the film won for Best Production Design and the 1989 Casting Society of America awards nominated the film with Best Casting for a Feature Film, Drama (Jane Jenkins and Janet Hirshenson).

COPPOLA MAGIC: Coppola's interest in creating inventive transitions between several scenes is one of the notable special effects of this film. The other, the use of split frames when characters are on the telephone to one another, is a direct refinement of these playful devices from *One From the Heart*. At one point, Tucker's move from one location to another would be physically impossible, and it's a very subtle optical match that makes it happen, Jeff Bridges having been shot in front of a blue screen and then incorporated into the background plate.

MOVIE SPEAK:
Preston Tucker: 'The car of tomorrow, today!'

Eddy: 'Who are we gonna sell it to? Buck Rogers?'

Preston (fixing coffee): 'How'd you like your coffee?' **Abe:** 'In the city.'

Eddy: 'No matter how much he makes, he always manages to spend twice as much.'

Abe: 'Don't get too close to people, you'll catch their dreams.'

Preston: 'It's the idea that counts. The dream.'

HOME VIEWING: The film is available on Region 1 DVD and, alongside the feature, the disc comprises: *Tucker: The Man and the Car* (1948 promo film, with commentary by Coppola), *Under the Hood: Making Tucker* (1988 documentary), commentary by Francis Coppola, widescreen, interactive menus, scene access. The film is unavailable on Region 2 DVD nor is it in print on VHS.

TRIVIA: Coppola had considered Brando for the role of Tucker back in the 1970s.

COPPOLA'S VIEW: For Coppola the film offers the chance to celebrate the maverick as the story pitches Tucker into a David and Goliath scenario. Coppola enjoys the showdown between the little guy and the corporation, with the little guy winning, and in *The Rainmaker* Coppola emphasises this clash again. As with *The Godfather* films, the power and support of family is there through difficult times. The film is the least melancholy of Coppola's entire career. This is a film with a smile on its face which embraces the notion of family as the most significant element in the success of an enterprise.

CRITICAL COPPOLA: *Time Out* commented, 'The cinematic sleight of hand parallels the bombast of its hero, but you never get a glimpse of either visionary.' From the *Washington Post*: 'heartfelt passion seems to have fuelled what could be a needed and satisfying commercial breakthrough for Coppola.' *Sight and Sound* observed that 'Through the soda fountains and cars and massive factories, Coppola suggests an America of almost limitless hope and commercial plenitude . . . psychologically fascinating but deeply disheartening as the latest chapter of Coppola's cinematic career.'

VERDICT: *Tucker: The Man and His Dream* is a highly entertaining film that pulls together the hints of playfulness present in some of Coppola's other films. It is a very warm and optimistic film that retains a sharp focus on the protagonist's dilemma. In a way Preston Tucker is as much a punk rebel as Rusty James and the Motorcycle Boy in *Rumble Fish*. Alongside *Rumble Fish* it is Coppola's most inspiring film in terms of reminding the audience of a positive take on life.

The project also proved Coppola and Lucas's long-standing friendship and it can only be hoped they will collaborate again.

COPPOLA NOW: 'Here's a story about a fellow who's got a better idea and he knows it.'

The Godfather Part III (1990)

(Colour – 161 minutes)

Paramount Pictures
Producer: Francis Ford Coppola for Zoetrope Studios
Executive Producers: Fred Fuchs and Nicholas Gage
Co-Producers: Fred Roos, Gray Frederickson and Charles Mulvehill
Associate Producer: Marina Geffer
Screenplay: Mario Puzo and Francis Ford Coppola
Cinematographer: Gordon Willis
Editor: Barry Malkin, Lisa Fruchtman and Walter Murch
Music: Carmine Coppola
Additional Music and Themes: Nino Rota
Production Design: Dean Tavoularis
Art Direction: Alex Tavoularis
Costume Design: Millen Canonero
Makeup: Dick Smith
Visual Effects: Industrial Light and Magic

CAST: Al Pacino (*Michael Corleone*), Diane Keaton (*Kay Adams*), Talia Shire (*Connie Corleone Rizzi*), Andy Garcia (*Vincent Mancini*), Eli Wallach (*Don Altobello*), Joe Mantegna (*Joey Zasa*), George Hamilton (*BJ Harrison*), Bridget Fonda (*Grace Hamilton*), Sofia Coppola (*Mary Corleone*), Raf Vallone (*Cardinal Lamberto*), Franc D'Ambrosio (*Anthony Corleone*), Donal Donnelly (*Archbishop Gliday*), Richard Bright (*Al Neri*), Helmut Berger (*Frederick Keinszig*), Don Novello (*Dominic Abbandando*), John Savage (*Andrew Hagen*), Franco Citti (*Calo*), Mario Donatone (*Mosca*), Vittorio Duse (*Don Tommasino*), Robert Cicchini (*Lou Pennino*), Rogerio Miranda (*Armand*), Carlos Miranda (*Francesco*), Jeannie Linero (*Lucy Mancini*)

BUDGET: $54 million

THE BOX OFFICE: $66.67 million

RELEASE DATE: 25 December 1990

MPAA: R

BBFC: 15

TAGLINE: Advance poster: Real power cannot be taken, it must be given. Release poster: All the power on earth can't change destiny.

SUMMARY: 1979, New York. Michael Corleone and his family attend a ceremony where he is bestowed with Papal Honours for his charitable contributions. At the party afterwards in his sprawling and expensive New York City home, Michael receives a range of guests in his den. Aging Don Altobello offers Michael his friendship and congratulations. Small-time crook Joey Zasa comes in to see Michael and asks for his help in dealing with one of his 'staff', Vincent Santini – Michael's nephew. Vincent wants to work for Michael, who agrees to employ him. Kay confronts Michael, telling him that their son Anthony does not want to go into the family business. Anthony says that he wants to be an opera singer. Michael is angry at this but eventually relents. Michael is now being advised and supported by his sister Connie. At the party outside the den, Vincent meets Mary, Michael's daughter, and there is an attraction between them.

Michael meets Archbishop Gliday, who informs Michael that a lot of Vatican money has been embezzzled and illegally spent. Michael strikes a deal to invest in, and take control of, the corporation Immobilare, which is owned by the Vatican. Michael presents his business plan to shareholders, who agree to it. The stumbling block is the need for the Pope to ratify the decision.

Back at home in New York, Michael is concerned about the attraction between Mary and Vincent. Mary then confronts her father about the legitimacy of The Corleone Foundation of which she is chairman.

Michael travels to Rome for a meeting regarding the Immobilare deal and its ratification. Because the Pope is ill it is creating delays in the deal being approved.

Back in America, Michael and Vincent fly to Atlantic City for a meeting of the families. Michael announces that it is time to dissolve their business relationship and he distributes cheques for all those who invested in the gambling interests Corleone once controlled. The gathering is then hit by a shower of bullets from above and many of the family bosses are killed. Someone is trying to kill Michael and Vincent protects him. Initially suspecting Joey Zasa, Michael then realises that the enemy is Don Altobello. This causes Michael to collapse with shock and he is hospitalised. If he dies then all the corrupt business between him and the Church will become public.

Michael is angry when, at an Italian festival, Joey Zasa is shot dead by Vincent.

Michael, Vincent and Mary travel to Sicily. Michael seeks the advice of Cardinal Lamberto and even asks the Cardinal to hear his confession. He then devises a plan to get back at Don Altobello.

Kay arrives in Sicily and she and Michael spend time together in an effort to reconcile. Don Tommasino, with whom the Corleones are staying, is then killed by Altobello's assassin. In the Vatican, Cardinal Lamberto is elected as Pope. Vincent informs Michael that Altobello has hired an assassin to kill him. Vincent wants Michael to give him the order to kill Don Altobello. Michael tells him that if he does so then Vincent cannot return to any normal life. Michael divests himself of responsibility as the Godfather and transfers power to Vincent.

The Corleone family attend the opera to watch Anthony's debut. The assassin enters the opera house preparing to kill Michael. In the Vatican, Bishop Gilday is killed. Lucchesi is then killed by Corleone killers and Don Altobello is killed by Connie, courtesy of a poisoned cannoli. The Swiss banker, Frederick Keinszig, hangs himself. The Pope is discovered dead in bed. As the family leave the opera, the assassin strikes, hitting Michael but killing Mary. She dies in Michael's arms.

Some years later, Michael sits alone in a garden in Sicily, old and weary. He dies and falls to the earth.

COPPOLA'S CONCEPT: With *The Godfather Part III*, Coppola evidently took a lot of satisfaction in rounding off the saga and bringing it full circle. In the sixteen years since *The Godfather Part II*, the possibility of a third instalment had been seriously considered and attempts to encourage Coppola to return had been made. For many years, he resisted the idea. Prior to his coming on board the process had been torturous.

As far back as July 1977, Michael Eisner (in his time at Paramount before going to Disney), had drafted a 'story arena' outline offering a general idea of what could be the basis of a story. A writer named Alexander Jacobs was also commissioned for a first draft screenplay for the proposed *The Godfather Part III*. This concept had Michael suffering from cancer and his son Anthony clearing the family name by selling off all illicit gambling interests in Las Vegas. Dramatic tension came in the shape of Tomasso, the son of Sonny Corleone (one of Michael's brothers), who gets the family involved in new conflicts with enemies. Tomasso becomes the Godfather and Anthony makes the family legitimate.

This idea was shelved and, in the summer of 1978, Mario Puzo and Charles Bludhorn (head of Gulf and Western who owned Paramount at the time) collaborated on an idea, but Paramount's Michael Eisner and Jeffrey Katzenberg did not care for it.

In 1979 Dean Riesner drafted a screenplay about the conflict between the Corleones, a rival family and the CIA. Nothing developed on the project until September 1985 when a treatment was submitted by Nicholas Gage which was set in the 1970s with Michael wanting to legalise the family business.

Again, this idea went further in advancing the possibility of a third film and, in 1986, Mario Puzo was asked by Paramount to write a draft screenplay. Puzo's story had Don Vito struggling to maintain inter-Family peace while trying to legitimise the family so that he could retire and let Vincent lead.

A second draft by Puzo soon followed which concentrated more on the present than the 1930s. In the script Tom Hagen dies and Vincent is aggressive about keeping the Family. A third draft by Nicholas Gage then followed in which Anthony discovers that his father lied about his past and, against Michael's wishes, Vincent takes control of the Family. In March 1987, a fourth draft was completed which was not significantly different than the third.

Finally, in the autumn of 1988 Frank Mancuso at Paramount called Francis Coppola to talk about the possibility of *The Godfather Part III*. With Coppola's most recent film *Tucker: The Man and His Dream* something of a commercial failure despite its great charm and entertainment factor, Coppola needed a success – his last hit had been with *Peggy Sue Got Married* in 1986. At this stage in his career Coppola had also spent a fair amount of his money on the development of a still-to-be-made project called *Megalopolis*, which was originally to have been shot at Cinecitta studios. Bankruptcy faced Coppola and American Zoetrope, and money was still owed for 1982's *One From the Heart*. Coppola agreed to return to the Corleone Family and stipulated a range of key story elements that he wanted to include. Coppola wanted to call the film *Mario Puzo's The Death of Michael Corleone*, but the studio vetoed that idea. That title was doubtless considered too downbeat even though it would correctly set up the sense of closure that the film possessed. Puzo's grand dream was for a *Godfather Part IV* to be set in the 1920s when Vito's power really begins to be exercised.

On 6 August 1989, in his office at his Napa Valley home, Francis Coppola drafted out his basic game plan for the structure of what would become *The Godfather Part III*. Coppola's story-map split the film into five acts and he titled his page of notes *The Tragedy of Michael*

Corleone. The notes include the phrases 'unravelling of puzzle', 'catastrophe' and 'Hagen's suicide'.

Coppola, in pursuit of a suitably grand and emotionally true conclusion, agonised about the ending of the film. In his and Puzo's original script Michael dies in a hail of gunfire. It was much later that Coppola changed it so that Mary dies, charging the movie with an unambiguous *King Lear* reference, wherein a ruler loses a daughter.

The film's verisimilitude is found partly in the way it refers to events that did indeed happen, notably the untimely death of John Paul I in the late 1970s, the Vatican Bank scandals and the fact that a Vatican banker did hang himself from London Bridge.

INFLUENCES: *The Godfather Part III* is most obviously influenced and haunted by the two preceding *Godfather* films, both thematically and stylistically. Shakespeare also informs the narrative, in particular with the plays *King Lear* (see **COPPOLA'S CONCEPT**) and *Titus Andronicus* – a revenge-based tragedy set in ancient Rome, an historical reference point all through *The Godfather* trilogy. The play hinges on acts of deceit, betrayal and violence. Titus is a victorious military leader who is offered the imperial mantle but turns it down. Over the course of the intricately plotted play, Titus eventually comes to recognise his enemies and dispenses violent retribution on them all.

The influence of Catholic dogma is also felt throughout the film, making more obvious and potent the allusions to the faith in *The Godfather* and *The Godfather Part II*.

COSTUME: With *The Godfather Part III* the saga enters its most modern era. Certain character traits remain consistent and are expressed through clothing. Michael still wears a cravat, as he did in *The Godfather Part II*, and at the end of *The Godfather Part III* he clearly resembles his father as an old man, so that in that closing moment character and theme fuse, not through dialogue or action, but just through attire.

With Michael as the old man of the story, young blood is manifest in Vincent, son of volatile Sonny Corleone from *The Godfather*. Vince is the flash young man whose more contemporary sensibility is marked, initially, by his leather jacket. As the film progresses his clothing changes, reflecting his willing immersion in the Corleone life. His smart brown suit and slicked-back hair recall memories of dapper young Michael and young Vito Corleone.

In *The Godfather Part III* it is the costumes for Connie that are the most memorable, for their severe and impenetrable design. As she becomes more powerful and threatening they resemble armour. She has come a long way from where she began in *The Godfather*, as the sweet-natured bride dancing in the sun. At the end of *The Godfather Part III* she lingers in the shadows of the opera house.

TEAM COPPOLA: In a sense, by directing *The Godfather Part III*, Coppola came full circle. The original *Godfather* had been the genesis of many of his long-standing collaborations and, in film history terms, the trilogy is one of the finest, in part due to the consistency of its returning talent. Gordon Willis returned as cinematographer and Dean and Alex Tavoularis oversaw production design and art direction, as they had done on the first and second instalments of the series. Coppola's regular editor Barry Malkin returned and the great Walter Murch, who had collaborated so creatively on *The Conversation*, *The Godfather Part II* and *Apocalypse Now*, also co-edited the movie. Coppola's regular production associates Gray Frederickson, Fred Roos and Fred Fuchs also signed up to produce the film.

CASTING: *The Godfather* trilogy is notable not just for the returning talent behind the camera, but also for its acting roster. Al Pacino, who returned to films refreshed in 1989 with *Sea of Love* (after a five-year time-out period), reappeared as the aging Michael. Talia Shire returned as Connie and Diane Keaton reprised her role as Kay. New faces Andy Garcia and Bridget Fonda also starred. Coppola had offered Frank Sinatra the role of Don Altobello but he pulled out when he realised he would be needed for two months on location. Coppola also wanted Gene Hackman as a wire tapper, something of an in-joke reference to *The Conversation*, though this might not have worked within the serious world of the *Godfather* films; Hackman, however, was busy. Eddie Murphy had also been considered by Coppola for a cameo. The significant absence from the film was Robert Duvall (as Tom Hagen), who had wanted a higher fee for appearing in the film. Coppola wrote to his long-time colleague, who had been in one of his earliest films *The Rain People* as well as *Apocalypse Now*, saying he hoped they would work together again.

For the role of Mary, many actresses were considered, including Uma Thurman, Diane Lane (a Coppola veteran), Mary Stuart Masterson, Madeline Stowe, Jennifer Grey, Molly Ringwald and Julia Roberts. Coppola settled on Winona Ryder. Ryder then pulled out very close to the start of production as she was suffering from exhaustion. Coppola cast his daughter Sofia, who, contrary to general comment, does *not* put in a terrible performance. In a film that is charged with big-time Hollywood performances, there is something very natural about her contribution.

For Vincent, Coppola had considered Alec Baldwin, Matt Dillon, Sean Penn, Nicolas Cage and Val Kilmer. He settled on Andy Garcia, who had co-starred in *Black Rain* (Ridley Scott, 1989), putting in a performance of charm and intensity that was the highlight of the film.

I KNOW THAT FACE: Andy Garcia has been in *The Untouchables* (Brian De Palma, 1987), *When A Man Loves A Woman* (Luis Mandoki, 1994) and *Ocean's Eleven* (Steven Soderbergh, 2001). In April 2003, Garcia talked with the Canadian press about returning for a potential *The Godfather Part IV*.

Sofia Coppola was the baby being baptised in *The Godfather* and has gone on to direct the accomplished *The Virgin Suicides* (1999). Eli Wallach has appeared in *Baby Doll* (Elia Kazan, 1956), *The Magnificent Seven* (John Sturges, 1960), *The Misfits* (John Huston, 1961) and *The Good, The Bad and The Ugly* (Sergio Leone, 1966). Joe Mantegna has appeared in *House of Cards* (David Mamet, 1987).

THE FILMING: Filming began on 27 November 1989 and finished in May 1990. The shoot lasted 125 days and went to New York, Atlantic City, Cinecitta Studios, and Palermo for the opera house sequence. The production ran smoothly. Coppola had to film twenty-three minutes of the Verdi opera *Cavalleria Rusticana*. During the shoot, Coppola commented to an interviewer that 'Every time you make a movie it's always interesting how it seems like the movie is about you, you know?'

Early in the *Godfather Part III* shoot, Coppola mentioned the possibility of a *Godfather IV* which would focus on Vincent with flashbacks to Don Vito in the 1940s and 1950s, but regretted that mention.

In a series of diary entries at the time, Eleanor Coppola charted the emotional highs and lows of the production, notably the pressure on Sofia Coppola to play a major role in the film at short notice. She writes about Gordon Willis's precision in lighting the film's opening party scene and how he would position each extra so precisely for his lighting design to work. Eleanor Coppola also notes how the Villa Malfitano (Don Tommasino's hideaway for the Corleones in Sicily) was refurbished for the shoot. The side and back walls of the garden room were painted with windows and views of tropical foliage that matched real windows and real views.

PROMOTION: When *The Godfather Part III* was released, sixteen years had elapsed since the previous instalment and the release generated a lot of hype. A teaser poster for the film showed Michael sitting in a chair, the backdrop a burnished window and floor, looking directly at us, though we cannot see his eyes as he is wearing his shades. The tagline on this poster stated that 'Real power cannot be taken, it must be given.' A release poster for the film remained consistent with the previous films, featuring one person, in this case Michael with sad eyes, and hands raised together in prayer.

An early screening of the rough-cut of the film at Paramount made Coppola anxious, as the response from the studio was not ecstatic. A short time later, the film was test-screened in San Francisco to a much better reception.

THE OPENING: The film begins by dovetailing neatly with the end of *The Godfather Part II*, just as the beginning of *The Godfather Part II* dovetailed neatly and arrestingly with the end of the original *Godfather*.

Images of the windswept, run-down, abandoned Corleone home at Lake Tahoe dissolve across one another, the camera tracking slowly across debris in the water. This is a fallen kingdom in need of clearance or resurrection just as in *Rumble Fish* the world of The Motorcycle Boy has fallen in his absence and is ultimately cleared away. Under dark skies there is a shot, in silhouette, of a statue of the Virgin Mary. *The Godfather* music plays over the images, emphasising an era that has gone. Michael's gruff, elderly voice is heard inviting his children to his Papal Honours ceremony, and the images dissolve to photographs on his desk of his family as he handwrites his invitation. Originally, the film was to have begun where Gliday tells Michael that the Vatican is in big financial trouble – a scene that would echo the very first scene of *The Godfather*. Gliday's confession even included a reference to Dante. However, the scene was cut and placed later in the film, after the Papal Honour investiture and family gathering, where all of the film's dramatic strands are laid down.

HEROES AND VILLAINS: Michael Corleone is attempting to pull out of the corrupt world he has lived in for thirty years, and throughout *The Godfather Part III* he is torn between evil and redemption. Michael is an exhausted, worn man at the beginning of the film and weakens as it proceeds. The final image of him dying in a Sicilian garden recalls Vito's death at the end of *The Godfather*. By falling to the earth, the metaphor of going back to the ground is captured and makes his corruption and angst-ridden life seem even more futile and meaningless.

Michael's cropped hair retains its severity but he is more prone to a smile and joke. The burden of his shadowy life culminates in his meeting with Cardinal Lamberto to whom he confesses thirty years of sin. Michael claims that 'I'm beyond redemption' and asks what use confession is if he does not repent. Michael is as guilty as Harry Caul in *The Conversation* and, corrupted by life, he pays the ultimate price when his daughter is murdered at the end of the film. Michael's growing sadness throughout the trilogy reaches its apogee in *The Godfather Part III*. He is a truly tragic figure, who began *The Godfather* trilogy with no connection with his family's business, only allowing himself to become involved when his sense of family loyalty overwhelmed reason.

Michael's fall is emphasised in the flashbacks at the close of the film, where he is shown dancing with Apollonia, the woman he married during his hideaway time in Sicily in *The Godfather*, and then with Kay at the party for their son's first Holy Communion. These moments of beauty and happiness have been suffocated by Michael's grasping for power and in the end rendered meaningless. At the start of the film Michael writes, 'The only wealth in the world is children.' An especially powerful moment is when Michael's son Anthony sings an old Sicilian song to him. The camera pushes in slowly on Michael, his eyes behind sunglasses, his head bowed, his sadness and worry etched right across him. He dries his eyes. When Michael realises that Don Altobello is his enemy he collapses and thrashes and rages like a beast. Michael's animalistic reaction emphasises the great shock of his realisation.

Michael's immense, crushing sense of failure and guilt builds throughout the film. As he sits next to the body of Don Tommasino lying in a coffin, Michael makes a confession of sorts saying, 'I wanted to do good. What betrayed me? My mind? My heart?'

The theme of history repeating itself, for the worst, is played out in *The Godfather Part III* through the character of Vincent. Just as hot-headed as his father Sonny (see **The Godfather**), Vincent is driven by revenge and assumes the position of Godfather by the film's end.

Consistent with *The Godfather* and *The Godfather Part II* , this third instalment dramatises the way in which history repeats itself, so that Michael's son, Anthony, recalls young Michael in his desire to have no part in the violence and corruption of the family business.

The most alarming fall into evil is that taken by Connie. In the first two *Godfather* films she was a bright-eyed young woman. As *The Godfather Part III* begins she is a more sinister presence, committed to supporting Michael in maintaining the Corleone name. Her black dresses, often covering even her neck, have a real severity to them and her gaunt face lends her the quality of a witch. Midway through the story she begins pulling some of the strings.

Michael's ex-wife Kay remains very much as she has always been in the story, an outsider wrestling with the family's bloody heritage, but she returns far stronger than in the previous instalments, fully aware of the corruption that engulfs the Corleone family.

Only Michael's daughter Mary seems innocent, but she too is tainted by corruption and ultimately becomes the sacrificial lamb so that the sins of the father are visited not on the son but on the daughter.

In the world of *The Godfather* films it is often the unassuming and frail who wield the most lethal power. As such Don Altobello is akin to Hyman Roth in *The Godfather Part II*, an old, frail, seemingly harmless man with more power than anybody else.

The biggest character loss in this final chapter is that of Tom Hagen who has died before the story commences. Hagen has been replaced by a less terse and invisible consigliere named George Hamilton, a slick and smart-talking adviser who, like Tom, is often framed on Michael's shoulder rather like a guardian angel.

The corrupt bureaucrats and Vatican members round out the matrix of evil, their potential for greed all the more culpable for the guise in which it is presented.

COPPOLA STYLE: *The Godfather Part III* concludes the great trilogy with consistency. The trilogy's emphasis on muted colours and shadow remains, and there is an overripe, burnished quality to many of the film's sequences, suggesting a world that can only crumble.

Michael is often framed in half light, expressing his moral dilemma: whether or not to move out of the illegitimate business world. The elegantly constructed multi-strand narrative is clearly established in the film's opening twenty mintues, where all the major players meet with Michael in his den. Unsurprisingly, the operatic shedding of blood that closed *The Godfather Part I* and *The Godfather Part II* is in place again here, this time literally tied to an opera. The film revels in the grandeur of its Rome locations, which plug the film into its associations with stories of the fall of the Roman Empire, where power was a corrupting influence. These stories have evidently influenced Coppola in his conceptual work on his project *Megalopolis*.

The Godfather Part III enjoys flip-flopping back and forth between the modern world of America, the ancient world of Rome and the quiet pastoral world of Sicily, each location informing the visual palette of the film. The tragic death of Mary Corleone is the perfect conclusion, and the location of her death enhances the trilogy's connection with classical dramas and intrigues of the ancient world.

IMAGE: *The Godfather Part III* stays true to the visual scheme of the previous instalments. Silhouettes and tableau arrangements remain a staple element of the visual design, for example when Michael and Connie talk on a balcony in Sicily. The camera holds on a wide shot of the two of them in silhouette against the bright sunlight.

The Catholic iconography that works its way throughout the trilogy is very much in evidence in *The Godfather Part III*. Examples are the crucifix on stage in the opera, Mary's name, the silhouette of the dead bishop falling to his doom and the body of the hanged Swiss banker, which recalls the notion of betrayal.

For the key scene where Michael confesses to the violence of his past, it is in the genteel surroundings of a garden. With Michael on the right of frame and Cardinal Lamberto on the left, and with a wall between them, it is very much as though Michael is in a confessional box.

In a way that recalls a tension-building flourish found in some of Steven Spielberg's films, such as *Jurassic Park* (1993), there is an image that presages the mass murder of family heads in Atlantic City – a highlight of the film. As an unseen helicopter swoops in for the kill the effect of its propeller turning causes an immense, food-covered dinner table to shake as though in an earthquake.

When Don Tommasino is killed by the assassin, the action is shown in a wide shot that distances the viewer from the action as though they are witnessing it almost secretly. This same device is used for the killing of young Vito's mother at the start of *The Godfather Part II*. These visual rhymes and symmetry are what organise and unify the story so magnificently.

Coppola's knack for building tension by emphasising a detail is as sure as ever. In the build-up to the death of Joey Zasa the camera returns to the stirrup and boot of a New York policeman on horseback.

For the climax of the film, Coppola intercuts between the opera staging of *Cavalleria Rusticana* (see **THE FILMING**), the assassin preparing to kill Michael and the deaths of the Corleone's enemies in the Vatican and elsewhere.

SOUND: The film shifts from the echoes of Vatican halls to the quiet of Sicily. The most prominent manipulation of sound is saved for the climax of the film. As Mary lies in Michael's arms (Pieta-like), the soundtrack goes mute as we watch Michael screaming. Finally his screaming explodes with startling power and, for all the wrong he has committed, one can only feel pity.

The crackle of gunfire is never accompanied by music, enhancing the believability of the moment. In the Atlantic City killing scene we hear the table rattle and the building rumble as the killing begins.

The sound of thunder pre-empts Michael's realisation of who the family's real enemy is.

COPPOLA TUNES: *The Godfather Part III* has the most music underscoring it of the trilogy. Carmine Coppola provides the music, building on Nino Rota's legendary theme music, which is played as a motif throughout the film. The film is also heavily scored throughout. For the multi-narrative climax of the film, Coppola scores it with music from *Cavalleria Rusticana* (see **THE FILMING**) and, for the death of Mary and the subsequent closing images, the opera music is used. The same piece underscored the opening image of *Raging Bull* (Martin Scorsese, 1980). It ties the movie to its cultural roots in Italian melodrama, which was referred to in *The Godfather Part II*. In *The Godfather Part III*, Michael comments on the operatic nature of Sicily. When Michael arrives in Rome this is accompanied on the soundtrack by a 'Gloria' investing the moment with a sense both of history and of the collision between a religious institution and crime. The hymn is intense.

Composed by Nino Rota, conducted by Carmine Coppola: 'Main Title', 'The Godfather Waltz', 'Marcia Religioso', 'Michael's Letter', 'Medley: The Immigrant/Love Theme from *The Godfather Part III*', 'The Godfather Waltz', 'To Each His Own', 'Vincent's Theme', 'Altobello', 'The Godfather Intermezzo', 'Sicilian Medley: Va Pensiero/Danza Tarantella/Mazurka' (Alla Sicilia), 'Promise Me You'll Remember' (Love Theme from *The Godfather Part III*), 'Preludio and Siciliana', 'A Casa Amiche', 'Pregliena', Finale, Coda: 'The Godfather Finale.'

HUMOUR: The film has more humour than the previous two *Godfather* films and much of it derives from Michael in his self-mocking, lighter-hearted middle age.

AWARDS: At the 1991 Academy Awards the film was nominated for Best Supporting Actor (Andy Garcia), Best Art Direction/Set Decoration, Best Cinematography, Best Director, Best Film Editing and Best Music (Song). At the 1991 American Society of Cinematographers awards Gordon Willis was nominated for Outstanding Achievement in Cinematography. The 1991 Directors Guild of America nominated Coppola for Directorial Achievement in Motion Pictures and at the 1991 Golden Globes the film was nominated for Best Director, Best Motion Picture Drama, Best Original Score, Best Original Song, Best Actor, Best Supporting Actor and Best Screenplay.

COPPOLA MAGIC: Coppola's great facility with intercutting across scenes for the climax of the film rounds the saga off powerfully and consistently with what has come before. The parallel of the action on stage at the opera with the broader story arc of the film is a smart stroke that expands on young Vito's visit to the theatre in *The Godfather Part II*.

The fast editing and chaos of the attack on Atlantic City has a real force and ugliness to it.

MOVIE SPEAK:
Michael: 'Times do change, don't they?'

Bishop Gliday (to Michael): 'The power to absolve debt is greater than the power of forgiveness.'

Michael (to his daughter Mary): 'I would burn in hell to keep you safe.'

Michael (to Vincent): 'Never hate your enemies, it affects your judgement.'

Michael: 'I command this family. Right or wrong.'

Lucchesi: 'Politics is knowing when to pull the trigger.'

Michael: 'The higher I go, the crookeder it becomes.'

HOME VIEWING: Both Region 1 and Region 2 DVD editions are the same: a stunningly comprehensive package as follows: Director's Commentary on all films, documentaries: *Francis Coppola's Notebook, On Location, The Godfather Family, Behind the Scenes 1971, The Cinematography of The Godfather, Coppola and Puzo on Screenwriting*, two featurettes on music, additional scenes, storyboards for *Part II* and *Part III*, character, cast and crew biographies, Academy Award acceptance speeches, photo galleries, theatrical trailers, widescreen 1.85:1. Individual VHS copies of each film are available and *The Godfather* trilogy boxed set presents the saga's events in chronological order as opposed to the format of the films when released theatrically.

TRIVIA: Martin Scorsese's mother is the old woman who talks to Vincent on the street and in the bar.
The killing of Lucchesi at the end of the film was initially very bloody and, subsequently, the film was certified with the NC17 rating in America, which is regarded as box office poison. Coppola therefore reduced the blood quotient so the film would get its R rating.

COPPOLA'S VIEW: The tragic implications of *The Godfather Parts I* and *II* reach their culmination in *The Godfather Part III*, completing a moral story that stays true to the maxim that you reap what you sow. The mournful sense of time passing and the world changing, that is so much a part of Coppola's finest work, runs right through *The Godfather Part III* to the point where the corrupt gangster intrigues are less important and intriguing than Michael Corleone's personal, emotional and spiritual dilemma. Again, the language in much of the film is operatic and biblical-sounding as the drama plays out its themes of revenge, betrayal, fear, horror and regret. It is in the theme of regret and the unity of the family that the trilogy holds its strongest appeal to audiences. Michael's business advice to Vincent also has an appeal in that it is so shrewdly thought out. The chilling precision of Michael's little life lessons is made all the more compelling because of the low-key way he expresses it. Just as his father used to.

Redemption is at the heart of *The Godfather Part III*, taking the spiritual element that runs through the first two instalments and amplifying it. In Coppola's *Bram Stoker's Dracula*, his protagonist seeks redemption over hundreds of years to atone for his fall from grace.

The power of power and its corollary, corruption, plays out in *The Godfather Part III* but, for all his power and smart thinking, Michael Corleone is still just a man whose greed and evil has led him to die alone.

CRITICAL COPPOLA: *Empire* said that 'Fans of the first two instalments are likely to find *The Godfather Part III* an unworthy heir to the tradition.' Pauline Kael noted that 'Coppola doesn't transform the sensationalist material; he just presents it, with an aura of solemnity . . . It's about a battered movie maker's king size depression.' However, a BBCi online review said, 'sympathetic filmgoers may find something of merit in Al Pacino's portrayal of a grey-haired, rueful Michael Corleone' and Peter Travers in *Rolling Stone* added 'It's still *The Godfather* and some of it's deeply affecting.'

VERDICT: Despite the reviews, *The Godfather Part III is* a worthy successor to *Parts I* and *II*. It is a softer film dealing with an attempt to shift from dark back into the light. At the time of its release, the excitement and anticipation could only lead to some sense of disappointment. When viewed as the culmination of the trilogy the film is very satisfying, elaborating further on the theme of guilt where the second film took revenge as its driving force.

The trilogy is a touchstone of popular American cinema and it has a personal core.

The classical and Catholic allusions fold back not only into the first two chapters but also tie the film to other Coppola movies. Its commitment to a story about codes of conduct link it to the professional concerns of Harry Caul in *The Conversation* and the men of The Old Guard in *Gardens of Stone*.

Its huge, all-encompassing melancholy is also worth noting in such a piece of American pop culture.

The Godfather series has cast an immense light and shadow over Coppola's body of work. Its success in two parts in the early 1970s gave him the freedom to make *The Conversation*, *Apocalypse Now* and *One From the Heart*. Conversely, it has put public perception of him in a straightjacket as to some extent he is seen as *The Godfather* guy. Subsequently many of his other, smaller films are overlooked.

COPPOLA NOW: 'This is the cathedral of the Godfather movies.'
'I absolutely had no idea how to do a *Godfather III* . . . The movie didn't and couldn't give to the audience what it loved about *The Godfather*, which was this cold, calculating Michael Corleone.'

Bram Stoker's Dracula (1992)

(Colour – 123 minutes)

Columbia Pictures Presents An American Zoetrope/Osiris Films Production
Producer: Francis Ford Coppola, Fred Fuchs and Charles Mulvehill
Executive Producers: Michael Apted and Robert O'Connor
Screenplay: James V Hart
Cinematographer: Michael Ballhaus
Editor: Nicholas C Smith, Glenn Scattlebury with Anne Goursand
Music: Wojciech Kilar
Production Designer: Thomas Sanders
Set Dresser: Garret Lewis
Costume Design: Eiko Ishioka
Makeup: Greg Cannom
Visual Effects: Roman Coppola and Michael Lantieri

CAST: Gary Oldman (*Dracula*), Winona Ryder (*Mina Harker*), Anthony Hopkins (*Abraham Van Helsing*), Keanu Reeves (*Jonathan Harker*), Sadie Frost (*Lucy Westenra*), Richard E Grant (*Dr Jack Seward*), Cary Elwes (*Arthur Holmwood*), Bill Campbell (*Quincey Morris*), Tom Waits (*Renfield*), Monica Bellucci (*Dracula's Bride*), Michaela Bercu (*Dracula's Bride*), Florina Kendrick (*Dracula's Bride*)

BUDGET: $40 million

THE BOX OFFICE: The film grossed around $85 million in North America and worldwide around $190 million. The commercial success of the film helped revive the fortunes of American Zoetrope, Coppola's company.

RELEASE DATE: 13 November 1992 (USA)

MPAA: R

BBFC: 18

TAGLINE: Love Never Dies.

SUMMARY: It is the year 1462 and the Turkish city of Constantinople has fallen as Christian armies fight the Muslim Turks. Count Dracula kisses his love Elizabeta goodbye and heads into battle for Christendom. The battlefield seethes with the silhouetted figures of the clashing armies and Dracula fights with animal ferocity. The voice-over (courtesy of Van Helsing) explains that the Turks informed Elizabeta that the Count has been killed in battle. She throws herself from the castle walls and dies. Dracula returns victoriously to his fortress and learns of Elizabeta's suicide. He is driven to rage and goes berserk in the castle chapel, vowing that 'I shall arise from my own death.' He drives his sword into a stone crucifix and renounces his faith in God.

London, 1897. At Carfax Lunatic Asylum, an inmate, Dr Renfield, speaks mysteriously and prophetically of the coming of the Master for whose arrival everything is prepared. Across London, young solicitor's clerk Jonathan Harker is informed that because of Renfield's condition (he had been to Castle Dracula to deal with the Count's business and returned a changed man) someone else must go in his place to Transylvania to deal with the various property concerns that Count Dracula has in England. Harker is happy to take the trip. He goes to Hillingham, a country house, to tell his fiancée Mina that he is going to be away for a short time. Deeply in love, the young couple say goodbye and Harker makes the journey to see Dracula. Standing in the mist and doom-filled darkness of the Transylvanian forest Harker watches an elaborate carriage approach to take him to Castle Dracula.

At the castle, Harker enters and is greeted by the Count who is a frail, deathly-looking man. Dracula and Harker begin discussing the Count's business and property interests in London. Dracula wants Harker to stay for a week and, though clearly uneasy about this, Harker is unable to decline.

Back in England, a party is under way at Hillingham. The principal guests arrive: the Texan Quincey P Morris, Dr Jack Seward and finally

Lord Arthur Holmwood. At the party, Dracula's phantom presence is made clear. He is able to traverse time and space. The Count sights Mina at the party – she looks just like the Count's lost love Elizabeta.

At the castle in Transylvania, Harker is confronted by Dracula who expresses his disillusionment with the Church. The Count leaves Harker alone. Harker explores the shadows and is seduced by the three brides of Dracula. The Count has a new victim. Deep inside the castle, the Count's gypsy servants fill boxes with earth to take to Carfax Abbey. There then follows a set-piece sequence which contracts time and events as the ship that Dracula has chartered sails stormy seas to England with Dracula aboard.

Mina receives a letter at Hillingham from Jonathan Harker explaining he will not return to London for a month. In contrast to this sad news, Lucy announces she is going to marry Arthur Holmwood. A storm rises and Lucy and Mina run through the rain and the garden maze. At London Zoo the animals are whipped into a frenzy as though sensing impending terror. At the asylum, Renfield announces Dracula's imminent arrival. Dracula arrives at Hillingham in the form of a wolfman. He attacks Lucy as Mina looks on in horror.

At Purfleet, the boxes from the castle are delivered and Dracula erupts from one of them in the form of a young man; essentially a more groomed version of the man in the film's prologue. The dashing Prince Vlad tours the streets of London where he meets Mina and begins his quest to seduce her.

Back at Hillingham, Dr Seward goes to see Lucy, whose senses have been heightened since the attack. Seward decides to contact his old mentor, Abraham Van Helsing. In London, Dracula tells Mina that he has been searching for her for many years. Mina is made anxious by the Count's passionate intensity, having pledged herself to Jonathan. Gradually, she is seduced by the Count.

In a distant lecture hall, Van Helsing's presentation about blood disease is cut short by Seward's telegram. Van Helsing goes to Hillingham and, after Dracula attacks Lucy again, he explains to Seward, Holmwood and Morris that they are up against some kind of monster. Unlike the young men, Van Helsing seems strangely thrilled by the situation. Mina goes to dinner with the Count and their bond strengthens.

In Transylvania, Harker escapes the castle, weakened and terrified, having been left at the mercy of the brides. Harker manages to reach the river, where he washes. It is near a remote convent and he is taken in by the sisters.

At Hillingham, Lucy has become increasingly vampiric in the wake of Dracula's attacks. The Count reads a letter from Mina explaining that she must go to Jonathan. In his fury, the Count conjures a storm. In a second set piece, Dracula goes to Hillingham, and in Romania Jonathan and Mina are married in the convent before returning to London. Dracula savages Lucy in his guise as a wolf and she dies. Some days later, Van Helsing, Seward, Holmwood and Morris go to Lucy's sepulchre and open it. Van Helsing's plan is to kill Lucy properly (as she is the Undead) and start bringing an end to Dracula's reign of deathly terror. Lucy is not in her tomb. She then enters the chamber in her vampire form and the men drive a stake through her chest and then behead her. On Jonathan's advice the men go to Carfax Abbey where Dracula is in hiding.

The Count's obsession with Mina continues and he seduces her again in a passionate and sensual meeting. Dracula bites Mina and begins her vampire transformation. The men arrive to rescue Mina and destroy Dracula, but it is, apparently, too late. They are confronted by Dracula in his grotesque bat manifestation. Van Helsing's attempts to kill Dracula fail and the Count flees. The race is on. The Count is going to return to Transylvania while Mina is left slowly dying in London.

A plan is made that involves separating Mina and Van Helsing from the other men. Dracula is returning to his fortress by boat; the men will travel there by train. Mina is to be used as a decoy. Van Helsing and Mina arrive at the walls of the castle ahead of the others and await Dracula's arrival. Mina attempts to seduce Van Helsing and the brides of Dracula close in on them. Van Helsing protects himself and Mina from the brides and at sunrise he enters the castle and beheads them.

En route to the castle a furious chase ensues with the men on horseback pursuing Dracula's gypsy wagon as it transports him from his boat across land to the castle. In the castle grounds, the men fight the gypsies. Quincey is injured and Dracula is stabbed and severely weakened. Van Helsing instructs everybody to back off. Only Mina can complete the mission. She goes with Dracula into the chapel. She kisses him and then finally beheads him. Sunshine fills the chapel and the Count is at peace.

COPPOLA'S CONCEPT: Given Coppola's theatrical and literary sensibilities, his adaptation of Bram Stoker's 1897 novel was to be one of the more faithful of the many already produced, most of which deviated from the narrative, using the concept and image of Dracula the vampire as a springboard for a wide range of movies.

Coppola wanted to stay true to the range of characters, locations and narrative thrust found in the source novel. To some degree, Coppola came full circle with *Bram Stoker's Dracula*. As a young, emerging hotshot director in the late 1960s he had directed the horror movie *Dementia 13* (1963) in Ireland for Roger Corman, king of the low-budget exploitation movie. The commercial success of *Bram Stoker's Dracula* led to Coppola serving as executive producer on *Mary Shelley's Frankenstein* (Kenneth Branagh, 1994) and *Sleepy Hollow* (Tim Burton, 1999). There was also talk of a series of Gothic horror stories for television, though that plan did not reach fruition.

In realising Stoker's novel for the cinema, Coppola saw an opportunity to create a florid and wilfully artificial movie. He acknowledged that, in his opinion, the best Dracula movie had been WF Murnau's *Nosferatu* (1922), starring Max Shreck, the actor whose namesake is the villain portrayed by Christopher Walken in *Batman Returns* (Tim Burton, 1992).

One of the key elements of Dracula that Coppola wanted to emphasise was the segment where Harker arrives at Dracula's castle and explores its terrifying places. Coppola relishes building the creep factor through an accumulation of detail for these scenes, notably a shot of rats defying gravity as they cross a supporting beam, and those moments when Dracula crosses a room without having to walk anywhere. For Coppola, this segment of the Dracula story had been a highlight of the Bela Lugosi *Dracula* film (Tod Browning, 1931), and it certainly makes one of the most enjoyable segments of Coppola's take on the story. The sequence hits its creepy high when Harker watches Dracula crawl across an exterior wall of the castle, rather like a nineteenth-century Spiderman.

To bolster the drama and fantasy element of the story Coppola emphasised Dracula's link to history. There had been a Prince Vlad the Impaler in the fifteenth century who campaigned against the Turks. Vlad's bloodlust was legendary and fuelled the legend that became the Count Dracula figure and narrative. This rich and lurid historical strain caught the attention of the man whose enthusiasm for the subject was the true first step in the creation of the film.

In 1977, aspiring Texan screenwriter Jim V Hart began work on an adaptation of Bram Stoker's *Dracula* novel. Hart began by tracking down a Dracula specialist named Leonard Wolf who, at the time, was Head of the English Department at San Francisco State University. Wolf was born in Transylvania. Hart got to work on his screenplay and it received a lot of rejection in Hollywood through the 1980s. In 1990, Peter O'Connor and Michael Apted committed to developing the project. For Hart, the novel had a 'wet' and 'feverish' quality which Coppola's film often expresses strongly and memorably. Hart's dream director for the film was David Lean. Instead, he got the director who, for many writers about film, and film makers themselves, stands as the greatest American director of the last thirty years, if the *Sight and Sound* poll of 2002 is anything to go by.

In March 1991, Coppola met Jim Hart to begin developing the script further. Of Hart's screenplay for the film, Coppola said at the time of the film's release, 'When I read Jim's script, I thought he had made a brilliant innovation by using (that) history of Prince Vlad to set the frame for the whole story . . . Also, I felt immediately that he had written it as a story of passion and eroticism.'

In a journal entry dated 9 August 1991, prior to the filming of *Bram Stoker's Dracula*, Coppola wrote, 'Above all it is a love story between Dracula and Mina – souls reaching out through a universe of horror and pathos . . . Blood is also the symbol of human passion.' Interestingly, at the time of Coppola's work on the screenplay for the film, he was also developing a film called *The Cure*, about the search for a cure for AIDS. A bloodline of social commentary runs right through *Bram Stoker's Dracula* and forms a powerful real-world subtext amid the fantasy of the scenario. It dramatises the unease that can surface around a fear of blood contamination and this underpins the film's sensual and melodramatic qualities with a real-world analogue in the fight against AIDS.

Another of Coppola's ambitions with this version of *Dracula* was to give the adaptation a sense of the 'old world' in which the story is set. The film luxuriates in layering the images and certain sequences with letters, diary entries and voice-overs. Throughout his career, Coppola has been compared to Welles, partly perhaps for the brilliance of his early career (though to ignore the later work is wrong) and partly for the scale of his storytelling. With *Bram Stoker's Dracula*, Coppola also shows a debt to DW Griffith and Carl Theodore Dreyer, whose films included *Intolerance* (1916) and *Vampyr* (1932) respectively.

INFLUENCES: Coppola, looking to historical fact, developed the film's powerful love story element. Clearly, Akira Kurosawa's battle scenes inspired him, especially the highly theatrical battle scenes from Kurosawa's *Kagemusha* (1980) on which Coppola and George Lucas were executive producers.

Other films that inspired Coppola were *Ivan the Terrible* (Sergei Eisenstein, 1942) and *Citizen Kane* (Orson Welles, 1941). Certain films produced by British film-making great Michael Powell, in collaboration with Emeric Pressburger, seem also to have influenced Coppola's thinking, especially their film *The Red Shoes* (1948).

COSTUME: Six stunningly flamboyant and detailed costumes were designed and created for the character of Dracula. The Dracula crest was a combination of a wolf, a dragon, snakes and birds. Although the name Dracula has become synonymous with the word 'vampire', the original meaning of Dracul is dragon.

For Coppola, the costumes were more important than the set design. His modus operandi was 'Let's dress these young actors in beautiful, exotic, erotic costumes that have so much of the emotion right in the fabric.'

TEAM COPPOLA: With many directors, a core team of key collaborators develops around them over the years. Subsequently, a creative shorthand comes into play, allowing directors to efficiently and coherently communicate their vision to the various film-making departments. For example, John Ford had his collaborators in producer CV Whitney and cinematographer Winston Koch, and his actors John Wayne and Victor Maclaglen; Scorsese has Thelma Schoonmaker as editor and Michael Ballhaus as cinematographer; Spielberg has Michael Kahn as editor, John Williams as composer and Janusz Kaminski as cinematographer. These long-standing teams develop an understanding about the director's sense of what cinema means to them and how the form can best be used to tell a particular story. Of course, the impact of these collaborative teams somewhat throws into question the concept of the auteur theory where the director is essentially the creator of a film.

For Coppola, on *Bram Stoker's Dracula*, the old and the new fused together. The costume design was handled by noted film and theatre designer Eiko Ishioka, who has designed costumes for the film *Mishima* (Paul Schrader, 1985) which Coppola and Lucas put their names to in order to secure backing for the project. Ishioka has also designed costumes for the stage play *M. Butterfly* and the Philip Glass opera *The Making of the Representative for Planet 8*. Her collaboration with Coppola began in 1979 when she designed the poster for the Japanese release of *Apocalypse Now*.

Michael Ballhaus began as a cinematographer in Germany working with one of New German Cinema's major directors, Rainer Werner Fassbinder, on such films as *The Marriage of Maria Braun* (1979). Ballhaus's credits also include *The Last Temptation of Christ* (Martin Scorsese, 1988), *The Fabulous Baker Boys* (Steve Kloves, 1989), *GoodFellas* (Martin Scorsese, 1990), *The Age of Innocence* (Martin Scorsese, 1993), *Air Force One* (Wolfgang Petersen, 1997), *The Legend of Bagger Vance* (Robert Redford, 2000) and *The Gangs of New York* (Martin Scorsese, 2002).

Screenwriter Jim V Hart has written the screenplay for *Hook* (Steven Spielberg, 1991). Since *Hook* and *Bram Stoker's Dracula*, Hart has been a producer on *Mary Shelley's Frankenstein* (Kenneth Branagh, 1994) on which Coppola was executive producer. Hart has also co-written the screenplays for *Contact* (Robert Zemeckis, 1997) and *Tuck Everlasting* (Jay Russell, 2002).

For production designer, Thomas Sanders, *Bram Stoker's Dracula* was a breakthrough. He has gone on to work in the same capacity on

Braveheart (Mel Gibson, 1995), *Saving Private Ryan* (Steven Spielberg, 1998), *Mission: Impossible 2* (John Woo, 2000) and *We Were Soldiers* (Randall Wallace, 2002).

Michael Lantieri, who handled the film's physical effects, has worked in special effects since the early 1980s when fantasy movies became a staple of Hollywood production. Lantieri's responsibility on *Bram Stoker's Dracula*, as on most films in which he is involved, was to oversee the realisation of practical effects achieved live on the set. Lantieri's credits include *Heartbeeps* (Allan Arkush, 1981), *The Last Starfighter* (Nick Castle, 1984), *Back to the Future Part II* (Robert Zemeckis, 1989), *Back to the Future Part III* (Robert Zemeckis, 1990), *Death Becomes Her* (Robert Zemeckis, 1992), *Jurassic Park* (Steven Spielberg, 1993), *The Flintstones* (Brian Levant, 1994), *Mars Attacks* (Tim Burton, 1996), *Deep Impact* (Mimi Leder, 1998), *Wild Wild West* (Barry Sonnenfeld, 1999), *AI: Artificial Intelligence* (Steven Spielberg, 2001) and *Minority Report* (Steven Spielberg, 2002).

Make-up artist Greg Cannom's work can also be seen in *The Howling* (Joe Dante, 1980), *The Mask* (Chuck Russell, 1994), *Titanic* (James Cameron, 1997) and *A Beautiful Mind* (Ron Howard, 2001).

Fred Fuchs is a Coppola collaborator of old. His work with Coppola and Zoetrope goes back to the late 1970s. As an executive producer, Fuchs worked on *The Virgin Suicides* (Sofia Coppola, 2000) and *The Godfather Part III*. As a producer he has worked on *The Rainmaker*, *Jack* and *Tucker: The Man and His Dream*.

Executive Producer Michael Apted is a British director who has established a successful Hollywood career with films such as *Coal Miner's Daughter* (1980), *Gorillas in the Mist* (1988), *The World is Not Enough* (2000) and *Enigma* (2001). He is also the guiding hand behind the generational *7 Up* series which, every seven years, has been documenting, for television, the lives of a group of children born in Britain in the 1960s. The lavish fantasy of *Bram Stoker's Dracula* is a long way from the down-to-earth realism of the documentary series.

The beautiful matte paintings for *Bram Stoker's Dracula* were achieved at Matte World. Craig Barron and Mike Pangrazio of Matte World were once at Industrial Light and Magic where they advanced the art of matte painting, creating beautiful images of worlds both far and closer to home. As such they extended the tradition of matte painting as practised by craftsmen like Peter Ellenshaw and Albert Whitlock.

CASTING: Coppola, as he had done in his role as producer on *American Graffiti* (George Lucas, 1973) and as director on *The Godfather*, *The Outsiders* and *Rumble Fish*, dedicated himself to fitting out *Bram Stoker's Dracula* with a cast of new film stars. Winona Ryder had read the screenplay when *Bram Stoker's Dracula* was originally being pitched as a television movie. She then talked to Coppola about it. Ryder had originally been due to star in *The Godfather Part III* as Michael Corleone's daughter. When Ryder pulled out due to exhaustion, Coppola cast his own daughter Sofia in the part. Ryder's starring in *Bram Stoker's Dracula* came during a run of successful movies for the actress.

Coming back into the Coppola fold was one of the director's 'stock company actors', the singer Tom Waits, who appears as the insane Dr Renfield. Waits has also appeared in *One From the Heart*, *The Outsiders*, *Rumble Fish* and *The Cotton Club*.

Coppola's love of theatre and his beginnings as a writer have always lead him to a rewarding series of collaborations with actors. His films have elicited some of the finest performances in American cinema. In his youth, Coppola had been a youth-camp counsellor, and this sense of community feeling and of getting to know one another has always informed his casting process and the development of the actors as an ensemble. For *Bram Stoker's Dracula*, Coppola gathered the actors at his base in Napa, northern California, for a two-week period of improvisations, games and trips, which included horseback riding and ballooning. The cast also convened at a San Francisco cabaret club to watch a staged reading, by radio actors, of the film's screenplay. In the two weeks before shooting began there was a further period of rehearsals at Hollywood's United Methodist Church. These rehearsals incorporated lighting and sound effects and were videotaped for reference during the shoot.

I KNOW THAT FACE: *Bram Stoker's Dracula* brims with familiar faces. Look out for Bill Campbell who starred in the underrated and charm-heavy *The Rocketeer* (Joe Johnston, 1991) and Cary Elwes, who remains most famous for *The Princess Bride* (Rob Reiner, 1986) and who also appeared in *Glory* (Edward Zwick, 1989). Keanu Reeves was just starting to see his career take off after appearing in *Parenthood* (Ron Howard, 1989) and *Bill and Ted's Excellent Adventure* (Steven Herek, 1988). Prior to portraying Jonathan Harker he starred as Johnny Utah in Kathryn Bigelow's kinetic, Buddhist action movie *Point Break* (1991). Reeves has gone on to star in such iconic Hollywood movies as *Speed* (1994) and *The Matrix* (The Wachowski Brothers, 1999).

In the early 1990s, Anthony Hopkins was experiencing a resurgent career after the success of *Silence of the Lambs* (Jonathan Demme, 1991). He has gone on to star in *Legends of the Fall* (Ed Zwick, 1994), *The Mask of Zorro* (Martin Campbell, 1998) and even supplied the voice-over narration for *The Grinch* (Ron Howard, 2000).

Gary Oldman has starred in *The Firm* (Alan Clarke, 1983), *Sid and Nancy* (Alex Cox, 1986), *State of Grace* (Phil Jouanou, 1990), *True Romance* (Tony Scott, 1993), *The Professional/Leon* (Jean Luc Besson, 1993) and played an intergalactic tyrant with shades of Bugs Bunny in *The Fifth Element* (Jean Luc Besson, 1997) and went on to direct the astonishing *Nil By Mouth* (1997).

Winona Ryder starred in dark teen drama *Heathers* (Michael Lehmann, 1988) and *Beetlejuice* (Tim Burton, 1988) before moving on to films that include *Great Balls of Fire* (Jim McBride, 1989), *Edward Scissorhands* (Tim Burton, 1990), *The Age of Innocence* (Martin Scorsese, 1993), *The Crucible* (Nicholas Hytner, 1994), *Little Women* (Gillian Armstrong, 1994), *How to Make an American Quilt* (Jocelyn Moorhouse, 1995), and *Girl, Interrupted* (James Mangold, 1999).

Richard E Grant made his movie breakthrough in *Withnail and I* (Bruce Robinson, 1985) and has remained a high-profile movie star since. He appeared in *The Age of Innocence* (Martin Scorsese, 1993), *Jack and Sarah* (Tim Sullivan, 1995) and *Gosford Park* (Robert Altman, 2001).

Sadie Frost went on to appear in *Shopping* (Paul WS Anderson, 1994), *An Ideal Husband* (William P Catlidge, 1998) and *Rancid Aluminium* (Edward Thomas, 2000).

THE FILMING: *Bram Stoker's Dracula* is notable for being shot entirely on sound stages. Based at Sony Studios (where Spielberg's equally theatrical *Hook* had been shot) the production possessed an old-fashioned magic with its huge sets and stunning costumes. The artifice enhanced the fantasy. At one point, Coppola had considered shooting the action against black drapes and backdrops onto which would be projected backgrounds. Like his long-time friend and colleague, George Lucas, Coppola has been committed to developing the process of filming and moving towards digital cinema. This term describes the process of filming whereby actors perform against a blue screen so that the appropriate background environment can essentially be painted in during post-production.

Digital cinema also refers to a way of organising the film-making process, in order to make it as fluid, economic, efficient and creative as possible. As far back as *One From the Heart*, Coppola integrated video with film production so that he could swiftly review and edit together scenes on video during the shoot. Speaking about the video element of *Bram Stoker's Dracula*, Coppola looked to the future of film production and commented, 'That's the way it's going to be in the future – images piped around studios like hot and cold running water.'

Bram Stoker's Dracula required the construction of 58 sets across six different sound stages. A team of 150 worked on the building of the sets and certain sets were still being designed during production because there had been a time delay when original designs for the film were not deemed appropriate. For the London street scenes, a set was built outside on the Universal Studios backlot and filming on those fake streets lasted just two days.

The Hillingham garden set was built on the Esther Williams stage named after the Hollywood star of the Golden Era, though her particular skill was not singing or dancing but swimming. All her major films featured some kind of impressive water-based sequences. The films included *Ziegfield Follies* (Vincente Minelli, 1946) and *Million Dollar Mermaid* (Mervyn LeRoy, 1952). The Esther Williams stage houses a watertank where the Dracula scenes were filmed. This allowed for the set to be built as a split-level structure so that the Hillingham set could feature a sunken garden as well as a pool and a maze. The expanse of the maze was suggested by a painting hung beyond the physical set.

The Borgo Pass set, seen at the end of the film as the heroes race to the castle, was built on Stage 15 at Sony, the largest stage in Hollywood. Real wolves were brought onto the set for this sequence.

Several of Coppola's earlier films, famously *Apocalypse Now* and *One from the Heart* had been gargantuan projects and, by the early 1990s, he was aware of the importance of being seen running a tight ship. This mindset also informed his 'work for hire' projects to follow, *Jack* and *The Rainmaker* – that is to say films that Coppola directed based on others' material, rather than generating and developing them himself as was the case with *The Conversation*, *One From the Heart*, *Apocalypse Now* and the forthcoming *Megalopolis*.

Storyboarding for *Bram Stoker's Dracula* was key to maintaining control and this effort was led by Coppola's son, Roman, with input from Michael Ballhaus and sketch artist Peter Ramsay. The film's tight preparation ensured that the production ran smoothly and efficiently. The storyboards were then videotaped with the script being read as voice-over.

This material was readily available on the set as a point of reference for the actors prior to shooting the scene for real. In effect, the video material functioned as a sketch from which to create the final painting.

The film was cut and edited on video and, as the shoot progressed, cutting was under way so that a comprehensive, basic version of the film was in place by the time shooting was complete. In August 1992, Coppola recorded a new Anthony Hopkins narration for the film and a new final shot. In September 1992, Coppola filmed a new opening shot.

The film went through thirty-eight different cuts before Coppola had the edit that was ready for release.

PROMOTION: In the 1990s, Coppola directed only a handful of films of which *Bram Stoker's Dracula* was his most elaborate and commercially successful, a real blockbuster on an opulent and richly cinematic scale. The other films of this decade were *The Godfather Part III*, *Jack* and *The Rainmaker*. Coppola had mounted other vast productions, notably the first two *Godfather* films, *Apocalypse* Now and *One From the Heart*.

In 1989, Tim Burton's film *Batman* took the marketing of a hoped for blockbuster to a new level. *Bram Stoker's Dracula* also benefited from the intense marketing process. There was a great deal of excitement about the film, notably because of Coppola's immense reputation as a visionary director, able to reinvigorate genre staples as he had done with *The Godfather* and *Apocalypse Now*. Whenever Coppola makes a film, people root for him to succeed because of their desire to see him approach the glory of his 1970s work.

For *Bram Stoker's Dracula* a teaser poster simply featured an image of a stonework gargoyle. The release poster featured Vlad and Mina in an embrace, emphasising the romance rather than the monstrous elements of the story. Science-fiction novelist Fred Saberhagen wrote a novel based on the screenplay. Saberhagen is the author of many novels, including the long-running Berserker series of novels and various vampire-themed novels, including *The Holmes–Dracula File* and *Séance for a Vampire*.

Dark Horse comics released a strong four-part comic book adaptation with art work by Mike Mignola, famous in the early 1990s for his *Hellboy* comic series, which are now being adapted for film by director Guillermo Del Toro, director of *Cronos* (1993), *Mimic* (1997) and *Blade II* (2002). Each issue of the comic came with a couple of trading cards. Yes, there was a trading card set courtesy of Topps Trading Cards.

There was also a very effective teaser trailer released in the summer of 1992. It simply showed drops of blood landing on a slab of stone. The droplets then skittered across the stone and formed the word Dracula.

THE OPENING: The film's opening sequence, highly theatrical in its depiction of the battlefield, establishes the somewhat unusual quality of the visuals that are to come. For all its intricate visual stylings, the film's opening sequence is refreshingly simple. The illusion of battle is suggested by silhouette cut-outs of soldiers moving across the battlefield. Much later in the film, this device is echoed in the sequence at the cinematograph in London where Dracula goes to confront Mina.

Despite the bloody nature of the film's logo on the poster for the film, when the title card appears it is as if the words *Bram Stoker's Dracula* have been forged in the fires of hell on a sheet of metal.

HEROES AND VILLAINS: As a genre piece, *Bram Stoker's Dracula* pits heroes of civilisation against the beast that is Dracula. Stoker's original novel explored the emerging sexuality and independence of women in the late nineteenth century and, with the exception of Van Helsing, the women characters are the strongest personalities in the film; strong and self-determining, like Kay in *The Godfather* films. Mina's character arc in the film moves from some level of repression and gentility to something far more impassioned and sexual, suggested as much by her costumes as her behaviour.

Like other Coppola heroes, from *The Godfather* to *Apocalypse Now* to *The Rainmaker,* Dracula is seeking out a better life as he moves through a corrupted world that threatens to demolish his sense of what is right. Although the villain of the piece, Dracula is made highly sympathetic, his apparently evil mission rendered believable and touching in its motivation. Much of Dracula's menace is physical, based on his ability to cross time and space in an instant – an ability frequently visualised by his shadow, as seen during the party scene at Hillingham.

The Count is heroic and menacing and, most importantly, somebody we feel sympathy for. When he first attacks Lucy there is a moment when we see his mournful human face beneath the wolf fur as he stares at Mina, the Dracula crest, momentarily burning bright on her chest, making clear the link between Mina and Elizabeta. Early in the film he is powerfully attired in blood-red, muscle-like armour, his long hair flowing, his eyes intense. As the film develops his villainy is fused with a strongly romantic quality which complicates his status as a force of evil, particularly when Mina is seduced by him.

For Coppola, Van Helsing is as evil and demented in his obsessive goal as Dracula is in his. Van Helsing's crazed determination and delight in pursuing Dracula recalls the dementia and intensity of the journey to find Kurtz in *Apocalypse Now* and the drive of Preston Tucker to create a better car in *Tucker: The Man and His Dream.*

COPPOLA STYLE: In this film Coppola emphasises the decadent, combining real cinematic verve in editing and camera placement with a highly theatrical feeling in terms of production design and lighting. There is an overwhelming flourish to the film, almost as though Coppola is saying 'You want to see a smart and artful blockbuster? I'll show you one.' From the moment the blood gushes from the stone crucifix in the opening moments the film asserts its theatricality. It is a theatricality we have seen at work throughout Coppola's films (notably in *One From the Heart*) and it is in full flow in this film. In what might be a nod to Stanley Kubrick's *The Shining* (1980), the most theatrical moment occurs at the moment of Lucy's death, with waves of blood crashing onto her bed from off screen. The moment is a visual crescendo, and the film's operatic quality is never clearer. Realism has no place in this film, yet the action is totally believable.

IMAGE: Coppola derives a lot of creativity from the spirit of early cinema and the Symbolist art of the late nineteenth century, with its emphasis on fantasy, history, myth and eroticism. All through the film there is an evident contrast between the blood-reds and shadows of Dracula's world and the airiness and lightness of Hillingham. Mina begins the film in softly coloured dresses and, as the story develops, her costuming reflects far more her emerging sexuality and independence. The lady is a vamp.

One of the film's strongest features is its inventive and rich transitions between scenes. This is illustrated in the moment when the peacock feather drops across the frame and the camera focuses on one of the blue spots which then dissolves to the menacing exit of the railway tunnel that runs through Transylvania.

A wide-angle lens is often used to distort the image slightly, in turn matching the distorted reality experienced by certain characters, as in the moment when Harker freaks out after being seduced by the brides of Dracula. Those shots of the crazed Renfield benefit hugely from the use of a wide-angle lens into which the character leans and looks directly, lending these scenes a comically bizarre quality.

Twenty years on from *The Godfather*, Coppola employs an especially powerful narrative device, that of intercutting between two starkly contrasting situations. One of the most celebrated moments in *The Godfather* is the baptism and killing scene where Coppola economically and powerfully intercuts between the two events. In doing so, love and death are fused and shown to be utterly connected. The same device is used during one of the set-piece sequences of *Bram Stoker's Dracula* during which Lucy is killed. The violence of this action is intercut with images of Mina and Jonathan being married in the warm glow of the Romanian convent.

Camera movement, in synchronicity with lighting and production design, is as important as the juxtaposition of scenes through editing. One of the most potent uses of camera motion is in the scene where Mina and Dracula kiss. The scene has a dreamlike quality, the camera fluidly drifting, the lighting blood-red, the sense of a location not important, the music deeply and achingly romantic. There is a sense of release in this sequence contrasting with the cluttered décor and restraint of the world that Mina has come from.

Coppola elegantly organises the various stories of his expansive narrative, combining voice-over and dissolving in-frame between images of diary entries and faces drifting in and out of shot.

The scene where Dracula tells Mina of his lost love feels very much embedded in the early traditions of film making as Coppola imposes an image of Elizabeta falling in the background behind Mina. It is as though the late nineteenth century has returned and filled this hi-tech movie with an old-world spirit.

SOUND: The film is scored dramatically and romantically by composer Wojciech Kilar. Sound effects also enhance the sense of location and terror. A notable example of this frenzied fusion of music and sound effects is when Dracula arrives in England and attacks Lucy in his wolfman form. Generally, the film's soundscape adds to the believability of the stage-bound settings.

COPPOLA TUNES: For *Bram Stoker's Dracula*, Coppola did not use an American composer, but a European one. In doing so the score is more richly steeped in a European musical tradition befitting the origins of Dracula. The Dracula score is strident, terrifying and deeply romantic. It was conducted by Anton Coppola. Kilar has worked as a film composer since the late 1950s and since *Bram Stoker's Dracula* he has worked with Roman Polanski on the films *Death and the Maiden* (1994), *The Ninth Gate* (1999) and *The Pianist* (2002). The track listing for the soundtrack to the film is: 'Dracula – The Beginning', 'Vampire Hunters', 'Mina's Photo', 'Lucy's Party', 'The Brides', 'The Storm', 'Love Remembered', 'The Hunt Builds', 'The Hunters Prelude', 'The Green Mist', 'Mina-Dracula', 'The Ring of Fire', 'Love Eternal', 'Ascension', 'End Credits', 'Love Song for a Vampire' (performed by Annie Lennox).

HUMOUR: The film has its share of humour to lighten and counterpoint the intensity. One of the best juxtaposes the beheading of Lucy with the cutting of a roast dinner. Economy is the name of the game. When Dracula reads Mina's letter his sadness is not shown so much by a heavy-going close-up but simply by slow-motion tears as they strike and distort the ink. Even Dracula's free-ranging, transcontinental shadow has a humour to it and is a direct homage to the menacing shadow in *Nosferatu* (FW Murnau, 1922). Such a simple effect is very powerful and dramatic.

AWARDS: *Bram Stoker's Dracula* won a slew of awards and nominations that particularly recognised the film's production design. The film was nominated for a Hugo for Best Dramatic Presentation and an MTV Movie Award for Best Kiss (Gary Oldman and Winona Ryder). It won the ASCAP Film and Television Music Award for Top Box Office Film, the award going to composer Wojciech Kilar.

At the Academy Awards in the spring of 1993, the film won the Oscar for Best Costume Design (Eiko Ishioka), Best Effects, Sound Editing (Tom C McCarthy and David E Stone) and Best Make-up (Greg Cannom, Michelle Burke and Matthew W Mungle). The film was also nominated for an Oscar in the categories of Best Art Direction (Thomas Sanders and Garret Lewis).

At the Academy of Science Fiction, Fantasy and Horror Films the film won the Saturn Award for Best Actor (Gary Oldman), Best Costumes (Eiko Ishioka), Best Director (Coppola) and Best Writing (James V Hart). At the BAFTAs the film was nominated for Best Costume, Best Make-up, Best Production Design and Best Special Effects, but won in none of those categories.

COPPOLA MAGIC: Though made in the early days of digital effects (the late 1980s and early 1990s), *Bram Stoker's Dracula* largely eschews such an approach, for both economic and aesthetic reasons. Instead, Coppola saw a way to suggest the era that Dracula was written and set in by referring to, and drawing on, the kinds of illusions and effects that would have been used by early cinema. The film is far more smoke and mirrors than cut and paste. The film also utilises many practical effects, that is to say illusions that are created in real space and time, as the cameras roll, such as the image of the rat-king that is left after Dracula, in his bat-man manifestation, confronts Van Helsing.

More often than not, the fact that a practical effect is physical and has a sense of mass and presence makes it more believable than something created in post-production and imposed onto the image.

Roman Coppola led the inventive and mesmerising effects work on *Bram Stoker's Dracula*. There was a relatively small budget for effects, and they have been realised masterfully, suggesting that a limitation is often a benefit and not a burden. The concept with the effects was to go for what Coppola termed a naïve approach, inspired by film makers such as Jean Cocteau. The effects have a winning cuteness to them, despite their frequently menacing allure, nowhere more so than when Dracula's eyes appear in the sky outside the train as Harker journeys to Transylvania.

The beautiful and dreamy matte paintings for the film can be seen in wide shots of London at night, of the train station in the mountains and, most notably, in shots of Dracula's castle. A matte painting (traditionally) was created on a sheet of glass and when seen in the film has a photorealistic quality to it. Matte paintings are combined with live action footage which, in the pre-digital era, was projected into a marked-out space in the glass and then refilmed.

Tricks that were used included running the film in reverse for the scene of Lucy writhing on her bed, thereby giving it an unreal quality. Another shot shows a droplet of blood falling upwards, and multiple exposures are used to combine Harker's face and a train in the same shot. Mirror effects were used extensively. Coppola's basic design sense for the visual effects was to make them appear weird. Models, miniatures and beautiful matte paintings formed the core of the effects work.

For those moments when we get Dracula's point of view, such as the camera racing up the steps at Hillingham to the window, the camera was fitted so as to click off frames erratically and then to click off several frames per second. One of the eeriest moments in the film is the arrival of Dracula's carriage to pick up Jonathan in the woods. The film runs in slow motion as it approaches and the action feels suitably unreal and unsettling.

The illusion of green mist (a form that Dracula takes) as it drifts through Carfax Abbey was created by pumping out dry ice and lighting it green. This was then filmed and superimposed onto the set.

Greg Cannom was in charge of make-up effects on *Bram Stoker's Dracula*. The Count's old age make-up, for example, was comprised of twelve separate pieces which took twelve hours to apply to Gary Oldman's face. The red contact lenses he wore could only be worn for thirty minutes at a time.

MOVIE SPEAK:

Dracula: 'Enter freely of your own will and leave some of the happiness you bring.'

Renfield: 'The Master of all life is at hand.'

Dracula: 'I have crossed oceans of time to find you.'

HOME VIEWING: The film was once available on now out of print Laserdisc and is currently available on VHS and DVD (both Region 1 and Region 2). The DVD includes a featurette about the making of the film. This featurette is especially valuable in its inclusion of video footage taken during rehearsals for the film. The most compelling footage shows the actors wrestling with Coppola to nail the drama of the scene towards the end of the film when the men confront Dracula after his seduction of Mina.

When the film was screened on American TV in 1997, the Renfield subplot was cut entirely.

Region 1 DVD Superbit Collection – optimised video quality because of the transfer process from film to disc widescreen 1.85:1. Standard DVD – interactive menu and scene access.

Region 2 DVD Extras – filmographies, trailer, documentary *Dracula: The Man, The Myth, The Legend*, interactive menu, scene access, widescreen 1.85:1.

TRIVIA: During the opening sequence of *Bram Stoker's Dracula*, when Vlad storms into the church and renounces Christianity, the bearded priest Cesare is played by Anthony Hopkins. The blue flame that appears close to Vlad's castle is inspired by a flame seen in FW Murnau's film *Faust* (1926).

In the establishing shots of the streets of London there is a sandwich board being worn advertising The Lyceum theatre. Bram Stoker was manager of The Lyceum theatre in London when he wrote *Dracula.*

An acting coach, Greta Seacat, worked with Winona Ryder and Sadie Frost to give them a sense of what life was like for well-to-do young women in the late nineteenth century.

To develop the historical accuracy, and also the necessary otherworldliness of his Dracula portrayal, Gary Oldman received lessons in Romanian for his vocal performance and in Tai Chi to enhance the elegance of his body movement.

When Vlad screams out in the church and drives his sword into the cross, the scream is not that of Gary Oldman but of Lux Interior, lead singer of The Cramps.

In the development of the film's look a 'bible' of reference images was compiled, covering art, architecture, design and film stills. Some of these images were incorporated into the videotape version of the script.

COPPOLA'S VIEW: Coppola's films have often contained images and references to the religious and sacramental, and beyond that a sense of the mythic. The Dracula story has become a myth of the modern age. Coppola's film is drenched in luxuriousness and the motifs and references to the Church continue through the film. The film's prologue is a stunning piece of work that gleefully draws on the blood associations of the Christian Church so that, as seen in *The Godfather*, the ritual of the Church is associated with the shedding of blood. A renunciation of God by the Count finds its equivalent in Michael Corleone, and both men battle with their own souls to somehow atone for their actions. In *Bram Stoker's Dracula* blood sacrifice gets a medieval and Victorian workout, fuelled by the theme of betrayal. The primal, heart of darkness of *Apocalypse Now* features too in Bram Stoker's Dracula where the transformation to a vampiric state of mind creates a savage and wild behaviour in stark contrast to the so-called advances of civilisation. For some, though, Coppola singularly misses the most intriguing dynamic of the Dracula figure, namely his alternative sexuality. Time's passing is as acutely present in the castles and mountains of Dracula as it is in the backalleys of Tulsa in *Rumble Fish* and the sunny, easygoing suburbia of *Jack*. Vlad fights against time in his appearance as a man who is eternally young.

As with *Apocalypse Now*, and to a less obvious extent *Rumble Fish*, *Bram Stoker's Dracula* carries some associations with the Fisher King myth, which tells of a wounded ruler whose physical injury matches an injury of the heart that must be healed. The notion of the wasteland, which is part of the myth's metaphor, represents the barren soul of the king. In this film, Vlad's quest is to restore his sense of being alive, to heal himself by finding his beloved Elizabeta. Her death is what wounded him and only she can heal him. The Catholic imagery and associations of other Coppola movies finds a very florid expression in this film and The Fisher King myth ties in with the Holy Grail legends, themselves a thrilling fusion of Christian and pagan legend.

The film dramatises the flip-side nature of love and violence and taps into the contemporary culture's concern with blood. At the time of the film's release, Coppola alluded to the AIDS epidemic and the film's second half pulses with shots of blood cells. The blood tie of family binds *Bram Stoker's Dracula* to the blood drama of *The Godfather* series in particular, despite the vast differences on the surface. Vlad is just as driven by a notion of vengeance and the need to continue the legacy of his rule as Michael Corleone is.

Bram Stoker's Dracula is a deeply romantic film that acknowledges the expected hits of a horror film but also transcends them and works as powerful drama. True love wins out and there is a strong sense of relief and peace at the film's end. There is an overriding fairy-tale sensibility at work when we see the Count's youthful face in peaceful repose, the sun touching his face, as a choir sings soothingly on the soundtrack. The final image of the painting of Dracula and Elizabeta, seemingly entwined, encapsulates the potency of love and its redemptive power.

CRITICAL COPPOLA: Roger Ebert in the *Chicago Sun-Times* wrote 'Coppola directs with all the stops out . . . the movie is particularly operatic in the way it prefers climaxes to continuity.' For Hal Hinson of the *Washington Post* the film was 'Francis Ford Coppola's magnificent, astonishing new telling . . . This is Coppola the master showman, the conjuror and maestro, directing at full tilt.' (Hal Hinson, *Washington Post*, 13 November 1992). *Newsweek* said the film was 'drowned in a tide of images'.

VERDICT: Coppola's adaptation of the classic novel is, at the very least, proof of how much fun Hollywood cinema can be, allied with intelligent drama and strong performances. The film draws on all the elements available to film making – performers, colour, camera movement, visual effects, light and shadow. It demonstrates cinema's enduring affinity for making fantasy subjects believable. The film brilliantly rides against anything naturalistic and reminds us of Coppola's flamboyance. As a fantasy movie it is exemplary. It is a beautiful film. The performances of Gary Oldman, Sadie Frost, Winona Ryder and Anthony Hopkins are especially strong. I can only hope that Hollywood will continue to produce (just occasionally) such wilfully artificial movies. The success of the film surely helped pave the way for others such as *Interview with the Vampire* (Neil Jordan, 1994) and gave a fresh dose of blood to the horror movie genre. Production company American Zoetrope has gone on to produce *Jeepers Creepers* (Victor Salva, 2001).

Like his contemporary Spielberg, Coppola is able to reach beyond the décor and fantasy elements to go for something recognisably human in the emotions and tensions being played out. The ending of the film is truly touching. It is one of the best Hollywood blockbusters of the past decade.

COPPOLA NOW: 'The vampire has lost his soul, and that can happen to anyone.'

Jack (1996)

(Colour – 113 minutes)

American Zoetrope/Great Oaks released through Buena Vista
Producer: Ricardo Mestres, Fred Fuchs and Francis Ford Coppola
Executive Producer: Doug Claybourne
Screenplay: James DeMonaco and Gary Nadeau
Cinematographer: John Toll
Editor: Barry Malkin
Music: Michael Kamen
Production Design: Dean Tavoularis
Art Direction: Angelo Graham
Costume Design: Aggie Guerard Rogers

CAST: Robin Williams (*Jack Powell*), Diane Lane (*Karen Powell*), Jennifer Lopez (*Miss Marquez*), Brian Kerwin (*Brian Powell*), Fran Drescher (*Dolores Durante*), Bill Cosby (*Lawrence Woodruff*), Michael McKean (*Paulie*), Don Novello (*Bartender*), Allan Rich (*Dr Benfante*), Adam Zolotin (*Louis Durante*), Todd Bosley (*Edward*), Seth Smith (*John-John*), Mario Yedidia (*George*), Jeremy Lelliott (*Johnny Duffer*), Rickey O'Shon Collins (*Eric*), Hugo Hernandez (*Victor*)

BUDGET: $45 million

THE BOX OFFICE: $58.58 million

RELEASE DATE: 9 August 1996

MPAA: PG

BBFC: PG

TAGLINE: He's a healthy ten-year-old who's growing four times faster than normal. Now he's about to take the biggest adventure of his life . . . 5th grade at school.

SUMMARY: A party. A conga line of adults in fancy dress slinks across the dance hall. The Tin Man and the Wicked Witch of the West dance by. The Wicked Witch of the West goes into contractions, seven months early. Rushed to the hospital, she gives birth to little baby Jack. The doctors inform Jack's mother and father that Jack's internal body clock is ticking at an accelerated rate. By the time Jack is ten he will look forty.

Ten years later. Jack watches the world from his bedroom as the local kids stand outside wondering who Jack is. They don't know him because he is tutored at home by Mr Woodruff, who suggests to Jack's parents that it is time Jack went to school.

Jack's arrival at school prompts curiosity and initially a kind of schoolyard fear. Miss Marquez encourages the children to see past Jack's abnormality. When Jack's height comes in useful in a game of basketball, he is soon accepted. In class, the students are set an essay to write about what they want to be when they grow up; we watch Jack fall for his teacher, Miss Marquez. Jack's adult appearance soon bonds him tighter to the boys. He buys *Penthouse* magazine for them and his friend Louis introduces Jack to his mother as the headteacher. Louis' mother then flirts outrageously with Jack.

Jack is invited to the boys' treehouse where they mess around. Jack takes Mr Woodruff to meet the boys in the treehouse, which then collapses. At home, Jack finds that his accelerated aging process is intensifying. His hair begins to fall out. After school, Jack asks Miss Marquez to go with him to the school dance but she has to decline. Jack takes the reply badly and collapses with a form of angina. Jack's mum keeps him safe at home. Jack is tired of staying home and sneaks out to the nightclub where Louis' mother goes. He meets her there and then becomes embroiled in a fight. Mr Woodruff returns to continue Jack's home education, but Jack is not interested – he just wants to be with his friends. Louis organises all of the friends to pass by Jack's house and ask Jack's mother if he can come out to play. Jack returns to school.

Seven years later, it is the high school graduation. Jack is only eighteen but looks like an old man and he is honoured as the school's valedictorian. He gives an upbeat speech before taking off with his pals.

COPPOLA'S CONCEPT: The screenplay for Jack was written by two New York University graduates, Gary Nadeau and James DeMonaco. Coppola connected to the film's statement of living fully, as everybody is on borrowed time. In an interview with *Premiere* magazine at the time of the film's release, Coppola referred to his late son Gio, and the film is dedicated to Gio's daughter, Gia-Carla.

By the time of *Jack*, the success of *The Godfather Part III* and *Bram Stoker's Dracula* had restored Coppola's financial complications, which had kicked off with *One From the Heart*. Coppola had originally been approached to direct *The Juror* which went on to star Demi Moore (Brian Gibson, 1996). Coppola declined as he felt the violence in the screenplay was too gratuitous and the studio wouldn't lessen it. When the screenplay for *Jack* finally arrived with Coppola he responded well to its sweetness.

Coppola regarded *Jack* as a fable in the same way that *Peggy Sue Got Married* was a fable – a smallscale story with a fanciful aspect, although the illness that propels the drama of *Jack* is all too real, if very rare: progeria prompts accelerated physical growth in children.

In preparing the film, Coppola ran a camp at his base in Napa for Robin Williams and the young actors he would be working with. As always, Coppola's belief was that this rehearsal period would enrich the work on set, giving the actors memories to draw on and a sense of connection.

The film seems to be very personal to Coppola, and just because it isn't *Apocalypse Now* or *The Godfather* does not mean it is not well made or heartfelt; it has an emotional authenticity within it.

To develop Mr Woodruff, Coppola wrote a whole backstory which told how the character's father was a country schoolteacher and his son (the Cosby character) went off to play music and then himself became a teacher.

INFLUENCES: Coppola's film *Peggy Sue Got Married* certainly influences the tone of the piece with its interplay of comedy (more raucous and appropriately childish in *Jack*) and sombre drama. For Coppola the film was a fairy tale.

In keeping with the fairy-tale quality, and the period in Coppola's career when *Jack* was made, it's worth noting that around this time he was in the middle of developing his cherished *Pinocchio* adaptation (see **Coppola the Producer and Showman**). Like the Carlo Collodi story, *Jack* concerns a hero who wants to be as real and normal as the other boys. Where Jack's congenital abnormality is accelerated growth rate, Pinocchio's is that he is made of wood and he wants to be real.

COSTUME: The film's naturalistic, contemporary setting does not demand that the costumes stand out from the natural suburban setting of the film, though the soft pastel colours of some of Jack's shirts hint at his gentleness.

The film's opening scene presents a fancy dress conga party at which Jack's parents are present. His dad is dressed as The Tin Man from *The Wizard of Oz* and Jack's mum is dressed as the Wicked Witch of the West, wearing Dorothy's red shoes. This makes clear the film's inclination to a sweet fable with strains of more serious concerns.

Mr Woodruff's beret marks him out as somewhat bohemian and recalls the beret Coppola has often been photographed wearing. Mr Woodruff's dedication and enthusiasm for kids seems mirrored by Coppola.

TEAM COPPOLA: *Jack* was the first film Coppola made after the florid, Victorian Gothic of *Bram Stoker's Dracula* and of all his films is the smallest. *Jack* reunited Coppola with Dean Tavoularis as production designer. Tavoularis's great success with *Jack* is the creation of a warm and nurturing sense of home. Jack's bedroom, especially, is a cosy place. Fred Fuchs, who produced *Tucker: The Man and His Dream*, returns in the same capacity on *Jack*.

CASTING: Coppola had long-admired Robin Williams's skills as both comic and dramatic actor. He had seen Williams perform at George Lucas's fortieth birthday party and been knocked out by it. By 1995, Robin Williams's career was at its peak and even he joked about how Jack was going to be the last part he played where he drew on the manic and childish. Indeed, Williams, best known for his roles in *Good Morning Vietnam* (Barry Levinson, 1987) and *Dead Poets Society* (Peter Weir, 1989), was initially reluctant to portray a child-man figure again as he had become famous for doing in films such as *Hook* (Steven Spielberg, 1991), *Toys* (Barry Levinson, 1992) and *Jumanji* (Joe Johnston, 1995); he would go on to perform in *Bicentennial Man* (Chris Columbus, 1999), *Insomnia* (Christopher Nolan, 2002) and *One Hour Photo* (Mark Romanek, 2002). Disney persisted in encouraging Williams to come on board *Jack* and, finally, Coppola interceded personally. Coppola put Williams on a three-week period with the child actors, including a camping trip. Williams's interest in, and connection with, the material concerned its themes of loneliness (he had been an only child), and its sad and often delicate tone. The film's expression of the power of connections also appealed to Williams's warm and fuzzy screen persona.

In a role that came before her breakthrough role in the brilliant *Out of Sight* (Steven Soderbergh, 1998), singer Jennifer Lopez appears as Jack's schoolteacher.

Diane Lane returns for her fourth Coppola movie after *The Outsiders*, *Rumble Fish* and *The Cotton Club*.

I KNOW THAT FACE: Robin Williams was a major star in the 1990s and has been starring in films since the early 1980s in *Popeye* (Robert Altman, 1980), *The World According to Garp* (George Roy Hill, 1982), *Moscow on the Hudson* (Paul Mazursky, 1983), *Good Morning, Vietnam* (Barry Levinson, 1987), *Dead Poets Society* (Peter Weir, 1989), *Hook* (Steven Spielberg, 1991), *The Fisher King* (Terry Gilliam, 1991), *Aladdin* (Ron Clements, John Musker, 1992), *Mrs Doubtfire* (Chris Columbus, 1993) and *Good Will Hunting* (Gus van Sant, 1997).

Jennifer Lopez is now a major singer and Hollywood star and appears in *The Cell* (Tarsem Singh, 2000), *The Wedding Planner* (Adam Shankman, 2001) and *Maid in Manhattan* (Wayne Wang, 2002).

Bill Cosby had been an iconic presence of American and UK TV in the 1980s thanks to his smash hit sitcom *The Cosby Show*.

THE FILMING: Shooting was preceded by Coppola's customary three-week rehearsal period, and filming began in September 1995. The film was shot on location around San Francisco where Coppola's Zoetrope Studio base is located.

PROMOTION: The film was marketed around Robin Williams's starring role and took $11 million on its opening weekend in early autumn 1996. The film's poster simply featured a photograph of Robin Williams in character as Jack with the film's title written and coloured as though by a child.

THE OPENING: The film begins with a carnivalesque craziness which keys us in to the tone of the film. The final scene has a similar sense of playfulness but is underpinned with a very real sense of sadness.) A trumpet sounds and the camera pulls away from the mouth of the trumpet to reveal a fancy dress party and conga dance winding its way around a hall. As the line proceeds a young woman dressed as the Wicked Witch of the West stops and experiences pains in her abdomen.

She is pregnant, but only two months so. Her husband, dressed as the Tin Man, helps her to sit down. This real-life setting, as the place where there is a sudden and bizarre twist of fate, most clearly recalls the opening of *Peggy Sue Got Married*. The action then shifts to the hospital as the expectant mother and father, still in fancy dress, rush in, followed by a partygoer in a cocktail glass outfit and a man dressed as a packet of cigarettes. Only when Jack is born does the tone of the scene become more intense. It is an absurd sequence that is playful and that makes a smooth transition from the everyday to the highly unusual, which is the backdrop against which the drama will play out. The titles roll, accompanied by a Bryan Adams song, over a montage of baby Jack being examined by medical staff using a range of medical devices.

HEROES AND VILLAINS: Jack is a typical boy, anarchic at times, but more often introspective and unsure of how to behave. Robin Williams, known for his manic performances, is especially strong at registering unease and a sense of loneliness without resorting to dialogue. When Miss Marquez says she cannot go to the dance with him, Jack's expression says it all. When Jack goes to Memories nightclub his confusion at the behaviour and thought-processes of adults is loaded. Like many other Coppola characters, Jack experiences a little of the corrupt adult world. Jack wants to be like everybody else but finally comes to delight in his difference. In *The Outsiders* Ponyboy also enjoys the fact that he is different from the crowd; he explains that his father was an original person, borne out by the inventive names he chose for his sons. The boys who befriend Jack begin as his enemies, watching his bedroom window from the street as though trying to sight a monster. To emphasise this sense of an unknown identity, the camera pulls away from the window to rest on Jack's shoulder. It does not immediately reveal Jack in his entirety. The basketball match in the school playground galvanises Jack's friendship with the boys, and Coppola sketches the tribal element that exists in the rough and tumble of a playground. When Jack plays basketball it recalls another Robin Williams film, *Hook* (Steven Spielberg, 1991), where basketball bonds the boys together. Jack's closing speech encapsulates the simple theme of the film and, like the coda to *The Outsiders*, is overtly romantic and committed to the young. The chances are Jack would enjoy knowing Johnny and Ponyboy; like them Jack can talk about sunsets, that time when one day ends but another is promised.

Jack's parents are the most perfect kind: loving, patient and understanding. But Jack's mother does insist on Jack remaining at home, wrapped too protectively in her care, understandable given his abnormality and illness. Jack must fight against that throughout the film.

Mr Woodruff is the voice of reason, saying that Jack needs to experience the outside world, no matter how fragile he is. Mr Woodruff is the 'Coppola character', the adult who understands kids; he even wears a beret. Late in the film Woodruff says to Jack, 'You were a shooting star amongst ordinary stars.'

The villain of *Jack* is time itself. This film has its bond with *Peggy Sue Got Married* in which a tale of eternal concerns and the swift passing of time is played out in sunny suburbia. In 1983, Coppola made *The Outsiders* and *Rumble Fish*, stylistically very different films to *Jack* but like *Jack* expressing the growing awareness of its young characters that time is fleeting. Life is to be grasped.

COPPOLA STYLE: Coppola adopts a very unfussy, low-key approach in *Jack*, occasionally alluding to the theme of time's transience by using the two motifs of a butterfly and racing, time-lapse clouds.

The film favours a locked-off camera and the autumnal colours and drying leaves suggest the more sombre emotions beneath the smiles of the film. The film's celebration of life, in its smallest joys, befits the playful tone of the material.

IMAGE: Some of Coppola's previously flexed, stylistic muscles are on show in *Jack*. The racing clouds of *Rumble Fish* return in *Jack* and this device also recalls the fast-setting sun of *Bram Stoker's Dracula*. In each film, time is fleeting and is the real enemy. The butterfly that features in *Jack* adds to the meaning of the fragility of life and even Jack's pillow and bedclothes are patterned with a sun and moon motif symbolising the cycle of a day. When Jack turns up for the graduation there is a long-lens close-up of him; over his shoulder hangs the setting sun, almost like a halo.

The theme of the movie is expressed early on in a shot of Jack lying on the grass looking at a butterfly breaking free of its cocoon. Over this image is heard the voice of Mr Woodruff talking to Jack's parents, encouraging them to let Jack out into the world. When the butterfly lands on Jack's window ledge and he cradles it in his hand, it is already dead. This presages Jack's own rapid decline. His loneliness is emphasised in a tableau shot of him sitting on a low wall under a tree on the edge of the playground on his first day, capturing that sense of detachment and outsider status which is so crushing.

Jack is a film in which the mother is a very protective and nurturing figure, as always in Coppola's films, where mothers exist beyond imperfection. Recalling the Virgin Mary imagery of *The Godfather*, *Jack* finds the space to include a statue of the Virgin Mary in the hospital lobby.

SOUND: The film's sound design is very naturalistic and the opening scene includes comic sound effects as Jack's father tries to get past the metal detector at the hospital in his fancy dress Tin Man costume.

COPPOLA TUNES: Michael Kamen's score is by turns tender and effusive. Kamen also composed scores for *Brazil* (Terry Gilliam, 1985), *Don Juan De Marco* (Jeremy Leven, 1995), *Band of Brothers* (TV), *Robin Hood: Prince of Thieves* (Kevin Reynolds, 1991), *The Three Musketeers*, *X-Men* (Bryan Singer, 2000), *What Dreams May Come* (Vincent Ward, 1998), *The Winter Guest* (Alan Rickman, 1998), *Die Hard* (John McTiernan, 1988), *Lethal Weapon* (Richard Donner, 1987) and *The Iron Giant* (Brad Bird, 2000). Kamen's music is sweet and playful and weighs in most heavily underneath Jack's graduation speech.

Jack composed and conducted by Michael Kamen: 'Jack Conga', 'Jack Scherzo', 'Sky', 'Butterfly', 'Basketball Game', 'Hello Jack', 'Louie's Mom (A Great School Day)', 'Treehouse Collapse', 'Jack's Collapse (Butterfly's Death)', 'Time to Grow Up', 'Children's Crusade (Can Jack Come Out and Play?)', 'Back to School (What Do I Want to be When I Grow Up?)', 'Valedictorian (Life is Fleeting)'.

HUMOUR: Known for the intensity and shadowy drama and territories of *The Godfather* triptych and *Apocalypse Now*, Coppola also has a deft hand for comedy. There is a sense of the carnivalesque in his work and this is played up in *Jack*. Being about young boys the film has its share of scatological and obvious humour, but there is also fun to be had in Jack's encounters with the adult world, as in the scene where he helps Louis by pretending to be the headteacher. Bill Cosby's warm and gentle humour, so famous from his legendary 80s sitcom *The Cosby Show*, is apparent, for example in his first scene early on in the film. The quirky mannerisms of children is something Coppola picks up on, as shown in the shots of kids around the basketball court. When all the kids come by Jack's house to ask him to come out to play, Coppola speeds the image up in a parade of infectious, childhood energy and creativity.

Robin Williams improvises his words slightly during the film notably in the scene where he goes to buy a copy of *Penthouse*.

The film is very much two movies; the first part being light-hearted, the second part more melancholy and dramatic. The humour serves as relief.

AWARDS: *Jack* won the 1997 NCLR Bravo Award for Outstanding Achievement in a Feature Film, the award going to emerging star Jennifer Lopez. The film was also nominated as Best Family Feature at the 1997 Young Artist Awards, and an award was made for Best Performance in a Feature Film to Supporting Actor Adam Zolotin.

COPPOLA MAGIC: For all the hugeness of visual design that Coppola has been associated with in his career, *Jack*'s most magical moment is one of the smallest in Coppola's body of work. It is the shot of the butterfly emerging from its cocoon, an effect that encapsulates all that the film is saying.

MOVIE SPEAK:

Jack: 'I just want to be a regular star.'

Jack: 'I made it mom. I'm a grown up.'

Jack: 'Life is fleeting and if you're ever distressed cast your eyes to the summer sky . . . make a wish.'

HOME VIEWING: *Jack* is available on Region 1 and Region 2 DVD and on VHS.

TRIVIA: One of the conga line dancers in the film's opening scene is dressed in a white leotard and, over it, wears a cocktail glass outfit. This is a direct homage to Coppola's hugely underrated *One From the Heart,* in which Leila is shown performing inside a neon-lit, oversized cocktail glass.

COPPOLA'S VIEW: Coppola's acknowledged love of family and its nurturing potential is central to *Jack*. Early in the film, though, the question raised is: when does mothering become smothering? – particularly when a child has an illness. The film celebrates individuality, being different and the alertness of young minds to the real beauties of life, the same themes that are at work in *The Outsiders*. 'How sweet it is!' Jack exclaims at the end of the film, this hopeful declaration ranking Jack alongside Ponyboy from *The Outsiders* and Preston Tucker (*Tucker: A Man and His Dream*) in their lust for life.

CRITICAL COPPOLA: *Sight and Sound* felt that *Jack* was 'further dispiriting evidence of the creative bankruptcy of Francis Ford Coppola' and the *Los Angeles Times* was also less than complimentary: 'A sappy comedy . . . so rich in wasted talents.'

VERDICT: *Jack* is a minor Coppola movie, better than its reputation would suggest, yet one which expresses a long-standing, major concern of his work. The drama of *Jack* is far from melodramatic. A genuinely heartfelt film for children, it focuses on human generosity. The parts may be better than the whole and the film is certainly stronger after the treehouse collapses. It contains several neat and emotionally true moments and the last scene is pure Coppola in young person mode and succeeds in tugging the heartstrings. By turns silly and genuinely heartfelt, the film is stronger in its second half because its focus narrows to straight drama rather than the sometimes clumsy mixture of melancholy and broad humour. People find it hard to equate a film like *Jack* with the sweep of *The Godfather*, but it articulates similar concerns, such as the value of family, though within the distinct genre of a childrens' film. For all its surface silliness, it is driven by a real melancholy. Watch it alongside *The Outsiders*, *Rumble Fish* and *Peggy Sue Got Married* to get the sense of how these films fit together despite their wide-ranging stylistic differences.

COPPOLA NOW: 'It's a fable, a fairy tale . . . if they're done with a lot of heart and a little bit of eccentricity so they aren't just the same as every other movie, then there's a place for them.'

The Rainmaker (1997)

(Colour – 130 minutes)

Constellation Films/Douglas/Reuther
Productions/American Zoetrope released through
Paramount
Producer: Michael Douglas, Steven Reuther and Fred Fuchs
Co-Producer: Georgia Kacandes
Associate Producer: Gary Scott
Screenplay: Francis Ford Coppola, based on the novel by
John Grisham
Cinematographer: John Toll
Editor: Barry Malkin
Music: Elmer Bernstein
Production Design: Howard Cummings
Art Direction: Robert Shaw, Jeffrey McDonald
Costume Design: Aggie Guerard Rodgers

CAST: Matt Damon (*Rudy Baylor*), Claire Danes (*Kelly Riker*), Jon Voight (*Leo F Drummond*), Mary Kay Place (*Dot Black*), Mickey Rourke (*Bruiser Stone*), Danny DeVito (*Deck Schifflet*), Dean Stockwell (*Judge Harvey Hale*), Teresa Wright (*Miss Birdie*), Virginia Madsen (*Jackie Lemancyzk*), Andrew Shue (*Cliff Riker*), Red West (*Buddy Black*), Johnny Whitworth (*Donny Ray Black*), Danny Glover (*Judge*

Tyrone Kipler), Wayne Emmons (*Prince Thomas*), Adrian Roberts
(*Butch*), Roy Scheider (*Wilfred Keeley*), Randy Travis (*Billy Porter*),
Michael Girardin (*Everett Lufkin*), Randall King (*Jack Underhall*),
Justin Ashforth (*F Franklin Donaldson*), Michael Keys Hall (*B Bobby
Shaw*)

BUDGET: $40 million

THE BOX OFFICE: $45.85 million

RELEASE DATE: 21 November 1997

MPAA: PG13

BBFC: 12

TAGLINE: They were totally unqualified to try the case of a lifetime . . .
but every underdog has his day.

SUMMARY: Memphis, the late 1990s. Rudy Baylor is a young law
student preparing to sit his bar exam. He secures work at the practice of
J Lyman Stone, also known as Bruiser. Rudy brings two cases to the
practice, one a will for an old woman and a second concerning an
insurance claim on behalf of a working-class Memphis family, the
Blacks, whose son Donny Ray is dying of leukaemia. The Blacks have
had their claim refused eight times. Rudy is introduced to Bruiser's
associate, Deck Shifflet, who has failed his bar exam six times. Rudy
visits his client, Miss Birdie, to discuss the will. He then accompanies
Deck to a local hospital to chase up business from patients and be taught
the finer points of ambulance-chasing as a lawyer. Rudy, recently evicted
from his home, takes a room on the premises of Miss Birdie. Bruiser
gives Rudy another ambulance-chaser job, which is to represent a young
woman called Kelly who has been hospitalised by her husband's
beatings. Rudy visits the hospital and revises for his bar exam in the
cafeteria there. He sees Kelly and her husband, who gets heavy with her
as she sits in a wheelchair, bruised and bandaged. Rudy then reads an
article about Bruiser; he is being investigated by the FBI for corrupt
practice. Rudy returns to the hospital and this time speaks to Kelly
saying that if she needs anything to ask him. Rudy sees Kelly again and
their relationship warms further. He encourages her to file for divorce
from Cliff.
   Rudy returns home to find Miss Birdie's son, Delbert, and his wife
there. Delbert says he hopes Rudy is not meddling with Miss Birdie's

will. Rudy picks up Donny Ray and brings him over to Miss Birdie's for some conversation. Rudy sits the bar exam and later learns he has passed. Deck, Rudy and Bruiser go out for lunch and Bruiser asks if Rudy is ready to present a case in court. When Bruiser leaves, Deck informs Rudy that something's wrong and they should sever their ties with Bruiser immediately. Deck reveals that Bruiser is being investigated for jury tampering and tax evasion. Deck suggests to Rudy that they should go into business. The FBI close Bruiser's business – he has disappeared.

Deck and Rudy go to court for the Black versus Great Benefit hearing. They meet with the judge and the defence lawyer, Leo Drummond. Rudy is sworn in by the judge who then says he is inclined to dismiss the case. Leo politely, but clearly, threatens Rudy and, in an attempt to avert a court case, offers an out-of-court settlement for the Black's. Rudy wants the case to go to court. He tells Deck that he was virtually ambushed by the judge and Drummond, but Deck says to accept the settlement. Rudy decides against this and advises the Black family that an out-of-court settlement has been offered. Mrs Black turns it down.

Donny Ray and Rudy talk. Rudy begins work on the case. Deck informs Rudy that the judge has died and is being replaced by Judge Tyrone Kipler, who is very anti-insurance corporations in his rulings. Kipler fast tracks the case, to the consternation of Drummond, who wants to stall it. Because of Donny Ray's ill-health his case is heard in his garden and a video statement is made.

Kelly and Rudy spend more time together and grow closer. For her protection, Rudy has Kelly go and stay with Miss Birdie and he persuades Kelly to file for divorce. Rudy then takes the bus to Cleveland for a meeting with members of the defence. Rudy realises that he is being stitched up when he learns that two of the Great Benefit members of staff he wants to call as witnesses are no longer employees there. Rudy challenges Drummond. Rudy returns to Memphis and attends the funeral of Donny Ray. Rudy and Deck discover their office is being bugged by Drummond and decide to fight dirty too by jury tampering. In court Mrs Black goes into the witness box and the trial begins. Drummond cross-examines her ferociously, sure that he will win.

Rudy and Kelly go back to Kelly's home to collect some of her belongings. Cliff arrives and a fight breaks out. Rudy goes to Kelly's defence, fights Cliff and strikes him down; Cliff dies. Rudy leaves before the police arrive and Kelly says she will say he was never there. Kelly is arrested but Rudy gets her released into his custody.

In court, Rudy's key witness, a former Great Benefit employee called Jackie Lemancyzk, is called to the witness box and reveals the extent of Great Benefit's corruption and efforts to pay out on the minimum number of claims. When Drummond challenges Rudy's case, Deck calls Bruiser, now somewhere in the Caribbean, for advice on a legal precedent with which to get back at Drummond. Bruiser names a case which Rudy then quotes in court. The CEO of Great Benefit is called and successfully challenged by Rudy. Rudy closes his case with an appeal to the jury and use of the video statement from Donny Ray. Rudy wins the case and Great Benefit go bankrupt after paying damages.

Rudy and Kelly are together. Rudy considers teaching law and not practising it. With the business closed, he says goodbye to Deck, joking about Deck trying the bar exam once more.

COPPOLA'S CONCEPT: No stranger to adapting source novels (see **The Godfather**) into compelling movies, Coppola read *The Rainmaker* on a flight from New York to Paris and decided he wanted to direct it as a film. By this time, four of John Grisham's legal novels had been publishing and movie-making hits: *The Firm* (Sydney Pollack, 1993), *The Client* and *A Time to Kill* (Joel Schumacher, 1994 and 1996) and *The Pelican Brief* (Alan J Pakula, 1993). In 1998 Robert Altman also directed *The Gingerbread Man* adaptation.

Coppola bought the rights to the book, wrote the screenplay and signed on to direct in April 1996. Michael Herr wrote the film's voice-over, reprising his collaboration with Coppola after their stunning work on *Apocalypse Now*. Coppola felt that working on such a popular novel would help him tap into the kind of stories that were appealing to mass audiences. Evidently, by the late 1990s Coppola felt that he was out of tune with audience taste when he had once been so in tune with it during the 1970s with *The Godfather*, *The Conversation*, *The Godfather Part II* and *Apocalypse Now*. Coppola's main interest in terms of what the movie expressed was sincerity. Even in the genre of the courtroom drama and the subgenre (or cycle, even) of John Grisham movie adaptations, Coppola found a way to run some sense of social comment through the expected beats of the story. With *The Rainmaker*, Coppola found a personal connection to the film, asking '. . . do you really want to be a lawyer if you're not going to help people? Do you really want to be a film maker if you're not going to make the films that are in your heart?' In a *Film Comment* article (online) entitled 'Grishamovies' Mark Olsen discusses the concept that Grisham adaptations have allowed a range of directors to flex their muscles more than is usual with this kind of material.

Like the other Grisham movies, there is a familiar structure to *The Rainmaker*, though Coppola's contribution carries some of his familiar preoccupations, albeit in a fairly distilled way. For Olsen, the films offer a real challenge to an auteur to continue expressing themselves, and

Coppola rises to the challenge with arguably the finest adaptation of Grisham to date.

INFLUENCES: As an adaptation the biggest influence of course is the source novel. Grisham's novels achieved great popularity in the early nineties and continue to do so. The key difference between the book and the novel is that Coppola has to really condense the relationship between Kelly and Rudy. The other major difference is that Coppola amplifies the tensions and uncertainties of the courtroom scenes. In the novel, it is fairly clear which route things will take but, in the film, Coppola works to keep the audience unsure until near the end.

This was the first time John Grisham's name was officially part of the film. It recalled the *Mario Puzo's The Godfather* titling and only served to show how Coppola's name carried less box office value than it had done when he was adapting other novels such as *The Outsiders* and *Rumble Fish*. Also, when Coppola directed the first of the *Godfather* trilogy, it was as a hired hand and expectations were not so big for its commercial success. The combined North American box office for Grisham adaptations at the time of writing is around $500 million.

COSTUME: The film's naturalistic style is conveyed very much through costume. Rudy Baylor wears a dark-blue suit – he is the clean-cut all-American guy venturing into the corrupt adult world where sharp suits disguise even sharper business practices and dubious morality.

In keeping with the rich panoply of quirky characters in the film, who move around straight-arrow Rudy, the costumes reflect their quirks. Deck Shifflet dresses in a bland brown suit and sometimes wears a hat. He is as crumpled as his cheap suits. The most vivid costume design is for Bruiser Stone with his bracelets, shades and snappy shirts. For the Black family, their working-class status is reflected in their simple, low-key, almost anonymous clothes, though Mr Black wears an arresting bright-red T-shirt that highlights him against the autumn leaves.

TEAM COPPOLA: Coppola worked with only a few of his regular technical collaborators. John Toll returned after his work on *Jack*. Toll's other credits include many of the major Hollywood movies of the past ten years, including *Wind* (Carroll Ballard, 1992), with Francis Ford Coppola as executive producer, *Legends of the Fall* (Ed Zwick, 1994), *Braveheart* (Mel Gibson, 1995), *The Thin Red Line* (Terrence Malick, 1998), *Almost Famous* (Cameron Crowe, 2000), *Captain Corelli's Mandolin* (John Madden, 2001), *Vanilla Sky* (Cameron Crowe, 2001) and *The Last Samurai* (Ed Zwick, 2003).

The production designer was Howard Cummings who has also designed *The Usual Suspects* (Bryan Singer, 1995), *The Long Kiss Goodnight* (Renny Harlin, 1996) and *Death to Smoochy* (Danny DeVito, 2002).

The costume designer was Aggie Guerard Rodgers, one of Coppola's oldest collaborators. Prior to her work on *The Rainmaker* she worked with Coppola on *The Conversation* and *Jack*. Her credits include *American Graffiti* (George Lucas, 1973), *Star Wars: Return of the Jedi* (Richard Marquand, 1983), *The Color Purple* (Steven Spielberg, 1985), *Beetlejuice* (Tim Burton, 1988), *The Fugitive* (Andrew Davis, 1993), *Evolution* (Ivan Reitman, 2001) and *Holes* (2003).

CASTING: One of the most notable features of Coppola's adaptation is the richness of the casting. The film brims with high-calibre actors who invest their supporting roles with real quirks and believability. Certainly, Jon Voight as bad guy Leo Drummond stands out in this capacity. The film's other ace in the hole is Mickey Rourke, who returns from *Rumble Fish*, as Bruiser Stone.

Matt Damon, who plays Rudy Baylor, was not at that time a movie star. That happened very shortly after *The Rainmaker* with the release of *Good Will Hunting* (Gus Van Sant, 1997). For Damon, the challenge was in affecting a believable southern accent. Damon hails from the northeastern state of Massachusetts but had been told that the way he spoke would be key to the success of the story because lawyers play with their accents to suit different occasions. Damon went to Tennessee for several weeks to soak up the dialect. He worked as a bartender in Knoxville over this period of research. Coppola, as he had with *The Godfather*, *The Outsiders* and *Rumble Fish*, used *The Rainmaker* as a way to put an emerging male movie star into centre frame.

Dean Stockwell, as in *Tucker: The Man and His Dream*, puts in another memorable cameo, this time as a wheezing, corrupt judge.

I KNOW THAT FACE: Matt Damon was an emerging star when Coppola cast him in *The Rainmaker*. Damon has appeared in *Chasing Amy* (Kevin Smith, 1996), *Good Will Hunting* (Gus van Sant, 1997), which he co-wrote with Ben Affleck, *The Talented Mr Ripley* (Anthony Minghella, 1999), *Saving Private Ryan* (Steven Spielberg, 1998), *The Legend of Bagger Vance* (Robert Redford, 2001), *Ocean's Eleven* (Steven Soderbergh, 2001) and *The Bourne Identity* (Doug Liman, 2002).

Jon Voight starred in *Midnight Cowboy* (John Schlesinger, 1969), *Deliverance* (John Boorman, 1976), *Coming Home* (Hal Ashby, 1979),

Runaway Train (Andrei Konchalovsky, 1985), *Heat* (Michael Mann, 1996) and *U-Turn* (Oliver Stone, 1998).

Danny Glover has starred in *Places in the Heart* (Robert Benton, 1984), *The Color Purple* (Steven Spielberg), the *Lethal Weapon* series (Richard Donner, 1987, 1989, 1992, 1999) and *The Royal Tannenbaums* (Wes Anderson, 2001).

Clare Danes starred in the hit American TV show *My So-Called Life* and has also starred in *William Shakespeare's Romeo + Juliet* (Baz Luhrmann, 1997).

THE FILMING: Coppola's mission with the design of *The Rainmaker* was to follow a realist line, not to play with the real world. Locations serve to massage the meaning of the story.

Filming began in Memphis in October 1996 with the shoot prepared by Fred Fuchs. Key to the filming in Memphis was The Memphis Pyramid. This is a venue in Memphis that sparked, in Coppola, an idea for the design of the fictional company in the film, Great Benefit. At the time of the film's release Coppola commented, 'When you go to a city you always look around to see what in the city you can use and how you can take advantage of what's there to tell the story.'

Two local Memphis homes were used for filming the scenes at Miss Birdie's and Dot and Buddy's. The interiors were also practical locations, within the houses where the exteriors were shot. The North End Bar was used for the scenes at Yogi's and The Butcher Shop where Bruiser takes Deck and Rudy for lunch played itself. The Arcade, the oldest diner in Memphis also features. Springdale Elementary School was another location for the Cypress Gardens Senior Centre. The fictional St Peter's Hospital was filmed at the Regional Medical Centre in Memphis and Baptist Memorial Hospital was also used. Drummond's office was filmed at a Union Planter's Bank site as was the hospital cafeteria location and the Great Benefits boardroom. The filming of the bar exam was made in the Continental Ballroom of the Peabody Hotel, and the Shelby County Courthouse was used for two days of filming. Rudy and Deck's office was filmed on location at the Bruce Printing Company.

The film was shot through the autumn of 1996 and, over the film's Christmas break, Coppola rewrote the courtroom scene, almost one third of the film.

PROMOTION: *The Rainmaker* certainly traded more on John Grisham's name than Coppola's directorial involvement, and the film's poster very simply showed an image of Rudy and Deck outside a lawcourt.

THE OPENING: As with *Apocalypse Now*, one of the key narrative features of *The Rainmaker* is its voice-over, sincere and ironic by turns in its observations about the legal profession particularly.

A voice-over begins the film and there is a shot of a courthouse building, a clear blue sky, the American flag and an image of Rudy Baylor, the film's hero, studying. The voice-over sets up Rudy's personal and professional roots. Rudy's father used to beat him and his mother and had no time for lawyers. After that, and hearing about civil rights lawyers, Rudy explains why he wanted to be a lawyer. *The Rainmaker* title appears on screen and a shark swims over it, a visual joke about the status of lawyers in the eyes of many. Idealism and corruption are drawn together in these opening moments, raising the key conflict of the drama.

HEROES AND VILLAINS: Rudy Baylor is a young man doing all he can to pull out of the shadow of his father in a way that recalls the struggle of Michael Corleone to do the same. Rudy's father behaved violently at home and certainly this charges Rudy's sense of protectiveness towards Kelly – 'All I want to do is protect her,' he says. He sees himself as her salvation. His commitment to the law in its most idealistic sense is challenged and, like Michael Corleone in *The Godfather Part III*, when Rudy feels himself being compromised, he realises it is time to get out before it is too late. Rudy is earnest and committed and like Michael Corleone he allows the personal and the professional to collide for both better and worse. Rudy's voice-over says, 'this is how the uninsured die . . . I sit here with this poor suffering kid and I swear revenge.' When Rudy enters court for the start of the case he says in voice-over, 'I haven't even been born yet.' The court case will be his baptism, and like Willard's far more intense journey upriver, the experience shows him the capacity for both light and dark in human behaviour. He is tested by the experience, and by his involvement with Kelly, when he becomes as violent as Cliff at the critical moment. Rudy is always redeemed by his sense of a larger justice and his desire to somehow save the world. At a critical meeting which amplifies how much the odds are stacked against Rudy and Deck, he asks Drummond, 'Do you even remember when you sold out?'

Kelly is a victim and, like Rudy, essentially a child beginning to grapple with the corruption of the world. Rudy and Kelly evoke the youthful quality of Vera and Dixie in *The Cotton Club*. Early in their relationship, the camera does all the work as Rudy carries Kelly to her hospital bed, a close-up showing their faces brushing together momentarily, followed by a more emphatic shot showing them holding hands.

Bruiser Stone is a comically corrupt individual whose flash dress code, has something unsettling about it, contrasting with the functional, but far from high-class, quality of his office décor. The fact that he keeps a shark in a fishtank behind his desk tells us all we need to know.

Deck Shifflet is a comic sidekick character to Rudy Baylor but also serves as a father figure to him, teaching him how to negotiate the tricky waters of the legal profession.

Judge Tyrone Kipler is a father figure to Rudy also, certainly on his side from their first meeting. 'You in over your head, son?' Kipler asks Rudy, who replies 'Absolutely.' Kipler smiles approvingly. Coppola, as always, is on the side of youth.

Leo Drummond is theatrically evil, the camera often at a low height as he performs in the courtoom, emphasising his imposing presence. His team of lawyers and associates has the quality of an army that Rudy is up against. Leo's calm, genteel demeanour barely conceals his capacity for wrath, rather like Don Corleone.

As in other Coppola movies, the mother in the story is a wellspring of strength. Mrs Black holds her fragile family together despite her husband's dependence on drink and his fists.

Donny Black is a saintly youngster, representing for Coppola the poor and defeated of America.

COPPOLA STYLE: Coppola imposes very little of his signature style on the film, instead working efficiently within the studio movie template and even more anonymously than he did in *Peggy Sue Got Married* or *Gardens of Stone*; yet he manages to elegantly structure the plot-heavy narrative, in the process offering up the most artful adaptation of a John Grisham novel to date.

IMAGE: *The Rainmaker* has a sombre, autumnal quality, the leaves and grey skies as much a part of the mood as they are in *The Godfather Part II*. John Toll's cinematography is unfussy and transparent. We are a long way from the heightened visuals and dreamy picture making of *The Godfather Part II, Apocalypse Now, Rumble Fish* and *Tucker*. Coppola's simple approach, which has been part of his work all along, serves this story very well, the camera often locked-off and rarely moving. Coppola enjoys his very wide shots of the courtroom, but his love of the tableau is not much in evidence with this film, though there is a brief shot in the courtoom where Rudy occupies the right of screen and on the left Donny Ray's grieving parents hold one another as they sit on the bench.

Coppola sides with the common American who, like all working classes, is exploited by the elite whose wealth is dependent on the labour of the masses. So, in the film, Rudy makes a stand for the common man. You can almost hear Aaron Copland's iconic 'Fanfare for the Common Man' playing as Rudy closes his case at the trial.

Coppola is most comfortable and at his most engaging with the domestic scenes where homes (the Black's and Miss Birdie's) are gentle and nurturing places of warm woods and sunlight softly coming in through the windows. This contrasts with the coldness of the grey hospital cafeteria scenes and the very flat lighting of the courtroom.

There is a shot of Donny Ray lying dead in bed, the sunlight rim-lighting his profile and investing this unfortunate young man with the quality of golden youth and innocence.

During the sound and fury of the trial there is an affecting image where Donny Ray's father cradles a framed photo of his dead son and kisses it.

SOUND: This film is absolutely naturalistic. In classic Coppola fashion, at the moment of high tension and jeopardy a thunder rumble fills the soundtrack as Rudy sits in his car after killing Kelly's violent husband, Cliff.

COPPOLA TUNES: In keeping with the low-key visual telling of the story, Elmer Bernstein's score is whispering, wistful and in its illustration of the Rudy and Kelly storyline it recalls his classic sweet theme for *To Kill A Mockingbird* in its gentility. Elmer Bernstein is a film score legend. His credits include *Far From Heaven* (Todd Haynes, 2002), *The Age of Innocence* (Martin Scorsese, 1993), *Cape Fear* (Martin Scorsese, 1991), *To Kill A Mockingbird* (Robert Mulligan, 1962), *Thoroughly Modern Millie* (George Roy Hill, 1967), *The Great Escape* (John Sturges, 1963), *The Magnificent Seven* (John Sturges, 1960), *The Ten Commandments* (Cecil B De Mille, 1956), *The Black Cauldron* (Ted Berman, 1985) and *The Man with the Golden Arm* (Otto Preminger, 1955).

Composed and conducted by Elmer Bernstein: 'Sharks', 'Last Ride', 'Donny', 'Kelly', 'Shenanagins', 'Plot Thickens', 'Fight, Jail, Who Is Jackie Lemancyzk?', 'Trial Ends', 'Goodbye Dot', 'Sharks' (Reprise).

HUMOUR: The film's wellspring of humour is the character of Deck Shifflett with all his quirks and tics. There is humour too in Rudy's voice-over as he criticises the legal profession.

In a darkly humourous way, there is something surreal about the scene where Donny Ray speaks his case in an impromptu court setting, including judge and stenographer, held in the backyard of Donny Ray's home on a cold-looking autumn day.

In a nod to *The Conversation*, the little scene with the surveillance expert, Rudy and Deck is warmly amusing, the nerdy expert a more caricatured version of Harry Caul in Coppola's great film.

AWARDS: The film received a nomination at the 1998 Golden Globes for Best Supporting Actor (Jon Voight).

The Las Vegas Film Critics Award – the Sierra Award – went to Matt Damon as most promising actor and the London Film Critics Circle Award nominated Damon as actor of the year. The Political Film Society USA nominated the film in 1998 for its Democracy Award and the 1988 Image Awards nominated Danny Glover as Outstanding Supporting Actor.

COPPOLA MAGIC: In a story that does not allow for any kind of fanciful design, action or tone, Coppola's one moment where reality is distorted is in the staging of the court hearing in the backyard of the Black family. In its low-key way it is a very surreal moment.

MOVIE SPEAK:
Rudy: 'There are too many lawyers in Memphis. This city's infested with them.'

Deck: 'There's nothing more thrilling than nailing an insurance company.'

Rudy: 'What's wrong with ethics?'

Rudy: 'I'm so hot after this case, there's no place for me to go but down.'

HOME VIEWING: The film is available on VHS and on both Region 1 and Region 2 DVD with an interactive menu and scene access, and formatted in widescreen 2.35:1. The Region 2 disc is formatted as 16:9 anamorphic.

TRIVIA: The end credits include a listing for Poet in Residence. To enrich performances on set, Coppola would play tricks. So that Clare Danes would shiver believably after being beaten, Coppola got Danes to sit on a block of ice. For a scene where Matt Damon's character was to be fired, Coppola went up to Damon and told him he might be replaced in the role by Ed Norton.

COPPOLA'S VIEW: As with *Tucker: The Man and His Dream*, *The Rainmaker* expresses the conflict between big, corporate business and the efforts of the little guy. For Coppola, the corruption of corporate affairs makes victims of all others. Sure enough, like Preston Tucker, some inventive thought and pluck go a long way in challenging the assumed power of big business. In Rudy Baylor, Coppola is able to repeat, albeit less vividly, the story of a man who is surrounded by corruption but who succeeds in avoiding its pitfalls. The creation of a family unit is as evident in *The Rainmaker* as it is in so many Coppola movies, as is Coppola's career-long interest in rituals, through the presentation of the courtcase.

Rudy's romantic sense connects him to characters like The Motorcycle Boy in *Rumble Fish*, Ponyboy and Johnny in *The Outsiders* and Willow in *Gardens of Stone*. All of these young men have a sense of duty to whatever their particular code is, and they carry a deeply romantic strain in the widest, truest sense of the term.

CRITICAL COPPOLA: *Empire* described this as 'a watchable courtroom drama as perfunctory and efficient as any other upmarket Hollywood product. It feels like the deadening of a true creative spirit' though the *San Francisco Examiner* felt that 'Coppola . . . shines his intelligence on . . . bestseller material'. However, *Time* magazine was more positive: 'Cheers for Coppola! *The Rainmaker*, cleverly adapted by Francis Ford Coppola, is honest fun!'

VERDICT: Alongside *The Cotton Club*, *The Rainmaker* is Coppola's most anonymous film and certainly a minor entry for him in his body of work. Coppola reins in his predilection for what some would call fussy film making. It is a very muted film and it is in Coppola's favour that he spends so much time on everything except the tedious legal exposition of these kinds of films. Nonetheless, it does express some familiar Coppola preoccupations. The strongest element of the film is its performances, lending a Dickensian quality to its oddball characters. Coppola gives the potentially clunky story some energy and seems far more interested in the Black family story and Rudy's relationship with Deck than with the legalese and courtroom drama. The most rewarding element of the story is the relationship between Rudy and Kelly.

COPPOLA NOW: 'You try to win, but in the end there are more important things than money prizes.'

Short Film Projects

In the 1980s, Coppola directed three short film projects; one was an adaptation of a fairy tale for American TV; another was called *Captain Eo*, for Disney theme parks; the third was *Life Without Zoe*, a short piece for a portmanteau movie called *New York Stories* with Martin Scorsese and Woody Allen.

Faerie Tale Theatre: Rip Van Winkle (1984)

Coppola was approached by Shelley Duvall, who had starred as Olive Oil in *Popeye* (Robert Altman, 1980), in her capacity as producer on *Faerie Tale Theatre*, a children's series for network television. The piece Coppola turned his imagination to was *Rip Van Winkle*. While the piece is ultimately a sideline (when set against the feature career), the Rip Van Winkle story does relate to Coppola's recurring theme of change and time passing, as this theme is at the heart of Washington Irving's story – one of the first American fairy-tale narratives. Coppola shot the piece in five days and caused the producers some frustration; he rehearsed his actors and imposed his own process on the well-oiled machine of network production in shaping the script and going with a highly theatrical design process.

Harry Dean Stanton, who had appeared in *The Godfather Part II* and *One From the Heart* starred as Rip Van Winkle and Talia Shire played Rip's wife. Sofia Coppola played their daughter. Eiko Ishioka provided the design for the piece, which was highly artificial and theatrical.

Captain Eo (1986)

(Colour – 17 minutes)

Walt Disney and Lucasfilm
Director: Francis Ford Coppola
Executive Producer: George Lucas
Production Designer: John Napier
Choreographer: Jeffrey Hornaday
Music: James Horner
Songs: Michael Jackson

CAST: Michael Jackson (*Captain Eo*), Anjelica Huston (*The Supreme Leader*)

BUDGET: $17 million

RELEASE DATE: 12 September 1986 (EPCOT opening), 18 September 1986 (Disneyland opening).

TAGLINE: We are here to change the world.

SUMMARY: A starfield and a swirl of a galaxy against which a meteorite spins wildly. An ominous-sounding voice says that this is 'a universe of good and evil where a small group struggles to bring freedom to the countless worlds of despair, a ragtag band led by the infamous Captain Eo.' Eo's ship explodes the meteorite and rockets towards a planet. On board the ship, the navigator, a creature called The Geex, announces that they have almost reached their destination. A claxon sounds but the panic is unnecessary: it is simply clumsy little Hooter entering. There is some cute interplay between the space critter crew before the brusque robot Major Domo announces that Captain Eo is about to enter. Eo says that the time has come to go into battle in order to prove their worth to The Command. Suddenly, the ship is rocked by an enemy ship passing by and the huge ship pursues Eo's tiny, bronze-tinted vessel. A hologram from The Command appears asking if Eo and his crew are fine. Eo says they are and then admits, in a nod to Han Solo in *Star Wars*, that they have 'a slight weapons malfunction'. Eo's ship races towards the planet's surface, a conglomeration of industrial buildings, towers and tunnels, rather like the Death Star in Star Wars. Eo's ship navigates a run of tight spots before crashlanding.

Eo and his crew emerge into the sinister darkness and are surrounded by guards hiding amid the junk. They take Eo and his crew to the lair of the Supreme Leader. The Supreme Leader hangs from the ceiling wrapped in cables and tubing. She sentences Eo and his crew and Eo passively accepts the punishment. He then declares that he comes with a gift for the Supreme Leader. Eo gestures to his crew and the music begins. Major Domo transforms into a guitar and drum set. Minor Domo becomes a synthesiser. The Geex plays the drums and Fuzzball strums the guitar strings. The Supreme Leader's guards close around Eo who forces them back with his music. Eo transforms the guards into dancers and he and his crew advance on the Supreme Leader, who calls on her Whip Warriors. Eo sends his power down the whips but it is deflected. He runs for a gate which closes before he reaches it. He transforms the Whip Warriors into dancers and the Supreme Leader rages. Eo lifts her into the air and transforms her into a beautiful woman. All around, the monochromatic, junkyard world becomes classically gorgeous and bright. The sky is a rich orange and the sun shines. Fuzzball waves goodbye to the audience as Eo salutes and exits. His ship rockets off on another adventure.

CONCEPT: Walt Disney Imagineering had been keen to build on the success of their Magic Journey 3D mini-movie experience at their North American theme parks. By the mid-1980s, George Lucas had assumed a Walt Disney-like stature in American pop culture through his films *American Graffiti* (1973), the Indiana Jones character (from 1981) and the *Star Wars* movies (from 1977 onwards). Disney were keen to work with him and had been developing the Star Tours (Star Wars) ride. When the subject of a short film collaboration with Michael Jackson (at the height of his popularity) was suggested, Lucas was intrigued. Several story premises were presented, devised by Walt Disney Imagineers, Rick Rothschild, Richard Vaughan, Tim Kirk and Joe Rohde. Lucas moved towards something with an outerspace setting, in keeping with his *Star Wars* world. Indeed, Captain Eo's spaceship was designed by former Industrial Light and Magic design ace, Joe Johnston. Like Coppola's *One From the Heart*, *Captain Eo* delights in the power of music to enrich lives. Fantasy can transform mundane reality, a classic motif of the musical form.

Francis Ford Coppola was brought on board, in his first collaboration with Lucas since *American Graffiti*. After the success of *Captain Eo,* they would collaborate again on *Tucker: The Man and His Dream*. With Coppola and Lucas on board the idea was revised further and the team of funky space creatures and robots developed.

The *Captain Eo* short film is akin to a movie by the Van Beuren brothers, called *The Sunshine Makers* (Ted Eshbaugh, Burt Gillett, 1935).

Captain Eo is about the power of art in the shape of song and dance to have a positive influence on the world.

TEAM COPPOLA: Rick Baker, the make-up master behind *An American Werewolf in London* (John Landis, 1981) and many years later *Men In Black* (Barry Sonnenfeld, 1997), served on *Captain Eo*. Vittorio Storaro, who shot *Apocalypse Now* and *One From the Heart*, returned to film *Captain Eo*. He would work with Coppola again on *Tucker: The Man and His Dream*. James Horner was a newly established Hollywood film composer, having begun working on the Roger Corman movie *Battle Beyond the Stars* (Jimmy T Murakami, 1980). He has since scored many movies including *Cocoon* (Ron Howard, 1985), *Aliens* (James Cameron, 1986), *An American Tail* (Don Bluth, 1986), *Field of Dreams* (Phil Alden Robinson, 1989), *Glory* (Ed Zwick, 1989), *Legends of the Fall* (Ed Zwick, 1994), Braveheart (Mel Gibson, 1995) and *Titanic*

(James Cameron, 1997). John Napier designed the costumes for *Captain Eo*. Napier has established himself as a stage designer on shows like *Cats* and *Starlight Express*. He went on to work as a visual consultant on the set design for *Hook* (Steven Spielberg, 1991).

By the mid-1980s, George Lucas was arguably at an all-time career high. He had completed his first *Star Wars* trilogy and also directed the classic *American Graffiti* (1973). As a producer he was also working with the late and truly great Jim Henson on *Labyrinth* (1986) and the *Indiana Jones* series had one more movie to come, *Indiana Jones and the Last Crusade* (Steven Spielberg, 1989).

Industrial Light and Magic provided visual effects for the film and the claymation effects for transforming characters was provided by the animator Will Vinton. Vinton provided stunning and charming effects for the sadly neglected and underrated film *Return to Oz* (Walter Murch, 1985). Murch, an old-time Coppola collaborator on *The Conversation*, *The Godfather Part II* and *Apocalypse Now*, came on board *Captain Eo* to edit it. The film's choreographer Jeffrey Hornaday had worked on *Flashdance* (Adrian Lyne, 1983), *A Chorus Line* (Richard Attenborough, 1985) and the *Say, Say, Say* music video with Michael Jackson and Paul McCartney.

Twenty years after they first met on the set of a feature musical, *Finian's Rainbow*, Lucas and Coppola were reunited on the set of a mini-movie musical.

CASTING: Michael Jackson and Anjelica Huston are the name actors in the movie.

I KNOW THAT FACE: Michael Jackson is a pop music phenomenon who redefined what pop music could be in the 1980s, integrating dance performance with vocals.

Anjelica Huston went on to appear in *Gardens of Stone* and has appeared in many films including *Prizzi's Honor* (John Huston, 1985), *The Dead* (John Huston, 1987) and *The Grifters* (Stephen Frears, Sy Richardson, 1990).

THE FILMING: The choreographer Jeffrey Hornaday worked with Lucas and Coppola to integrate dance into the story. Jackson improvised his dances and Hornaday devised ways for these moves to be echoed and expanded on by his dance troupe. For the shoot, Disney employed its two unique 65mm 3-D cameras. *Captain Eo* shot for two weeks in July 1985.

Eric Brevig served as the 3-D consultant on the film. Some of the film's footage was incorrectly shot because the cameras were not aligned with total accuracy. Subsequently about twelve shots are not quite right, though to the untrained eye it is not noticeable. Joe Johnston, ace designer on the original *Star Wars* trilogy, designed Eo's little bronze spaceship.

The film features 150 effects shots. Back in the mid-1980s a feature movie would reach its limit at this number so for a fifteen-minute movie this was quite something. Matte artist Harrison Ellenshaw, who had worked on George Lucas's 1977 film *Star Wars: A New Hope* – on the paintings of the Death Star chasm and the Millennium Falcon in the Death Star docking bay – worked on *Captain Eo* as an effects supervisor. Initially the film was budgeted for just sixty shots. The film drew on the full arsenal of effects techniques in the pre-digital age. *Captain Eo* was made before morphing had been tried and tested. There were motion control ships, blue-screen elements, high-speed explosions, stop-motion and hand-drawn animation elements. Some effects shots had twelve and thirteen layers to them.

There was a post-production period (editing, completing visual effects and incorporating them into the live-action footage) of seven months and the project soon found itself behind schedule. It was originally planned for release at Easter 1986, but was delayed for a few months. DreamQuest provided the film's starfield backdrops.

Will Vinton's animation studio in Portland, Oregon, provided two key elements, namely the transformation of Minor Domo into a synthesiser and of high-tech pillars into Grecian style columns. These two pieces of material took four months to complete, amounting to seven shots in all. For the moment, where Major Domo turns into a set of drums a full-scale stop-motion model was created.

It was not just the film that was a 3-D event, the theatre itself was rigged with lighting and smoke effects matched to the on-screen action so that it immersed the audience that bit more in the experience.

PROMOTION: The short was heavily promoted but was only shown at the Disneyland and Disneyworld theme parks in North America, before being screened at Disneyland Paris and the Disney theme park in Japan. The film ceased running at the theme parks around 1999. When the movie opened at Disneyland in mid-September 1986, it ran for sixty continuous hours such was the excitement for it, and 150,000 people saw it in that time. There was even a special opening ceremony attended by Coppola, Huston and Lucas, in almost the only instance where Lucas was photographed unbearded.

The film was regarded as a triumph of big names coming together on a film of little emotional substance but lots of whiz bang. The film is part movie, part ride, in keeping with the spirit of the theme park. *Captain Eo* has never been seen outside the theme parks.

For Coppola, the project was certainly high profile and must have appealed to the showman in him, quite apart from the appeal of collaborating with George Lucas again. For Michael Jackson the project built on his music video trailblazing. For Lucas, it was a chance to apply his great success to another format and to see his work fold back into a source of inspiration: Walt Disney. Thematically, the film has the sense of play and charm present in some of Coppola's films.

HEROES AND VILLAINS: Captain Eo is a mythological kind of figure in the broadest sense, part Luke Skywalker, part Michael Jackson, part painter. You could even say that Captain Eo and his gang represent youth, and the villains embody the adults who have forgotten the power of play. A similar theme gets less vivid expression in Coppola's short film *Life Without Zoe* (1989).

Captain Eo's crew are Hooter, a green elephant with a saxophone-like trunk and a propensity for clumsiness, rather like that other alien fellow Jar Jar Binks in *Star Wars: Episode 1 The Phantom Menace* (George Lucas, 1999). Then there is the gruff, military-styled Major Domo, a blue robot that can transform into a drum kit. His sidekick is, inevitably, Minor Domo, who can turn into a synthesiser and guitar. Filling out the corps is a shaggy golden-haired, two-headed creature called the Geex, its very Muppet-like heads named Idy and Ody. Finally there is a cute little hamster-like creature with butterfly wings called Fuzzball, who sits on Eo's shoulder most of the time. Originally there was a butterfly on the crew called Flutter, but this creature was combined with Fuzzball.

In *Captain Eo*, the Supreme Leader is the force of darkness. Darth Vader with mascara, and rather attractive for all the claws and armour. An almost unrecognisable, but still gorgeous, Anjelica Huston took her cue from Cruella de Ville and the witch from *Snow White*. She resembles the biotech look of HR Giger's designs fused with a good old-fashioned witch. Anjelica Huston's eyes are rimmed with dark circles and her face is ash white. Pipes and pieces of metal armour encase her, as she hangs from a ceiling. By the end of the film she is wearing a flowing pink dress looking quite classical.

COPPOLA TUNES: James Horner's orchestral score is a driving, symphonic piece in the grand tradition of space opera. Jackson sings two songs in this mega music video, which build on the tradition he helped begin with promos for his *Thriller* album for tracks such as 'Billie Jean', 'Beat It' and of course 'Thriller' (John Landis, 1983). Jackson's *Captain Eo* tunes are 'We Are Here to Change The World' and 'Another Part of Me.'

TRIVIA: Eo is the Greek word for sunrise. To watch the film, audiences wore 3-D glasses. Mylar balloons bought at the Disney theme parks could not be taken into the *Captain Eo* theatre because the live laser effects would ricochet off the balloons.

COPPOLA NOW: '(the film is like) one of those little children's stereo reel masters, that spins while the viewers see beautiful three-dimensional fairy tales, making you wish you could just step in and sit down next to the white rabbit.'

New York Stories: Life Without Zoe (1989)

(Colour – 35 minutes)

Touchstone Pictures
Producer: Fred Fuchs and Fred Roos
Screenplay: Francis Ford Coppola and Sofia Coppola
Cinematographer: Vittorio Storaro
Editor: Barry Malkin
Music: Carmine Coppola
Production Designer: Dean Tavoularis
Art Direction: Speed Hopkins
Costume Design: Sofia Coppola

CAST: Heather McComb (*Zoe*), Talia Shire (*Charlotte*), Giancarlo Giannini (*Carlo*), Gia Coppola (*Baby Zoe*), James Keane (*Jimmy*), Don Novello (*Hector*), Selim Tlili (*Abu*), Carmine Coppola (*Street Flautist*)

BUDGET: $5 million (*Life Without Zoe*), $15 million (whole *New York Stories*)

THE BOX OFFICE: $10.7 million (whole *New York Stories*)

RELEASE DATE: 26 February 1989

MPAA: R

BBFC: 15

TAGLINE: One city. Three stories tall.

SUMMARY: New York City, the late 1980s. A voice-over by Zoe explains how once upon a time flute-playing was banned because it caused all the world's virgins to fall in love. Zoe is the daughter of a well-to-do flautist, her father, and a globetrotting writer, her mother. Zoe lives in a suite at the Sheraton Hotel where she is cared for by the family butler, Hector. She is an artistic girl with dreams of far-off lands and merely sweet memories and thoughts of her far-off parents. Zoe heads off for school, taking a taxi when she misses the bus. At school, she and her friends interview the new boy for their paper. The boy is called Abu, the young son of a Middle-Eastern prince. Zoe and Abu befriend one another and go on a shopping spree. Returning to the hotel late at night, Zoe gets caught in the midst of an armed robbery. Her father's safe box is robbed and in their haste to escape the thieves drop a package. Zoe grabs it before the robbers realise what has happened.

With the robbers gone, Zoe looks inside the package. It contains a gorgeous earring. Zoe tells Hector what has happened. He thinks that the reason her father has the earring is because the Sheikh's wife, the Princess, heard his flute-playing and loved it so much she had to give him a gift. But does this mean that the Sheikh is angry at Zoe's father for being the object of the Princess's affections? Zoe learns that the earring in her father's possession had been given to him as a gift when the Sheikh's wife heard him play the flute. The wife of Sheikh Omar has sent Zoe's absent parents an invite to a lavish party. Zoe decides to throw her own party for her friends in the apartment. Zoe attends the party dressed like a character from *The Arabian Nights*, with the earring as the centre piece of her turban. The party is under way when first Zoe's mother unexpectedly returns, and then her father. Zoe's parents are attempting to reconcile their marriage. At the lavish party, Zoe is taken by Abu to meet the Sheikh's wife. At the apartment, Zoe's parents make up their differences. Zoe's dad then gets a telegram. He is being asked to perform in Europe, starting off in Athens. He goes. Zoe purchases plane tickets for herself and her mother to go and see him. They sit with the audience in the ruins of the Parthenon at sundown, united as a family on the move.

COPPOLA'S CONCEPT: Originally the concept for *New York Stories* was that it would be a movie of three short films solely by Woody Allen, the director most associated with New York. Woody Allen's cinema has always offered a very different glimpse of New York City than the work of his contemporary Martin Scorsese, with Scorsese's emphasis on the meaner streets and behaviour of The Big Apple.

It was Allen's producer, Robert Greenhut, who suggested that Allen should be one of three hotshot directors. Orion were not prepared to finance a $15 million movie of this nature. They can be hard to market. However, with Martin Scorsese and another name director on board perhaps it would be a more marketable project. Initially, Steven Spielberg was invited but it was not to be. The studio, Touchstone Pictures (Disney) turned to Francis Ford Coppola, at the time re-established as an under-control director after the successes (commercial and artistic) of *Peggy Sue Got Married, Gardens of Stone* and *Tucker: The Man and His Dream* and Coppola's short film for Disney, *Captain Eo*. In hindsight, though, one has to ask how committed Coppola was to the project. When Coppola's daughter Sofia expressed a creative idea he teamed up with her to draft the screenplay. Martin Scorsese's movie is about an artist and his intense relationship with his assistant. Allen's is a comic tale about a middle-aged man and his monstrous mother. Coppola's concept is essentially about a rich kid.

INFLUENCES: Dean Tavoularis called the short a sort of Noel Coward story for kids and Coppola derived some insspiration from *The Arabian Nights* stories.

COSTUME: Sofia Coppola designed the costumes for the film and they establish the mood more so than the décor and setting. The costumes carry a delicate fairy-tale quality and do more for the tone of the piece than the sets. Coppola repeated this kind of design sense on *Bram Stoker's Dracula* where the costumes were consciously meant to carry as much tonal and, in some cases, thematic weight as other elements of the film.

TEAM COPPOLA: Even for this small film, Coppola's big-time collaborators worked with him. Fred Fuchs and Fred Roos worked as producers. Fuchs had served as producer on *Tucker: The Man and His Dream* and Roos had worked with Coppola on virtually every film since *The Conversation*.

CASTING: *Life Without Zoe* is very much a family affair. Coppola's sister, Talia Shire, plays the mother. Coppola's granddaughter, Gia, plays Baby Zoe. Giancarlo Giannini is Carlo. Coppola's father appears as a street flautist.

I KNOW THAT FACE: Talia Shire appears as Connie in the *Godfather* trilogy. Giancarlo Giannini can be seen in *Hannibal* (Ridley Scott, 2001).

THE FILMING: Production on the film began in June 1988 shooting on location in New York over a period of about four weeks.

PROMOTION: The film was sold on the strength of the star directors. The original release poster was of an apartment block; in three of the windows the central characters for each film are shown.

THE OPENING: Coppola's often playful spirit is evident, as is his love of art which imbues the opening with soft dissolves and shots of a sculpture. On the voice-over Zoe talks about how flute-playing was once banned because of it causing virgins to fall in love. One shot has the camera tracking to the right revealing Zoe finishing a painting of an Arabian prince and princess. The film's playful tone is at its most charming in the opening credits, apparently hand-drawn, and all the cast and crew credited just with first names, emphasising the sense of family.

HEROES AND VILLAINS: As with many Coppola movies, a young person is the centre of the action. Like young Vito and Jack, to name two characters, who are polar opposites in utterly contrasting Coppola movies, Zoe is lonely. She has built herself a rich imaginative life that evidently does more for her than the comfort of her surroundings. Hector is Zoe's 'guardian'. He is a childlike personality, sleeping with a bedside light on.

Zoe's parents, Charlotte and Carlo, are warm and loving towards her. Indeed, Zoe is more the adult and her parents more the children.

COPPOLA STYLE: The film has a very sweet and luxurious look to its interior apartment and party scenes contrasting with the sharper images of the outside world. It is essentially a kind of heightened naturalism. The film, for the most part, shows a genteel New York, in contrast to the more familiar imagery we associate with the city.

IMAGE: Vittorio Storaro lends the apartment scenes a warm and comforting orange tone, and for the shots out on the streets of New York, the vast scale of the city, its height, is emphasised by placing the camera low down, looking up at the young children in the story.

As in *One From the Heart* and *Tucker: The Man and His Dream*, Storaro finds appropriate opportunities to bring lighting effects to the fore. When Zoe holds up the Princess's earring, her face is awash with blue light which elevates the discovery's sense of magic and importance. When Zoe is taken by Abu to meet the Princess, a blue light engulfs the image, separating it from a sense of reality. Coppola and Storaro work hard to build the atmosphere of a sweet fairy tale. There is a feeling of a picture book, never more clear than when the camera pushes in slowly and gently on Abu and Zoe sitting under a tree in Central Park.

For the scene where the hotel is being robbed, the tone of the images is appropriately different to the rest of the film, with its titled camera angles and low-key lighting.

For the elaborate party scene at the Sheikh's apartment, the golden lighting and graceful camera moves again place the action apart from reality and also set the moment as some fictional, heightened, storybook sense of an Arabian night. Coppola has long been intrigued by these stories and the culture of the Middle East.

Coppola's love of tableaux shines through, nowhere better than in the wide shot of Zoe and Abu going up the immense staircase at the party. With the archways and vividly bright festivities filling the frame, the image is like one of Zoe's paintings made real.

SOUND: The film has a naturalistic sound design.

COPPOLA TUNES: Carmine Coppola's father wrote the score for the film, played on a flute, and resembling 'Twinkle Twinkle Little Star'.

HUMOUR: Hector provides a degree of humour. Zoe lives in a world where all adults care about her. Out on the streets there is a comic interruption to her pleasant life when the hand of a homeless person reaches out to her from inside their cardboard box. While the scene acknowledges the extremes of life in the city, it works predominantly as a source of quirky humour. It is almost cartoony.

AWARDS: Despite the calibre of talent involved in this portmanteau movie, it failed to gain any awards recognition.

COPPOLA MAGIC: The film's most magical moment is when Zoe discovers the jewel.

HOME VIEWING: *New York Stories* is available on VHS and DVD in America and on VHS in the UK.

TRIVIA: Coppola's wife Eleanor puts in a cameo as the school teacher. Coppola's father, Carmine, is the flautist on the street.

COPPOLA'S VIEW: Thematically, just about, the film ties in with Coppola's familiar preoccupation with the bonds of family and lonely protagonists. During the 1980s, Coppola held the rights to *Peter Pan* and had wanted to focus on that character's essential loneliness. One senses that as the concept comes from Sofia, who has gone on to direct the fantastic *The Virgin Suicides*, it is really her reaction to her father's globetrotting as a film maker. People often acknowledge Coppola's playful side and certainly this film belongs much more in this zone.

CRITICAL COPPOLA: Pauline Kael noted of the short that 'the Arabian Nights . . . conceit never takes hold.'

VERDICT: Sadly, *Life Without Zoe* does not really warrant much scrutiny. Often, short films offer very concentrated expressions of a film maker's larger works. Perhaps the big problem with the film is its premise. Should the audience be that interested in the life of a little girl who lives so comfortably? Nonetheless, the motifs of art and fantasy do link in with other Coppola movies, so there is some value in it. Maybe its most winning aspect is its gentility. Alongside the edgy intensity of Scorsese's *Life Lessons* and Woody Allen's very funny *Oedipus Wrecks*, the weakness of *Life Without Zoe* is emphasised all the more than by watching it in isolation. The film begins with playful promise, and yet, once it has established its premise, there is not far for it to go, and the ending lacks any real sense of resolution. Throughout the film, Zoe does not seem to miss her parents that much, so the fact they are all together at the end does not carry the weight it perhaps might have done.

COPPOLA NOW: 'It's sort of like Pippi Longstocking.'

Works Still to Come

On the Road

Given Coppola's affinity for the Beat writers it is no surprise that he has owned the rights to Jack Kerouac's seminal, road trip novel *On The Road* for many years and, as of late 2003, is some way to seeing it hit the screen in his capacity as producer. In the early 1980s it looked as though Jean-Luc Godard might direct it for American Zoetrope. In fact Joel Schumacher has, apparently, been signed to direct with Brad Pitt and Billy Crudup in the lead roles. The project would tie in nicely with Coppola's loose bohemian interests and San Francisco base. Michael Herr has been engaged to write a voice-over narration, with Russell Banks writing the screenplay which, by the summer of 2002 had been approved by Coppola. In 1994, Zoetrope had considered casting Ethan Hawke and Brad Pitt in a film version. As an interesting point of Beat and film history, Jack Kerouac contacted producer Jerry Wald in 1958 when there was the prospect of a movie version of *On the Road*. Kerouac wrote that the film should be about 'goodhearted kids in pain of soul doing wild things out of desperation. I find life much less violent than the movies and TV make it out.' Coppola's 1983 and 1984 movies *The Outsiders* and *Rumble Fish* are awash with young people going wild because they despair.

Pinocchio – The Unmade Dream

At one point in his career, during the 1980s, Coppola had held the movie rights to the JM Barrie novel *Peter Pan*. Coppola's concept had been to zero in on the notion of loneliness were he ever able to mount the film. Sadly, it never came to pass and is surely one of the great lost films of his career. Nonetheless, Coppola would pursue another iconic modern fairy-tale project which has also become a lost dream.

All through the 1990s one of Coppola's obsessions was to bring a new version of Carlo Collodi's story *Pinocchio* to the screen. The material has been adapted many times and even folded into the bigger story of Spielberg's astonishing *AI:Artificial Intelligence*. Roberto Benigni made a big-budget version in Italy in 2002 which was met with critical negativity but proved popular. Typically, Coppola's concept was innovative. He considered framing the story within the context of the Bosnian war of the mid-1990s with the story being read to children in the war zone.

Coppola's desire to see the film made was not fulfilled. He had initially approached Warner Brothers with the idea, as part of a deal that was in the offing for him to make three films for the studio. In 1993, Coppola took the completed screenplay for his Pinocchio story to Columbia. When Coppola's foreign financing for the film fell through, Columbia lost interest and withdrew their financing.

In 1998, the case went to court and Coppola's representatives argued that Warner never had a deal for Coppola to produce it for them. When Coppola took it to Columbia, Warners stepped in and unlawfully stopped the project, just as a slap on the wrist. Warners said there had been an agreement for Coppola to produce the movie for them and that as soon as *Bram Stoker's Dracula* was a hit for Coppola at Columbia he took the movie to them. Coppola appealed against a post-trial order throwing out a jury award for $60 million which was then reduced to $20 million. Coppola appealed, wanting the higher figure reinstated. Warner Brothers appealed for $20 million in compensatory damages. Coppola argues that he would never have made Pinocchio at Columbia but for Warner Brothers' assertion that it owned the rights to the film. This certificate gave Warner Brothers the right to inform Columbia that it reserved all rights to Coppola's Pinocchio film.

In 2000 a California Court of Appeal reversed the $80 million jury verdict that Coppola had won and this ended the project once and for all. Although Coppola had not signed a contract, he had signed a certificate of employment with the studio.

Coppola allowed his friend the ballet choreographer Michael Smuin to use one of the songs Coppola had written for his hoped for movie to be included in Smuin's 2000 Pinocchio ballet in San Francisco. The song was called 'Little Moon'. One of Coppola's conceptual collaborators, Ian McCaig, was one of the most influential artists of the past fifteen years in the field of fantasy and visual effects films. He has contributed to George Lucas's *Star Wars: Episode I – The Phantom Menace* (1999), *Star Wars: Episode II – Attack of the Clones* (2002) and *The Young Indiana Jones Chronicles* (1992–3) as well as *Hook* (Steven Spielberg, 1991), the abandoned ILM all digital feature *Frankenstein, Bram Stoker's Dracula, Interview with the Vampire* (Neil Jordan, 1994), *Terminator 2: Judgment Day* (James Cameron, 1991), *Star Trek VI: The Undiscovered Country* (Nicholas Meyer, 1991) and *Dinotopia* (Marco Brambilla, 2002).

One can readily see why the prospect of adapting Collodi's novel appealed to Coppola. It is an Italian story with a strong fairy-tale quality. In a very different way to the *Godfather* stories, it details the relationship between a father and son and also explores the tension between the civilised and the wild.

A Dream to Come: Megalopolis

On 10 April 2003, MGM issued a press release. It stated that Francis Coppola was stepping down from the board. Why? Because of the 'intense focus he's placing right now on getting *Megalopolis* made'.

Megalopolis is the project that everybody is waiting for from Francis Coppola. He has been developing it since the early 1980s (by early 1983, Coppola had generated 400 pages of notes and script segments over two months) and from all the information available it suggests a fusion of the contemporary and the classical on the scale of *Apocalypse Now*, and with a screenplay more akin to *The Conversation*. In an interview in 1996, Coppola said, 'I feel that I owe it to myself to have a shot at something with original writing where I can use the epic level that I'm capable of at least once in my life.' Of thematic interest is Coppola's statement that one of the concerns of the story is time, just as it is in *The Godfather*, *The Outsiders*, *Rumble Fish*, *Peggy Sue Got Married* and *Jack*. For all the historical elements and reference points and indeed the tensions and corruptions of the world, what seems to shine through in Coppola's talking about the project is that the film will embrace life and offer a very positive vision of how the world could be. For all his challenges and bruisings, Coppola the young man is still very much the heartbeat pulsing away.

In his childlike enthusiasm for an idea, Coppola is just excited to have the script. 'It's funny, I don't feel any sense of accomplishment or pride about anything I've done in the past. If I didn't have this script, I would just be totally deflated . . . What I live for is the idea that I'm going to make this beautiful film, not that I've made a few good films.'

In the concept, which is all the movie watching world knows of right now, New York City assumes the quality of ancient Rome. Coppola has been inspired by an incident called *The Catiline Conspiracy*, which is related in Cicero. Coppola even talks about the film in the *Apocalypse Now* documentary *Hearts of Darkness*.

Coppola's deal for the film is apparently with United Artists. Many big name actors have been attached to the potential film, including Nicolas Cage, Russell Crowe, Robert De Niro, Paul Newman, Parker Posey, Kevin Spacey and Warren Beatty. In the very early 1980s while working on *Rumble Fish*, Coppola mentioned the *Megalopolis* concept to Matt Dillon and Dillon was even in the running for a starring role in the proposed film as a West Point cadet who goes AWOL and becomes a window cleaner in New York City.

The film's proposed director of photography is Ron Fricke, who has worked with Godfrey Reggio on the Coppola-backed *Koyaanisqatsi* (1982) and *Powaqaatsi* (1988). Dean Tavoularis is on board as production designer and Jim Steranko has been generating concept art just as he did many years ago for *Raiders of the Lost Ark* (Steven Spielberg, 1981).

The basic premise of *Megalopolis* is that an architect dreams of building a city of the future in order to create a utopia. The mayor of the city, however, wants to preserve the city's heritage, but the architect is for looking to the future. A massive renovation project is planned for a vast area and it is here that the conflict begins over scale, profit and vision and goes on to affect all stratas of society.

Coppola's other phrasing for the film is that it will be futurist, akin to the look of the Chrysler building with a 1930s Parisian, film noir, art deco spin to the design. For Coppola, the movie would grandly encapsulate a statement about life with the city a metaphor of society. 'I'm interested in believing that we have the talent, we have the scientists or engineers, the genius to control a world that would be extremely beautiful and harmonious.'

In the aftermath of the terrorist attacks on New York in September 2001 Coppola has had to find a way to reconcile his screenplay with real events as he had framed his story around a city rebuilding itself after a tragedy. Coppola had thirty hours of footage by the autumn of 2001 and he shot again in New York two weeks after the Twin Towers tragedy.

In terms of characters, Coppola's central dynamic is to chart how a good man becomes evil and an evil man becomes good, a concept played out across *The Godfather* story.

Locations proposed for the film include Montreal and New York. By late 2002, Coppola had shot a wealth of material on high definition video. George Lucas in an interview with *American Cinematographer* said, 'Coppola has just shot some unbelievably gorgeous material, wide shots of cities with detail at magic hour and all kinds of available light material.'

The film's budget is pitched at $65–70 million. Concept artist Maura Borrelli has generated concept art for the movie.

In an interview with Business Week in September 2000, Coppola said, 'I confess that this screenplay I'm writing is a bear. It just fights me back. . . . It's a kind of a shape-of-things-to-come film . . . It's a little bit like an Ayn Rand novel.' Ayn Rand's novels include *The Fountainhead* which concerns a dazzling architect who stands for social integrity in a compromised world. The *Megalopolis* concept also recalls the astonishing work of American novelists Frank Norris and John Dos Passos with its vast span of society from workers, labour unions, financiers and, of course, the man on the street.

In a diary entry of 31 March 1993, Coppola noted that his characters in *Megalopolis* were committed to the Ultrafuture and others were locked in the past. And what's the betting that at the heart of his dream film might be some young hero and dreamer, rather like Francis Ford Coppola always was, is and will be.

Coppola the Producer and Showman

Every director worth his salt has had films that, for a range of reasons, have taken much effort to bring to the screen. Other projects simply elude the creative grasp and never reach the screen, existing as tantalising 'almost projects' that often say as much about a film maker's creative identity as the material they do bring to life.

Francis Coppola has had a range of projects that he has wanted to realise in his capacity as a writer and director.

What follows is an overview of the work he has wanted to put the smoke and mirrors of movie making to, but which has not come to pass.

In the 1980s one of Coppola's grand plans was to adapt Goethe's novel *Elective Affinities* to the screen across four movies made over a ten-year period, so that the performers returned, genuinely aged. The story was built on the idea that a husband and wife take in a young girl and the man falls in love with her and the wife has a relationship with another man.

Coppola considered a movie with Joseph Papp, a screen version of *The Pirates of Penzance*. The film was eventually made but not with Coppola's involvement.

Thy Neighbour's Wife was another project, based on a bestselling novel by Gay Talese about marital infidelity.

In the early 1980s, Coppola was interested in developing a TV project for NBC called *Sweat Shop* about illegal Mexicans in America.

Coppola had wanted to back movie adaptations of Gabriel Garcia Marquez's novel *One Hundred Years of Solitude* and Michael Shaara's *The Killer Angels*. Coppola also wanted to raise $20 million to allow Werner Herzog to make a movie called *The Conquest of Mexico*.

Energised and enthused by his status and influence, and his love of historical subject matter, Coppola presented Abel Gance's silent classic epic *Napoleon* in January 1981 at Radio City Music Hall. The film presentation was accompanied by a new score written by Coppola's father Carmine Coppola.

Coppola's associate, Tom Luddy, introduced Coppola to Jean-Luc Godard. Coppola gave Godard $250,000 to develop his project about Bugsy Seigel. The film was eventually abandoned and in return Godard offered Coppola the US rights for his most recently completed film *Sauve qui Peut* and American Zoetrope released the film through New Yorker Films in October 1980.

In 1979, Coppola bought the rights to Hans Jurgen Syberberg's film *Hitler: A Film From Germany*.

In the 1980s, Coppola planned to make a film based on Carl Sagan's novel *Contact*. It was eventually made by Robert Zemeckis. In 1997 Coppola wanted to block the release of the film, but was unable to do so. In 1978, his lawsuit stated, Coppola had agreed with Sagan to create a TV series based on the book, which Sagan was still developing at the time. Their agreement was that should the project come to fruition they would share any profits from related projects. The lawsuit was dismissed in February 1998 because the contract was never enforced and statute of limitations expired.

When Coppola and Lucas backed Akira Kurosawa's movie *Kagemusha* (1980) it became Japan's most popular film at the time and can only have introduced Kurosawa's work to a wider Western audience.

In spring 1980, Paul Schrader told Coppola how much he wanted to make a film based on the life and work of Japanese novelist Yukio Mishima. In April 1980, Kurosawa invited Coppola to the premiere of the film Coppola and Lucas had sponsored, *Kagemusha*. Coppola and Luddy arranged to meet with the executor of the literary rights to Yukio Mishima's work in order to realise Schrader's dream. By spring Coppola wanted Paul Schrader's movie *Mishima: A Life in Four Chapters* to be a fully fledged Zoetrope production but, in the shadow cast by the commercial failure of *One From the Heart*, that did not happen. Ultimately, the movie went to Warner Brothers. Teaming up with George Lucas, Coppola rode to the rescue, and Lucas convinced Warner Brothers to put $5 million into the film; he and Coppola presented the film as executive producers.

In January 1989, Coppola announced he and his family were going to relocate to Italy to make two films over a five-year period. One of them was *Le Ribellion di Catilina*, which may have been some kind of precursor to *Megalopolis*. This move did not occur, though Coppola did spend some of 1989 and early 1990 in Italy shooting *The Godfather Part III*.

Word went round that Coppola was working on a sequel to *Apocalypse Now* with John Milius.

Coppola went into discussions with Ted Turner concerning a project called *Century* about key twentieth-century events.

In the autumn of 2000, Coppola was to have produced a movie about the life of Frida Kahlo starring Jennifer Lopez and directed by Luis Valdez (*La Bamba*). This film would have been part of Coppola's new deal with MGM/UA. The film did not reach fruition. In late 2002 a film called *Frida* was released starring Salma Hayek and directed by Julie Taymor.

Coppola's TV interests expanded in the autumn of 2000 as a raft of projects went into development with the American networks.

Boulevard of Dreams was a concept for a TV series about a family of police officers working the Hollywood beat. Coppola was to have been executive producer and co-writer of the screenplay.

American Zoetrope and Alliance Atlantis also entered into an agreement on the following projects: *Hollywood Land*, about the transformation of Tinsel Town; *The Brooklyn Bridge*, a miniseries about the building of the bridge; *The Gold Rush*, a miniseries about settling the West; *Mr and Mrs Macbeth*, a TV movie adaptation of the Shakespeare play set in the world of professional sports; *Brave New Word*, about a boy who invents a new word to describe his feelings; and *Christiana Claus* in which Santa's daughter takes over the family business.

Coppola considered adapting a novel, called *Brotherhood of the Grape*, about an Italian–American bricklayer in his seventies living in California. Robert Towne was to have written the screenplay at some point in the mid-1980s. By the late 1980s Curtis Hanson (*L.A. Confidential* (1997), *The Wonder Boys* (2000), *8 Mile* (2002)) was preparing the project for Zoetrope, but it was never produced.

One of Coppola's most high-profile films as a producer was his involvement on the Godfrey Reggio film, *Koyaanisqatsi*. Released in 1982, the film was a dazzling dream of a documentary about modern life. It formed the first part of what has become a trilogy, *Powaqqatsi* (1988) and in 2002 *Naqoyqatsi,* presented by Steven Soderbergh. *Koyaanisqatsi* was distributed by American Zoetrope. The movie's title mesmerising to the ear and to the eye is drawn from the Hopi language of the American southwest. Reggio had lived and worked in the region for many years, prior to becoming a film maker, on a range of community development projects. Powaqa is Hopi for a negative sorcerer who lives selfishly to the detriment of others. Qatsi means life. *Koyaanisqatsi*, then, explores the notion of life out of balance, where the urban and technological collide with the natural. *Powaqqatsi* means life in transformation and focuses on the passing of ancient cultures and traditions while celebrating their diversity. *Naqoyqatsi* means war as a way of life, so appropriate at the time of writing in the spring of 2003. One of Zoetrope's editors, Dennis Jakob, worked with the film's editors Alan Walpole and Ron Fricke. The costume designer for *Bram Stoker's Dracula*, Eiko Ishioka, provided the arresting poster for the release of *Koyaanisqatsi*.

American Zoetrope also distributed globally a film called *The Grey Fox* starring Richard Farnsworth, who starred as Alvin Straight in *The Straight Story* (David Lynch, 1999). *The Grey Fox* was about a train robber.

A sequel to the *Black Stallion* was made, entitled *The Black Stallion Returns*, but was not as successful as the original. *The Escape Artist* received terrible reviews and quickly disappeared after release.

Fresh from his success with *Bram Stoker's Dracula*, Coppola served as executive producer on *Mary Shelley's Frankenstein*, directed by Kenneth Branagh (1994). The film has much in common with the florid extravagance of Coppola's adaptation of the vampire tale and some of the same, very appealing self-conscious artifice. The film starred Robert De Niro as the monster and Kenneth Branagh as Frankenstein.

In 1999, Coppola served as executive producer on the beautifully realised *Sleepy Hollow* (Tim Burton), which was lavish, funny, tense and moving.

Ever a fan of innovation and reinvention, Coppola has even had something to say about the state of the music video. In *Res* magazine he is quoted as saying on air when hosting a VH1 Music Cinema programme in the late 1990s: 'This short form, basically commercials for records, is losing energy. Why not have a longer form . . . an audiovisual piece, not just two minutes, but forty minutes? The sky is the limit for the new music cinema.'

In 1998, Coppola came on board a troubled sci-fi project called *Supernova* to edit it into a workable shape for the studio. Around this time he was also attached for a brief period to the Film *Thirteen Days* starring Kevin Costner (Roger Donaldson, 2000) after Costner's *Field of Dreams* (1989) director, Phil Alden Robinson, left the project.

In keeping with his genuine, career-long commitment to world cinema and new work, in the spring of 2002 Coppola teamed up with Thai film maker Chatrichalerm Yukol to prepare Yukol's film *Suriyothai* (a big hit in Thailand) for Cannes in 2003. The film cost around $13 million and Coppola secured another $2 million and worked with Yukol in trimming the film from 185 minutes to 150. Coppola also worked on the film's soundtrack. Some scenes were cut, and other scenes, not shot for the original version, were brought to life for the Western audience version. Yukol and Coppola were classmates at UCLA in the 1960s.

In the spring of 2000 Coppola made a deal with MGM/UA for a three-year, ten-picture run of films to be produced through American Zoetrope and released through United Artists. *Jeepers Creepers* was one of these projects as was *Taking on the Neighbourhood* (about a woman caught between the Latino and Irish communities in New York) and *CQ* (directed by Roman Coppola). Robert De Niro has gone on to direct his second feature, *The Good Shepherd* with Coppola as executive producer. The other project of particular satisfaction for Coppola must be *The Girl's Guide to Hunting and Fishing* which began as a short story in the *Zoetrope: All Story* magazine, then became a novel and finally a movie. This proved Coppola's belief that that magazine could function as a springboard for movie projects.

In the spring of 2001, plans were up and running for Coppola to be involved in a teen surf musical to be staged in London's West End. It was to have been titled *Gidget*, co-written by Coppola, with *Grease* songwriter John Farrar.

The *Zoetrope: All Story* magazine and online edition is maybe Coppola's best contribution to storytelling in quite a while. Through the magazine new writers are nurtured and given exposure. Big names, such as Gabriel Garcia Marquez, David Byrne and David Bowie have all contributed to the magazine. Through the Zoetrope website, there is also a Virtual Studio that offers a range of advice and resources for film makers. There is something democratic about this open-access concept, something remaining of Coppola's early days in theatre work where you rolled your sleeves up and got stuck in.

Famously, Coppola has been in the wine business for twenty years or so now and it has been the huge financial success of this that has contributed to his being independent of the studios. Coppola also owns a restaurant in San Francisco, with Robin Williams and Robert De Niro, called Rubicon. In Belize, Coppola owns a small resort called The Blancaneaux Lodge. In 2000 in San Francisco, Coppola opened the Café Niebaum-Coppola with a small shop on the side. Coppola regards all these ventures as aspects of show business.

Coppola the Writer

Coppola's mega success very early in his Hollywood career was based not just on his great capacity as a director but also as a writer. Alongside his own writer–director projects he also wrote the screenplay for two major period Hollywood movies. One was *Patton* and the other was *The Great Gatsby*. Coppola became involved as a writer on *Patton* back in 1967 when he finished working on his feature *You're A Big Boy Now*. By this time, Coppola had begun to establish a reputation in Hollywood as a writer. He had been given six months to create a script about the soldier in 1964. Coppola had immersed himself in books on Patton (a larger-than-life US General who, once, even hit a shell-shocked soldier) such as *Patton: Ordeal and Triumph* by Ladislas Farago and Patton's own diaries. As with the Coppola movie characters Michael Corleone, Colonel Kurtz and even Count Dracula, there is a linking obsession with power, and certainly Patton's life held this appeal as a source of drama. In 1970 the film was finally ready to be made but George C Scott would only commit if Coppola's screenplay was used. Other writers had attempted to shape up a story since Coppola left the project in the late 1960s. The film's famous opening speech showing Patton against a frame-filling United States flag, was Coppola's idea. Patton's monologue in Sicily was a specific Coppola contribution. The film's attributed co-writer was Edmund North, who restructured some of Coppola's original screenplay. Coppola never met North though they shared an Academy Award for the screenplay. The film was directed by Franklin J Schaffner.

Coppola's screenplay for *The Great Gatsby* was written in 1972, during the post-production period on *The Godfather*. When Truman Capote had been unable to write a screenplay that satisfied Paramount's Robert Evans, Evans turned to Coppola for help in writing the adaptation of the novel. F Scott Fitzgerald was one of Coppola's favourite writers. Robert Evans had wanted Ali McGraw (a massive star at the time) to star as Daisy Buchanan. Coppola stayed in Paris for three weeks in the run up to the premiere of *The Godfather* and wrote the screenplay at L'Hotel, taking the Oscar Wilde Room. Coppola went with the novel's visual qualities and also integrated certain pieces of dialogue from other Fitzgerald texts.

In 1982, Coppola was an unpaid and uncredited script doctor on the screenplay for the James Bond film *Never Say Never Again* (Irvin

Kershner, 1983). Coppola's material and contributions were never used. His focus had been to return to the Fleming novel *Thunderball* and do a real adaptation of it, emphasising the romance between Bond and Domino.

Zoetrope Studios: Filmography

This list represents films directed by Coppola and also the many on which he has been producer and executive producer. American Zoetrope's films have received fifteen Academy Awards and sixty-eight nominations. Four of their films have been included in the American Film Institute's top 100 American films and *The Godfather* and *Apocalypse Now* have been enshrined by the American Congress in the National Film Registry.

These are the films:
1963 *Dementia 13*   Francis Ford Coppola
1966 *You're A Big Boy Now*   Francis Ford Coppola
1968 *Finian's Rainbow*   Francis Ford Coppola
1969 *The Rain People*   Francis Ford Coppola
1970 *THX-1138*   George Lucas
1972 *The Godfather*   Francis Ford Coppola
     Ludwig: Requiem for a Virgin King   Hans Jurgen Syberberg
1973 *American Graffiti*   George Lucas
1974 *The Conversation*   Francis Ford Coppola
     The Godfather Part II   Francis Ford Coppola
1977 *The Perfumed Nightmare*   Kidlat Tahimik
1978 *Our Hitler*   Hans Jurgen Syberberg
1979 *Apocalypse Now*   Francis Ford Coppola
     The Black Stallion   Carroll Ballard
     Every Man for Himself (Sauve qui peut)   Jean-Luc Godard
1980 *Kagemusha* (The Shadow Warrior)   Akira Kurosawa
1981 *Napoleon* (restored version of Abel Gance's 1927 film)   Abel Gance
1982 *The Escape Artist*   Caleb Deschanel
     One From the Heart   Francis Ford Coppola
     Passion   Jean-Luc Godard
     Parsifal   Hans Jurgen Syberberg
     Hammett   Wim Wenders
     Too Far To Go   Fielder Cook
1983 *The Grey Fox*   Philip Borsos
     Koyaanisqatsi   Godfrey Reggio
     The Black Stallion Returns   Robert Dalva
     The Outsiders   Francis Ford Coppola
     Rumble Fish   Francis Ford Coppola
1984 *The Cotton Club*   Francis Ford Coppola

1985 *Mishima: A Life in Four Chapters*   Paul Schrader
1986 *Peggy Sue Got Married*   Francis Ford Coppola
     Captain Eo   Francis Ford Coppola
1987 *Gardens of Stone*   Francis Ford Coppola
     Barfly   Barbet Schroeder
1988 *Tucker: The Man and His Dream*   Francis Ford Coppola
     Clownhouse   Victor Salva
     Powaqqatsi   Godfrey Reggio
1989 *New York Stories* (*Life Without Zoe* segment)   Francis Ford Coppola
     Wait Until Spring, Bandini   Dominique Deruddere
1990 *The Godfather Part III*   Francis Ford Coppola
     The Spirit of '76   Lucas Reiner
1991 *Hearts of Darkness: A Filmmaker's Apocalypse*   Fax Bahr, Eleanor Coppola and George Hickenlooper
1992 *Wind*   Carroll Ballard
     Bram Stoker's Dracula   Francis Ford Coppola
1993 *The Secret Garden*   Agnieszka Holland
1994 *Mary Shelley's Frankenstein*   Kenneth Branagh
     Tecumseh: The Last Warrior (TV series)   Larry Elikann
1995 *My Family/Mi Familia*   Gregory Nava
1996 *Titanic* (TV miniseries)   Robert Lieberman
     Jack   Francis Ford Coppola
1997 *John Grisham's The Rainmaker*   Francis Ford Coppola
     Buddy   Caroline Thompson
1998 *Moby Dick* (TV miniseries)   Frank Roddam
     Outrage (TV)   Robert Allan Ackerman
     First Wave (TV series)   Bill Corcoran, Holly Dale, Ken Girotti, Rob LaBelle, Michael Robinson, Mike Rohl
1999 *The Third Miracle*   Agnieszka Holland
     Sleepy Hollow   Tim Burton
2000 *The Virgin Suicides*   Sofia Coppola
2001 *Jeepers Creepers*   Victor Salva
2002 *Assassination Tango*   Robert Duvall
     Pumpkin   Anthony Abrams, Adam Larson Broder
     CQ   Roman Coppola
     No Such Thing   Hal Hartley
2003 *Jeepers Creepers 2*   Victor Salva

virgin film **COPPOLA** Zoetrope Studios: Filmography

273

Index of Quotations

Introduction
1   'Most of my life . . .' Francis Ford Coppola quoted by Stephen
     Farber, *Coppola and The Godfather*, *Sight and Sound*, autumn
     1972, p. 220
2   'I'm more like a kid . . .' Francis Ford Coppola quoted by Jonathan
     Romney, 'At The Court of Coppola', *Guardian* G2 Section, 21
     January 1993, p. 2
4   'You know, I have been . . .' Francis Ford Coppola quoted by
     Cyndi Stivers, 'Family Reunion', *Premiere*, January 1991, vol. 4,
     no. 5, p. 106
4   'ravaged Hollywood genius'. Comment by Michael Sragow in
     Salon online article
13   'ice breaker' Walter Murch describing Coppola and his helping
     colleagues in *Walter Murch: Designing Sound for Apocalypse
     Now*, *Projections* 6, Faber and Faber, 1996, p. 150
15   'I was very anxious . . .' Coppola quoted by Ann Nocenti in
     Scenario online interview
16   'Characters are always nesting . . .' Kent Jones, 'Mythmaker: The
     Great Conductor of Cinema', in *Film Comment*, www.
     Filmcomment.com archive, spring 2002
17   'personal battleground' Walter Murch quoted by Michael
     Ondaatje, *The Conversations: Walter Murch and the Art of Editing
     Film*, Bloomsbury, 2002
17   'I think Francis was far . . .' John Milius, interviewed by Kenneth
     Plumen, www.filmforce.net, May 2003

Finian's Rainbow
26   'I was like a fish out of water . . .' Francis Ford Coppola in a BBC
     TV profile 6 April 1985 quoted by Peter Cowie, in *Coppola*, Faber
     and Faber, 1990, p. 38

The Rain People
28   'a loose confederation of . . .' George Lucas
29   'remains American Zoetrope's . . .' Coppola in *The Creative
     Impulse*, Charles Champlin
29   'Have I become an old man . . .' Francis Ford Coppola
33   'a fascinating early . . .' Tom Milne, *Time Out* in *The Time Out
     Film Guide*, 1991, p. 548
33   'I wanted the film to be . . .' Coppola on a BBC TV profile, quoted
     by Peter Cowie, April 1985, pp. 50–1

in *The Conversations: Walter Murch and the Art of Editing Film*, Bloomsbury, 2002, p. 179

62 'Confession, at first . . .' Coppola interviewed by Marjorie Rosen, *Film Comment,* July–August 1974, p. 44, vol. 10, no. 4

64 'The film is doing to him . . .' Francis Coppola quoted in *Scenario Online* interview by Annie Nocenti, 'A Talk with Francis Ford Coppola', 2002

69 'remarkably ambitious and serious . . .' David Denby, *Sight and Sound*, summer 1974, vol. 43, no. 3, p. 131

69 'A bleak . . .' Tom Milne, *Time Out* magazine, reprinted in *The Time Out Film Guide*, Penguin Books, 1991, p. 135

69 'Coppola's cerebral classic', Peter Bradshaw in *Guardian*, 1 March 2002

70 'I'm interested in films . . .' Francis Coppola quoted in *The Films of Harrison Ford* by Lee Pfeiffer and Michael Lewis, The Citadel Press, 1996, p. 63

The Godfather Part II

85 'converging and diverging . . .' Jonathan Rosenbaum, *Sight and Sound*, summer 1975, vol. 44, no. 3, p. 187

85 'this is nothing short . . .' Kim Newman, *Empire*, issue 86, August 1996, online

85 'masterful . . . a telling' BBCi *Online* review

85 'far superior to . . .' Anne Bilson, *Time Out, Time Out Film Guide*, Penguin Books, 1991, p. 259

85 'They were siblings . . .' Francis Coppola quoted in *Scenario* magazine, 'A Talk with Francis Ford Coppola' by Annie Nocenti, online

Apocalypse Now

89 'I'll be venturing into an area . . .' Francis Ford Coppola quoted by Laurence Said in *Hollywood and Vietnam, Film Comment*, September–October 1979, vol. 15, no. 5, pp. 20–1

98 'I felt as if Francis . . .' Jerry Ziesmer, *Ready When You Are, Mr Coppola, Mr Spielberg, Mr Crowe*, The Scarecrow Press Inc, Lanham, Maryland and London, 2000, p. 233

103 'The original idea . . .' Vittorio Storaro quoted by Rick Gentry in *A Journey into Light*, interview with Vittorio Storaro, *Projections 6*, Faber and Faber 1996, p. 265

112 'Vietnam as an epic . . .' *Empire*, issue 17, November 1990, online

112 'brilliant as movie making . . .' Chris Auty, *Time Out, The Time Out Film Guide*, Penguin Books, 1991, p. 28

112 'We had access . . .' Coppola quoted in *Coppola* by Peter Cowie, Faber and Faber, 1990, p 127. This famous comment was originally given in an interview with Roger Ebert in May 1979 for *Chicago Sun-Times*.

112 'This new, complete . . .' Coppola's address in *Apocalypse Now Redux* DVD booklet

One From the Heart

115 'We're on the eve . . .' Francis Ford Coppola quoted in 'Making Film with Video for *One From the Heart*', *American Cinematographer*, January 1982, vol. 63, no. 1, p. 22

119 'we tried to use . . .' Vittorio Storaro in *American Cinematographer*, January 1982, vol. 63, no.1, p. 93

119 'He is gifted . . .' Garret Brown on Francis Ford Coppola, 'The Steadicam and *One From the Heart*', *American Cinematographer*, January 1982, vol. 62, no. 1, p. 83

124 'physiology of colour . . .' Vittorio Storaro lighting mission statement presented in *American Cinematographer*, January 1982, vol. 72, no. 1, p. 24

124 'The unlimited desire . . .' *American Cinematographer*, January 1982, vol. 62, no. 1, p. 24

129 '*One From the Heart* is like . . .' Pauline Kael, review of the film reprinted in *Taking It All In: Film Writings 1980–1983*, Arena, London, p. 296

129 'the picture comes . . .' Sheila Benson in the *Los Angeles Times*

129 'Coppola has thrown' Andrew Sarris in the *Village Voice*

129 'a likeable . . .' Kevin Jackson, *Time Out*, *The Time Out Film Guide*, Penguin Books, 1991, p. 486

129 'I'm on the side of the audience . . .' Francis Coppola quoted in Kenneth Von Gunden, *Postmodern Auteurs*, McFarland and Co, 1991, p. 49, originally quoted by David Ansen and Martin Kasindorf, *Coppola's Apocalypse Again*, Newsweek, 16 February 1981, p. 79

The Outsiders

140 'surprisingly . . .' Chris Peachment in *Time Out*, *The Time Out Film Guide*, Penguin Books, 1991, p. 497

140 'small, sincere . . .' John Engstrom, *Boston Globe*

140 'The fault lies . . .' *The 3rd Virgin Film Guide*, 1994, p. 634

141 'One of the central concepts . . .' Francis Ford Coppola, quoted in *Idols of the King,* David Thomson and Lucy King interview with FFC, *Film Comment*, vol. 19, no. 5, September–October 1983, p. 66

141 'I got so saccharine . . .' Coppola quoted by Chris Nashawaty in *Entertainment Weekly* online interview in November 1997

Rumble Fish
153 'Coppola seemed to trade . . .' *Empire* issue 22, April 1991, no writer credited online
153 'Camus for kids . . .' Chris Peachment, *Time Out, The Time Out Film Guide*, Penguin Books, 1991, p. 576
153 'an unabashed art film . . .' *The 3rd Virgin Film Guide*, 1994, p. 740
153 '*Rumble Fish* was (more) . . .' Coppola interviewed by Chris Nashawaty, *Entertainment Weekly* online, November 1997

The Cotton Club
165 'Another of Francis Coppola's . . .' Kim Newman, *Empire* 145, July 2001, online
165 'Francis Coppola . . . seems to have . . .' Pauline Kael, *State of the Art*, Arena, London, 1987, p. 293. Original review *The New Yorker,* 7 January 1985
165 'The misconception . . .' Brian Case, *Time Out, The Time Out Film Guide*, Penguin Books, 1991 p. 137
165 'Lavish, interesting . . .' *The 3rd Virgin Film Guide*, 1994, p. 157
165 'It's not even . . .' Coppola quoted by Chris Nashawaty in an interview for *Entertainment Weekly* online, November 1997

Peggy Sue Got Married
168 'I decided . . .' Coppola quoted by Chris Nashawaty in an interview for *Entertainment Weekly* online, November 1997
174 'it has a golden . . .' Pauline Kael, *Hooked*, p. 220
174 'More relaxed . . .' Chris Peachment, *Time Out, The Time Out Film Guide*, Penguin Books, 1991, p. 511
174 'a human comedy . . .' Roger Ebert in *Chicago Sun-Times*, 10 August 1986, available online
174 'some fuzzy Capraesque homilies . . .' Terrence Rafferty, *Sight and Sound*, winter 86/87, vol. 56, no. 1, p. 33
175 'My model was . . .' Coppola quoted in *Francis Ford Coppola – A Filmmakers Life* by Michael Schumacher, Bloomsbury, London, 2000, p. 371. The quote originally appeared in *Direct Approach*, *TV Guide*, 2 March 1985

Gardens of Stone
183 'Francis Coppola's soulful . . .' *Empire* online, issue 17, November 1990, no reviewer credited

207 'It's still . . .' Peter Travers, 'A Mob King Lear', *Roling Stone*, 29 January 1991
208 'This is the cathedral . . .' Francis Ford Coppola quoted in *Coppola* by Peter Cowie, Faber and Faber, 1990, p. 232
208 'I absolutely . . .' Coppola quoted by Chris Nashawaty, *Entertainment Weekly* online, November 1997

Bram Stoker's Dracula
213 'When I read . . .' Francis Ford Coppola, *Bram Stoker's Dracula: The Film and The Legend*, Pan Books, 1992, p. 3
213 'Above all it is . . .' Francis Ford Coppola diary entry, *Francis Coppola Journals 1989–1993* reprinted in *Projections 3*, Faber and Faber, 1994, vol. 3, p. 19
213 'Let's dress . . .' Francis Ford Coppola in *Bram Stoker's Dracula: The Film and The Legend*, Pan Books, 1992, p. 126
217 'That's the way . . .' Francis Coppola in *Bram Stoker's Dracula: The Film and The Legend*, Pan Books, 1992, p. 149
226 'Coppola directs . . .' Roger Ebert, *Chicago Sun-Times* online review
226 'Francis Ford Coppola's magnificent . . .' Hal Hinson in *Washington Post* review, online, 13 November 1992
226 'drowned in a tide . . .' David Ansen review, *Newsweek*, 23 November 1992
227 'The vampire has . . .' Francis Ford Coppola in *Bram Stoker's Dracula: The Film and the Legend,* Pan Books, 1992, p. 5

Jack
235 'further dispiriting evidence . . .' Philip Kemp, *Sight and Sound*, October 1996, vol. 96, no. 10, p. 42
235 'A sappy comedy . . .' Kenneth Turan in the *Los Angeles Times*, 9 August 1996, available online
236 'it's a fable . . .' Francis Ford Coppola in *Premiere*, September 1996, *The Filmmaker Series* no. 1, Peter Biskind, pp. 53–61, vol. 10, no. 1, p. 54

The Rainmaker
239 'do you really . . .' Coppola quoted by Chris Nashawaty in an interview for *Entertainment Weekly*, November 1997
242 'When you go . . .' Coppola quoted in *Creating John Grisham's The Rainmaker* by Annette Cotton, online report
247 'a watchable courtroom drama . . .' Ian Nathan, *Empire* online, issue 105, March 1998

Short Films

Picture Credits

The following pictures are from the Ronald Grant Archive:
Page 1 (top) courtesy Seven Arts Pictures; Page 1 (middle) courtesy
Warner Bros/Seven Arts; Page 1 (bottom) courtesy American Zoetrope;
Page 2 (top) courtesy Paramount Pictures; Page 3 (top) courtesy
American Zoetrope/Paramount Pictures; Page 3 (middle and bottom)
courtesy Zoetrope Studios; Page 4 (top) courtesy Zoetrope Studios; Page
5 (all three pictures) courtesy Zoetrope Studios; Page 6 (bottom right)
courtesy American Zoetrope; Page 6 (bottom left) courtesy Paramount
Pictures; Page 7 (top) courtesy American Zoetrope; Page 7 (bottom right)
courtesy LucasFilm/Disney; Page 8 (top) courtesy Touchstone Pictures;
Page 8 (bottom) courtesy American Zoetrope
　　The following pictures are from the Kobal Collection:
Page 2 (bottom) courtesy Paramount/The Kobal Collection; Page 4
(bottom) courtesy Warner Bros/The Kobal Collection; Page 6 (top)
courtesy LucasFilm Ltd, Paramount, The Kobal Collection; Page 7
(bottom left) courtesy American Zoetrope/Hollywood Pictures/The
Kobal Collection

Bibliography

Campbell, Joseph, *The Masks of God: Creative Mythology*, Penguin Books, London, 1976

Campbell, Joseph, *The Power of Myth*, Transworld Publishers Ltd, London, 1989

Champlin, Charles, *George Lucas: The Creative Impulse*, Virgin Books, London, 1997

Collodi, Carlo, *Pinocchio*, Penguin Classics, 2002

Coppola, Eleanor, *Notes: On the Making of Apocalypse Now*, Faber and Faber, London and Boston, 1991

Cowie, Peter, *The Godfather Book*, Faber and Faber, London and Boston, 1997

Cowie, Peter, *The Apocalypse Now Book*, Faber and Faber, 2001

Cowie, Peter, *Coppola*, Faber and Faber, London and Boston, 1990

Dougan, Andy, *Robin Williams*, Orion Media, 1998

Drabble, Margaret (ed), *The Oxford Companion to English Literature*, Oxford University Press, 1989

French, Karl, *Apocalypse Now: Pocket Guide*, Bloomsbury, 2000

Hughes, Robert, *American Visions: The Epic History of Art in America*, The Harvill Press, London, 1997

Kael, Pauline, *Taking it All In: Film Writings 1980–1983*, Arena, London, 1987

Kael, Pauline, *State of the Art: Film Writings 1983–1985*, Arena, London, 1987

Kael, Pauline, *Hooked: Film Writings 1985–1988*, Marion Boyars, London, 1990

Kael, Pauline, *Movie Love: Film Writings 1988–1991*, Marion Boyars, 1991

Lyons, Christopher (ed), *The International Dictionary of Films and Filmmakers: Directors*, Papermac, 1987

Lyons, Christopher (ed), *The International Dictionary of Films and Filmmakers: Films*, Papermac, 1987

Milius, John and Coppola, Francis Ford, *Apocalypse Now: The Screenplay*, Faber and Faber, 2001

Ondaatje, Michael, *The Conversations: Walter Murch and the Art of Editing Film*, Bloomsbury, 2002

Room, Adrian, *Brewer's Dictionary of Phrase and Fable*, Cassell, 15th Edition, 1997

Schumacher, Michael, *Francis Ford Coppola: A Filmmaker's Life*, Bloomsbury, 1999

Spignesi, Stephen, *The Robin Williams Scrapbook*, A Citadel Press Book, 1997

Ziesmer, Jerry, *Ready When You Are, Mr Coppola, Mr Spielberg, Mr Crowe*, Scarecrow Press, 1999

Projections, numerous volumes, Faber and Faber series published annually.

The Virgin Film Guide 3 (James Pallot, ed.) Virgin, 1994

The *Lucasfilm Fan Club* magazine – a magazine, published quarterly, of the late 1980s through to 1994.

The following is a list of material not consulted directly for this book but which may be useful and enlightening for readers:

'The Youth of Francis Ford Coppola,' interview by R Koszarski in *Films in Review* (NY), November 1968

'The Dangerous Age', interview by John Cutts in *Films and Filming* (London), May 1969

Francis Ford Coppola, interview in *The Film Director as Superstar* by Joseph Gelmis, Garden City, New York, 1970

'Francis Ford Coppola on the Director,' *Movie People*, (Fred Baker ed.), New York, 1973

'Conversation avec Francis Ford Coppola', by G Belloni and L Codelli in *Positif* (Paris), September 1974

'The Making of *The Conversation*' interview by Brian De Palma in *Filmmakers Newsletter* (Ward Hill, Massachusetts), May 1974

Interview with Francis Ford Coppola by Max Tessier and JA Gili in *Ecran* (Paris), July 1974

Playboy Interview: 'Francis Ford Coppola' by William Murray in *Playboy* (Chicago), July 1975

'Entretien avec Francis Ford Coppola' in *Cahiers du Cinema* (Paris), July/August 1979

'Testimonianze: la storia di *Apocalypse Now*' in *Filmcritica* (Rome), May 1979

'Journey Up the River', interview by G Marcus in *Rolling Stone* (New York), 1 November 1979

'Francis Ford Coppola habla de *Apocalypse Now*' interview in *Cine* (Mexico), March 1980

The Godfather Journal by Ira Zucherman, New York, 1972

Francis Ford Coppola by Robert Johnson, Boston, 1977

'A National Anthem' by Joseph Morgenstern in *Newsweek*, 20 February 1967

'Francis Ford Coppola' by JR Taylor in *Sight and Sound*, winter 1968/9

'San Francisco's Own American Zoetrope' by Christopher Pearce in *American Cinematographer,* October 1972

'Francis Ford Coppola' by David McGilivray in *Focus on Film*, autumn 1972

'The Making of *The Godfather*' in *The Godfather Papers* by Mario Puzo, Greenwich, Connecticut, 1973

'Directors Guild Winner: Francis Ford Coppola' by Charles Higham in *Action* (LA), May/June 1973

'Coppola's Conversation' by A Madsen in *Sight and Sound*, autumn 1973

'The Final Act of a Family Epic,' *Time*, 16 December 1974

'Godfather of the Movies' by Maureen Orth in *Newsweek*, 14 November 1974

'Coppola's Progress' by William Pechter in *Commentary*, July 1974

'Outs' by Jay Cocks in *Take One*, December 1974

'Conversation secrete in Avant Scène du cinéma', November 1974

'Francis Ford Coppola: A Profile' by Susan Braudy in *Atlantic Monthly*, August 1976

'Zoetrope and *Apocalypse Now*' by Audie Bock in *American Film*, September 1979

'Dossier: Hollywood 1979: Francis Ford Coppola' by P Carcassonne in *Cinematographer*, March 1979

'Francis Coppola Discusses *Apocalypse Now*' by GR Levin in *Millimeter*, October 1979

'Meet Me in Las Vegas' by Mike Bygrave and Joan Goodman in *American Film*, October 1981

'Coppola on the Beat' by P McGilligan in *Films and Filming*, December 1981

Index

Horner, James 250, 253
Hoskins, Bob 159
Howell, C Thomas 133, 134
Hughes, Howard 191
Hughes, John 141
Hughes, Langston 157
Hugo Award 222
Hunt, Helen 169
Huston, Anjelica 178, 251, 252

Industrial Light and Magic 127, 215, 251
Is Paris Burning? 15
Ishioka, Eiko 214, 223, 248, 267
It's A Wonderful Life (Capra) 168

Jack 4, 6, 7, 8, 11, 12, 16, 25, 136, 140, 141, 149, 174, 179, 190, 215, 219, 225, 227–36
Jackson, Joe 192
Jackson, Michael 250, 251, 253
Jacobs, Alexander 196
Jakob, Dennis 93, 152
Jeepers Creepers (Salva) 227, 268
Jein, Greg 127
Johnston, Joe 252
Jones, James Earl 178
Jones, Kent 16
Julia, Raul 118
Jurassic Park (Spielberg) 204
Juror, The (Gibson) 229

Kael, Pauline 129, 165, 174, 183, 207, 259
Kahlo, Frida 266–7
Kama, Pete 110
Kamen, Michael 234
Karatz, Abe 188
Kasdan, Lawrence 62
Katzenberg, Jeffrey 197
Kaufman, Victor 177
Kazan, Elia 44, 76, 132
Keaton, Diane 41, 42, 76, 199

Keitel, Harvey 95
Kelly, Gene 117
Kennedy, William 158
Kerouac, Jack 5, 149, 260
Kerr, Michael 177
Kershner, Irvin 57
Kilar, Wojciech 222
Killer Angels, The (Shaara) 265
King Lear 198
Klein, Dennis 118
Knight, Shirley 30
Korty, John 29
Koyaanisqatsi (Reggio) 262, 267
Kurosawa, Akira 2, 5, 11, 20, 37, 38, 47, 58, 115, 213, 266

Landau, Martin 187, 188, 192
Lane, Diane 134, 139, 145, 151, 158, 159, 199, 231
Lanterna Film 29
Lantieri, Michael 215
Las Vegas Film Critics Award 245
Le Ribellion di Catilina 266
Lean, David 11
Lear, Norman 120
Lester, Richard 15
Life Without Zoe (*New York Stories*) 248, 253, 254–9
Lipset, Hal 57
Lombardi, Joe 107–8
London Critics' Circle Film Awards 107, 246
Lopez, Jennifer 231, 234, 266
Lovell, Dyson 157, 164
Lowe, Rob 133, 134
Lucas, George 3, 7, 9, 11, 22, 28, 29, 30, 31, 37, 39, 41, 43, 53, 80, 88, 91, 94, 96, 110, 115, 127, 135, 168, 186, 187, 188, 189, 213, 214, 217, 230, 250, 251, 252, 253, 263, 266
Lucas, Marcia 41
LucasFilm 3, 187